CHINA'S DEVELOPMENTAL MIRACLE

—— ASIA AND THE PACIFIC ——

Series Editor: Mark Selden, Binghamton University

Exploring one of the most dynamic and contested regions of the world, this series includes contributions on political, economic, cultural, and social changes in modern and contemporary Asia and the Pacific.

Asia
and
the
Pacific

CHINA'S DEVELOPMENTAL MIRACLE

Origins, Transformations, and Challenges

Alvin Y. So
Editor

AN EAST GATE BOOK

M.E. Sharpe
Armonk, New York
London, England

An East Gate Book

Library of Congress Cataloging-in-Publication Data

China's developmental miracle : origins, transformations, and challenges / [edited by]
Alvin Y. So.
　　p. cm. — (Asia and Pacific)
"An East gate book."
Includes bibliographical references and index.
ISBN 0-7656-1037-X (alk. paper) — ISBN 0-7656-1038-8 (pbk.: alk. paper)
　1. China—Economic policy—20th century. 2. China—Economic conditions—20th
century. 3. China—Social conditions—20th century. 4. China—Politics and
government—20th century. I. So, Alvin Y., 1953– II. Asia and Pacific (Armonk, N.Y.)

HC427 .C55975 2002
338.951—dc21
　　　　　　　　　　　　　　　　　　　　　　　　　　　　　　2002029409

Printed in the United States of America

BM (c)　10　9　8　7　6　5　4　3　2　1
BM (p)　10　9　8　7　6　5　4　3　2　1

Contents

Part III. Challenges

Tables and Figures

Tables

Figures

Acknowledgments

This volume is a selection of papers that appeared in a special issue of *Asian Perspective*. Therefore, I would like to thank Mel Gurtov, Taik-young Hamm, and Su-Hoon Lee, the editors of *Asian Perspective*, for their support of the special issue and their encouragement in turning the journal articles into a book. I would also like to thank Mark Selden for including the manuscript in his M.E. Sharpe series.

In addition, I want to express my gratitude to the chapter authors for their support of this volume. Once they agreed to write for the volume, they took their assignments seriously. Not only did they deliver their manuscripts on time, they were willing when asked to make one or two rounds of revisions.

In producing the manuscript for publication, I had the good fortune of enlisting Josephine Wong, the secretary of the Division of Social Science, for technical support. Josephine taught me how to use the Microsoft Word program, helped to prepare the endnotes, and made sure that all the chapters had the same formatting. It has been a pleasure to work with her for the past four years.

An Emerging High Impact Areas (EHIA) grant from the Hong Kong University of Science and Technology (HKUST) helped to cover the expenses incurred in preparing the manuscript for publication. I therefore want to thank Professor Pang-Hsin Ting, the Dean of the School of Humanities and Social Science, for his support since I became affiliated with HKUST in 1998.

CHINA'S DEVELOPMENTAL MIRACLE

1

Introduction

Rethinking the Chinese Developmental Miracle

Alvin Y. So

The Chinese Developmental Miracle

Suppose you could travel through time to Maoist China in the mid-1970s, and you told the Chinese that their country would soon become an economic powerhouse of the capitalist world economy in twenty years. No Chinese would have taken your words seriously, because they knew that China had experienced very serious developmental problems during the revolutionary period (1949–1976).

First, China faced the problem of forced withdrawal from the world economy.[1] Before the Chinese communist state could barely consolidate its power in the early 1950s, the United States quickly had sent warships to patrol the Taiwan Strait and supported the defeated Nationalist Party (the Guomindang) in Taiwan, sent soldiers to fight against the Chinese soldiers in Korea, imposed an economic embargo on mainland Chinese products, prevented mainland China from gaining a seat in the United Nations, and waged ideological attacks on Chinese "communist totalitarianism" in the mass media. Intense hostility from the United States during this Cold War era served to preclude certain developmental options for socialist China. Cut off from contacts with capitalist states, the Chinese communist state could not possibly pursue either export-oriented industrialization (owing to the closure of Western markets) or import-substitution (owing to the economic embargo) in the global economy. Thus, the Chinese state was forced to lean toward the Soviet bloc and miss the golden opportunity of achieving ascent during the post-war economic boom. Furthermore, as Yi-min Lin argues in this volume, the Cold War had created a resource strain on the Chinese economy. From 1952 to 1977, defense spending on average accounted for 5.5 percent of China's gross domestic product (GDP).

Second, like other communist regimes, China experienced the structural problems of a planned economy. Chinese state enterprises were highly inefficient and paid little heed to productivity, since they had been operating under a "soft budgetary constraint" and could rely on the state for more subsidies if they ran into losses. State enterprises also tended to stock up more resources and manpower than necessary, leading to waste, misuse of resources, and acute shortages of raw materials. Moreover, workers had little incentive to work harder, because revolutionary socialism guaranteed job security and fringe benefits regardless of job performance, and because there were few consumer goods on which they could spend their salaries. As a result, China's per capita annual income was still very low in the early 1970s, due to the extraordinary growth of its population from around 500 million in 1953 to one billion in 1980. Yi-min Lin reports in this volume that despite the fact that over 70 percent of the total workforce was deployed in agriculture and the adoption of a "grain first" policy, China could not even produce enough food to sustain a barest level of consumption for the population. Thus, China still ranked among the poorest nations in the world, and the standard of living of its people remained very low.

Third, there was the problem of political alienation. The long period of political struggles during the Cultural Revolution had alienated the general population, making them highly cynical about the slogans of class struggle and absolute egalitarianism. It seems ironic that in just a few years, the revolutionary fervor and the intense ideological struggles of the late 1960s were replaced by widespread disillusionment in the mid-1970s. In sum, by the mid-1970s, the Chinese state had suffered from the problems of forced withdrawal from the world economy, the structural problems of a planned economy, and political alienation.

What a complete turnaround in just twenty years! Although Eastern Europe and the Soviet Union (now Russia) were in economic decline during the 1980s and the 1990s, the Chinese developmental miracle had already begun to take shape as early as the mid-1990s.

First, economic growth in China in the same period was nothing but spectacular. The average annual growth rate of real GDP was 9 percent from 1978 through 1994 and 10.7 percent from 1990 through 1999. Even in the aftermath of the Asian financial crisis,[2] China still recorded an 8 percent GDP growth rate in 2000 and a projected 7.3 percent GDP growth rate in 2001. If such impressive economic growth rates continue, China could be transformed into the world's second largest economy in a decade or so. The real GDP grew from 681 billion yuan in 1978 to 8,190 billion yuan in 1999; Chinese per capita income rose from 316 yuan in 1978 to 6,456 yuan in 1999.[3] China recorded a trade surplus of almost US$44 billion in 1998, a current account surplus (about 1 percent of GDP in 1996 but close to 3 percent in 1997), and held a very large foreign exchange reserve of US$200 billion in 1999.[4]

Second, China has experienced a long period of political stability. The communist state withstood the challenges from below by mercilessly crushing the pro-democracy movement on June 4, 1989. Since then, the Chinese democracy movement has been forced to go underground. Despite an increase of activities among the dissidents in the late 1990s, the democracy movement has yet to regain its strength to challenge the power of the Chinese communist state from below. In addition, there has been a smooth leadership transition from the founding fathers to a younger generation of technocrats in the communist state. The collective leadership led by Jiang Zemin has emerged stronger from the Fifteenth Communist Party Congress in the fall of 1997, after senior leader Deng Xiaoping passed away.

Third, the Chinese state has played a more active role in the inter-state system and even had the capacity to deal with the complicated issue of national reunification.[5] In the early 1980s, when the British government refused to turn over Hong Kong to China, the Chinese government stood firm on the sovereignty issue, engaged in stormy negotiations with the British over two years, and finally pressured the British to sign the 1984 Joint Declaration to return Hong Kong's sovereignty to China in 1997. In the 1990s, China hosted the Asian games, tried to bid to be the host of the Olympics, and actively sought to enter the World Trade Organization (WTO). Finally, in 2001, China successfully won both the Olympics and the accession to WTO.

What is the origin of this Chinese developmental miracle? How could China overcome the serious developmental problems in the 1970s to achieve rapid economic development, political stability, and an empowered state in the 1990s? What was the impact of the developmental miracle on Chinese politics, economy, and society? The chapters in this volume will examine the origins and characteristics of the Chinese developmental miracle as well as discuss the challenges China is facing today and the future prospects for China's development in the twenty-first century.

The contributors to this volume include four sociologists, four institutional economists, two geographers, one political scientist, and one political sociologist. Coming from different disciplines, these contributors have highlighted various prominent issues, such as institutional changes, property rights, regional integration, migration, nationalism, religious evolution, civil society, gender politics, and class relations in their chapters. Although their chapters have different emphases and have presented contrasting findings, they often do not amount to competing theses. The aim of this Introduction is to bring these divergent views together to show that they have as a whole presented a sophisticated explanation of the origins of the Chinese developmental miracle, the transformations that have been taking place over the past two decades, and the various challenges that China is facing in the twenty-first century.

To start the discussion, the sections below will examine the following questions: What explains the transformation of a revolutionary state under Maoism to a developmental state since 1978? What are China's developmental strategies and why did they work? And why was the Chinese developmental state able to endure the initial challenges in the late twentieth century?

From a Revolutionary State to a Developmental State

The Legacy of a Strong Party-State

In the field of Chinese studies, it is often pointed out that the communist experiment under Mao was a disaster. The Great Leap Forward commune policy in the late 1950s led to famine and the death of tens of millions of Chinese. The ten years of Cultural Revolution (1966–1976) turned Chinese society upside down and resulted in political anarchy. In this scenario, China's march to modernization began only in 1978, after the rise of Deng Xiaoping, a pragmatist, who paid little attention to the revolutionary ideology of Mao. Hence, Deng became the hero of Chinese modernization, while Mao was held responsible for the economic backwardness and political turmoil in the first phase of Chinese communist rule.

What is missing in the above account, however, is that the present developmental miracle of China actually owes much to the historical heritage of the Maoist era.[6] Despite many shortcomings, the Maoist legacy has provided China with a strong Leninist party-state, with a concentration of power in the communist party. Only political organizations (like peasants' associations and labor unions) formally sponsored by the party were allowed to operate; other organizations were either made ineffective or simply banned from operation. This Leninist party-state was all-powerful in the sense that it extended both vertically and horizontally to every sphere in Chinese society. Vertically, the Leninist party-state was the first Chinese state that was able to exert its political control all the way down to village, family, and individual levels. Horizontally, there was a great expansion of state functions. The Leninist state did not just collect taxes and keep social order; it also oversaw such functions as education, health care, marriage, culture, and economic policy. After 1978, although the Chinese state was no longer interested in promoting revolutionary socialism, it still had inherited a strong state machinery to carry out its developmental policy.

The critical issue, then, is what explains the dramatic transformation of the revolutionary state under Maoism to the developmental state in the re-form era? This chapter argues that the fading of the Cold War provided the pre-condition for China to re-enter the world economy, the success of the Asian Newly Industrializing Economies (NIEs) and their industrial reloca-tion provided the incentives for the Chinese leaders to pursue developmental objectives, and the passing of the old generation and natural disasters pro-vided the triggering events to overcome the inertia of the status quo.

The Fading of the Cold War

If the Cold War and the forced withdrawal from the world economy pre-vented China from pursuing either export-oriented industrialization or im-port substitution, the fading of the Cold War since the 1970s provided the pre-condition for China to re-enter the world economy to pursue develop-mental objectives.

The late 1970s was a period of declining American hegemony. Economi-cally, the United States faced the problems of inflation, low productivity, and recession. Its products were under strong competition from Japanese and German manufactures in the world market. Politically, the United States was still plagued by its defeat in Vietnam and its failed attempt to fend off global Soviet expansionism. At this historical conjuncture, the United States wel-comed China back to the world economy. China could be a new regional power to counterbalance Soviet military expansion and Japanese economic expansion in East Asia. Moreover, the vast Chinese market, cheap Chinese labor, and abundant Chinese raw materials and minerals could considerably increase the competitive power of American industry in the world market.

East Asian Industrial Relocation

In addition, the Chinese state was impressed with the economic success of its East Asian neighbors. With U.S. support in the 1950s and the 1960s, Ja-pan, South Korea, Taiwan, and Hong Kong had become highly industrialized and their people enjoyed a much higher living standard than that of China. Thus, the Chinese state was motivated to follow the path of its successful East Asian neighbors to engage in export-oriented industrialization.

Furthermore, as Hong Kong, Taiwan, and South Korea were upgraded to the status of NIEs in the late 1970s, they gradually lost their geopolitical privileges with the United States. They, too, had to face the trade restrictions (tariffs, quotas, and rising foreign currency value). Due to their economic success, there were also labor shortages, increasing labor disputes, escalat-ing land prices, and the emergence of environmental protests—all of which served to raise the cost of production in the East Asian NIEs. As a result, the East Asian NIEs felt the need to promote an industrial relocation in order to secure a stable supply of cheap, docile labor, and other resources in the 1980s.

Industrial relocation of the NIEs provided a strong incentive for the Chinese state to promote developmental objectives. From the Chinese perspective, China could be a favorable site for the NIEs' relocation because it had abundant cheap labor, land, and other resources. China was also quite close to Hong Kong, Taiwan, and South Korea, and these areas all share a common Confucian cultural heritage. Therefore, China set up four special economic zones (SEZs) in 1979, opened fourteen coastal cities and Hainan Island in 1984 and three delta areas in 1985 for foreign investment, and pursued a coastal developmental strategy to enhance export industrialization in 1988.[7]

Triggering Events

Even though the fading of the Cold War and the NIEs' industrial relocation provided the precondition and an incentive for the Chinese state to transform itself into a developmental state, it still required several triggering events to overcome the inertia of the communist status quo.

In this volume, Yi-min Lin points out that the critical event that set in motion the efforts to reform the economic system was the passing of the old generation of revolutionary leaders. The death of Mao in 1976 was followed by the rise of a new coalition of political leaders who were leaning toward or receptive to some form of economic institutional change. Most of them were victims of the Cultural Revolution. Their return was accompanied by a national rehabilitation of lower-level party-state functionaries. Most of these functionaries had prior experience in formulating and implementing economic policies.

Yi-min Lin further explains that the shift in policy focus from socialist egalitarianism to economic development and the reshuffling of local leaders opened the way for bottom-up institutional innovation. In provinces like Anhui, pro-reform leaders gave tolerance and even encouragement to certain attempts made by grassroots officials. This significantly changed the political risk perceived by the rank-and-file of the local state apparatus. Subsequently, when severe national disasters hit from 1977 through 1979, some local officials resorted to various forms of family production and justified their rule-breaking on the grounds of coping with natural disaster. The good results of family farming in turn provided grounds for the arrangement to be introduced to other provinces, which later led to decollectivization and the institutionalization of the household responsibility system in the countryside. The great success of the economic reforms in the agricultural sector—

as shown by the crop output growth from 2.5 percent from 1954 to 1978 to 5.9 percent from 1978 to 1984—further empowered the Chinese state to develop various developmental strategies.[8]

Developmental Strategies and Why They Worked

The Legacy of the Maoist Era

Once the Chinese state decided to pursue developmental objectives, it found itself blessed with many legacies of the Maoist era. To start with, the Maoist legacy of economic backwardness ironically worked to the advantage of the economic reforms in the late 1970s. As Andrew Walder points out, at the outset of the reforms, employment in China was 75 percent in agriculture; in the Soviet Union, 75 percent in industry. Since the Soviet Union was already an urbanized industrial society, Soviet economic reforms necessitated technological and organization innovations to boost industrial productivity in the urban sector. On the other hand, since China was still mostly agricultural, the state could achieve rapid growth rates by simply taking labor out of agriculture and increasing its productivity by putting it to work in industry.[9]

Second, the Maoist legacy of "self-reliance" resulted in a debt-free economy for pre-reform China. Instead of relying on external support (such as Soviet aid, technology, and expertise), Mao focused on a "self-reliance" model of development, stressing national autonomy, pride in being a poor country, mass mobilization, local development, and labor-intensive industries. As a result, China incurred almost no foreign debt when the state started its economic reforms in 1978. In stark contrast to many Eastern European states and Russia, China did not need to devote huge resources to servicing foreign debt, nor did China need to resort to crushing bailout packages by the International Monetary Fund to shore up its economy.

Third, the Maoist legacy provided the much-needed rural infrastructure and local institutions to carry out the economic reforms. It was during the Maoist era that reservoirs were constructed, the irrigation system strengthened, and the drainage network improved. During the Great Leap Forward, the state mobilized millions of peasants to construct dams, reservoirs, and large-scale irrigation systems for the communes. It was also during the Maoist era that rural industries and enterprises were set up in the communes, local officials accumulated managerial experience through running commune and brigade enterprises, and local governments were asked to promote development in the community. The Maoist commune model and its decentralization policy provided the medium to tap local resources, to train local leaders, and to arouse local initiatives. Without all these infrastructure and institutional

foundations built in the Maoist era, it is doubtful whether agricultural productivity could have increased so rapidly in the early 1980s, and whether
local village and township enterprises could have played the leading role in
China's industrialization since 1978.[10]

Finally, China benefited from adopting the strategy of "reform from above."
Even though China faced many serious developmental problems in the mid-
1970s, the situation was not desperate. The Chinese state was not under the
threat of foreign invasion, economic bankruptcy, or rebellion from below. As
such, the party-state still had the autonomy and capacity to propose and implement various structural reforms under its control. The state could select certain types of reform, could vary the speed of reform, and most importantly,
had the freedom to correct its mistakes.

Therefore, different from the "one bang" approach in Eastern Europe, the
reform in China has been a gradual, adaptive process without a clear blueprint. John McMillan and Barry Naughton remark that "the reforms have
proceeded by trial and error, with frequent mid-course corrections and rever-
sals of policy."[11] In other words, the economic reforms were not a complete
project settled in the first stage, but an ongoing process with many adjustments. There was no rapid leap to free prices, currency convertibility, or
cutting of state subsidies; nor was there massive privatization and the quick
selling off of state enterprises. This gradualist approach practiced by the
Chinese state was quite different from those "one bang" and "shock therapy"
approaches practiced in Eastern Europe, which called for the dismantling of
the centrally planned economy as soon as possible. As Andrew Walder remarks, "Where in Europe shock therapy and mass privatization are designed
in part to dismantle Communism and strip former Communists of power and
privilege, in China gradual reform is intended to allow the Party to survive as
an instrument of economic development."[12]

With the Chinese state in control, it carried out the following strategies of
development: decentralization and local development, mobilizing diaspora
capitalists, labor migration, and reform sequence.

Decentralization and Local Development

Attracted by the policy of fiscal decentralization through which local governments could keep part of the tax revenue, local governments quickly engaged in market activities. The product was the formation of township and
village enterprises (TVEs), which were not bound by the central plan and
were free to seek out market opportunities. Kyung-Sup Chang in this volume
remarks that for local cadres, running rural industries was no new experience
since they had been in charge of rural industries since the Great Leap Forward

in the late 1950s. Seizing the golden opportunity created by the policy of fiscal decentralization, many rural cadres created a favorable political and administrative environment for new industrial ventures, renovated or built factories, set up corporate organizations, mobilized villagers' economic resources, secured financial and technical cooperation from urban enterprises, and staffed the management of rural industrial enterprises.

Focusing on the South China case, George Lin in this volume further points out that a new "bottom up" development mechanism is taking shape in which initiatives are made primarily by local governments to solicit overseas Chinese and domestic capital, mobilize labor and land resources, and lead the local economy to enter the orbit of the international division of labor and global competition. As a result, South China has experienced rural industrialization through which a great number of surplus rural laborers have entered the TVEs without moving into the city. In the South Chinese countryside, it is common to find industrial and agricultural activities standing side by side. Lin stresses that the geographic outcome of intense rural-urban interaction in the countryside has been the formation of a dispersed pattern of spatial distribution that does not confirm to the classic definition of urban or rural but displays the characteristics of both types.

Mobilizing Chinese Diaspora Capitalism

In Eastern Europe, ethnic divisions are reinforced by religious conflict and national conflict, leading to ethnic violence and making ethnic separatism a highly explosive issue. It was the constant rebellions in ethnic minority regions that weakened the communist state, eventually leading to its downfall and the breaking up of the Soviet Union.

However, in China, ethnicity is generally a valuable asset for economic development, instead of becoming a source of political instability. Before 1978, Chinese diaspora capitalism thrived in Hong Kong, Taiwan, Singapore, and overseas Chinese communities. After the Chinese state adopted an open door policy for foreign investment in 1978, Hong Kong accounted for the bulk of China's foreign investment and foreign trade. By the early 1990s, Taiwan became the second largest trading partner and investor in mainland China.

Drawing upon Guangdong's Dongguan County as a case study, George Lin shows in this volume that the local government has sought every possible opportunity to cultivate kinship ties and interpersonal trusts with the diaspora capitalists in Hong Kong in order to encourage them to invest in Dongguan County. Special policies, including taxation concessions and preferential treatment regarding the import of necessary equipment and the handling of foreign currency, were announced to attract foreign investment. A special office was set up by the county government to serve Hong Kong investors with efficient personnel and simplified bureaucratic procedures. Economic cooperation between Dongguan and Hong Kong was arranged creatively and flexibly in a variety of forms, including joint ventures, cooperative ventures, export processing, and compensation trade. The general pattern is that designing and marketing are handled in Hong Kong, while labor intensive processes are performed in Dongguan. Access to cheap labor enables Hong Kong diaspora capitalists to compete effectively in the global market, and export processing has created jobs and income for mainland China.

In discussing the case of Fujian Province, Hsin-Huang Michael Hsiao points out in this volume that Chinese diaspora capitalists have played an important role in the economic development of Fujian. In the 1980s, many Southeast Asian Chinese business groups with Fujian origins, such as the Philippines' Tan Yu and Lucio C. Tan, Indonesia's Liem Sioe Liong, and Malaysia's Robert Kuok, made substantial investments in Fujian. By the early 1990s, Taiwan capital began to enter Fujian on a massive scale. By 1997, Fujian had attracted more than 4,900 Taiwanese enterprises, with the total realized investment exceeding US$6.9 billion. Taiwan capital has been highly diversified, ranging from small-scale labor-intensive manufacturing industries to capital-intensive heavy industries and high-tech industries.

Controlling Labor Migration

Before the reform era, the household registration (*hukou*) system had kept farmers in the countryside. In order to transfer resources from the rural to the urban sector, the Chinese state has loosened the household registration system since 1978, starting a trend of migration of the non-*hukou* migrant population from the countryside, which by the late 1990s had reached the size of about 100 million migrants.

In this volume, Kam Wing Chan contends that economic development in the reform era in China is intimately linked with migration. Migration is a redistribution of labor that helps balance China's regional supply and demand. The vast pools of rural migrants provide a plentiful supply of cheap labor in sustaining China's urban economic boom. This labor force is also flexible, able, and willing to move quickly into new growth areas. In the cities, the full cost of hiring a migrant worker is only about one-quarter of that of hiring a local worker. Migrant workers are also willing not only to work for less and for long hours, but also often to work under unsafe conditions with minimal protection. The increasing supply of labor from outside has fostered the development of an urban labor market.

Kam Wing Chan also reveals the generally positive impact of migration for rural areas. Out-migration is an effective and cheap way to siphon off surplus rural labor and to ease pressure on local land and resources. In addition, remittances by migrant workers to their families back home have become a major contribution to the economy. Chan estimates that remittances in the size of 180 billion yuan are sent back to rural areas every year, equivalent to 15 percent of China's agricultural sector's GDP.

Furthermore, working in the cities is an important opportunity for many farmers to learn about the modern world and skills. It is not uncommon for returnees to use the savings, skills, and business contacts they bring back to start up or invest in small businesses. And the remittances allow those working on the farm to purchase fertilizers and other needed modern inputs (such as better seeds) for farming.

Reform Sequence

Finally, the Chinese state benefited from carrying out reforms in the countryside before proposing any reform on the urban economy. Rural reforms were much less complicated than urban reforms. In the late 1970s, the Chinese state increased procurement prices for agricultural products, encouraged peasants to engage in cash crop and rural industrial production, and allowed peasants to work in nearby market towns and faraway cities. After the rural reforms succeeded, the Chinese state was more confident about working on the complicated urban reforms in the 1980s. Rising agricultural productivity, in turn, released surplus labor from the countryside, providing a large number of cheap laborers to urban factories.

Furthermore, in the Soviet Union, political reforms were carried out before economic reforms, with the hope that democratization would provide the communist party with the needed support to overcome bureaucratic resistance toward economic reforms. The Soviet Union also carried out reforms in urban areas first because of the deep-rooted problems in the countryside. However, political reforms unintentionally released new political forces that opposed the communist party, and urban unrest eventually led to the overthrow of the communist state in the Soviet Union.

In contrast, the Chinese state promoted economic reforms before carrying out major democratic reforms. In the late 1970s, communes were dismantled, and peasants were asked to be responsible for their own living. In the early 1980s, the Chinese state tried to promote enterprise reforms to increase the power of managers. In the mid-1980s, the Chinese state went further and opened fourteen coastal cities to attract foreign investment. In the reform period the Chinese state showed more tolerance toward dissent, granted more freedom to its citizens, and allowed local elections at the village level, but the Chinese state was reluctant to promote any serious democratic reform to allow multi-party elections at the provincial and national levels. As a result, the Chinese state could retain the Leninist structure. Not only did it not need to share power with other political parties, it also did not need to worry about the critical democratic voices in the civil society and the uncertainty of election outcomes. Without being distracted by democratic reforms, the Chinese state was able to concentrate on the economic front to promote its modernization programs.

Managing New Ideas and Social Forces

Still, new ideas and social forces were unleashed during the economic reforms to challenge the Chinese state. What explains the ability of the Chinese state to be able to maintain political stability and to promote economic development in spite of these challenges?

Communitarianism

First of all, as Suzanne Ogden explains in this volume, the Chinese state is now confronting the problem of how to fill the void created by the collapse of communitarian values fostered by Marxism-Leninism-Mao Zedong Thought. Furthermore, the Chinese state is facing the divisive and destabilizing forces of capitalism, individualism, commercialism, and modernization, forces that have undercut the sense of community in China. The search for communitarian values to replace those of communism has led to official support for the values of nationalism, patriotism, and the reinvention of Chinese popular culture. In particular, the Chinese state tried to revive Chinese culture as part of an effort to confront a "fever" for Western ideas. Its overall goal was to use culture to bolster the power of (cultural) nationalism. Also, to be a "patriot" in today's China means to support the national community and its goals, notably national reunification, economic growth, and political stability.

Suzanne Ogden argues that the Chinese people have embraced cultural nationalism and patriotism with a passion, as shown by the fact that even Chinese dissidents have overwhelmingly taken the government's side in defending China's claims to Taiwan and Tibet, their extraordinary pleasure in Hong Kong's return to Beijing rule in 1997, and their anger at what they interpret as the West's support for Japan's military expansion and containment of China, including U.S. consideration of plans to build a "theatre missile defense" in Northeast Asia that would protect Japan, and possibly Taiwan, from attack.

Egalitarianism

Second, the legacy of egalitarianism during the Maoist era helped to slow down the reforms and make their impact less disruptive. In this volume, James Kung shows that in the countryside, although decollectivization gave the farmers the right to decide on how land and labor are to be deployed, land ownership rights continue to reside in the hands of the village authorities, or more appropriately the villagers, given that in practice land is divided more or less equally among members of the village community. Thus, decollectivization turned out to be highly egalitarian. James Kung further refutes the claim in the mainstream literature that communal ownership has been the primary cause of a stagnant crop output growth and an obstructive force to the development process. There is empirical evidence to show that despite the lack of private property rights in land, the rural land market is quite active, which is how people view the market in "use-rights" of the land. Also, the transfer of rural surplus labor has also occurred without secure land rights, so Kung argues China has had the luxury to assess the possible consequences of privatization before rushing into it.

In addition, Yi-min Lin shows that ideological constraints have slowed the growth of the private sector. Until the mid-1990s, capitalists not only faced weak and unstable protection for their residual rights, but they were actually discriminated against in licensing, credit, land use, material input allocation, and the supply of utilities. Such a policy bias forced many capitalists to disguise their private businesses as public or collective enterprises in order to survive.

The pace of urban reform has been constrained by the ideological claim that the working class is the master of society and the state sector represents the foundation of the socialist economy. Thus, in this volume, Kyung-Sup Chang points out that urban workers are somehow provided by the state with various shock-absorbing mechanisms against layoffs and unemployment. In March 1999, Zhu Rongji announced that redundant workers who had been asked to leave their jobs, called *xiagang* (off-the-post) employees in Chinese, would be given a grace period to stay in the *xiagang* category.

As Carsten Holz and Tian Zhu further explain, a *xiagang* employee is to enter a "reemployment service center," which is usually located within the state-owned enterprise, for a period of three years. During these three years, the center helps find reemployment, and during the period of unemployment, it pays a "basic living allowance" as well as the laid-off workers' pension contributions, medical insurance, and unemployment insurance. After three years, the relationship between the state-owned enterprise and its former workers is severed and the former workers receive regular unemployment insurance payments or social relief support.

Holz and Zhu further point out that the three-year *xiagang* program was in part preceded and in part accompanied by a complete overhaul of the social security system. Traditionally, all social security tasks were concentrated within a state-owned enterprise. State-owned enterprise reform required these social security tasks to be shifted to an external institution. This led to the establishment of a provincial-level pension system beginning in 1997, a new urban medical insurance system in 1998, and an unemployment insurance system in 1999.

In a report to the National People's Congress in 2002, Premier Zhu Rongji further highlighted the needs of the poor as the government's top priorities in the coming year. Zhu declared that the government would target retired and redundant workers from state enterprises by ensuring that they received their pensions and stipends on time. Zhu wanted to set up a minimum living standard protection scheme to provide a level of protection for those who were unable to find a job for more than two years and were no longer covered by unemployment funds.[13]

Corporatism

Finally, after experiencing two decades of capitalism since the late 1970s, many new social actors and civic organizations have emerged in China. These new actors include private business owners, employers, operators, and those employees and laborers working for foreign and private enterprises. Accompanying the appearance of these new actors has been the emergence of many new semi-autonomous social organizations in the coastal provinces, such as the Private Enterprise Association, the Enterprise Owners Civic Associations, and the Local Federations of Industry and Commerce. These new social organizations help to expand the horizontal linkages and alliances among different societal units and individuals.

However, despite the rise of these new actors and social organizations, business politics in China has yet to take the form of the democratic or human rights movements. Why then did the business class not protest or fight back against state suppression of its civil organization? This is because business activity in China is mediated through state institutions.

On the one hand, as Hsin-Huang Michael Hsiao explains in this volume, a new kind of corporatism has emerged during the reform era. The state surely recognized the business class as a powerful social force to challenge the existing order. That was why the state was determined to bring new business organizations under its control through the rubric of corporatism. The essence of corporatism is that the state holds the power to approve which business association can represent the private sector, who are the businessmen who can be chosen as the leaders, and what activities can be seen as legitimate.

Corporatism generally allows that only one business association can be recognized as representing a given economic sector in an administrative unit, that the association leaders have gained the trust of the communist party, and their association activities cannot be anti-state.

On the other hand, the business class cultivates *guanxi,* a gift economy, and clientelism in order to form an alliance with the local state. Given that the local state has had almost complete control over the economy, this business class's alliance with the local state is a pragmatic political tactic of survival and self-protection. The space that private business has enjoyed is handed down from the local state, and businesspeople have to know their political limits. As a result, instead of challenging the state, businesspeople use clientelism to work with state officials in order to attain a high degree of managerial autonomy in their enterprises. This clientelism enables business people to re-impose the nineteenth century despotic factory regime in South China (such as unpaid overtime, disrespect, cursing, deduction of wages and bonuses, arbitrary firings, body searches, lack of medical or industrial accident insurance, and a ban on unions), even though the central state has set up rules to protect Chinese labor from capitalist abuses.[14]

Aside from unleashing the social forces in the private sector, the reforms have also activated gender politics. Ping-Chun Hsiung examines in this volume Chinese women's political participation as it is experienced and articulated by professional women. By conceptualizing the political arena as an engendered site of discontent, Hsiung investigates how women professionals have come to challenge the gender system in post-Mao China and what forces have sustained these women in times of uncertainty and defeat. Hsiung shows that a women professional's desire for self-realization is interlocked with her yearning for collective group emancipation. Together, these aspirations form an oppositional, engendered identity that inspires the everyday activism of women professionals. Nevertheless, Chinese gender politics is mediated by the official Women's Federation. Hsiung argues that the Federation has had an ambivalent relationship with the Chinese Communist Party (CCP). Mandated to follow the directives of the CCP and to represent women's interests, the Federation is never free to advocate women's causes that would compromise its party function.

In sum, even though the dynamics of the reforms have set off new actors and organizations in China, these nascent actors and organizations are more interested in working with the existing state structure than in transforming it. Since the Chinese state was not weakened by the dynamics of capitalism, it was able to impose a "corporatist" civil society in China, absorbing the new social forces into the existing state framework to maintain political order and to promote economic development.

Characteristics

Similarities with the East Asian Developmental States

From the above discussion, it is obvious that the Chinese pattern of develop-ment shares many similar characteristics with the developmental states in South Korea and Taiwan during their industrial take-off phase (between the 1960s and the mid-1980s). First, there was an autonomous state that had the capacity to formulate and implement developmental policies. In China, since the strong Leninist party-state remained largely intact in the reform era, the Chinese state had the capacity to introduce certain types of economic pro-grams, to vary the speed and the sequence of reform, and to make correc-tions or even reverse its policy if it should become necessary.

Second, the developmental states adopted authoritarian policies to deacti-vate civil society, discipline labor, and suppress dissent in order to maintain a favorable environment to attract foreign and domestic investment and to maintain political stability. In China, the legacy of the Leninist party-state and corporatism helped the Chinese state deal with the emerging social forces unleashed by the economic reforms.

Third, since the developmental states did not carry out any democratic reforms but relied upon suppression and corporatism for political control, they needed a different basis of legitimacy from that of the Western demo-cratic states. In China, like other East Asian developmental states, the basis of legitimacy was mainly derived from "GNPism" and nationalism. The claims were that the citizens should support the state because their incomes had greatly improved, their living standards were much better than those of the older generation, and they should unite behind the state in order to create a rich and powerful nation free of domination by the foreigners.

The China Difference

Despite the above similarities, the pattern of Chinese development differs from that of the East Asian developmental states in the following ways.

First, China has exhibited a strong tendency toward state entrepreneur-ship. Although developmental state officials, like those in South Korea, tar-geted industry, provided incentives such as subsidies and lower tax rates, and monitored corporate performance, they seldom directly engaged in running the companies themselves. In China, however, not only were state officials asked to be good managers and turn state enterprises into profit-making busi-nesses, but also in many cases informally turned public assets into quasi-public, quasi-private properties, or even into simply private companies. As it is well documented in Chinese studies, there is a fuzzy boundary between state enterprises and collective/private enterprises, and it is difficult to draw a clear boundary between state officials and private capitalists in China. Rather, the Chinese characteristic is a hybrid "state-capitalist" walking on two legs in both the state sector and the private sector.[15]

In Russia and Eastern Europe, former state officials also engaged in stripping the assets of state enterprises. However, although such activity in Russia and Eastern Europe had led to rent-seeking and the decline of their economies, state officials in China often invested in productive, profitable enterprises in a competitive market. While it is true that stripping the assets of state enterprises greatly enriched Chinese officials, their productive investments also helped promote economic development, leading to a very respectable growth rate for the Chinese economy over the past decade.

Second, China has exhibited a pattern of local, "bottom-up" development. The East Asian developmental states had adopted a centralized policy, and it was their central governments that played the most active role in development. However, in China, owing to the legacy of the communes, the present policy of fiscal decentralization, and the vast territory of China, local officials in provincial, county, and village governments played a much more active role than their counterparts in the East Asian developmental states. Instead of promoting urban industrialization and mega-cities (like that of Seoul), Chinese local state officials promoted rural industrialization and small and medium-size cities. This pattern of dispersed development will have a profound impact on China in the future.

Third, although the Chinese state relied mostly on "GNPism" and nationalism as its bases of legitimacy, it also paid more attention to egalitarianism than the East Asian developmental states during their industrial take-off phases. Having gone through the legacy of revolutionary socialism under the Maoist regime, and having a constitution still proclaiming that workers and peasants are the masters of society, the Chinese "communist" state was much more vulnerable to charges of inequality, poverty, and exploitation than its East Asian development state counterparts. Thus, the Chinese state many times backed off from carrying out those policies that could lead to the massive layoffs and the elimination of the social safety net of the urban residents.

Challenges

China is facing four challenges: how to carry out the proposed economic reforms, how to handle the increasing pressures from global competition after WTO entry, how to manage the emerging social conflicts, and how to position itself in hegemonic struggles with the United States.

The Challenge of the Implementation of Economic Reforms

Despite achieving a developmental miracle over the past two decades, China is not without serious challenges in the twenty-first century. Carsten Holz and Tian Zhu explain that China is facing three financial crises: bad loans in the state banks, losses in the state-owned enterprises (SOEs), and government budget deficits. First of all, by the mid-1990s, estimates of the state banks' bad loans ranged from 20 percent to about 50 percent. The 20 percent estimate of bad debts tended to cover only nonperforming loans and loan losses, while the higher 50 percent estimate usually included overdue loans. Second, the financial performance of industrial SOEs deteriorated sharply over the reform period. Losses of industrial SOEs increased drastically in the late 1980s and continued to rise through the late 1990s. The ratio of the profits of profitable enterprises to the losses of money-losing enterprises after 1985 fell to an all-time low in 1997. Third, with regard to government budget deficits, the fiscal balance deteriorated from a small budget surplus in 1978 to a deficit equivalent to more than 10 percent of expenditures in 1990s. From 1995 to 2000, approximately 20 percent of total annual expenditures were financed through borrowing, gradually increasing over time. In 2000, the budget deficit was equivalent to 4.55 percent of GDP. Domestic debt grew rapidly from zero in 1978 to a minimum of 9.68 percent of GDP in 2000.

Holz and Zhu further stress that these three financial crises are intricately linked. For example, social security payments could be made either by SOEs or through the government budget. If they are made by an SOE, they reduce SOE profit; if they are financed through the government budget, they increase the government budget deficit. Infrastructure projects could either be financed through government budget appropriations, increasing the government budget deficit, or through state-ordained low-interest loans from the state banks, reducing bank profits. In this respect, reforming one sector (either the banks, the SOEs, or the government budget) without reforming the other two will not have an effective outcome. The extent of the banks' bad loans, SOE losses, and government fiscal shortfalls reflects more than a political decision on where within the state sector to place the financial deficit attributable only to the state sector as a whole.

Up to now, these financial crises have been ameliorated by China's rapid economic development. However, once China's high-speed economic growth slows down, the problem of bad loans, SOE losses, and government deficit will become explosive.

The Challenge of Globalization and Development

The crucial question then is whether China's rapid economic development can continue and for how long. During the Asian financial crisis in the late

1990s, China's foreign investment and exports experienced a slight decline. Only after the Asian financial crisis passed did foreign investment and exports return to the previous level. However, at the beginning of the twenty-first century, both the U.S. and Japan have moved into economic recession. If a global economic recession continues for a fairly long period, it could produce a dampening effect on the Chinese economy, leading to a decline of foreign investment and exports, a rapid rise of unemployment, new pressures to devaluate the Chinese currency, and other consequences.

Furthermore, globalization through WTO accession is likely to produce significant competitive pressures on the agriculture sector. Kam Wing Chan estimates that China will lose about 3 million jobs in agriculture due to the competition of imported farm products. Another report quoting government sources said 20 million rural jobs will be lost because of China's WTO entry.[16] In the urban sector, many old and less competitive industries and enterprises will lose out in the short term after WTO entry. In this respect, the problem of job losses and unemployment will rise to the top of the agenda of the Chinese state in the first decade of the twenty-first century.

Accession into the WTO may have a negative impact on China's telecommunications, automobile, and banking industries as well. For example, the Asian Development Bank points out that China's banking sector, one of the most protected in the world, is particularly vulnerable. In the short to medium term, net interest margins of local banks will narrow, and profitability will be squeezed. To face the challenges from international banks after WTO accession, reform of the finance sector must be accelerated. The key problem is to tackle the problem of nonperforming loans and to establish an effective corporate governance system.

Furthermore, China was less affected by the Asian financial crisis in the late 1990s because its currency was not convertible, because it had strong control over the banking sector and foreign trade, and because the Chinese economy drew greatly on domestic markets and thus was less exposed to international market fluctuations than many of its neighbors. However, WTO entry will increase China's global economic integration. Any global recession in the early twenty-first century will exert a more serious impact on the Chinese economy than before.

The Challenge of Social Conflict

Although the Chinese state has been successful in incorporating new social forces and suppressing democratic reforms, these political issues will become more explosive once they are combined with the economic issues of enterprise bankruptcy, unemployment, and global recession.

Kam Wing Chan estimates that about 10 million workers are expected to be laid off in the state sector in the next five years, and layoffs carry the risk of triggering urban political turmoil. In addition, despite a massive outflow of rural migrant workers, 90 million laborers in the countryside need jobs. The sluggish performance of the urban economy, job competition from laid-off workers in the state sector, and increasingly protectionist policies by the local states against the migrant workers will make it harder and harder for them to find jobs in the cities. A large "floating population" could easily become the source of social conflict.

In this volume, Kyung-Sup Chang further laments that even when migrant workers do find employment, they must endure all kinds of social and economic hardships because of the constraints imposed upon them by the old household registration system. For example, it is extremely difficult, if not impossible, for migrant workers to acquire social services (such as education and health care for their children), while such services are offered to regular urban residents as a sort of citizenship rights.

At the same time, the wealth gap is growing very rapidly. According to a World Bank report in 1997, the Gini coefficient (an international measurement of income disparity) rose from 0.28 in the 1980s to a dangerously high 0.43 last year. The richest 20 percent of Beijing residents owned 11 times as much in assets as the poorest 20 percent.[17]

Subsequently, there is a serious possibility that grassroots people's frustration and resistance will be expressed not only against richer neighbors but also much more crucially against the state and its local agents. The numerous stories about corruption, favoritism, abuses of power, and extravagant life-styles of cadres reported in the Chinese newspapers and magazines are an expression of this grassroots frustration. In this context, state authority can easily be identified with economic injustice. Such grassroots sentiment could express itself in strikes, street demonstrations, social movements, and riots across the country. Kyung-Sup Chang reports that over the past few years peasants in many inland provinces rioted against corrupt and extorting local cadres, and in many big cities unemployed and impoverished groups staged rallies against their local governments for their economic mishaps. Even anti-corruption campaigns can be seen as a form of class politics catering to the desire of grassroots peasants, workers, and migrants.

Aside from class conflict, there could be religious conflict as well. Richard Madsen reports in this volume that in July 1999 the Chinese state officially declared the Falungong an evil cult and began a massive campaign to suppress it. The supposed evils of Falungong bolstered the officials in charge of religious affairs to tighten control over all manner of unofficial religious activity. Thus, over the past two years, the Chinese state demolished hundreds of nonregistered church buildings, stepped up arrests of underground bishops and priests, and established new local branches of the Catholic Patriotic Association. According to Madsen, the above conflicts with the Catholic Church stem from general weaknesses in the Chinese state's capacity to create new forms of soft power sufficient to contain a rapidly developing informal, unofficial social realm. The state seems too insecure to make the political concessions necessary to coopt such developments. Madsen argues that attempts to suppress the Catholic Church are often counterproductive. They succeed only in increasing the level of hostility of some citizens toward the regime, which renders peaceful political reform all the more difficult. Besides revealing weaknesses in governing capacity, the conflicts with the Catholic Church reveal weaknesses in the state's capacity to represent morally a richly pluralistic, evolving national identity.

The Challenge of Hegemonic Rivalry

The rapid economic development of China over the past two decades has also made the U.S. worry that in the near future China may challenge its global hegemony. Suzanne Ogden in this volume points out several ways that the United States has exerted its influence over China:

- Since 1989, it has used human rights as a pretext to threaten the end of China's most-favored-nation trade status (normal trade status), deny China the right to host the year 2000 Olympics, and block China's entry into the World Trade Organization for years;
- The United States has accused China of "stealing" U.S. nuclear secrets and making illegal contributions to the U.S. Democratic Party in the 1996 elections;
- The United States has continued to support Taiwan militarily and sent two U.S. aircraft carrier battle units to Taiwan in 1996;
- The United States bombed the Chinese Embassy in Belgrade, Yugoslavia in May 1999 during the war over Kosovo;
- It carried out air surveillance of China, which precipitated the crash of a Chinese jet, the death of its pilot, and an emergency landing of the U.S. plane on the island of Hainan;
- It decided to build a theatre missile defense system that might include Taiwan, as well as a national U.S. defense, that would deny China a second strike capability.

Although the war against terrorism in late 2001 temporarily overshadowed hegemonic rivalry between the United States and China, it is too early to tell whether such rivalry can be rekindled when the war against terrorism ends.

Prospects

What is the prospect for China's developmental miracle? There are three possible scenarios in the near future: failing to deal with the above challenges, succeeding in handling the above challenges, and muddling through.

The Developmental Mirage

If the Chinese state fails to implement economic reforms, if the accession to WTO brings more harm than benefit to China, if the global economic recession is long and serious, and if the United States sees China more as a strategic competitor than as a strategic partner, the developmental miracle could be transformed into a developmental mirage in the near future.

John Fernald and Oliver Babson mention the following pessimistic scenario:

> Suppose that growth slows sharply . . . , reflecting a plunge in exports and non-state investment, an overhang of inventories, and widespread consumer unwillingness to spend. Social and political pressures are mounting in response to rising unemployment and stagnating real wages. The perception that China might devalue (in order to spur exports) leads to a widening of black market premium and capital flight (evading capital controls). Foreign investors become less willing to invest in and lend to China, reducing investment further. In the face of slowing growth, steadily falling foreign exchange reserves, and lobbying by exporters, China devalues. Economic weakness could potentially lead to political infighting in China as well, thereby raising uncertainty and exacerbating all of the problems above.[18]

In this scenario, the Chinese communist state may not be able to hold on to power for long as a result of economic recession and political instability.

The Developmental Miracle Continues

However, the optimists cite Beijing's long-term commitment to reform and the pragmatic nature of its leadership. Jiang Zemin and Zhu Rongji have steadily reduced the role of the SOEs and are experimenting with novel solutions to financing, including stock ownership plans. The Chinese leaders also understand the important role of township and village enterprises, which, along with export industries, were the engines of China's economic growth. The optimists are persuaded that China will be spared from the turmoil of the marketization.

The two decades of generally uninterrupted economic growth have greatly strengthened the Chinese economy, providing breathing space for the Chinese state to try all sorts of policies to deal with the problems of enterprise reforms and banking reforms. For example, the Chinese government in 2002 proposed to boost the economy by investing in infrastructure projects, developing the western provinces, upgrading technology for state-owned enterprises, improving education, and developing a project to transport water from the Yangtze River to the northern provinces.[19] Massive state investments, China's abundant reserves (materials, food, and foreign exchange), and huge domestic market should help China meet the challenges of development. Thus, by the end of the second decade of the twenty-first century, the Chinese state will have gained the experience to handle the challenges of WTO accession and global market fluctuation, while China's vast domestic economy will be able to provide an economic powerhouse for the developmental miracle to continue. Economic miracle in turn enhances the state's capacity to solve the emerging social conflict in society, and the Chinese Communist Party will hold on to power for a fairly long time.

Muddling Through

Apart from the above pessimistic and optimistic scenarios, there is a muddling through scenario. Given the successful record of the Chinese state in handling challenges from below and from outside, the Chinese state should have the capacity to hold on to power and to promote economic development. On the other hand, as time goes by, the Chinese state will find it harder and harder to accomplish its goals. The Chinese state may be forced to slow down, change direction, or even reverse its reform policies. With economic growth rates declining, with social problems getting more acute, and with unending calls for political reforms and democratization, China may soon look more and more like other developing countries in East Asia.

In sum, will the miracle become a mirage? Will the miracle continue? Or will the miracle be tuned down allowing China to only muddle through? It depends. History never follows a predetermined path but is always subject to the intervention of human agency. Prospects for the developmental miracle, therefore, depend very much on how Chinese state leaders handle the issues of state enterprise reform, global recession, WTO entry, growing social conflicts, and hegemonic rivalry in the early twenty-first century.

Notes

I want to express my sincere thanks to Yi-min Lin and David Zweig for their helpful comments and criticisms on an earlier draft of this paper. I appreciate having these two colleagues read the chapter very carefully and make insightful comments page by page.

1. Alvin Y. So and Stephen Chiu, *East Asia and the World Economy* (Newbury Park, Calif.: Sage, 1995).

2. Alvin Y. So, "China Under the Shadow of the Asian Financial Crisis: Retreat from Economic and Political Liberalism?" *Asian Perspectives* 23, no. 2 (1999): 83–110.

3. On November 21, 2001, 8.2765 yuan (Renminbi) = US$1.

4. Far Eastern Economic Review, *Asia 2002 Yearbook* (Hong Kong: Far Eastern Economic Review, 2001).

5. See also David Zweig, "China and Its Neighbors: Strategic, Economic, and Transnational Perspective," paper prepared for the Northeast Asia Cooperation Project, Institute of Asian Research, University of British Columbia, September 15, 2001.

6. Chris Bramall, *In Praise of Maoist Economic Planning: Living Standards and Economic Development in Sichuan Since 1931* (Oxford, U.K.: Clarendon Press, 1993).

7. Alvin Y. So, "Introduction: The Origins and Transformation of the Chinese Triangle," in Alvin Y. So, Nan Lin, and Dudley Poston, eds., *The Chinese Triangle of Mainland China-Taiwan-Hong Kong* (Westport, Conn.: Greenwood Press, 2001), pp. 1–22.

8. David Zweig, *Agrarian Radicalism in China, 1968–1981* (Cambridge, Mass.: Harvard University Press, 1989).

9. Andrew Walder, *China's Transitional Economy: Interpreting its Significance* (London: Oxford University Press, 1996), p. 9.

10. Zweig, *Agrarian Radicalism in China, 1968–1981*.

11. John McMillan and Barry Naughton, "How to Reform a Planned Economy: Lessons from China," *Oxford Review of Economic Policy* 8 (1992): 781–807.

12. Walder, *China's Transitional Economy*, p. 10.

13. *South China Morning Post,* March 6, 2002, p. 8.

14. Hsin-Huang Michael Hsiao and Alvin Y. So, "Economic Integration and the Transformation of Civil Society in Taiwan, Hong Kong, and South China," in Shu-min Huang and Cheng-Kuang Hsu, eds., *Imagining China* (Taipei: Institute of Ethnology, Academia Sinica, 1999), pp. 221–252.

15. Alvin Y. So, "The Making of a Cadre-Capitalist Class in China," in Joseph Cheng, ed., *China's Challenges in the Twenty-First Century* (Hong Kong: City University Press of Hong Kong, forthcoming).

16. *South China Morning Post,* March 7, 2002, p. 6.

17. *South China Morning Post,* March 5, 2002.

18. John G. Fernald and Oliver D. Babson, "Why Has China Survived the Asian Crisis So Well? What Risks Remain?" *Board of Governors of the Federal Reserve System: International Finance Discussion Papers,* no. 333 (February 1999) at www.bog.frb.fed.us.

19. *South China Morning Post,* March 6, 2002, p. 8.

Part I

Origins

2

Economic Institutional Change in Post-Mao China

Reflections on the Triggering, Orienting, and Sustaining Mechanisms

Yi-min Lin

Introduction

Since the late 1970s China has undergone a fundamental transformation from a centrally planned economy based on public ownership to a market-oriented, increasingly private economy. Three factual aspects of this process of change are noteworthy. It began in the immediate aftermath of what is known as the Cultural Revolution (1966–1976). The pace and extent of reform have varied across different sectors, regions, and types of institutions. And, despite strong initial and persistent resistance from within and without the state apparatus and several major setbacks, the rules governing economic activities have evolved farther and farther away from state socialism.

There is a large and growing amount of research on the driving forces behind these facts. This essay examines some prominent explanations and seeks to piece together from them complementary clues to the causal mechanisms at work. As will be shown below, although there are many contrasting findings from different studies on the same issue or issues, they often do not amount to competing theses, and thus can be combined to form more illuminating explanations. Where competing theses do exist, their differences may also lead to more fruitful findings if they are used as bases on which to formulate further hypotheses that specify under what conditions which of the causal linkages identified is likely to predominate. Since elaborate descriptions of the process of reform are widely available, the discussion below will center on some focal issues in the interpretation of empirical findings.

The Triggers

The Third Plenum of the Eleventh Central Party Committee of the Chinese Communist Party (CCP) in December 1978 is widely regarded as the starting point of China's post-Mao reform.[1] It shifted the focus of government policy from class struggle to economic development. It called for a relaxation of a rigid, centralized system of economic management and emphasized the importance of adjusting agricultural policies. Moreover, it consolidated the political power of Deng Xiaoping and his associates by "rectifying" the verdicts on a number of high-ranking officials (including Deng) who had been purged or persecuted in the Mao era and by embracing the pragmatic principle of "seeking truth from facts." All this cleared the way for the subsequent introduction of a series of substantive reform measures in agriculture, foreign economic relations, fiscal administration, and industry.

There are, however, criticisms about both the treatment of the Third Plenum as the watershed of profound economic institutional change and the emphasis on the role of central leaders in the initiation of economic reform.[2] The common counterargument is that local forces started the process of reform, especially reform in the rural economic sector.

The Local Initiative Thesis

White contends that economic reform started in the early 1970s, when the violence of the Cultural Revolution had ended.[3] What happened subsequently was that "local networks"—coalitions of local officials and managers —began to promote the development of rural industry. This course of economic action not only deviated from the central planning system, it undermined planning by diverting resources and attracting demand for output away from centrally designated parties. As the problems (e.g., erosion of centrally controlled revenue bases and growth of financial burdens on the central authority) engendered by such divergent behavior gained momentum during the mid- to late 1970s, central leaders were forced to adopt measures to reform the economic system.

Kelliher argues that early components of rural reform—that is, decollectivization, commercialization, and the rise of a private economy—were all initiated by peasants rather than the state.[4] Motivated by the desire to escape their economic plight, peasants went beyond the limits set by central leaders to change the commune system. The economic alternatives that they pursued, such as family farming, proved to be more viable than the old arrangements in addressing the policy imperatives of the state. In consequence, central leaders eventually gave recognition to what peasants innovated.

Yang traces the origin of the economic alternatives pursued by local actors in the late 1970s to the Great Leap Forward campaign in the late 1950s.[5] He claims that the massive famine and deaths in the wake of the campaign and the contrast between the tragedy (as well as the practice under agrarian radicalism during the Cultural Revolution) and the economic improvement subsequently achieved through short-lived adoption of family farming in some localities during the early 1960s had a lasting disillusioning impact on the beliefs of both peasants and officials in the commune system. When the political climate changed after Mao's death, peasants and grassroots cadres took the lead in restructuring rural economic organization on the cognitive bases formed during the preceding two decades. The multiplication of such actions created a groundswell that compelled the central leadership to decollectivize agriculture in the early 1980s.

These arguments point to some important forces that developed from the bottom of the system and converged to drive economic institutional change beginning in the late 1970s. They provide a useful reminder that actions of central leaders are not an adequate explanation of what drove the initial process of reform. To account for the origins of reform, however, a broader view and a sharper focus on the causal linkages are needed.[6] In particular, it is important to identify and separate what created the growing pressures for reform and what triggered these pressures into a chain of interactive actions that shook loose the cornerstones of the Maoist system.[7]

Cumulative Pressures

White's observation about the eroding effect of rural industry on central planning is indeed insightful, as it points to a source of contradictions and inconsistencies within the system.[8] But the development of rural industry was by no means a local affair.[9] Its effects on central planning were not always damaging either, as rural enterprises did help alleviate the supply gaps under the plan, especially in the production of consumer goods.[10] Also, the magnitude of rural industry was quite limited.[11] More important, there were a number of concurrent problems or developments that added to the cumulative pressures for reform of the economic system;[12] yet their causes cannot be simply reduced to the exacerbating effect of rural industry on the central planning system.

One of the major problems faced by the Chinese economy was a heavy reliance on the increase in productive inputs for output growth rather than efficient use of inputs.[13] Related to this was a mismatch between demand and supply, as embodied in the coexistence of widespread shortages and huge inventories.[14] These problems were compounded by the political disruptions during the Cultural Revolution. A major consequence was a low standard of living,[15] which was further exacerbated by fast population growth before the mid-1970s,[16] when the government began to institute compulsory family planning.[17] The problem was particularly acute in the rural sector. Despite the fact that over 70 percent of the total work force was deployed in agriculture where a "grain first" policy was adopted, China could not even produce enough food to sustain the barest level of consumption for the population.[18] In fact, from 1961 to the late 1970s, China was a net importer of grain.[19] These situations called into question the official claim about the superiority of the Maoist development strategy as well as the legitimacy of the CCP's political rule.

Internationally, the Cold War created a resource strain on the Chinese economy,[20] though the depleting effect perhaps did not reach the same degree as that for the former Soviet Union.[21] From 1952 to 1977, defense spending on average accounted for 5.5 percent of China's GDP.[22] Geopolitical considerations also led Chinese leaders to make massive and costly relocations of industrial facilities from the coastal to inland areas from 1964 through 1971.[23] Moreover, the postwar economic growth and the concurrent uplifting of the standard of living in China's capitalist neighbors, such as Japan and the four industrializing mini-dragons of East Asia (Taiwan, South Korea, Singapore, and Hong Kong), posed another serious challenge to the CCP's claim about the superiority of state socialism.[24] The improvement of relations between China and the West after President Richard Nixon's visit in 1972, on the other hand, opened up an opportunity for China to derive an early (versus the Soviet bloc) peace dividend of sorts and benefit from participation in international divisions of labor.

There seems to be little doubt that these internal and external conditions combined to generate and intensify what Oksenberg and Dickson call a "perception of crisis" among CCP leaders.[25] Yet, as Naughton points out,[26] the economy "had clearly not exhausted growth potential under the old system" by the mid-1970s. How the subsequent drastic departure came about thus cannot be readily explained only with an account of the cumulative forces.

The Triggering Events

The most obvious event that set in motion the efforts to reform the economic system was Mao's death in September 1976. It was followed by the rise of a new coalition of political leaders who were leaning toward or were receptive to some form of economic institutional change. Most of them were victims of the Cultural Revolution. Their return was accompanied by a nationwide rehabilitation of lower-level party-state functionaries purged under Mao.[27]

There were a few possible, mutually nonexclusive links between this personnel reshuffling and the start of reforms.

First, the rehabilitated leaders were not only victims of the Cultural Revolution. Many of them had prior experience in formulating and/or implementing economic policies that rivaled or deviated from Mao's radicalist approach to socialist economic development. What they witnessed during the Cultural Revolution only reinforced their determination to move away from the excesses under Mao. Deng Xiaoping, the central figure among the rehabilitated politicians, was particularly keen on reviving what he had attempted unsuccessfully during the early to mid-1970s.[28] During the mid-1970s, visits by several top leaders to countries that had adopted Western-type systems also revealed the economic gaps between China and the capitalist world, thus further heightening their sense of urgency for change.[29]

Second, despite the removal of the Maoist faction within the CCP in the fall of 1976, there remained a power struggle between the group of leaders (headed by Hua Guofeng) who wanted to maintain the status quo and the pro-reform leaders associated with Deng Xiaoping.[30] To strengthen and consolidate their power, Deng and his associates needed to distance themselves from the old regime. Blaming Mao and the Gang of Four for China's economic problems was useful but insufficient. Bringing about concrete improvement in economic conditions through reform was a much more effective way to demonstrate Deng's leadership and legitimize the growing political power of those associated with him.[31]

Third, the political transition after Mao was accompanied by a trial-and-error process of economic policy making in which the central leaders muddled along for alternatives to address China's many pressing problems. Although many new leaders sought to introduce economic change, they did not have a clear blueprint for reform. The initial actions Deng and his associates took in economic readjustment from 1976 to 1978 followed the revisionist approach they had previously pursued within the institutional parameters of the old system. But such attempts were largely unsuccessful.[32] This outcome, coupled with the political need to deliver concrete results of improvement, prompted them to search for alternative measures. Therefore, according to Naughton,[33] the reformist leaders inadvertently stumbled on the kinds of reform programs that fed upon one another and touched off the process of departure from central planning.[34]

Fourth, the shift in policy focus from class struggle to economic development and the reshuffling of local political leadership opened the way for bottom-up institutional innovation. In some provinces (such as Anhui and Sichuan), pro-reform leaders tolerated and even encouraged attempts initiated by grassroots officials to bend existing rules for economic liberalization.[35] This significantly changed the political risk perceived by the rank and file of the local state apparatus. It is not surprising that these provinces became the spearhead of decollectivization.[36]

None of those scholars who share the local initiative thesis appears to dispute these links, especially the last one.[37] In essence, therefore, the thesis does not provide a competing argument against studies that focus on the actions of central leaders. This, of course, by no means implies that political change at the center was the main story, especially with regard to the start of rural reform. A contribution of the studies emphasizing "bottom-up" driving forces is that they illustrate that the initiatives taken by local actors were an important part of the process in which decollectivization was started. Since there is no evidence to dispute that local and central forces were both necessary conditions for this process of change to take place, it is analytically more useful to focus on the interplay between them rather than to weigh the relative significance of the role played by one or the other.

A key issue that needs to be closely examined in this connection is why some local actors, especially grassroots officials, responded to the changing political climate by breaking the rules. It is possible that in the localities where various forms of family farming were first adopted the rural cadres were under considerable pressure from peasants to abandon the commune system, as noted by Kelliher. There is also a plausible element in Yang's argument that in the wake of the Great Leap famine many local officials lost faith in the commune system and regarded family farming as a better alternative.[38] Perhaps one can further argue that among all party-state functionaries rural officials had the weakest incentive to maintain the central planning system because under that system they had the least resource power, whereas urban industrial bureaucracies were most favored in resource allocation.

Yet all these were cumulative forces conducive to change. Even if one takes into account the chain of central political changes set in motion by Mao's death and their repercussions for local politics, questions remain as to whether the presence of a more tolerant provincial leadership, as in the cases of Anhui and Sichuan, was a sufficiently strong trigger for peasants to intensify their pressure on grassroots cadres and for grassroots officials to take matters into their own hands—with or without increased pressure from peasants. A close reading of the history of rural reform suggests that rural cadres were divided over the issue of family farming, even in a "pioneering" province like Anhui.[39] How did the reform-minded cadres overcome or defuse the opposition from hardliners?

A fact that is widely noted in the accounts of decollectivization in Anhui is that it was started and spread from 1977 to 1979, when severe natural disasters hit the province. In response, officials in some communes and counties resorted to various forms of family production and justified their rule-breaking behavior on the ground that there was a desperate need to cope with natural disaster.[40] The same justification was used by provincial leaders to fend off criticisms from those who opposed family farming at the center.[41] The good results of family farming in turn provided a further ground of justification for the arrangement to be institutionalized and introduced to more localities in the entire country.[42]

Anhui was not alone. Sichuan, another "pioneering" province, was also hit by serious natural disasters when rural cadres in some localities ventured to experiment with family farming. In the nation as a whole,[43] the total size of rural areas that were affected by natural disasters from 1977 to 1978 rose to the highest level after the peak reached from 1959 to 1961.[44] More systematic evidence is needed to establish the link between the rule-breaking behavior of rural cadres and the severity of natural disasters in the late 1970s.[45] But it is not far-fetched to hypothesize that, by creating an extraordinarily difficult situation that the commune system was ill-equipped to tackle and thereby reducing the political risk for reformist cadres to trespass, Mother Nature provided a major trigger for a snowballing process of reform to derive from interactions between social forces at the grassroots and political forces at the center.

It should be noted that, while rural reform has been the focus of contention about the origins of reform, concurrent with commercialization and decollectivization of agriculture, major reform measures were also taken in other economic sectors, such as foreign economic relations, fiscal administration, and industry. As compared to agriculture, these sectors demonstrated much weaker local initiatives and lower initial inconsistencies between local and central actions,[46] though they joined agriculture in leading China away from the state socialist system.

In sum, the start of reform was an interactive process driven by diverse forces. The basic facts about this process are well known, yet the interpretations vary among different scholars. The foregoing discussion suggests that to reveal the complexities in the origins of China's economic reform, it is more useful to examine the full range of cumulative forces conducive to economic reforms than to single out a particular one as predominant. It is also important to identify the causal triggers that transformed the cumulative forces into an interactive process where their potential was played out. Mao's death triggered a chain of political events at the center that culminated in the landmark decision at the Third Plenum in 1978. Such events changed the balance of power at the center as well as the parameters of cost-benefit calculation by local actors. In the rural sector, these changes, probably coupled with natural disasters, created strong impetus for the start of an interactive process between central and local forces that led to decollectivization. In other economic sectors, these changes paved the way for the introduction of mostly centrally initiated reform programs that were incrementally adapted and expanded through subsequent central-local interactions.

Pace-Setting Mechanisms

The reform in China has been a gradual, adaptive process without a clear and thorough blueprint. Virtually all reform measures were started as experiments. But some (e.g., decollectivization of agriculture and opening up of the economy) have gained momentum more quickly than others (e.g., industrial and financial reforms). Some provinces (e.g., those in the coastal region) have moved away from the old system much faster than others (inland provinces). And some types of institutions (e.g., migration control) have been changed earlier and more extensively than others (e.g., public ownership).

Naughton notes that the Chinese reform has taken a path of least resistance.[47] What, then, are the sources of resistance? And what accounts for the variations in the intensity of resistance across different sectors, regions, and institutions?

Much of the resistance to reform can be traced to forces in three broad areas: bureaucratic interests, interests of ordinary citizens, and ideological constraints perceived and enforced by different political leaders. Obviously, none of these areas is internally homogeneous or necessarily coherent, and each has multiple linkages to different dimensions of the pre-reform system. The interplay among them has nevertheless shaped the sequencing of reform. Findings from research on the process of reform suggest that, other things being equal, the more convergent the forces in each area toward a particular reform, the less difficult the reform, and vice versa; and the stronger the combined resistance from the three areas toward a reform, the more difficult the reform, and vice versa.

Sectoral Variation

As noted above, agriculture was one of the sectors where substantial reform was first carried out. Despite initial confusion and hesitation, the reform received broad support from both rural cadres and peasants. A possible reason is that the rural sector was most disadvantaged under central planning, which concentrated the allocation of resources in urban industrial activities.[48] The reform promised and indeed delivered great gains for most peasants, who were given considerable freedom in decision making and allowed to retain a large part of the fruit of their own labor. The growth of output under family farming and the concurrent acceleration of rural industrialization also enlarged the revenue sources of local authorities, thus providing a major incentive for rural cadres to move along.[49] On the other hand, decollectivization did not require an immediate change in the existing pattern of resource allocation, thus limiting the resistance from powerful vested interests based in the urban industrial bureaucracy.[50] Also, the ideological constraint on the restructuring of the rural economy was softened by the fact that public ownership of land, which constitutes the most important resource in agriculture, was preserved despite the reversion to family farming. Thus, once the central leadership gave the go-ahead, the reform was carried out rather swiftly.

The pre-reform pattern of bureaucratic interests also had a direct bearing on the relatively fast pace of reform in foreign economic relations.[51] Under central planning, foreign trade was monopolized by a small number of trading companies under the auspices of the central government. No foreign direct investment was allowed. As a result, centrally instituted relaxation of restrictions on local participation in foreign trade and opening up of the country to foreign investment tended to produce very few losers but potentially very large numbers of winners, including both party-state functionaries and ordinary citizens.[52] The initial political and economic risk was also contained by the practice of limiting the adoption of new reform programs to selected localities as "experiments."[53] Moreover, while seeking to contain the "undesirable" aspects of opening up (e.g., cultural influence from abroad), the central leadership under Deng was able to legitimize the reform in foreign economic relations by drawing a contrast between the prosperity associated with economic opening and the backwardness associated with the Maoist strategy of economic autarky. Despite periodic setbacks due to blocking attempts by bureaucratic interests threatened by further opening, therefore, the reforms have spiraled onward.[54]

In fiscal administration, the pre-reform system, featuring unified revenue and spending, gave the central authority considerable control over the allocation of financial resources.[55] Yet, it created serious constraints on the revenue-generating capacity of the government, as the top-heavy system provided little incentive for local authorities to increase revenue and fostered local attempts to dodge centrally imposed financial obligations.[56] The revenue sharing system introduced in 1980 initially created a win-win situation for the parties involved. It was therefore carried out rather smoothly. In fact, many local governments even went further to expand the "gray area" under the arrangement to increase their discretion in revenue and spending. This led to serious erosion of the central government's share in the expanded revenue bases as well as its influence over investment,[57] prompting the introduction of the tax reform in 1994 to curb the imbalance.

In contrast, the pace of reform has varied significantly among different segments of the industry sector. Its traditional core—state-owned enterprises (SOEs)—has made much slower progress in reform.[58] A major obstacle lies in the closely coupled, highly complicated web of bureaucratic interests in which the industrial system has traditionally been lodged.[59] Many of the changes needed, such as removal of entry barriers, price decontrol, delegation of decision-making authority, restructuring of debt, and reduction of the workforce, have direct or ripple effects on the vested interests of the pertinent supervising authorities as well as on the streams of revenue accruing to different levels of government.[60]

Moreover, the transition from a centrally planned system of industrial and financial management to a market-driven system inevitably increases job insecurity for urban employees, especially those in the state sector. To contain the potential social unrest that massive organizational restructuring of SOEs may touch off, a comprehensive social security system that provides minimal benefits or cushion for unemployment, health care, housing, and pension is needed.[61] Yet, resource constraints and bureaucratic gridlocks have made it difficult to convert quickly to such a system from the enterprise-based arrangement of social welfare benefit provision that urban China inherited from the Mao era.[62] The pace of reform has also been constrained, especially in the early years of reform, by the ideological claim that working-class people are the masters of society and the state sector economy is the spearhead of socialist economic development. It was not until the mid-1990s, when agency problems became widespread and seriously worsened in the state sector and the cumulative financial burdens on the state significantly increased,[63] that the pace to reform industrial SOEs and, relatedly, the banking system was accelerated.

Among non-SOEs in the industrial sector, however, the pace of change has been much faster. Under the central planning system, the leading role of SOEs in industrial development was supplemented with a second group of enterprises,[64] known as urban collective enterprises.[65] Mostly small in size, they operated under the sole purview of sub-provincial governments, produced mainly low-end consumer goods, and received the lowest priority in resource allocation. Their weaker resource ties with central planning and relatively simpler regulatory structure made it possible for these enterprises to depart earlier than SOEs from the plan to pursue market-oriented economic activities as an alternative for survival.[66] They have been joined by large numbers of market-oriented enterprises newly formed outside the state sector, including urban and rural collective enterprises, private entities, and foreign-invested enterprises. Most of these newcomers operate under the jurisdiction of grassroots governments, which had the weakest resource power under central planning and have been keen on exploring alternative sources to generate revenue and address unemployment pressures. To promote and facilitate market-oriented industrial growth outside the state sector, many local officials have bent existing rules on a variety of issues, such as entry, accounting, financing, price, labor practices, and taxation. As will be discussed below, such rule-bending behavior and the growth of competition from outside the state sector have created an important impetus for economic institutional change.

Spatial Variation

A salient feature of China's recent economic change is that its pace and outcome have varied across different regions.[67] Except in the case of agricultural reform, where some inland provinces actually took the lead,[68] most coastal provinces have moved away faster from the old economic system.[69] In contrast, most inland provinces have been trend followers rather than trendsetters in a wide range of reforms, including those concerning foreign economic relations, rural industrialization, SOEs, social security, fiscal relations, and laws and regulations. The slower pace of economic institutional change in turn has constrained the ability of inland provinces to narrow the gap in economic development with coastal provinces.

A common source of such spatial disparity is found in the preferential policies adopted by the central authority to concentrate experimental measures of reform as well as resources in coastal provinces. Wang and Hu, for example, argue that in the first decade of reform, the central leaders followed a "trickle-down" approach to regional disparity and deliberately favored coastal provinces to boost the aggregate rate of economic growth.[70] The leadership increased attention to the interior in the 1990s, but the shift did not produce significant results because the center's capacity to redistribute resources through the fiscal process had been seriously weakened due to fiscal decentralization during the preceding decade.

Yang also regards differential treatment by the center of different provinces in liberalization as the main cause of regional disparity in the pace and outcome of economic change.[71] What has led to such treatment, he argues, is a dominance of coastal interests (hence an underrepresentation of the interior) in the central leadership. This has left inland provinces in a disadvantaged position to bargain with the center.

While recognizing the importance of central policies, a number of studies emphasize the role of provincial leadership and strategies.[72] According to one characterization, provincial leaders fall into three categories: "pioneers," who seek to innovate and actively expand the boundaries of reform;

"bandwagoners," who follow the predominant policy line defined by the center; and "laggards," who resist or lack enthusiasm for major changes to the status quo.[73] Economic reform tends to be most successfully carried out in provinces that are led by "pioneers." They pursue shrewd strategies that aim to achieve several objectives: to mobilize resources and adopt enabling policies for the development of local comparative and competitive advantages, to contain the political risks of reform programs, and to cultivate support and soften resistance from both local social forces and the center. A number of coastal provinces appear to have followed this path, yet few inland provinces have done so.

This perspective complements the analyses focusing on the impact of central policies and actions. It illustrates an important factor that may bring about changes beyond the limits set by the center and/or lead to different outcomes in the implementation of existing reform measures. Along this line of inquiry, an issue that needs to be further explored is what shapes the variations in the local political environments that are conducive to the predominance of different types of leadership. Although the perspective of a top provincial leader holds enormous sway over policy making, those who make up the policy circles at the provincial and sub-provincial levels of the local state are also important in the formulation and implementation of reform policies. The behavioral tendencies of these people are likely to be diverse and responsive to the incentives and constraints that they face. What drives a critical mass of them to pursue a pioneering, centrist, or resistant approach to reform thus merits close examination.

Obviously, extensive research is needed to address this complex issue. A clue, though, may lie in a common feature shared by many inland provinces: poor endowment in financial and human resources, physical infrastructure, and connections with international markets. This not only directly affects the level of economic development, as widely noted;[74] it also imposes some constraints on the process of reform.

First, poor resource endowment and infrastructure make it difficult to achieve quick and significant improvement in economic conditions through rule bending in the "gray area" of centrally set limits,[75] especially in the face of competition from provinces with better endowment and preferential policy treatment, where the marginal effect of such "multipliers" tends to be much greater. Second, poor financial endowment makes it difficult to tackle many problems that bold reform may trigger, such as various social welfare provisions for SOE employees. This, in turn, tends to increase the difficulty in cultivating popular support for reform, raising the political risk for the more reform-minded leaders. Third, poor endowment in human resources, especially the undersupply of technocrats at various levels of local government administration, may make it difficult for local authorities to formulate effective reform policies. The reason is that for reform to succeed, a simple hands-off approach is not only inadequate but also potentially disastrous in the absence of a well-functioning governance structure to minimize negative externalities and stimulate synergy among political and economic actors.

These problems have important implications for local officials in inland provinces.[76] Given the uncertain gains and high risks of adopting unauthorized new rules governing economic activities beyond farming, centrists tend to prevail over reformists in decision-making. Cosmetic or short-term maximizing measures of change are more likely to be adopted than substantive programs of reform. Unable to champion alternative reform programs that are politically viable and promise to offer better economic trade-offs, reformists are also likely to face formidable criticisms from conservatives about the downside of economic reform, especially during periods of centrally engendered political retrenchment, which for the same reason may also last longer on the local level.

Institutional Variation

Another interesting feature of the Chinese reform is that the process of marketization has outpaced the changes in ownership institutions. Although private economic activities reemerged in the late 1970s, they were confined to family farming and self-employment outside the farming sector for a decade. It was not until 1988 that the government changed its policy of limiting the workforce of private organizations to no more than seven persons. And it was not until after 1992 that the development of the private sector began to gain momentum—through growth and multiplication of entities set up by private owners and through privatization of existing public enterprises.[77]

Ideological constraint has been a major obstacle to the growth of the private economy.[78] Unlike the former Soviet bloc, China started the transition toward markets without a political revolution that abandoned, among other things, the dominance of public ownership. Socialism has remained the goal of economic change embraced by CCP leaders of all factions. Such constraint was most severe at the outset of economic reform, when private owners were not only faced with weak and unstable legal protection for their residual claiming rights, but were actually discriminated against in many important areas, such as licensing, credit, land use, material input allocation, and the supply of utilities. In view of such policy bias, some private owners had to disguise themselves as "public" enterprises in order to survive.[79]

The policy bias was further reinforced by bureaucratic interests. When the reform was started, many local governments formed locally controlled public enterprises, such as township and village enterprises (TVEs), which were not bound by the central plan. These enterprises were free to explore and benefit from the market opportunities to produce products in short supply in the emergent economic space outside the plan. Since they helped address two key policy imperatives of local officials—creation of government revenue and provision of local employment—they received most favorable treatment from local authorities in resource allocation and regulation.[80] As a result, these enterprises became the spearhead of early marketization. This added to the competitive disadvantage of small private entities. The convergence of centrally imposed ideological constraint and local bureaucratic interests thus created an initially adverse environment for private economic activities despite the desire of many citizens to pursue them.

What, then, accounts for the rising significance of the private sector in the 1990s?[81] Kung and Lin argue that an answer lies in the forces that early marketization led by local public enterprises unleashed.[82] First, the growth of TVEs created mounting competitive pressures on urban state-owned enterprises, eroding their profits as well as the taxes paid to the government and weakening their ability to provide urban jobs. To address growing revenue gap and unemployment pressure, urban authorities had to search for alternative solutions. This led them to relax the restrictions on private economic activities, which in turn created pressures for the central authority to follow suit. The deterioration of performance among large numbers of urban SOEs also placed heavy financial burdens on the government, prompting efforts to speed up reform in SOEs, including outright privatization of poorly performing enterprises.

Second and ironically, the same impact that the growth of TVEs exerted on SOEs also affected TVEs themselves, restraining their ability to expand revenue and employment and forcing them to take a more receptive or even accommodating approach toward private enterprises. Third, the expansionary strategy pursued by local authorities to promote the growth of TVEs weakened the monitoring capacity of local governments and spawned various agency problems. The deterioration of performance and increase of financial liabilities due to reckless management and opportunism made it increasingly imperative for a growing number of TVEs to be privatized.[83]

Sustaining Forces

The economic change in China since the late 1970s and its ramifications in all dimensions of social life have far exceeded the initial expectation of both policy makers and observers. And the process of change under way continues to bring about surprises. What has pushed the process of change increasingly away from the state socialist system in which China was anchored? In particular, what has made the old system increasingly unsustainable, and what has shaped the formative rules governing the activities pursued by economic and political actors in the emergent economic space outside central planning?

Economic Actors

A number of economists argue that competition among economic actors has played a key role in driving China's economic institutional change.[84] According to them, growing competition in product and factor markets developed from the periphery of central planning has drawn increasing numbers of enterprises from the plan to market-oriented economic activities by rewarding those that can make efficient use of resources and penalizing those that fail to do so. The leading force in this process of change has been the nonstate economic sector, which includes both public enterprises under grassroots authorities and enterprises of private or semi-private ownership. Most of them have not been bound by the central plan and their activities have been driven by the pursuit of profits through self-arranged market transactions. The growth of competition in the product and factor markets that they created has hardened the financial discipline on these enterprises and forced them to improve efficiency. Such competition has also made it difficult for SOEs to obtain inputs and sell output, whereas the profits made by many non-SOEs have illustrated the opportunity cost for SOEs to stick to rigid government plans. The resultant erosion of the financial performance among SOEs and the intensification of their lobbying for change have forced the government to reduce the scope of the plan and increase the freedom for SOEs to participate in market-oriented economic activities.

To cope with the many problems triggered by growing competition, the government has made numerous adaptations, mostly in a piecemeal fashion, in economic policy and regulation. Consequently, central planning has gradually succumbed to markets and market institutions.

This account of economic change is criticized by another group of economists—those associated with the so-called "big bang school."[85] In particular, they question the argument that by participating in the creation and expansion of markets (and hence intensifying competition), public enterprises (especially TVEs) in the nonstate sector and SOEs have both contributed to a virtuous cycle of reform.[86] They claim that incremental reforms in the rural public sector and among urban SOEs have been largely unsuccessful due to political meddling and persistence and even exacerbation of agency problems under public ownership. The real driving force of economic change in post-Mao China has instead stemmed from economic actors' pursuit of private profits, which was revitalized by drastic measures to decollectivize and commercialize agriculture and to liberalize trade in the late 1970s and early 1980s. It accounts for much of the economic growth that China achieved in the first two decades of reform.[87] On the other hand, restrained by the government's ideological commitment to state ownership and reluctance to institute measures to safeguard private ownership, the pursuit of private profits in what has nominally remained as the public sector has taken various hidden forms, such as registration of de facto private entities as public enterprises, embezzlement, and asset stripping. The growth of these subversive forces has in turn intensified the pressures on the government to privatize poorly performing public enterprises and relax the restrictions on private enterprises.

It appears that this criticism does not constitute a direct challenge to the core argument of the gradualism thesis with regard to the role of economic competition in institutional change, as it does not provide an alternative account of what triggered many reforms in the public sector (especially during the 1980s), regardless of their outcomes. In fact, it implicitly acknowledges the importance of competition in China's economic liberalization. Yet, the criticism does point out an issue that is not clearly explored in the gradualism thesis, that is, the agency problem in public enterprises and its undermining effects on the central planning system. As such, the mechanisms identified by the two theses may not be mutually exclusive, and their analyses may be seen as capturing different convergent forces in a complex process of change.

Political Actors

What is commonly missing in both accounts highlighted above is an elaborate analysis of the role played by the interests and actions of state agents. This is the focus of a number of other studies.

Based on research on the restructuring of central-provincial fiscal relations,[88] Li argues that an important mechanism that has carried the reform process forward is the search for mutually beneficial arrangements in place of the top-heavy fiscal practice before the reform. Also focusing on vertical bargaining between interdependent parties within the state apparatus, Shirk argues that the formulation of central government policies on industrial reform has been greatly influenced by "particularistic contracting" involving communist party, ministerial, and provincial leaders.[89] The essence of such "enfranchisement" of authority is a give-and-take relationship, where in exchange for political support, higher-level leaders have made ad hoc allowances for subordinate parties to accommodate their parochial interests and increase discretionary power. The competitive bargaining to reduce existing institutional unevenness while seeking special treatment has spread the effects of ad hoc reforms and brought about incremental change to more and more aspects of the system.

Looking at the ramifications of changing central-local relations, Oi and some other scholars have developed a theory about the role played by local state policies in economic development and institutional change.[90] Their analyses center on the responses of local governments to the incentives created by fiscal decentralization during the reform, which has significantly strengthened the tie between local officials' financial and career rewards and the growth of local government revenue. According to them, fiscal decentralization makes local officials interested in promoting market-oriented growth and running the local economy like a public corporation. Efforts to expand the revenue base have led local officials to mobilize resources and bend existing rules for local enterprises' market-oriented activities that compete with those promoted by governments in other localities. The result is a weakening of commitment to the plan and a broadening and institutionalization of avenues to markets.

This thesis is predicated on the assumption that the formal fiscal incentives faced by local officials are strong enough to align their pursuit of self-interest with the accomplishment of local public policy goals. Yet, some other studies point to the moral hazard problem under decentralization as well as its implications for economic institutional change.[91] Since local officials are not true owners of the public assets under their purview and thus do not bear the ultimate risk for failure to make economically efficient use of such assets, they may seek to advance their careers by pursuing economic policies, such as expansionary investment in capital construction and promotion of sales growth of local public enterprises at the expense of efficiency, that boost the short-term economic growth record but create long-term problems for the local state. The impact of such behavior on the old economic institutions is twofold. It increases the difficulty of maintaining the central planning system by siphoning resources away from centrally designated users, and it creates problems (e.g., deteriorating performance of local public enterprises) that cannot be tackled within the framework of the old system based on public ownership.

Another source of the eroding effects of state agents' self-seeking behavior lies in the decay of the state's own organizational health in the post-Mao era.[92] The main driving force of this change is the growth of exchange relations between state agents and economic actors and among state agents themselves.[93] It has created a competing incentive for party-state functionaries to advance their private interests at the expense of the announced public agendas of the state. As a result, resources have been channeled away from the plan, and competition has grown to seek political rent and to couple special treatment by state agents with pursuit of profit-making opportunities outside the old system.[94] The efforts to address the inconsistencies and problems caused by state agents' rule bending and resource diversion have made the central planning system unsustainable and led to the adoption of new rules to govern the changing political economy.

It appears that the studies focusing on central-local interactions and those focusing on the local state have much more to inform than to contradict each other. But the different drivers of institutional change identified by the local developmental state thesis and the accounts about the divergence between public policy goals of the local state and local officials' self-seeking behavior are unlikely to be found under the same structure of incentives and constraints. Yet there seems to be evidence of their presence in separate localities and periods. To make sense of such a seemingly puzzling outcome of research, it is important to investigate what may tilt the behavior of local officials in one direction or the other.

An important factor that merits close attention is the internal monitoring system of the state, which has long relied upon mutual monitoring between administrative levels, between agencies, and between officials to maintain its own organizational health and contain deviations in policy implementation. To capture the different possibilities identified by the two competing theses, it can be hypothesized that where and when the local state's internal monitoring system remains relatively effective, the causal linkages identified by the local developmental state thesis are more likely to be the way changes have occurred, and vice versa. Further analyses of what constitute the components of the party-state's mutual monitoring system and under what conditions the (local) state is able or unable to maintain the system will probably lead to the discovery of more revealing clues to the driving forces of economic institutional change.[95]

International Forces

Along with the actions and interactions of economic and political actors, China's integration into the world economy has also generated some input to and impetus for economic institutional change. Three convergent mechanisms appear to have been at work in this connection. First, adapting institutional arrangements from abroad to address domestic problems has begotten further need or pressure for the introduction of more institutions compatible with the ones already adopted. Second, interactions with foreign investors and trading partners have added to the pressures on the Chinese government to adopt measures to reform the basic framework of economic regulation. Third, some domestic political and economic actors have actively sought to advance their own interests and agendas by exploiting or reshaping existing economic regulation with the leverage of foreign connections, resources, and influence.

A major change in the post-Mao era is that many economic practices previously labeled as "capitalist" (e.g., bankruptcy, contracts, financial and managerial accounting, marketing, shareholding, and trademarks) have been redefined as neutral and thus usable in the service of socialism. To govern and regulate increasingly marketized economic activities, the Chinese government has sought to adapt certain established practices in the West to address the inadequacies of the central planning system.[96] In the twenty years after the start of the economic reform, the National People's Congress enacted 253 new laws and issued 106 directives on existing or new laws; the State Council (SC) enacted over 800 ordinances and regulations; and provincial legislatures enacted or approved over 7,000 local laws and regulations.[97] Many of these new laws and regulations are concerned with economic issues, and their formulation has often drawn upon existing practices governing market economies. With the deepening of marketization, especially with the unfolding of reforms in the more complex secondary and tertiary sectors based in urban areas, the limited number of Western-style economic institutions initially adopted or adapted in a piecemeal fashion has become increasingly inadequate. To make them work, many parallel institutions have to be established. Thus the 1990s saw the enactment of a growing body of new laws and regulations modeled on Western practices, including those concerning accounting, capital controls, competitive practices, corporate governance, land use, securities, and taxes.[98]

In the late 1970s, China opened its doors to a limited extent in an effort to attract foreign investment and benefit from international divisions of labor through trade. To explore the full potential of this opportunity, however, it has had to reform its industrial and commercial regulations, make changes in existing trade practices, and conform to pertinent international standards. Foreign investors have pressured the Chinese government to lower or remove entry barriers, increase transparency in policy making and implementation, reduce interference in managerial decision making, and liberalize the flow of resources and products.[99] Over time, such pressures have led to a series of modifications in economic regulation.[100] Since the mid-1980s the Chinese government has sought accession to the General Agreements on Tariffs and Trade/World Trade Organization (GATT/WTO). Along the way, the negotiations between the Chinese government and many foreign governments and trade organizations have exerted considerable pressure to go beyond the initial open policies to revamp a host of institutional arrangements concerning trade and nontrade issues.[101] Such interactions culminated in

China's agreement in the late 1990s to make most of the required changes over a period of time.

It is important to note that the adoption of Western-style economic institutions has by no means been a linear process. Despite considerable pressures, for example, the Chinese government has made very slow changes in some areas, such as entry barriers to certain economic sectors and protection of intellectual property rights.[102] Also, although newly instituted laws and regulations have changed the constraints and parameters under which political and economic actions are taken, what has been adopted on paper is not necessarily what functions in practice.[103] The formal and informal rules that are coexistent but inconsistent or even in conflict with newly adopted formal rules thus merit close examination. Moreover, the changes that have resulted from responses to pressures from international forces have had diverse impacts on domestic parties.[104] Therefore, the influence of international forces on economic institutional change cannot be properly assessed without a close examination of their interplay with the roles played by domestic political and economic actors.

An interesting aspect of China's economic internationalization after Mao is that it has been coupled with domestic actors' efforts to advance their interests and agendas by leveraging pertinent opportunities in the process of opening up. Some local governments, for example, have combined the promotion of foreign trade and investment with the efforts to gain greater autonomy and discretion over issues beyond both foreign economic relations and central planning.[105] Some reformist leaders at the center may also have played the "WTO card" to reinforce their domestic reform agendas by bringing direct international pressures to bear on the long-standing monopolies protected by entrenched bureaucratic interests in certain economic sectors (e.g., telecommunications and financial services) and by pitting such interests against other sectoral/regional (e.g., export-oriented) interests in a broader equation of trade-offs among different components of the "national interest."[106] In view of the rent (extra-ordinary gain) embedded in various special policies and regulations (e.g., those regarding taxation, imports and exports, foreign exchange, etc.) for foreigners, some Chinese organizations have actively sought links with foreign-invested entities or simply faked themselves as such entities.[107] Like those of the political actors just mentioned, the actions of these economic actors have not only increased the speed and scope of China's opening up but exerted corrosive effects on the old economic institutions. [108]

Summary

This cursory discussion of the pertinent literature suggests that no single explanation is adequate to account for the diverse driving forces of the Chinese reform. To bring to light the origins of the reform, the cumulative pressures to change the organizing principles of economic activities should be separated from the events that triggered the interactive process in which the effects of such pressures were played out through the behavior of political and economic actors. It is more useful to discern the concrete causal linkages in this process than to single out any particular source of cumulative pressure, triggering event, or group of actors as the most important contributing factor to the start of reform.

The path that the reform has taken cannot be clearly explained without examining closely the initial conditions of the reform. This does not imply that sectoral, spatial, and institutional variations in the pace and extent of reform have certain predetermined patterns. Rather, tracking the evolving opportunities, constraints, and interactive strategies of different actors may lead to useful insights into where and why resistance to reform has been strong and what may have weakened it.

The transformation of economic institutions in post-Mao China has been an evolutionary process driven and shaped by a multitude of factors. Some of the changes have taken place by design or imitation, but many others are the outcomes of responses and adaptations to contingencies, problems, pressures, and opportunities engendered by the actions and interactions of political and economic actors as well as international forces under the existing rules of the economic game. Much research has been produced to illuminate the causal mechanisms at work, yet more insights can be gained by integrating the analytic thrusts from largely complementary findings and by developing testable hypotheses to address the contradictions posed by competing theses.

Notes

1. See, for example, Joseph Fewsmith, *Dilemmas of Reform in China* (Armonk, N.Y.: M.E. Sharpe, 1994); Harry Harding, *China's Second Revolution: Reform After Mao* (Washington, D.C.: Brookings Institution, 1987); Dwight H. Perkins, "Reforming China's Economic System," *Journal of Economic Literature* 26 (June 1988): 601–645; Elizabeth Perry and Christine Wong, eds., *The Political Economy of Reform in Post-Mao China* (Cambridge, Mass.: Council on East Asian Studies, Harvard University, 1985); Carl Riskin, *China's Political Economy: The Quest for Development Since 1949* (Oxford: Oxford University Press, 1987).

2. Economic institutions as discussed in this essay refer to the formal and informal rules that govern economic activities.

3. Lynn T. White, III, *Unstately Power* (Armonk, N.Y.: M.E. Sharpe, 1998).

4. Daniel Kelliher, *Peasant Power in China* (New Haven, Conn.: Yale University Press, 1992). A very similar account is offered in Kate Xiao Zhou, *How the Farmers Changed China: Power of the People* (Boulder, Colo.: Westview, 1996).

5. Dali L.Yang, *Calamity and Reform in China: State, Rural Society, and Institutional Change since the Great Leap Famine* (Stanford, Calif.: Stanford University Press, 1996).

6. To prove that "local" forces were more important in initiating the process of economic reform, one needs to demonstrate that actions of the central leadership assumed only secondary importance and always followed the lead of local actors. Yet, none of these studies appears to have clear evidence to establish this.

7. White calls such triggers "spark causes" of reform (but downplays their importance), whereas Harding refers to them as the "immediate causes" of reform. See White, *Unstately Power,* and Harding, *China's Second Revolution.*

8. There remain questions, however, as to what motivated those in "local networks," which by his definition included virtually all the political and economic decision-makers below the central government, and what held their actions together.

9. The initial impetus for the formation of commune and brigade enterprises (CBEs) came from the central government's call for agricultural mechanization in the early 1970s. The central authority also granted local governments the right to determine taxes on rural industry and injected resources for rural industrial development. Moreover, the actions of local officials with regard to rural industry were conditioned by the shift in the balance of power between different factions in the central leadership throughout the final years of the Mao era. See William A. Byrd and Qingsong Lin, eds., *China's Rural Industry: Structure, Development, and Reform* (New York: Oxford University Press, 1990); Jiesan Ma, ed., *Dangdai Zhongguo de xiangzhen qiye* (Township and Village Enterprises in Contemporary China) (Beijing: Dangdai Zhongguo Chubanshe, 1991); and Susan Whiting, *Power and Wealth in Rural China: The Political Economy of Institutional Change* (Cambridge: Cambridge University Press, 2000).

10. Byrd and Lin, *China's Rural Industry;* Ma, *Dangdai Zhongguo de xiangzhen qiye.*

11. In 1976 the gross industrial output from CBEs totaled 24.4 billion yuan, which was equivalent to 7.4 percent of the gross industrial output of China. Ma, *Dangdai Zhongguo de xiangzhen qiye,* p. 59; National Bureau of Statistics (NBS), *Zhongguo tongji nianjian 1990* (Statistical Yearbook of China 1990) (Beijing: Zhongguo Tongji Chubanshe, 1990), p. 415. See also Barry Naughton, *Growing Out of the Plan: Economic Reform in China* (Cambridge: Cambridge University Press, 1995), pp. 144–146.

12. While White emphasizes the growing problems under central planning, Bramall argues that despite its many defects the central planning system served China relatively well, especially in the formation of infrastructural foundations (in energy, irrigation, transport, and heavy industry), which paved the way for subsequent economic takeoff. Chris Bramall, *In Praise of Maoist Economic Planning: Living Standards and Economic Development in Sichuan since 1931* (Oxford: Clarendon Press, 1993).

13. Riskin, *China's Political Economy,* p. 256.

14. Naughton, *Growing Out of the Plan,* p. 49.

15. Perkins, "Reforming China's Economic System."

16. Judith Banister, *China's Changing Population* (Stanford, Calif.: Stanford University Press, 1987).

17. From 1949 to 1975, the natural growth rate of the population averaged 2.07 percent, whereas in the subsequent twenty-four years it declined to 1.27 percent. NBS, *Xin Zhongguo wushi nian tongji ziliao huibian 1949–1999* (Comprehensive Statisti-

cal Data and Materials on Fifty Years of New China, 1949–1999) (Beijing: Zhongguo Tongji Chubanshe, 1999), p. 1.

18. For discussions of food rationing in urban and rural areas, see William L. Parish and Martin King Whyte, *Village and Family in Contemporary China* (Chicago: University of Chicago Press, 1978), and Martin King Whyte and William L. Parish, *Urban Life in Contemporary China* (Chicago: University of Chicago Press, 1984).

19. NBS, *Zhongguo tongji nianjian 1981*, pp. 384, 386.

20. A major concern that Deng Xiaoping had when he sought to introduce reforms in the army before his second political fall in early 1976 was the "swollen" size of the military force. See Jin Chen, ed., *Xin Zhongguo* (New China) (Hong Kong: Joint Publishing [H.K.] Co. Ltd., 2000), p. 171.

21. For a discussion of the exhaustion that the Soviet Union experienced from international military competition, see William Odom, *The Collapse of the Soviet Military* (New Haven, Conn.: Yale University Press, 1998).

22. In contrast, the average share for 1978 to 1999 was 2.1 percent. NBS, *Zhongguo tongji nianjian 2000*, pp. 53, 262.

23. See Naughton, *Growing Out of the Plan;* Shaoguang Wang and Angang Hu, *The Political Economy of Uneven Development: The Case of China* (Armonk, N.Y.: M.E. Sharpe, 1999).

24. Nee and Lian argue that inter-state competition (and the international pressure resulting from this) was the main factor leading to the start of the Chinese reform. Victor Nee and Lian Peng, "Sleeping with the Enemy: A Dynamic Model of Declining Political Commitment in State Socialism," *Theory and Society* 32, no. 2 (April, 1994): 253–296; see also Perkins, "Reforming China's Economic System," and "Completing China's Move to the Market," *Journal of Economic Perspectives* 8 (1994): 23–46.

25. Michel Oksenberg and Bruce Dickson, "The Origins, Processes, and Outcomes of Great Political Reform," in Dankwart A. Rustow and Kenneth Paul Erickson, eds., *Comparative Political Dynamics* (New York: HarperCollins, 1991), pp. 235–261. For accounts of major central leaders' perceptions about the problems facing China after Mao, see Zhiyong Xiong, *Zaisheng Zhongguo: Zhonggong shiyijie sanzhong quanhui de qianqian houhou* (The New Life of China: Before and After the Third Plenum) (Beijing: Zhonggong Dangshi Chubanshe, 1998); Guangyuan Yu, *Wo qinli de naci lishi zhuanzhe: Shiyijie sanzhong quanhui de taiqian muhou* (The Historic Turning Point I Personally Experienced: The Front and Back Stages of the Third Plenum) (Beijing: Zhongyang Bianyi Chubanshe, 1998).

26. Naughton, *Growing Out of the Plan*. See also Riskin, *China's Political Economy*, and Perkins, "Reforming China's Economic System."

27. Olson conjectured that the repeated purges in the Cultural Revolution shook loose the foundations of stable coalitions of bureaucratic interests that were strongly motivated to defend the old system, thus paving the way for the start of economic reform. Mancur Olson, *Power and Prosperity: Outgrowing Communist and Capitalist Dictatorships* (New York: Basic Books, 2000).

28. In 1975, for example, Deng drafted documents on reform measures in foreign trade and investment. In 1977, immediately after his comeback to power, Deng began to revive those measures, though the pace of the new programs, which lacked a clear blueprint, was uneven and not coordinated with other domestic reforms. Harding, *China's Second Revolution;* Nicholas Lardy, *Foreign Trade and Economic Reform in China, 1978–1990* (Cambridge: Cambridge University Press, 1992).

29. Chen, *Xin Zhongguo.*

30. The term "pro-reform" here does not imply that these leaders had a clear and thorough plan on how to reform the economic system.

31. Fewsmith, *Dilemmas of China's Reform;* Harding, *China's Second Revolution.*

32. Naughton, *Growing Out of the Plan;* Riskin, *China's Political Economy.*

33. Naughton, *Growing Out of the Plan.* It should be noted, though, that Naughton argues against the view that the political leaders' economic perspectives played a central role in the start of reform. In his words, "neither chronic nor acute political factors can explain the initiation of reform, nor does it make sense to see some fraction of China's veteran leaders as being innately reformist" (pp. 63–64). Rather, it was political and economic expediency that opened the way for the start of a virtuous cycle of reforms.

34. See also Perkins, "Reforming China's Economic System" and "Completing China's Move to the Market."

35. Fewsmith, *The Dilemmas of China's Reform;* Jae Ho Chung, *Central Control and Local Discretion in China: Leadership and Implementation During Post-Mao Decollectivization* (Oxford: Oxford University Press, 2000).

36. Commercialization and decollectivization are the central themes of early rural reform. The former was encouraged by the central authorities from the very beginning; the latter was endorsed by some local authorities but initially opposed by the center. It was not until early 1983 that the center endorsed family farming.

37. As a matter of fact, those sharing the local initiative thesis do note these links. Yet, they downplay the importance of the actions of central leaders. The basic argument is that what was actually carried out in the reform process was not what the central leaders intended in the first place. An implicit assumption here is that intentionality is an indispensable element in the cause of a social phenomenon. This essentially functionalist assumption, however, may not even serve well the argument that the actions of peasants and local cadres were the real drivers of reform. The initial outcomes of rural reform, for example, might exceed or fall short of the varying expectations of the rural cadres and peasants who ventured to break the rules.

38. In Yang's book, however, other than statistical inference there is little direct evidence that the main driving force behind the initial rule-breaking actions taken by some rural cadres to adopt family farming indeed stemmed from their traumatic memories of the Great Leap famine and the resultant belief in the inferiority of the commune system. Yang, *Calamity and Reform.*

39. Chung, *Central Control and Local Discretion.*

40. Xiong, *Zaisheng Zhongguo.*

41. Ibid.

42. Much of this is documented in Yang's book, for example. But it is puzzling that instead of investigating the role of such a direct causal linkage, he makes broad assertions about the link between the depth of traumatic memory and the likelihood of early reform efforts without much direct evidence. Yang, *Calamity and Reform.*

43. Information about natural disasters can be found in NBS, *Zhongguo zaiqing baogao, 1949–1995* (Reports of the Damage Caused by Disaster in China, 1949–1995) (Beijing: Zhongguo Tongji Chubanshe, 1995). Statistics about the size of the rural areas affected by natural disasters can be found in NBS, *Xin Zhongguo wushi nian.*

44. In 1978, for example, natural disasters affected about one-third of the sown acreage in the nation. NBS, *Zhongguo zaiqing baogao,* p. 389.

45. What happened in the "pioneering provinces" is important, though. The

groundswell of spontaneous rule-breaking did not occur in most other provinces, which, as Chung illustrates, pursued a bandwagon approach to follow what was later legitimized by the center. Chung, *Central Control and Local Discretion.*

46. Another reform that somewhat resembled the process of rural reform is relaxation of control on rural-urban migration, which was initiated by local authorities and initially opposed by the central leadership (it was not until 1988 that the ban on rural-urban migration was lifted by the center).

47. Naughton, *Growing Out of the Plan.*

48. Perkins, "Reforming China's Economic System," and Riskin, *China's Political Economy.*

49. Although neither group was homogeneous, the contrast between breaking the rules for change and sticking to a position where there was not much for local officials to gain in terms of financial rewards and career advancement quickly led to massive defection from the old system. The ideologically most committed leaders lost out. As far as peasants are concerned, the risk takers and bandwagon followers outnumbered the laggards. See David Zweig, *Agrarian Radicalism in China, 1968–1981* (Cambridge, Mass.: Harvard University Press, 1989).

50. Susan L. Shirk, *The Political Logic of China's Economic Reform* (Berkeley, Calif.: University of California Press, 1993).

51. Jude Howell, *China Opens Its Doors: The Politics of Economic Transition* (Boulder, Colo.: Lynne Rienner, 1993); Lardy, *Foreign Trade and Economic Reform*; Susan L. Shirk, *How China Opened Its Doors: The Political Success of the PRC's Foreign Trade and Investment Reforms* (Washington, D.C.: Brookings Institution, 1994).

52. Also, since there was no foreign investment in China before the start of reform, opening up was largely a matter of who would gain more rather than who suffered net losses.

53. Shirk, *The Political Logic of China's Economic Reform;* Ezra Vogel, *One Step Ahead in China: Guangdong under Reform* (Cambridge, Mass.: Harvard University Press, 1989).

54. Howell, *China Opens Its Doors.*

55. Christine P. W. Wong, Christopher Heady, and Wing T. Woo, *Financial Management and Economic Reform in the People's Republic of China* (Hong Kong: Oxford University Press, 1995).

56. Rulong Chen, ed., *Dangdai Zhongguo de caizheng* (Public Finance in Contemporary China) (Beijing: Zhongguo Shehui Kexue Chubanshe, 1988); Shaoguang Wang and Angang Hu, *Zhongguo guojia nengli baogao* (A Report on China's State Capacity) (Hong Kong: Oxford University Press, 1994).

57. Wang and Hu, *Zhongguo guojia nengli baogao.*

58. The same is true for the banking system, which has long focused its functions on the financing of SOEs. Nicholas Lardy, *China's Unfinished Economic Revolution* (Washington, D.C.: Brookings Institution, 1998).

59. Shirk, *The Political Logic of China's Economic Reform.*

60. Yi-min Lin and Tian Zhu, "Ownership Restructuring in Chinese State Industry: An Analysis of Evidence on Initial Organizational Changes," *China Quarterly*, no. 166 (June 2001): 305–341.

61. In the event of job loss, rural migrants working in urban industrial and commercial entities can return to their home villages to survive on the land that their families contract out from the village. SOE employees, however, do not have such a last resort. They have been totally dependent on their work units for a wage income

and a wide range of basic social service and welfare provisions, such as housing, health care, and pensions.

62. Lin and Zhu, "Ownership Restructuring in Chinese State Industry."

63. The banking system, for example, has been extensively used to subsidize poorly performing SOEs instead of forcing them to improve efficiency through tighter financial discipline. A result of this is the growth of "bad loans." Lardy, *China's Unfinished Economic Revolution*.

64. For more detailed discussions of different industrial enterprises and their varying paces of reform, see Yi-min Lin, *Between Politics and Markets: Firms, Competition, and Institutional Change in Post-Mao China* (Cambridge: Cambridge University Press, 2001).

65. In rural areas, there were also growing numbers of commune and brigade enterprises toward the end of the Mao era. They were much less tightly integrated with the central planning system than urban collective enterprises.

66. For the same reason, small SOEs similar to urban collective enterprises tended to move away from the plan earlier than large and medium SOEs producing capital goods and operating under the direct control of central or provincial authorities.

67. Peter T.Y. Cheung, Jae Ho Chung, and Zhimin Lin, eds., *Provincial Strategies of Economic Reform in Post-Mao China* (Armonk, N.Y.: M.E. Sharpe, 1998).

68. With regard to the variations in the pace of agricultural reform, Yang argues that the legacy of the Great Leap famine was the most important determinant, as noted above. Yang, *Calamity and Reform.*

69. Anhui, for example, was a pioneer in agricultural reform, but has lagged behind in all other reforms.

70. Wang and Hu, *The Political Economy of Uneven Development.*

71. Dali L. Yang, *Beyond Beijing: Liberalization and the Regions in China* (London: Routledge, 1997).

72. A collection of such studies is offered in Cheung et al., eds., *Provincial Strategies of Economic Reform in Post-Mao China.*

73. Peter T.Y. Cheung, "Introduction," in Cheung et al., eds., *Provincial Strategies of Economic Reform in Post-Mao China,* pp. 3–48. See also Chung, *Central Control and Local Discretion in China.*

74. David S. G. Goodman, ed., *China's Regional Development* (London: Routledge, 1989) and Goodman, *China's Provinces in Reform: Class, Community and Political Culture* (London: Routledge, 1997).

75. Going beyond such areas bears a high political risk, as the CCP has continued to maintain rather tight control over its functionaries throughout the state bureaucracy despite the shift of policy focus from ideological indoctrination and political mobilization to economic development. Chung, *Central Control and Local Discretion;* Yasheng Huang, *Inflation and Investment Controls in China: The Political Economy of Central-local Relations During the Reform Era* (Cambridge: Cambridge University Press, 1996).

76. It is important to note that there is great diversity within both the interior and the coastal region. Guangxi, for example, is a coastal province, but it has features in economic institutional change that are more similar to many inland provinces than other coastal provinces.

77. For accounts of the development of the private sector, see Sheng Han Sun and Clifton W. Pannell, "The Geography of Privatization in China, 1978–1996," *Economic Geography* 75 (1999): 272–296; Susan Young, *Private Business and Eco-*

nomic Reform in China (Armonk, N.Y.: M.E. Sharpe, 1995); Xuwu Zhang, Minggan Xie, and Ding Li, eds., *Zhongguo siying jingji nianjian, 1978–1993* (Yearbook of China's Private Sector Economy, 1978–1993) (Hong Kong: Xianggang Jingji Daobao She, 1994), and *Zhongguo siying jingji nianjian, 1996* (Yearbook of China's Private Sector Economy, 1996) (Beijing: Zhonghua Gongshang Lian Chubanshe, 1996).

78. Chun Chang and Yijiang Wang, "The Nature of the Township-village Enterprise," *Journal of Comparative Economics* 19 (1994): 434–452; Hehui Jin and Yingyi Qian, "Public versus Private Ownership of Firms: Evidence from Rural China," *Quarterly Journal of Economics* 113, no. 3 (1998): 773–808; David Li, "A Theory of Ambiguous Property Rights in Transition Economies: The Case of the Chinese Non-state sector," *Journal of Comparative Economics* 23, no. 1 (1996): 1–19. Victor Nee, "Organizational Dynamics of Market Transition: Hybrid Forms, Property Rights, and Mixed Economy in China," *Administrative Science Quarterly* 37 (1992): 1–27; Wing Thye Woo, "The Real Reasons for China's Growth," *China Journal*, no. 41 (1999): 115–137.

79. Zhang et al., eds., *Zhongguo siying qiye nianjian 1978–1993, 1996.*

80. Jean C. Oi, "Fiscal Reform and the Economic Foundations of Local State Corporatism in China," *World Politics* 45 (1992): 99–126, and Oi, *Rural China Takes Off: The Institutional Foundations of Economic Reform* (Berkeley, Calif.: University of California Press, 1999).

81. Zhang et al., eds., *Zhongguo siying qiye nianjian 1978–1993, 1996.*

82. James Kung and Yi-min Lin, "The Evolving Ownership Structure in China's Economic Transition: An Analysis of the Rural Non-farm Sector," working paper, Division of Social Science, Hong Kong University of Science and Technology, 2000.

83. The changes driven by these mechanisms have been uneven across different regions, however. The predominance of public ownership tends to decline at a slower pace where local authorities are able to mobilize financial resources to fuel expansionary growth and have stronger organizational infrastructure to contain agency problems. See Kung and Lin, "The Evolving Ownership Structure of China's Transitional Economy."

84. For elaborate accounts of this view, see Gary Jefferson and Thomas Rawski, "Enterprise Reform in Chinese Industry," *Journal of Economic Perspectives* 8 (1994): 47–70; Jefferson and Rawski, "How Industrial Reform Worked in China: The Role of Innovation, Competition, and Property Rights," *Proceedings of the World Bank Annual Conference on Development Economics*, pp. 129–156; Naughton, *Growing Out of the Plan;* Rawski, "Implications of China's Reform Experience," *China Quarterly*, no. 144 (1995): 1150–1173.

85. Woo, "The Real Reasons for China's Growth." See also Jeffrey Sachs and Wing Thye Woo, "Structural Factors in the Economic Reforms of China, Eastern Europe, and the Former Soviet Union," *Economic Policy* 18 (1994): 102–131, and Sachs and Woo, "Experiences in the Transition to a Market Economy," *Journal of Comparative Economics* 18 (1994): 271–275.

86. As noted above, the "nonstate" sector in China consists of "collective (hence public) enterprises" controlled under the jurisdiction of local authorities and non-public enterprises (e.g., private entities and foreign-invested entities).

87. The rationale is that decollectivization (and concurrent commercialization) of agriculture led to significant improvement in the use of rural labor, which constituted the mainstay of the workforce. Rural labor, because of trade liberalization, has been drawn increasingly into export-oriented, labor-intensive manufacturing, producing great value outside farming. Woo, "The Real Reason for China's Growth."

88. Linda Chelan Li, *Centre and Provinces–China 1978–1993* (Oxford: Clarendon Press, 1998).

89. Shirk, *The Political Logic of China's Economic Reform.*

90. Oi, "Fiscal Reform and the Economic Foundations of Local State Corporatism in China," and *Rural China Takes Off.* See also Byrd and Lin, *China's Rural Industry;* Gabriella Montinola, Yingyi Qian, and Barry Weingast, "Federalism, Chinese Style: The Political Basis for Economic Success in China," *World Politics* 48 (1995): 50–81; Andrew Walder, "Local Governments as Industrial Firms: An Organizational Analysis of China's Transitional Economy," *American Journal of Sociology* 101 (1995): 263–301.

91. Lance Gore, *Market Communism: The Institutional Foundation of China's Post-Mao Hyper-Growth* (Hong Kong: Oxford University Press, 1998); Gore, "The Communist Legacy in Post-Mao Economic Growth," *China Journal,* no. 41: 25–54; Kung and Lin, "The Evolving Ownership Structure of China's Transitional Economy"; Susan Whiting, "Contract Incentives and Market Discipline in China's Rural Industrial Sector," in John McMillan and Barry Naughton, eds., *Reforming Asian Socialism: The Growth of Market Institutions* (Ann Arbor, Mich.: University of Michigan Press, 1996), pp. 53–110; Whiting, *Power and Wealth.*

92. Lin, *Between Politics and Markets*; Xiaobo Lu, *Cadres and Corruption: The Organizational Involution of the Chinese Communist Party* (Stanford, Calif.: Stanford University Press, 2000).

93. A detailed account is offered in David Wank, *Commodifying Communism: Business, Trust, and Politics in a Chinese City* (Cambridge: Cambridge University Press, 1999).

94. Lin, *Between Politics and Markets.*

95. Lin makes a preliminary effort to address this issue in *Between Politics and Markets.*

96. The adoption of Western-style laws and regulations has also been touted by the Chinese leadership as a major step toward modernizing China's economic institutional infrastructure. Doug Guthrie, *Dragon in a Three-piece Suit: The Emergence of Capitalism in China* (Princeton, N.J.: Princeton University Press, 1998).

97. *Renmin ribao* (People's Daily, Beijing), November 10, 1999.

98. Lin and Zhu, "Ownership Restructuring in Chinese State Industry."

99. Howell, *China Opens Its Doors;* Lardy, *Foreign Trade and Economic Reform;* Margaret Pearson, *Joint Ventures in the People's Republic of China: The Control over Foreign Direct Investment under Socialism* (Princeton, N.J.: Princeton University Press, 1991).

100. An example of such modification is the change in the policy with regard to rural-urban migration. Despite central restrictions, many local governments in the coastal region began to relax migration control in the early 1980s to maintain a supply of cheap labor for foreign-invested entities. Such actions led to the central authority's decision in 1988 to recognize what had already been adopted in practice.

101. Fred Hu, "China's WTO Accession as a Catalyst for Capital Account Liberalization," *Cato Journal* 21, no. 1 (Spring/Summer 2001): 101–111; Shirk, *How China Opened Its Doors.*

102. Lardy, *China's Unfinished Economic Revolution.*

103. Lin, *Between Politics and Markets.*

104. For discussions on the impact of FDI-related labor practices, see Anita Chan, *China's Workers Under Assault: The Exploitation of Labor in a Globalizing Economy*

(Armonk, N.Y.: M.E. Sharpe, 2001), and Howell, *China Opens Its Doors*. Shaoguang Wang offers a comprehensive discussion on how China's accession to WTO may exacerbate inequalities in "The Social and Political Implications of China's WTO Membership," *Journal of Contemporary China* 9, no. 25 (2000): 373–405. The September 2001 issue of *China Quarterly* carries a wider range of analyses about the impact of WTO membership on China's political economy.

105. Shirk, *How China Opened Its Doors;* David Zweig, *Internationalizing China: Domestic Interests and Global Linkages* (Ithaca, N.Y.: Cornell University Press, 2002).

106. Josepth Fewsmith, "The Political and Social Implications of China's Accession to the WTO," *China Quarterly,* no. 167 (2001): 573–591.

107. Nicholas Lardy, "The Role of Foreign Trade and Investment in China's Economic Transformation," *China Quarterly*, no. 144 (1995): 1065–1082; Pearson, *Joint Ventures in the People's Republic of China.*

108. Since foreign-invested entities are not effectively subject to the central plan, conversion of enterprises under the plan into such entities reduces the scope of the plan. Also, those transformed from public enterprises previously under the plan may not completely sever their ties with allocating authorities and channels and thus may be in a position to divert resources away from the planned economy. The competitive edge of the entities that are able to obtain special regulatory treatment for foreign-invested entities, along with the increased inflow of foreign products through the brokerage of some of these entities, poses a growing threat to enterprises operating under the plan while bringing to bear on them a demonstration effect about the potential gains of breaking away from the plan. The interaction and collusion between those seeking rent through illicit or even illegal avenues to internationalization and the officials who are coopted to bend the rules further have weakened the capacity of the old system to sustain itself. See Lin, *Between Politics and Markets.*

3

The Role of Property Rights in China's Rural Reforms and Development

A Review of Facts and Issues

James Kai-sing Kung

Introduction

The reform of China's rural economy has remained to this day one of the most radical reforms the post-Mao leadership has attempted in the past two decades. With the rapid and eventual dismantling of the collective farms, peasants in China have since then been able to farm on an individualized basis. Commonly known as the household responsibility system (HRS), the family farm is an institution that frees the farmers from the stranglehold typical of a collectivized agriculture; above all, it allows them to earn an income commensurate with the effort that they and their family members honestly and industriously expend on the soil of the clearly demarcated plots. The overall success of this reform is beyond dispute: both peasant incomes and crop output experienced the sharpest growth during this brief period (roughly between 1978 and 1984) in the history of Communist China.[1]

While farmers have importantly regained the right to decide how land and labor are to be deployed—no doubt in a manner consistent with the postulate of income maximization, the reform remains incomplete in one major respect; namely, that farmers have not been made the legal owners of the land which they have the right to cultivate and, accordingly, to obtain an income from optimally using it.[2] Farmers still do not have the complete triad of property rights. A useful approach to the study of property rights is to divide them into the following triad of "bundles": namely, the right to use a scarce economic resource; the corresponding right to derive an income from its use; and, not the least, the right to transfer or sell the former two bundles for a profit. Ownership rights in land continue to reside in the hands of the village authorities, or more appropriately the villagers, given that in practice land was divided more or less equally among members of the village community. As membership is naturally acquired by birth or through marriage, or lost in the event of death or sometimes as a result of permanent migration, change in community membership is inevitable. Accordingly, this change in family demographics necessitates land to be reallocated; sometimes only among families that have experienced membership change, but where the change is massive, the existing allocation of the entire village needs to be undone altogether.

For some time now, this communal nature of property rights in land has attracted a great deal of analytical (and perhaps also emotional) attention from scholars and policy makers alike. Sparked by an unexpected stagnation of crop output growth from around the mid-to-late 1980s, critics of common property rights have linked the lackluster performance of the crop sector to the tenure insecurity generated by the universal practice of periodic land reallocations.[3] Uncertain about the fruits of their plot-specific investments (in that the land in which investments have been made may be redistributed away in subsequent reallocations), farmers rationally refrain from committing these investments. Long-term land investments, of which the application of organic matters is a key input, are especially discouraged as a result of insecure tenure. The collective outcome is therefore an inevitable decline in crop output growth and a deterioration of soil fertility.

More recently, this lack of transfer rights among China's farmers is seen as having a restrictive effect on rural labor mobility. Whether villagers are prohibited outright by the local authorities from renting out the contracted plots, or simply fear that by leaving their farms behind, they may risk losing them in the next reallocation, the result is the same: people with a strong proclivity to work off the farms are forced to stay behind in the villages, possibly underutilizing their labor in an activity—farming—that offers the lowest economic return. To the extent that economic development, broadly conceived, is a process in which workers in the "traditional" or "subsistence" sector (namely agriculture) are gradually transferred to a "modern" sector (namely industry), common property rights are seen to retard such a crucial process, or what essentially is the centerpiece of modernization. Taken together, these two allegations point to the urgent imperative of fundamentally overhauling the remaining hurdle to economic growth —common property rights in land.

The overriding goal of this chapter is to critically examine the role played by property rights both during the reform period and in the ensuing development process. The main arguments that we would like to advance are as follows. First, we regard the changes in property rights during the initial reform period of the late 1970s and early 1980s as being extremely critical to the success of that reform. They were important because collectivized agriculture suffered from an immense *incentive* problem, so severe that work incentives could only be invigorated via the reassignment of rights to the peasantry, which in turn could only be achieved by means of breaking up the collective farms. By comparison, the right to transfer use and income rights were less important; in part that is because farmers were primarily concerned with increasing their long stagnated income at that time; but in part also because the prevailing rural economic structure then had yet to become sufficiently diversified for occupational change to take place. Second, although greater security associated with transfer rights is seen as a precondition upon which sustained agricultural growth as well as the development of an off-farm economy crucially depend, there is little empirical evidence to suggest that either process has been severely held back by weak property rights in land. In contrast, recent evidence shows that the substantial earnings gap between agriculture and off-farm work has been a powerful engine behind the development of a rural labor market, which in turn has induced the development of a land rental market. If this conjecture *is* correct, there appears to be no immediate urgency for China to privatize her land ownership system, in view both of the costs required for setting up such a system, and the unknown, near-term social consequences associated with privatization.[4] Indeed, unlike the situation two decades ago, what China is currently facing is a "*development* problem," and crucial to this is an uninterrupted process of gradually moving the rural population away from agriculture and the countryside. Insofar as this is happening, which we believe has been the case, reform of an incremental nature is perhaps a safer alternative—both economically and politically.

The remainder of this chapter is organized as follows. First, in order to highlight the importance of property rights in the reform process, the problem facing collective agriculture is analyzed from a historical perspective. Sections 2 and 3 offer two distinctly different but not mutually exclusive explanations of why work incentives were poor on the Chinese collective farms, whereas Section 4 examines the change that occurred to farmers' use and income rights as a consequence of agricultural decollectivization. In Section 5, the problems caused by common property rights in general and restrictive transfer rights in particular are analyzed. They are rejected in light of the lack of supportive evidence for such allegations. Section 6 provides a short summary to the chapter.

Collectivized Agriculture in Historical Perspective: Why Were Work Incentives Poor on Collective Farms?

Despite the enormous impact that collectivized agriculture had on the livelihoods of hundreds of millions of Chinese farmers, its existence, dating from around the mid-1950s to the early 1980s, had been a brief one. For a long time—hundreds of years to say the least—it was private farming that had been the *modus operandi* for the farmers in China. But as soon as the Communist government embarked on the path of rapidly industrializing the country, agriculture was destined to provide the "surplus" required for achieving this noble goal, with collectivization being an inevitable organizational counterpart to that strategy. A collectivized agriculture was deemed inevitable, in light of its role of providing a powerful mechanism through which farm surpluses could be tapped at rates conducive to socialist industrialization.[5] Through a rapid but on the whole little contested process of collectivization, the people's communes were eventually established in 1958. Although serious policy mistakes made during such a process inadvertently led to a famine on an unprecedented scale, resulting in an estimated excess deaths of as many as 30 million people, this organizational framework remained in place for more than two decades before it eventually was dismantled in 1984. Between 1962, the year when China began to gradually recover from its severe famine, and the late 1970s or early 1980s, depending on individual provinces, farmers in China could be broadly characterized as farming on a collectivized basis within the organizational framework of the commune.

There is little doubt that the commune was a mammoth organization: it consisted of an average of 1,800 farm households. Fortunately, enough production was actually carried out in much smaller accounting units—the production team. As the lowest tier of a three-tiered organizational structure, the production team had an average of only twenty-five to forty farm families, with forty-five to sixty full-time farm workers. It was at this level of organization that decisions regarding day-to-day farm work were made and executed. For labor-intensive agriculture, or agriculture that relies primarily on human and draft animal power, however, even a size as compact as the production team may be too large and unwieldy for eliciting an optimal effort from the individual workers who are part of it, according to critics of collective farms.[6] The reason appears intuitively straightforward. Economic theory suggests that an optimal wage should be set equal to the marginal product of labor ($w = MP_L$). The question then is how this condition could be achieved in reality. The corresponding answer is via piece-rate adoption.[7] To the extent that a worker's effort, its quality dimension included, can be enumerated, it follows that the optimal wage should be set equal to the last unit (hence marginal) of that worker's measurable effort. A classic example is an assembly line setting in which a group of workers are typically assigned to perform a homogeneous (albeit monotonous) task in a repetitious manner closely monitored by a supervisor.

There are however several conditions that need to be met before piece rates can be feasibly adopted. First, one's effort must be readily quantifiable. Second, equally if not more important, is the condition that the quality of effort can be verified. It is important because an income-maximizing worker has powerful incentives and therefore proclivities to skimp on the quality of his work under piece rates, as long as he manages to get away from managerial scrutiny. A procedure or mechanism must exist, in other words, for inspecting the quality of a worker's effort if piece rates are to be profitably adopted. Third is the equally stringent requirement that, once determined, rates should remain stable and not be easily susceptible to changes in production conditions, such as the vagaries of weather, as in the case of agriculture.[8] The constant revisions of such rates are not only costly; they also easily generate conflicts between the management and the managed, in which case the incentives of the managed would be adversely affected.

While piece rates can be feasibly employed in a manufacturing-type setting, the same is not true for labor-intensive agriculture. In the first place, the degree of specialization in nonmechanized agriculture is so low that farm workers are required to perform repeatedly a variety of idiosyncratic tasks from one phase to another, and as such it militates against the profitable use of piece rates (which, as we have seen, requires a high degree of standardization). Second, unlike manufacturing, in which operations can be brought under the same roof, agricultural production is spatially far too dispersed for management to efficaciously supervise labor effort. Third, and also in sharp contrast to manufacturing, agriculture does not have a well-delineated set of intermediate products for which a quality dimension readily lends itself to easy managerial scrutiny.[9] Finally, even though it may be technically feasible to establish "work norms" or piece rates, they are unlikely to remain stable due to the highly stochastic nature of agricultural production.[10] Combined, these problematic features of labor-intensive agriculture ruled out the remotest possibility for China to adopt piece rates on its collective farms.

Unable to adopt the piece rate payment scheme in the collectives, the Chinese were thus forced to adopt what is essentially a time rate–based remuneration scheme. As this method of remuneration purports to pay individual workers based on a combination of both observable (age, sex, seeming physical strengths, and farming skills) and unobservable characteristics (how hardworking one is), it essentially amounts to payment according to potentials. The fundamental problem is this: after one obtains a certain rating based on the former assessments, it is up to the individual and his supervisor to jointly determine how much effort he will put into work. To the extent that it is difficult to ascertain the actual effort expended by a particular individual when work is jointly performed within a team context, "shirking" behavior, or the purposive withdrawal of effort, becomes inevitable.[11] Unable to differentiate effort, team leaders simply assigned similar ratings to individual members, a practice, while convenient from an administrative standpoint, frustrated those who originally were prepared to work hard.

Viewed from this perspective, the poor work incentives that afflicted China's collective farms were the result of having adopted a low-powered incentive scheme, one that failed to forge an intimate link between work effort and material rewards. There was however little that the Chinese could do to correct this except by decollectivizing agriculture, insofar as the adoption of time rates was forced upon them by the production characteristics of a nonmechanized agriculture.

The Commune's "Tragedy": An Alternative Interpretation

While it was probably difficult to effectively supervise labor on China's collective farms, it is unlikely the only reason why incentives were poor: evidence suggests that there was at least one other mechanism through which work incentives had been negatively impacted. It is indisputable that (time) rates—determined on the basis of such factors as age, gender, farming skills, and physical strength—were narrowly differentiated among individual workers within the team.[12] Consider, however, the case that even in a context where individual wage rates are strictly identical, income differentials may still result insofar as households differ in their labor endowments, or simply the absolute number of full-time adult workers.[13] The important question then is whether households with better labor endowments are more prepared to work harder, in light of their greater ability to earn higher incomes within the collective context. While no definite answer can be given, it would be equally presumptuous to rule out the possibility that potential income differentials between families may indeed provide the necessary motivations for at least some members of the production team to supply a larger amount of effort (and presumably also work of a better quality). With that being a distinct possibility, it is thus not necessarily the case for incentives and correspondingly effort to be as poor on the collective farms as critics have made out. Of primary importance here is the question of whether production teams in rural China strictly committed to distributing income on the aforementioned basis.

Available evidence suggests that production teams commonly resorted to distributing income to farm families on criteria other than, or at least combined with, those based strictly on merit, or specifically work points in the Chinese case.[14] A brief description of the income distribution practices in pre-reform rural China may be useful in elucidating this alternative view. First of all, it is important to note that rural income in pre-reform China actually consisted of two parts: an in-kind income, consisting mainly of food grains, distributed primarily on the basis of household size or the number of mouths a family had to feed; and a cash component to only those households credited with sufficient "surplus" work points.[15] What that means in actual practice is that a farm household would be allocated an amount of grain equivalent to the product of the community consumption norms and its size, regardless of the category—be it "surplus" or "deficit"—under which it was classified. While in principle a deficit household had to make up for its shortfall in work points with cash payments to the team authorities, in actual practice such repayments were few and far between. Neither the dates of the repayment were stringently set—to the effect that a family in debt was implicitly allowed to extend its obligations to the community far into the future until his children reached the working age of 16—nor were interest payments accrued to the debt appropriately charged.

Might that have impaired the incentives of those households with surplus work points and therefore presumably higher potential incomes? It depends. Where the production teams were able to honor the remaining cash balance accrued to these surplus households, we cannot rule out the possibility that they might continue to work hard. In contrast, for teams with a good proportion of families landed on the deficit side and whose local authorities did not have sufficient funds with which to pay the surplus families, incentives of the latter would most certainly be impaired. What may further have undermined work incentives, in addition, was the team practice of rationing food grains to families without adjusting for differences in age and correspondingly laboring and consumption requirements. As deficit households were typically those with proportionately more children and correspondingly lower consumption requirements, many ended up having surplus grain and were in fact able to sell it in the local market and at higher market prices for an income. On the other hand, the rationed quantity often proved insufficient for at least some of the surplus households, who were then forced to make up for the shortfall in consumption by purchasing extra grain from the market at higher prices. To the extent that the deficit households were able to sell their surpluses at the higher market price while their nominal debt—even if it were to be settled sometime in the distant future—was fixed at the lower state purchase price, the difference in prices amounted to yet *another* subsidy. This must have further weakened the work incentives of the labor-cum–work point–abundant households.

Agricultural Decollectivization and the Invigoration
of Work Incentives

Regardless of which of the two interpretations better explain the incentive failure experienced on China's collective farms, it is certain that, when presented with a choice, as they had been during the late 1970s and early 1980s, farmers in China were unwilling to continue with just any variant of team farming; collectively, and without any planned coordination on their part, they voted for a return to family farming.[16]

The term decollectivization refers to a process whereby the former production team or the organization within which production was planned and carried out on a day-to-day basis became dismantled. A hallmark of this change, therefore, lay in the breaking up of the formerly consolidated holdings owned and held by the team into strips of small, scattered plots earmarked for return to the farm families who were members of this team for individualized use.[17] Decollectivization was not without its paradoxical feature, however, judging by the manner in which it was implemented. Most notably, just as a major chanted goal of the rural reforms was to "combat egalitarianism," the land division rule adopted in the majority of instances, however, ironically turned out to be highly egalitarian in itself. It was probably due to the legacy of the collective agricultural era (or perhaps even to the earlier land reform). Available evidence shows that land was overwhelmingly allocated to the farm households on the basis of their size, with a few taking into account a household's laboring capacity in determining its share of the assigned land.[18] An interesting question arises as to whether this seemingly egalitarian practice of dividing scarce resources impaired efficiency, or specifically output and income growth in the immediate ensuing period, just as an egalitarian income distribution scheme had dampened work incentives in the collective period?

Evidence suggests not. Compared with the lackluster growth rate of a mere 2.5 percent per annum for crops during the period from 1952 through 1978, the 5.9 percent attained within a short span of five years clearly suggests that the rural reforms in general, and decollectivization in particular, was a great policy success. According to one widely accepted estimate, the institutional change from collective to family farming is responsible for almost half (48.69 percent) of the output increase during the period from 1978 through 1984; a magnitude equal to the combined effects of the policy of simultaneously increasing chemical fertilizer supply and raising state purchase prices (respectively 32.2 percent and 15.98 percent).[19] To the extent that output performance depended closely on effective labor input, which we believe was the case, the question of key importance is why farmers now worked so hard on the delineated plots assigned to them after the breaking up of the collectives. In particular, is it possible to make sense of this monumental change in behavior within the analytical framework of property rights theory?

Two factors are crucial to produce this sea change of incentives on the farmers' part. First, the fact that they no longer have to work together in a team context implies that effort can now be clearly delineated; after all, how much is being produced on the single delineated plots depends critically on the effort of the farmer and his family who farm these plots, and nobody else.[20] To the extent that effort monitoring within a team context was a key detriment prohibiting team farming from being a viable alternative to private farming, this "individualization" of production effectively eliminates the problem of "free riding" or "shirking."

A second reason behind farmers' preference for family farming has to do with the abolition of the system of centralized income distribution. We have seen that under the commune system income was distributed in an exceedingly narrow manner. While such an egalitarian income practice may very well have served as a safety net in protecting the "demographically weak" households, it nonetheless impaired the incentives of those prepared to work hard. This explains why farmers in China eventually chose that variant of family farming called *baogan daohu;* for it is only under this particular institutional arrangement that the mechanism of a centralized income distribution practice became finally abolished.[21]

With respect to explaining the radical change in farmers' behavior in terms of property rights theory, we can simply restate the above observations in the following manner. What the farmers have gained are two important "bundles" of rights. First, the farmer and his family are now able to use the land "rented" to him by the village authorities as he sees fit, subject to the payment of a tax and an obligation to sell a certain amount of his output to the state at prices fixed by the latter (dubbed "procurement," or "grain quota sales"). In short, first decollectivization has conferred to a farm family the distinct right to use the land with which it does not have full legal ownership, insofar as it fulfills the procurement obligations. Second, and as a corollary, the right to derive an income is implicitly "bundled together" with the assignment of the use right. The fact that they are able to sell their output to both the government and the market implies the existence also of this income right. What farmers have not gained from decollectivization is the right to "transfer" the foregoing bundle of rights, as ownership in land continues to reside in the defunct "collectives." As we shall see in the subsequent section, this legacy of communal land ownership has been the center of controversy for some time for the allegedly adverse impact it has on both future agricultural growth and labor mobility—both of which arguably impede the development process.

China's Unfinished Agricultural Reforms: Some Consequences of Common Property Rights

Our discussions thus far show that China's rural reforms—in particular the switch from collective to household farming—have been a major source of efficiency gains. As with all institutional change whose effect is typically once-and-for-all, decollectivization is no exception. Crop output growth slipped precipitously to a lackluster 1.4 percent between 1984 and 1987 after having reached a peak of 5.9 percent between 1978 and 1984. A number of reasons have been proposed to explain this sudden plummeting of crop output.

The first argument attributes the output decline to a reduction in the government's purchase price. As part and parcel of the reform package, the government increased procurement prices as a means to stimulate farmers' production incentives. On the other hand, the government's commitment to the urban class of a low cost of living meant that the urban resale price of grain could not be raised, to the effect that the sale price failed even to cover the cost of purchase, thereby resulting in a fiscal deficit that the government found difficult to sustain. At about the same time (1984), a bumper harvest exceeding 400 million metric tons of grain was recorded for the first time, giving rise to the illusion that the "grain problem" that the country had grimly faced for a long time had eventually been resolved. These considerations, taken together, led to the sharply reversed decision of effectively lowering the state purchase prices of grain from 1985 onward. This decision is alleged to have resulted in a stagnation of crop output growth in the remaining decade.[22]

A second view attributes the decline in crop output growth to an exodus of villagers out of the farm sector and into a variety of off-farm activities that were beginning to develop in earnest from around the late 1980s.[23] Finally, and this is the view that has attracted the most attention from both academics and policymakers, is one that links declining crop output growth to the common or communal nature of property rights in land. Our remaining discussions will focus on this last view. Specifically, this view sees the restrictions that China's farmers face in renting out their plots as a major source of economic efficiency: either they fail to sustain continuing crop output growth by discouraging land-specific investments, or they reduce rural labor mobility more generally, thereby slowing down the process of rural surplus labor transfer.

Common Property, Tenure Security, and Land-Specific Investments

As noted earlier, when the collectives distributed land among the farm households during decollectivization the majority did it on a highly egalitarian basis, by simply using family size as a distributional yardstick. The adoption of such a criterion carries with it a very important implication underpinning the nature of property rights in land; namely, that it is a communal resource owned by virtually all the members of the village community or, previously, the production team. As such, every member of the community, of which membership is usually acquired either by birth or through marriage, is entitled to an equal opportunity of *using* this scarce economic resource.[24]

A salient institutional arrangement arising from this underlying premise is that land will be reallocated on a periodic basis in response to family demographic and other larger structural changes in the village economy. While evidence clearly suggests that villages do vary with respect to both the frequency and magnitude of these reallocations, there are few instances in which villages have completely avoided reallocations altogether since decollectivization.[25] The crux is therefore this: to the extent that people anticipate land reallocations, tenure becomes inherently insecure, as part, if not all, of one's current allocated plots could be redistributed away from him in the next assignment. For those who have invested in their currently assigned plots today, any premature redistribution in the absence of compensation amounts essentially to the effect of a "confiscation."[26] Of course, as long as farmers anticipate this and behave rationally, the collective outcome is that none will be committed to making such "plot-specific" investments. It is this alleged lack of incentives on the part of the farmers in China to invest in their assigned plots that powerfully explains the decline in crop output growth, according to the critics.[27] To restore the growth initiative, property rights in land must be made private. Unlike its communal counterpart, a regime of private property rights will encourage the owner to optimally invest in his land, for land of a better quality can fetch a higher price when he either sells it or rents it out.[28]

A number of "symptoms" associated with the alleged poor investment incentives have been invoked by these critics, chief amongst them has been the under-application of organic fertilizers. Unlike chemical fertilizer, which helps to increase yields, organic fertilizers serve the important purpose of preserving long-term soil fertility, and their use is thus a measure critical for a sustainable agricultural growth. The predominant reason why farmers in China are using much less organic fertilizer today relative to its chemical counterpart is therefore largely the consequence of a deficient property rights regime, according to the logic reviewed earlier.

Logically plausible as it may appear, none of these criticisms are nonetheless supported by sound empirical evidence. Thus far, only one study has made a specific attempt to compare farmers' input behavior between plots characterized by differing property rights regimes.[29] Specifically, by examining the fertilizing behavior of some eighty farmers respectively on the private plots and plots that are due for reallocation in Hebei Province in North China, Li et al. (1999) found that inputs on the former were about 25 percent higher than those on the latter.[30] While certainly not negligible, such a magnitude is still not substantial when compared to the difference between private and collective plots in the commune era—one that was in excess of 100 percent.[31]

A major drawback of the criticism in question is that it overlooks the larger trend toward which China is gravitating. Like countries whose trajectory of agricultural development has historically relied heavily on irrigation and chemical fertilizers (Japan and other East Asian economies, for example), China has similarly reached a stage of relying increasingly on the use of chemical fertilizers for raising yields. Decreases in the use of organic fertilizer relative to its chemical counterpart are therefore part and parcel of this evolutionary process. In fact, a careful examination of the relevant statistics reveals that organic fertilizer use has not declined in absolute terms after decollectivization, what *has* declined is only its relative share in overall fertilizer usage, a finding that corroborates the thesis of China going through a process of secular change.[32]

A second problem is that the criticism overlooks how the reform has fundamentally changed both the institutional environment and the incentive structures embedded in that environment with respect to the accumulation of organic fertilizers. Prior to the reform, the chronic shortages of chemical fertilizer and the collective framework within which production activities were structured were conducive to the purposive collection and use of a wide variety of organic fertilizers.[33] The rural reforms changed this. As part of a deliberate policy to raise farm outputs and peasant incomes, the government supplied more chemical fertilizers to be used as farm inputs. This effectively reduced the scope of organic fertilizer usage. On the other hand, the gradual rise of an off-farm economic sector has increasingly relegated farming to secondary importance insofar as income is concerned. As the rural labor force becomes increasingly absorbed into the orbit of off-farm work—temporary though much of such employment maybe—it effectively raises the opportunity costs of labor in terms of the time spent on farming.[34] At any rate, organic fertilizers have become much less available in the post-reform period, and as such their use has to be rationed. The remaining question is what supplies the criteria of rationing, the answer to which requires a study of farmers' fertilizing practices at the level of the villages.

The only available study of this nature indeed shows that fertilizing behavior may be regarded as largely subject to the forces of "demand" and "supply," and is patterned upon sharp differences in village characteristics.[35] In villages where a substantial proportion of households are engaged in off-farm economic activity, for example, a dominant behavioral "mode" is that only plots near and around one's homestead would be fertilized. In addition to the time constraint just alluded to the low returns to farming are also a factor predisposing these relatively well-to-do households to reduce their effort supply in agriculture, given that transporting organic fertilizers—which are often mixed with mud and other heavy bulky substances—is a typically onerous task. Contrarily, in villages that remain heavily dependent on agriculture, farmers are found to be putting more of their similarly inadequate organic nutrients into plots that they believe are most elastic in terms of supply response. While one should remain cautious in interpreting these findings, they do support the idea that the rise in the opportunity cost of labor may powerfully explain the declining usage of organic fertilizers.[36]

Restrictive Transfer Rights and Labor Immobility

Another area in which common property institutions are expected to have a profoundly negative effect is labor mobility, in particular the mobility of those villagers who wish to work off the farm. In the absence of private property rights in land, a prospective migrant is unable to sell the land that he farms and is thus unable to receive the scarcity land value essential for his relocation.[37] Given that the Chinese government is unlikely to privatize rural land rights in the near term, a more relevant issue is whether farmers in China are allowed to engage in land rental transactions. Insofar as government policy is concerned, the answer lies firmly in the positive. Research has found, however, that such a right varies considerably across villages. While in some villages farmers appear to be able to freely engage in land rental activities, in others such a freedom seems rather restricted.[38] In particular, transfer rights seem more restrictive in areas where village authorities are particularly concerned with fulfilling the state grain quotas, or the quantity of grain that farm households are supposed to sell to the government.[39]

Even in the less restrictive instances, survey evidence tends to corroborate the idea that the lack of transfer rights does hamper rural labor mobility, if only to a lesser extent. A study conducted in Henan Province of North China, for instance, finds the virtual absence of a land rental market and, concomitantly, that the male migrant workers have to return to their home villages during agricultural peak seasons for time-critical tasks, therefore shortening the duration of their migration and reducing their off-farm earnings.[40] This observation may lead one to arrive at the possible policy implication that a migrant worker would need not return to his home village if only he were allowed to rent out his land.[41] While little is known about the magnitude to which farmers across China are able to engage in land rental activities, the finding that land rental activity occurs on no more than 3–4 percent of the country's arable land appears to vindicate the popularly held view that transfer rights are probably highly restrictive. In fact, it is not necessary to refer to the restrictive behavior of local authorities to account for the low incidence of land leasing activity. Insofar as one will invariably obtain her share of this communal resource under the regime of common property rights, land rental activity will inevitably be reduced.[42] Further, to the extent that rural labor mobility depends crucially on how efficient the land rental market operates, a logical corollary is to suppress the administrative reallocation of land, the latter of which can only be accomplished by abolishing common property rights.

If the rural land rental market were indeed in a highly nascent stage up to the mid-1990s as the available scant evidence suggests, then recent survey evidence shows a considerable leap in the percentages both of the households engaging in such an activity and the magnitude of land that has entered into such transactions.[43] On the whole, close to 25 percent of the surveyed households indicated that they rented in land in the previous year (1998), with the proportion of land rented in by these households accounting for 14.3 percent of the land of all the surveyed households (including those not engaged in land rental transactions).[44] With exactly one-third of the surveyed households having rented in land and the percentage of land rented in amounting to a substantial 35 percent, the land rental market in Zhejiang, a province located on China's eastern seaboard, is unusually active. A question of key analytical importance, in this connection, is whether property rights in this province are especially secure, to the effect that farmers do not worry about the potentially negative consequences that may arise from renting out land.[45] Should that really be the case, then secure property rights are arguably an important precondition for bringing about the emergence of a rural labor market.

While the survey does not contain questions that allow one to directly answer such a question, indirect evidence suggests that transfer rights in this province are far from secure. The most telling feature, in this regard, is perhaps that a significantly larger proportion of those engaged in land rental transactions in this province, close to 60 percent, have done so with their relatives within the same village group, as opposed to the average of a mere 34.5 percent.[46] This disproportionate reliance upon one's relatives for rental transactions reveals, among other considerations, the concern that renting out one's land might risk losing it. Insofar as the economic returns to off-farm activities prove too tempting, however, one needs to work out a strategy that reaches a compromise between (reduced) risks and (higher) incomes. In addition, that the direction of causality is likely to run from labor to land markets instead of the other way around is bolstered by the substantial earnings gap that exists between farm and nonfarm work. For example, whereas the per capita net income obtained from farming is 2,381 yuan, wage incomes range between 5,589 and 5,900 yuan, depending on whether such employment involves migration.[47] In view of such enormous earnings differentials between the two sectors, and the greater demand for off-farm employment opportunities relative to supply, chances are more likely that an income-maximizing farmer would jump on the off-farm opportunity first and worry about the prospects of renting out land later. As a province known for its extraordinarily active local off-farm labor market but otherwise similarly weak property rights in land, we believe the reasons enumerated above provide strong support to the thesis that the process of rural surplus labor transfer has not been obstructed by insecure land rights, or at least not entirely so.[48]

That it is important to identify the causal nature of the underlying relationship between the two factor markets in question has to do with our assessment of how important property rights are at this current stage of China's reform and development. If a regime of unrestricted transfer rights were indeed crucial for moving the surplus rural workers in the development process, then it would be imperative to reform property rights in land; a move, while maybe costly in the near-term, can arguably no longer be delayed. However, if labor mobility has not been severely obstructed by insecure land rights, as it appears to have been demonstrated by the Zhejiang experience, it calls into question the urgency, if not necessity, of committing to a course of reform that may in the near-term produce certain unstable consequences, not to mention the wide array of "institutional costs" required for the establishment of a system of private land rights. Indeed, from this particular vantage point, might it not make better strategic sense for China to postpone completing her ultimate reform in property rights until greater proportions of her rural labor force and their families have become more thoroughly disengaged from agriculture, or at least until they no longer rely considerably on land for a livelihood? While more evidence is clearly needed to provide a solid basis for making a sound assessment, the rush for a wholesale privatization program in the entirety of rural China also appears unwarranted. We remain concerned with the *timing* issue, and not with whether privatization should be altogether avoided.

A Short Summary

Our mission in this chapter is to review the role of property rights in China's earlier rural reforms, and to assess its near-term significance. There is little dispute that property rights played a distinctly important role in the reform process: regardless of what was ultimately responsible for the incentive problem in collectivized agriculture, the reassignment of "residual" income right to the peasant household was by any measure a powerful institutional change that brought about the sharp increase in both farm incomes and crop output. The problem that China faced some two decades ago was a collectivized agriculture wherein the problems pertaining to an excessive egalitarian income distribution practice and weak work incentives viciously reinforced one another to the extent that only a restoration of the family farm as the primary unit of accounting could resolve the incentive problem that had long afflicted the collective farms.

While the dismantling of the collective farms may be regarded as radical in its own right, there is no denial that the reform was far from complete from a property rights standpoint. The ultimate "triad" of the three bundles of property rights, namely, the right to transfer use and income rights, was not reassigned to the farmers upon decollectivization. This "tail" of communal ownership, according to some, has been the primary cause of a stagnant crop output growth in the remaining reform decade (the 1980s), as well as, more recently, an obstructive force to the development process more generally. Without the security which land rental transactions typically require, or in the presence of local governmental restrictions, a land rental market remains arguably underdeveloped, with the corollary that a rural labor market—whose emergence is central to the development process— cannot accordingly come about. Needless to say, such a view is consistent with the mainstream postulate that connects sustained economic growth with a well-defined and effectively enforced system of property rights. Contrary to such a claim, recent empirical evidence nonetheless shows that the two rural factor markets—land and labor—have in fact been more active than was previously believed. By alluding to the substantial earnings gap between agriculture and off-farm work, we are able to link the emergence of a land rental market in rural China to the robust development of a rural labor market, at least in areas where such activities have been thriving. To the extent that this process of rural surplus labor transfer could occur in the absence of secure land rights, China has the luxury to assess the possible consequences of privatization before embarking on it in a rush.[49]

Notes

1. Income soared noticeably from a mere 2 percent from 1954 through 1978 to 6.3 percent per annum during the first six years of the reform, approximately 1978 through 1984, whereas crop output growth for the comparable periods were 2.5 percent and 5.9 percent, respectively.

2. Typically, the less attenuated or unrestrictive these rights are, the stronger are the incentives for pecuniary gains. It is important to note, however, that rights do not have to reside in the same person. In the Chinese case, for example, use and income rights are in the hands of the farmers, whereas ownership rights—which implies the right to transfer use and income rights, belong to the village authorities. For a general discussion of the theory of property rights see Armen Alchian and Harold Demsetz, "The Property Rights Paradigm," *Journal of Economic History* 33, no. 1 (1973): 16–27.

3. Crop output growth, for example, had slowed from 5.9 percent during 1978 to 1984 to a mere 1.4 percent during 1984 to 1987.

4. A cadastral system of land titles, and with it an infrastructure required for exchange and contract enforcement, for example, needs to be instigated with the establishment of private ownership. Depending on whether and if so how much the privatization of land rights will result in widening income inequality, the potential social instability which privatization may generate could potentially threaten the reform progress.

5. The model of "socialist" industrialization as it was being conceived in China in the 1950s necessitated state-owned enterprises to generate exceedingly high profit rates. This in turn required farm prices, among other input prices (such as workers' wages), to be kept artificially low. In the absence of collectivization, the state would have had to deal not only with many more independent farm producers, the farm households, but also with the much higher prices that they would have demanded, likely to be more than the state was willing to pay for.

6. See, among others, Peter Nolan, *The Political Economy of Collective Farms* (Oxford: Polity Press, 1988).

7. By piece rates, we are referring to a mechanism whereby a worker's income is based solely on the number of physically countable items he or she produces. Typically, each different item corresponds with a specific rate, the latter of which is determined by, among other considerations, the degree of skills required (for example the dexterity of fingers).

8. For a more detailed discussion on the economics of piece rates and time rates, see Steven N.S. Cheung, "The Contractual Nature of the Firm," *Journal of Law and Economics* 26 (1982): 1–21.

9. For example, it is arguably unclear how a thoroughly fertilized field should look.

10. The Chinese once made an attempt to establish a system of remuneration in collective agriculture whose properties resemble remarkably those of piece rates. For a detailed analysis of this "work norm management system," see James K. Kung, "Transaction Costs and Peasants' Choice of Institutions: Did the Right to Exit Really Solve the Free Rider Problem in Chinese Collective Agriculture?" *Journal of Comparative Economics* 17 (1993): 483–503. For a general discussion of the problems inherent in collectivized agriculture, see Michael Bradley and Michael Clark, "Supervision and Efficiency in Socialized Agriculture," *Soviet Studies* 23 (1972): 465–473.

11. See Armen Alchian and Harold Demestz, "Production, Information Costs, and Economic Organization," *American Economic Review* 62 (December 1972): 777–795. An alternative perspective from which to understand why effort is low under time rates is because there is no incentive for a worker to presumably increase his effort and produce more units when his income is tied to the amount of time he spends on the job, not the amount he actually produces (although the two are supposedly correlated under effective monitoring).

12. Male laborers, for instance, would typically be assigned a rating of between 8.5 and 10.

13. Only full-time workers—men aged between 16 and 60 years and women up to 55—were allowed to work and earn an income in the collective sector.

14. In China's collectivized agriculture, a work point system was used for determining individual income. Under the time rate system, for example, a worker would be assigned a rating, with 10 being the highest rating for a day's work. In the course of a crop cycle, a worker accumulated his work points, and then multiplied the sum total with the work point value to obtain his income after the harvest. How then was the work point value determined? Did each worker have his or her individual work point value? While individual workers may earn different work points, the work point value, which was obtained by dividing the team's income (net of expenditures) by the total amount of work points the production team had credited to its members, was common to all. To put the above ideas in the form of a simple equation, suppose y_i is the income of worker i, $y_i = wp_i * vwp$, where wp_i represents the amount of work points accumulated by worker i, and vwp is the abbreviation of the value of the work point, where $vwp = Y_T/(wp_T + wp_j + wp_k, \ldots + wp_n)$, Y_T stands for the production team's net income, and $wp_i + wp_j + wp_k, \ldots + wp_n$ are the sum total of work points credited to the team members.

15. Technically, the team would first divide the total amount of work points with which they had credited the households by the total team population; this yielded average or per capita work points for the team as a whole. As a simple numerical example, suppose that this number is 400. Assume further that subsistence consumption is set at 400 kilograms of grain, which means that one work point is required for exchanging each kilogram of grain. Now consider a household of four. According to our hypothetical example it should require 1,600 work points in order to be entitled to an amount of grain required for subsistence consumption. Labor deficiency, however, allowed it to earn only 1,200 work points. From the accounting perspective of the team, this household is a deficit household (short 400 work points). Now there is another household of the same size but one that has more family members able to work in the collective sector, thereby enabling it to earn more work points, say 2,000. It therefore has 400 surplus work points left after the initial distribution of 1,600 kilograms of food grains.

16. The amount of literature written on this subject matter is enormous. For a

detailed documentation of the process, see Robert Ash, "The Evolution of Agricultural Policy," *China Quarterly*, no. 116 (December 1988): 529–555. For an interpretative account by an economist, see Joseph C.H. Chai, "Property Rights and Income Distribution under China's Agricultural Household Responsibility System," in C.K. Leung and J.C.H. Chai, eds., *Development and Change in China: Selected Seminar Papers on Contemporary China, VI* (Hong Kong: University of Hong Kong Press, 1985).

17. In this process other erstwhile collective assets—ranging from farm implements and draft animals to the bricks of a building—were either sold to the individuals or simply shared among them.

18. James K. Kung, "Egalitarianism, Subsistence Provision, and Work Incentives in China's Agricultural Collectives," *World Development* 22, no. 2 (February 1994): 175–187.

19. See Justin Y. Lin, "Rural Reforms and Agricultural Growth in China," *American Economic Review* 82, no. 1 (March 1992): 34–51.

20. Effort delineation becomes superfluous, in fact, when one works only for oneself.

21. Translated literally, this variant of family farming means "contracting everything to the farm household." Even under *baochan daohu*, also an individualized family farming arrangement, income remained centrally distributed; specifically, the practice of equally distributing food grains to the households based on their sizes was retained.

22. It was not until 1990 that grain output in China reached a noticeably higher level—10 percent above the 1984 amount. See *Zhongguo nongcun tongji nianjian* (China's Rural Statistical Yearbook) (Beijing: Zhongguo tongji chubanshe, 2000), p. 23. For further details regarding the change in procurement arrangements and prices, see James K. Kung, "Food and Agriculture in Post-Reform China: The Marketed Surplus Problem Revisited," *Modern China* 18, no. 2 (April 1992): 138–170.

23. The output value of nonagriculture in 1987 surpassed that of agriculture for the first time, signifying that a major change in the rural economic structure was underway.

24. See James K. Kung, "Equal Entitlement versus Tenure Security under a Regime of Collective Property Rights: Peasants' Preference for Institutions in Post-Reform Chinese Agriculture," *Journal of Comparative Economics* 21, no. 1 (1995): 82–111.

25. Land reallocation is unavoidable insofar as it is a universal right for new members of the village community to have access to land use. For a study of land reallocation behavior, see James K. Kung, "Common Property Rights and Land Reallocations in Rural China: Evidence from a Village Survey," *World Development* 28, no. 4 (April 2000): 701–719.

26. By "premature," we are referring to a time horizon being too short to allow the investor to recoup the returns to his investments.

27. See, among others, G.J. Wen, "The Land Tenure System and its Saving and Investment Mechanism: The Case of Modern China," *Asian Economic Journal* 9, no. 3 (1995): 223–259. Some even link China's ability to feed her population to its current system of property rights in land. See, for example, R. Prosterman, T. Hanstad, and Ping Li, "Can China Feed Itself?" *Scientific American*, no. 5 (November 1996): 90–96.

28. It is implicitly assumed that, with the existence of a market for land transactions (either outright buying and selling or merely renting), the concomitant institu-

tions or mechanisms required for assessing the value of the good being exchanged will be there to facilitate the exchange.

29. Guo Li, S. Rozelle, and L. Brandt, "Tenure, Land Rights, and Farmer Investment Incentive in China," *Agricultural Economics* 19, no. 1–2 (1999): 63–71.

30. Obviously, one should be careful when drawing generalizations from such a small sample. There are two reasons why the sample in question is small, despite the fact that these authors have in fact surveyed over 1,000 farm households. First, in order to control for differences in input behavior arising from different cropping patterns, a necessary condition is for households to grow essentially the same crop(s) on both private and responsibility plots, or plots due for reassignment. Traditionally, however, because farmers in China customarily grew crops of a higher economic value on private plots, the chances of finding households cultivating the same crops on both types of land in question are inevitably rare. Second, with the switch to household farming, many villages no longer make a clear distinction between private and contracted plots. Moreover, even where that distinction is made, many families have used the former for new housing construction. See James K. Kung and Yongshun Cai, "Property Rights and Fertilizing Practices in Rural China: Evidence from Northern Jiangsu," *Modern China* 26, no. 3 (July 2000): 276–308.

31. Shahid Burki, *A Study of Chinese Communes*, 1965 (Cambridge, Mass.: Harvard University Press, 1969). The small difference, according to Li et al., "Tenure and Investment Incentive in China," is attributable to the small output elasticity of the organic nutrients.

32. It should be noted, in addition, that it was government policy that fueled the sharp increase in chemical fertilizer usage. See Kung and Cai, "Property Rights and Fertilizing Practices in Rural China," pp. 283–284.

33. The accumulation was indeed made a purposive economic activity; members of the production team who were assigned to be responsible for this specific task were indeed credited with work points upon delivery of this soil nutrient, which came from a variety of sources. For further detail see Kung and Cai, "Property Rights and Fertilizing Practices in Rural China," pp. 290–291.

34. Ibid., p. 292.

35. In villages where a good proportion of the household income comes from animal husbandry, for example, more organic fertilizers are applied.

36. Without necessarily implying any connections between the drop in organic fertilizer use and the decline in crop output growth, the preliminary assessment made here is nonetheless consistent with an observation that the decline in crop output growth since around the late 1980s is attributable to the ongoing process of transfer of surplus rural laborers, or what Lin calls "exodus of the farm workers." See Lin, "Rural Reforms and Agricultural Growth in China."

37. Dennis T. Yang, "China's Land Arrangements and Rural Labor Mobility," *China Economic Review* 8, no. 2 (Fall 1997): 101–115; D. Gale Johnson, "Property Rights in Rural China," mimeographed, University of Chicago, 1995.

38. Empirical studies have indeed confirmed the large variations found between villages in respect to how liberal or restrictive transfer rights across space have been. See, for example, Shouying Liu, Michael Carter, and Yang Yao, "Dimensions and Diversity of Property Rights in Rural China: Dilemmas on the Road to Further Reform," *World Development* 26, no. 10 (1998): 1789–1806.

39. See, for example, Scott Rozelle, Guo Li, Minggao Shen, Amelia Hughart, and John Giles, "Leaving China's Farms: Survey Results of New Paths and Remaining Hurdles to Rural Migration," *China Quarterly*, no. 158 (1999): 367–393. For an

explicit treatment of the effect of grain quotas on how households allocate their labor between farm and nonfarm activities, see Bryan Lohmar, Colin Carter, and Scott Rozelle, "Grain Quota Policies and Household Labor Allocation in China," paper presented at the Annual Meetings of the American Agricultural Economics Association, Chicago, Illinois, July 31–August 3, 2000.

40. Denise Hare, "'Push' versus 'Pull' Factors in Migration Outflows and Returns: Determinants of Migration Status and Spell Duration among China's Rural Population," *Journal of Development Studies* 35, no. 3 (1999): 45–72.

41. Although the absence of a land rental market is typically used to explain the return of the male household laborer during the peak seasons, the latter can be caused by reasons that are totally unrelated to government restrictions. We know, for example, that the demand for agricultural labor varies considerably between the slack and the peak seasons. While in the absence of the household male laborer family members are usually sufficient for the amount of farm tasks required during the slack seasons, an extra pair of expert hands can make a world of difference during the peak seasons, a time when many time-critical tasks need to be carried out close on the heels of one another. On the other hand, renting out the small parcels of land may not be a viable alternative, in view of the "surplus" family members who stay behind in the villages.

42. Matthew Turner, Loren Brandt, and Scott Rozelle, for example, view land rental activity and administrative land reallocations as "substitutes" for one another; the more a village reallocates land, the thinner the land rental market. See Matthew Turner, Loren Brandt, and Scott Rozelle, "Local Government Behavior and Property Rights Formation in Rural China," mimeographed, University of Toronto, 2001.

43. Conducted by the Ministry of Agriculture in 1999, the study surveyed 825 farm households in roughly 36 villages in the provinces of Hebei, Shaanxi, Zhejiang, Anhui, Sichuan, and Hunan.

44. Owing to the under-enumeration of households engaged in renting out activity, as many of these households (or at least the head of these households) have left their villages for off-farm work, only renting in activity is examined here.

45. By renting out land, a farm household risks the possibility of "signaling" to the village officials its low utility in land.

46. For a more detailed analysis of this issue, see James K. Kung, "Off-Farm Labor Markets and the Emergence of Land Rental Markets in Rural China," *Journal of Comparative Economics* 30, no. 2 (2002): 395–414.

47. Local wage income is slightly higher according to the results of this survey. See ibid.

48. Granted the magnitude of rural surplus labor transfer may arguably have been larger had the right to transfer been made more secure (assuming that some are unable to rent out their land to the people they trust), let us however not lose sight of the fact that the overall size of the rural labor market is determined also by the demand for such laborers.

49. Above all, a well-formulated reform strategy requires not merely an enumeration of the benefits of a certain course of action, but also a cognizance of its possible costs. We are merely pointing out the obvious virtues associated with incremental reforms.

4

An Emerging Global City Region?

Economic and Social Integration Between Hong Kong and the Pearl River Delta

George C.S. Lin

Introduction

The ongoing processes of globalization have had significant implications for the functional and territorial organization and reorganization of human activities in different world regions. While the flexible movement of capital and manufacturing activities on a global scale continues to prevail, a distinct process of regional economic integration has been under way not only in Europe and North America but also in the Asia Pacific. The formation of continental trade blocs on both sides of the Atlantic and the emergence of "global city regions" have been well documented in the West.[1] What has received less attention than it deserves is the fact that many Asian countries on the Pacific shore have been undergoing fundamental readjustment in response to the recent economic downturn and financial instability.[2] A system of regional cooperation is taking shape to meet the challenges of intensified international competition in the new era of "volatile globalization."[3]

Despite the growing scholarly attention to the changing role of the Asian-Pacific region in the world economy, there is considerable ambiguity and confusion in conceptualizing the processes and consequences of the economic integration of the region. The real extent of this integration, for instance, has troubled scholars and inspired continued debates.[4] The nature of such integration has been perceived by some as deriving from the common culture and tradition shared by countries within the region, but it has been seen by others as a result of internal differences and complementarities.[5] The dynamism of regional integration has also been the subject of various interpretations ranging from scholars who stress the role of state intervention through those who emphasize the operation of free market forces to those who argue for the emergence of a new "region-state."[6] While the constitution, nature, and dynamism of the integration of countries along the Asia-Pacific Rim continue to inspire endless speculations and unsettled debates, the real-world practice of regional integration and its spatial consequences remain poorly understood. Although numerous case studies have been done, the primary unit of analysis has tended to be either the entire region or an individual country in the region.[7]

This study examines the processes and consequences of regionalization in China by using the integrated Hong Kong–Guangdong economic region as a case. Although much has been written on the intensified interaction between Hong Kong and Guangdong Province as a result of implementing the open door policy initiated in 1979,[8] the actual operating mechanism of regionalization in the context of a transitional socialist economy and its theoretical implications remain controversial and vague. How has a regional economy under socialism been transformed after the intrusion of global market forces? To what extent and in what manner have the relocation of industrial facilities from Hong Kong to the mainland contributed to the growth and restructuring of the economy of the target region? How has the global force of flexible accumulation interacted with local conditions and facilitated spatial reorganization of economic activities, population, and land use? Given the fact that the process of globalization has extended beyond the confines of the Western capitalist world, what are the similarities and differences, if any, between the Chinese case of spatial transformation and the well-documented Western experience of transition from the era of Fordist mass production to the new age of post-Fordist flexible specialization? These questions are crucial to understanding the mechanism of regionalization in China, and they require further investigations.

This chapter is organized in three sections. It begins with an assessment of the changing national context in which the economic integration of Hong Kong and Guangdong Province takes place. This is followed by a detailed study of Dongguan, a county-level economy illustrative of the structural and spatial consequences of integration with Hong Kong. The final section summarizes major findings from this case study and discusses their theoretical implications. The assessment is based on data and information gathered through documentary research, unstructured interviews, and field investigations conducted in 1984, 1992, and 2000. The emphasis of analysis is on the economic and spatial transformation of the region in the post-reform era. Special reference is made, however, to the changing historical and national context to better understand the contemporary and local issues discussed.

National Context

Despite the existence of traditional cultural links, intensified interaction between Hong Kong and Guangdong Province has essentially been a recent phenomenon that has taken place since the late 1970s as a response to the restructuring of the political economies at both the national and global levels. As the world capitalist economy moved from the stage of Fordist mass production to the new era of post-Fordist flexible specialization, from Keynesian welfare-statism to global capitalism, and from managerialism to entrepreneurialism, the Chinese economy has gone through an unprecedented process of transition from central planning to market coordination and from state monopoly to decentralization.[9] Almost parallel with the ascendance of the Ronald Reagan and Margaret Thatcher "new right" administrations, which popularized the ideas of deregulation, privatization, and industrial rationalization, the pragmatic leadership of Deng Xiaoping, who took power after the demise of the radical Maoist regime, adopted a new approach that favored efficiency over equity, individual creativity over collectivization, and outward looking over self-isolation. While the emergence of the new regime of flexible accumulation in North America and Western Europe has been primarily a response to a deepened international division of labor and intensified global competition, the formation of liberal economic policies in China has stemmed from a keen recognition that endless revolutionary upheavals in the past several decades had brought little improvement to the lives of the Chinese people and that drastic policy changes had to be made to lead the nation out of the deadlock of isolation and stagnation.[10]

One of the most important actions taken by the new Chinese leaders has been the introduction of an open door policy as a means to attract foreign investment, bring advanced technology and know-how into the country, and promote export production. Under the open door policy, foreign investors are given preferential treatments, including tax concessions, duty-free imports of machinery and equipment, and other benefits, to facilitate their investment and production in China. As a major objective of the open door policy was to attract foreign capital, it is not surprising that the geographical focus of this new practice has been on the coastal zone which is more easily accessible than the interior to potential overseas investors (Figure 4.1).

The open door policy has been implemented through a process of spatial reorganization, which allowed China to enter the world step by step. It began with the establishment of four Special Economic Zones (SEZs) in the southern provinces of Guangdong and Fujian, where overseas connections are extensive and the tradition of international trade is strong. This was fol-

Figure 4.1   **China's Three Macroregions, Open Cities, and SEZs**

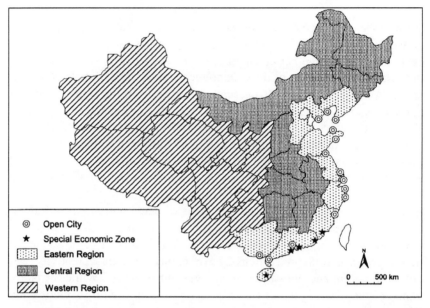

lowed by the opening up of fourteen port cities along the eastern coast in 1984 and the designation of three major river deltas as open economic regions in 1985. Finally, the policy was further extended to cover all coastal provinces in 1988. Increasingly, China's coastal zone has been seen as a "development catalyst" or a stepping-stone for the country to move up to the stage of Pacific regional cooperation and the new international division of labor.[11]

Although Chinese coastal provinces are now all open to receiving foreign capital, the most dynamic region capturing much international attention thus far has been the province of Guangdong, which is located at the southern end of the mainland facing Hong Kong across the border. When measured by its size of population or land area, Guangdong is not a prominent province in China. With a population of 67 million and a territory of 212,000 square kilometers, Guangdong is ranked fifth among China's provinces in population and accounts for only 2 percent of the country's land area.[12] The province is, however, distinguished by its geographic proximity to Hong Kong, which used to be a British colony but has just been returned to Chinese rule. Despite their political and economic differences, Hong Kong and Guangdong share a common Cantonese culture on which extensive social ties had been developed over the past several decades. Even in the Maoist era, when Guangdong's connections with Hong Kong were limited, the two territories maintained minimum economic exchanges because the city-state of Hong Kong had to rely on Guangdong for the supply of fresh water and farm products. However, social and economic linkages between Hong Kong and Guangdong were not extensive at the time. Nor did they benefit the development of Guangdong because the province's frontier location close to Hong Kong was perceived to be highly vulnerable to the penetration of capitalism and to possible military invasion by overseas enemies including Taiwan and the United States. For this and other reasons, Guangdong had never become a prime location to receive sizable state capital investment for most of the years since 1949.[13]

The implementation of the open door policy since 1979 has not only renewed traditional social and economic linkages between Hong Kong and Guangdong but also greatly facilitated the intertwining of the two neighboring territories. The opening up of Guangdong coincided with a time when Hong Kong was seeking ways to cope with growing competition from countries of the capitalist world and other newly industrializing economies. As the cost of labor and land continued to rise, low-price production outlets had to be found to accommodate the labor-intensive manufacturing facilities so that Hong Kong's industry could meet the challenges of the new international division of labor and global competition.[14] With its geographic proximity to and special connections with Hong Kong plus a newly introduced open door policy, Guangdong has naturally become the first choice for those Hong Kong manufacturers who have been desperately looking for low-price production outlets for relocating manufacturing facilities.

The combined effect of the forces of globalization and national policy changes has been intensified economic interaction between Hong Kong and Guangdong and the emergence of an integrated economic region in southern China. It has been estimated that of the total direct foreign investment received by Guangdong, 70 percent came from Hong Kong.[15] As many as three million workers in Guangdong have been hired to work for Hong Kong manufacturing firms, more than the total manufacture labor force of Hong Kong itself.[16] From the national point of view, available data clearly identify Hong Kong as the single largest source of foreign direct investment flown into China. From 1992 to 1999, for instance, China received a total of US$282.574 billion foreign direct investment from all over the world. Of this amount, US$140.688 billion or 49.7 percent came from Hong Kong alone. The inflow of foreign capital in China has been highly concentrated in Guangdong Province. In the two decades from 1979 to 1999, China received an estimated US$459.564 billion utilized foreign capital investment, of which US$110.67 billion or 24 percent of the national total ended in Guangdong Province. Of the total US$305.922 billion foreign direct investment that China received during

Table 4.1

Economic Restructuring in Hong Kong 1971–1996
(percent of total employment)

	1971	1981	1991	1996	1971–1996
Manufacturing	47.7	41.3	28.2	18.9	−28.8
Construction	5.3	7.7	6.9	8.1	+2.8
Wholesale, retail and import/export trades, restaurants and hotels	16.0	19.2	22.5	24.9	+8.9
Transport, storage, and communication	7.2	7.5	9.8	10.9	+3.7
Financing, insurance, real estate and business services	2.6	4.8	10.6	13.4	+10.8
Community, social, and personal services	14.7	15.6	19.9	22.3	+7.6
Others	6.5	3.9	2.1	1.5	−5.0
Total	100.0	100.0	100.0	100.0	

Sources: Complied from Hong Kong, Census and Statistics Department, *Hong Kong Population and Housing Census (1971 Main Report)* (Hong Kong: Hong Kong Government, 1972), p. 86; *Hong Kong 1991 Population Census (Main Report)* (1993), p. 95; and *1996 Population By-census (Summary Results)* (1996), p. 32.

this period of time, as much as US$86.58 billion or 28 percent was found in Guangdong Province alone.[17] Hong Kong and Guangdong, as the major origin and destination of the foreign capital investment flown into China, have played leading roles in the rearticulation of China within the global economy.

The integration of Hong Kong and Guangdong has resulted in a process of economic restructuring in both places. As many industrial facilities have been relocated from Hong Kong to Guangdong, employment in the manufacturing sector in Hong Kong dropped from 755 thousand in 1971 to 574 thousand in 1996 and its share of total employment declined from 48 percent to only 19 percent (Table 4.1). Meanwhile, employment in the service sector rose from 640 thousand to 2.18 million and its share of the economy increased from 41 percent to 72 percent for the same period, 1971 to 1996. While Hong Kong was undergoing a process of deindustrialization and tertiarization, Guangdong started to experience accelerated industrialization and urbanization. The emphasis of the regional economy shifted from the primary sector to the secondary and tertiary sectors, with the proportion of employment in the primary sector dropping from 71 percent to 42 percent and the percentage of people engaged in the secondary sector increasing from 17 percent to 31 percent during the years of 1980 to 1999

(Table 4.2). The composition of GDP also demonstrated a similar pattern of restructuring.

The process of regional integration has been most remarkable in the area extending from Hong Kong to the Pearl River Delta which is both the core of Guangdong Province and the immediate hinterland of the capitalist enclave. Tables 4.3 and 4.4 list some of the major economic and geographic indicators of the Pearl River Delta region in the provincial and national context. It is clear that the Pearl River Delta has played an exceptionally significant role in both exports and the attraction of foreign investment. The remarkable growth of the Pearl River Delta region has owed a great deal to its geographic proximity to and extensive economic linkages with Hong Kong. The dramatic expansion of the regional economy in South China has been the subject of intense scholarly attention. Much work has been done on the social and economic linkages between Hong Kong and Guangdong,[18] on the incentives of relocating manufacturing facilities from Hong Kong to the Pearl River Delta,[19] and on the implications of regional integration for the development of Hong Kong.[20] Little is known, however, about how a local Chinese economy under socialism is transformed after the intrusion of global market forces. The following section assesses the impacts of regional integration on the transformation of a local Chinese economy, with the case of Dongguan as illustration. The assessment focuses on the structural and spatial effects of regional integration in the Chinese context. Attempts are also made to examine social and cultural aspects of the interaction between local and global forces.

Dongguan: A Case Study

Among the counties and cities in the Pearl River Delta, Dongguan is a typical case of how a regional economy under socialism can be transformed by global market forces penetrating into it primarily from the capitalist city-state of Hong Kong. In terms of its relationship with Hong Kong, Dongguan is a small projection of Guangdong Province in a national context. Located at the eastern wing of the Pearl River Delta within close proximity to Hong Kong (Figure 4.2), Dongguan had a total population of 1.5 million in 1999 and has a land area of 2,465 square kilometers. Its economy is distinguished by an external orientation, particularly by the important role it has played in attracting foreign capital and promoting exports. Table 4.5 lists Dongguan's disproportionate contribution to the province and the nation in terms of foreign investment and export. The remarkable performance of Dongguan in foreign economic relations has been based on some locally specific social relations and geographic conditions. Geographically, Dongguan is about the

Table 4.2

Economic Restructuring in Guangdong Province, China, 1980–1999

Sector	Employment (percent)					GDP (percent)				
	1980	1985	1990	1995	1999	1980	1985	1990	1995	1999
Primary	70.7	60.3	53.0	41.5	41.5	33.2	29.8	24.7	15.1	12.1
Secondary	17.1	22.5	27.2	33.8	31.1	41.1	39.8	39.5	50.2	50.4
Tertiary	12.2	17.2	19.8	24.7	27.4	25.7	30.4	35.8	34.7	37.5
Total	100.0	100.0	100.0	100.0	100.0	100.0	100.0	100.0	100.0	100.0

Source: Compiled from Guangdong Statistical Bureau, *Guangdong Statistical Yearbook (2000)* (Beijing: China Statistical Press, 2000), pp. 86 and 127.

Table 4.3

The Pearl River Delta in National and Provincial Context, 1999

Items	Unit	Value	Delta As % of Guangdong	As % of China
Population	Million	22.62	31.11	1.80
Land area	Square Km	41,698.00	23.43	0.43
GDP	Billion yuan	643.89	76.07	7.86
Retail sales	Billion yuan	248.71	68.03	7.99
Exports	Billion US$	67.44	86.79	34.60
Utilized foreign investment	Billion US$	12.02	83.07	22.82

Source: Compiled from China State Statistical Bureau, *China Statistical Yearbook (2000)* (Beijing: China State Statistical Press, 2000), pp. 22–27; Guangdong Statistical Bureau, *Guangdong Statistical Yearbook (2000)* (Beijing: China State Statistical Press, 2000), pp. 58–63, 293, and 596.

Table 4.4

Selected Economic Indicators for the Pearl River Delta, Guangdong Province, and China, 1999

Indicator	Unit	Pearl River Delta	Guangdong	China
Population Density	Persons/km^2	542	408	132
Nonagricultural population as % of the total population	Percent	47.70	31.19	25.07
Per capita GDP	Yuan/Person	28,465	11,642	6,505
Per capita export output	US$/Person	2,981	1,068	154
Per capita realized foreign investment	US$/Person	531	199	41

Source: China State Statistical Bureau, *China Statistical Yearbook (2000)* (Beijing: China State Statistical Press, 2000), pp. 22–27; Guangdong Statistical Bureau, *Guangdong Statistical Yearbook (2000)* (Beijing: China State Statistical Press, 2000), pp. 58–63, 293 and 596.

same distance as the Shenzhen Special Economic Zone in terms of the distance to Hong Kong; but historically, it has fared better than Shenzhen in developing personal kinship ties with Hong Kong primarily because of its higher population density and its well-established historical tradition. It was estimated that Dongguan residents had at least 550,000 relatives in Hong Kong and Macao, a number significantly higher than those from Shenzhen.[21] The middle position of Dongguan in the Guangzhou–Hong Kong corridor means that it can easily access both the export outlet of Hong Kong and

Figure 4.2   **The Location of Dongguan in the Pearl River Delta Region, China**

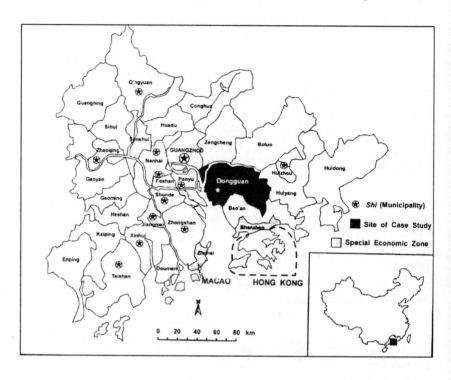

Table 4.5

Basic Economic Indicators for Dongguan, 1999

	Dongguan	Dongguan as % of Guangdong	Dongguan as % of China
Total population* (million)	1.500	2.06	0.12
Area (thousand Km²)	2.4650	1.39	0.02
GDP (billion yuan)	41.280	4.87	0.50
Export (billion $)	15.130	19.47	7.76
Realized foreign investment (billion $)	1.457	10.07	2.77

Source: Compiled from Guangdong Statistical Bureau, *Guangdong Statistical Yearbook (2000)* (Beijing: China Statistical Press, 2000), pp. 94, 121, 498, 510; China State
Statistical Bureau, *China Statistical Abstract (2000)* (Beijing: China Statistical Press, 2000),
pp. 4–5.
    *Total population does not include temporary residents from outside. There were 1.44
million temporary residents in Dongguan in 1997, of which 1.13 million were from places
outside of Guangdong Province.

the traditional urban center of Guangzhou. Such a geographical location has also enabled Dongguan to develop an export processing industry by merging capital, technology, and industrial components from Hong Kong in the south with interior cheap labor transferred mainly from Guangzhou in the northwest (Figure 4.2).

The favorable geographic features of Dongguan, however, brought no benefit to its development in the Maoist era when traditional connections between Hong Kong and the mainland were artificially cut off. Under the then prevailing radical ideology of anticapitalism, the proximity of Dongguan to the capitalist territory of Hong Kong was considered unfavorable since it was vulnerable, not only to the "contamination" of decaying capitalism, but also to possible naval attacks from counterrevolutionary enemies overseas, including those in Taiwan and the United States, which had constantly threatened to undermine the Chinese revolution. The perceived vulnerability of Dongguan's location to capitalist attack explains the fact that for decades Dongguan never became the focus of infrastructure development funded either by the central or provincial government.

There were few alternatives to working in the rice fields to build a self-reliant agrarian economy for the people of Dongguan. On the eve of economic reform in 1978, a total of 390,000 people, or 82 percent of the total labor force, were engaged in agricultural production. Annual income on a per capita basis was a mere 193 yuan (US$64).[22] In some places, such as the southern border township of Changan, annual per capita income was recorded as low as 83 yuan (less than US$20).[23] Tens of thousands of young people attempted to escape to Hong Kong. It was reported that about 20 percent of the young people in Dongguan had managed to get across the border into Hong Kong in the pre-reform years primarily because there was no hope for them to have a reasonable future in their hometown.

The demise of the radical Communist leadership in the late 1970s and the subsequent opening-up practice have brought dramatic economic changes to Dongguan. As Hong Kong is now seen as a bridge linking China with the capitalist world, geographic proximity to and wide-ranging personal connections with Hong Kong, which used to be detrimental factors, have now become valuable assets that can be utilized to attract Hong Kong investment and to develop an export-oriented economy.

Development of the Export Processing Industry

Once the people of Dongguan realized that their advantageous connections with Hong Kong could be utilized to create jobs and raise income, they began to seek every possible opportunity to draw capital investment from Hong Kong and overseas. Special policies, including taxation concessions and preferential treatment regarding the import of necessary equipment and the handling of foreign currency, were announced to attract foreign investment. A special office was set up by the county government to serve Hong Kong investors with efficient personnel and simplified bureaucratic procedures. Economic cooperation between Dongguan and Hong Kong was arranged creatively and flexibly in a variety of forms, including export processing (*lailiao jiagong*), compensation trade (*buchang maoyi*), joint ventures (*hezi jingying*), and cooperative ventures (*hezuo jingying*). It was reported that by the end of 1995, a total of 21,691 contracts had been signed between Dongguan and manufacturers from Hong Kong and overseas, of which 11,254 were already in operation.[24]

Economic cooperative ventures developed between Dongguan and Hong Kong since 1979 have varied in form and in size, but the most popular one has been the processing of imported materials (*lailiao jiagong*) or assembling of product components provided by Hong Kong manufacturers (*laijian chuanpei*). Known as "three supplies one compensation" (*sanlai yibu*), the arrangement requires the Hong Kong side to supply raw materials, components, and models for what is to be processed while the Chinese side provides labor, land, buildings, electricity, and other local utilities necessary for production. The Hong Kong participant of the contract does not hire or pay workers directly. Instead, a lump-sum payment is usually made available to the Dongguan participant for the contracted goods. The payment from Hong Kong, usually in U.S. or Hong Kong dollars, is paid in installments until the products are completed. The contracted Dongguan participant hires workers and pays them in Chinese dollars on a piecework basis. Needless to say, local governments and cadres of Dongguan, who serve as middlemen in this process, are able to make sizable profits, either by paying low salaries or by exchanging U.S. and Hong Kong dollars for Chinese yuan at a high rate on the "black market." Arrangements are also made on a compensational basis, in which the Dongguan side does the processing or assembling jobs for a specialized period of time, for example five years, and at the end of this period assumes ownership of the machinery or equipment provided by the Hong Kong firm as compensation.

Cooperation in the form of "three supplies one compensation" has become popular not only in Dongguan, but also in other parts of the delta region because it benefits substantially both the Hong Kong and Chinese participants in the contract. With designing and marketing handled in Hong Kong and labor-intensive work done cheaply in Dongguan, small Hong Kong manufacturers are able to compete effectively in the international market.

As for the Chinese side, export processing has created jobs and income for local cadres and the general population. By the end of 1987, some 2,500 processing firms on the basis of "three supplies one compensation" had been set up in Dongguan, creating up to 171,000 employment opportunities and receiving 107 million U.S. dollars mostly from Hong Kong, which accounted for about 40 percent of what was received by the whole Guangdong Province.[25] By the end of 1990, the number of export processing firms established in Dongguan had reached 4,680. These establishments produced a total export output of 150.06 million U.S. dollars, which was ahead of all cities and counties in the province except the Shenzhen Special Economic Zone.[26] A survey conducted by the Federation of Hong Kong Manufacturers in July 1991 identified Dongguan as the second most-favored location, next only to Shenzhen, for Hong Kong investment.[27] The considerable success of Dongguan in attracting foreign investment and developing export manufacturing enabled it to be promoted from a county to an officially designated municipality at the county level in 1985 and, further, to a higher level municipality directly subordinate to the provincial government in 1988.

Reasons for Developing an Export Processing Industry

Why has Dongguan, formerly a frontier agrarian county, proved so attractive to Hong Kong manufacturers? What are the driving forces that have helped Dongguan attract capital investment and manufacturing facilities from Hong Kong and overseas? In answering these questions, local officials of Dongguan frequently quote the words of a well-known ancient Chinese scholar and strategist Zhuge Kongming that "timing, location, and public relations" (*tianshi, dili, renhe*) are three essential factors in seeking any success.[28] Implied in this explanation is the importance of the implementation of the open door policy (timing), geographic proximity (location), and extensive personal connections between Dongguan and Hong Kong (public relations). From a geographic standpoint, however, three special factors are particularly important to the rapid development of the export processing industry in Dongguan.

First, good personal connections existing between Dongguan and Hong Kong have provided easy and reliable links between investors and their manufacturing partners. With over 550,000 relatives (*gang'ao tongbao*) in Hong Kong and another 150,000 (*huaqiao*) in other foreign countries, mostly in North America, the people of Dongguan have less difficulty than those of other parts of the nation in seeking investors or partners from Hong Kong and overseas. It was estimated by local officials that about half of the contracts they had signed was with their countrymen in Hong Kong. Many personal contacts are with former Dongguan residents who escaped from their hometown to Hong Kong during the pre-reform period.[29]

A second critical contributing factor that has often been overlooked in the assessment of the growth of export processing is the creation of a transportation infrastructure as a necessary means to attract foreign investment. In this regard, the local government of Dongguan has played a leading role in the development process. It was reported that in the eight years from 1980 through 1987 a total of 1.034 billion yuan (US$216 million) was raised by the local government through various channels for infrastructure development. Such a huge amount of capital was obtained primarily from local resources such as bank loans (33 percent), collective enterprises (31 percent), stocks and bonds (14 percent), and foreign capital (11 percent). Budgetary allocations from the central and provincial governments accounted for only 11 percent of all construction expenses.[30]

Heavy investment in infrastructure has resulted in significant improvements. The existing road system has been substantially extended, with the mileage of paved roads increasing from 600 kilometers in 1985 to 1,808 kilometers in 1995. By the end of the 1980s, Dongguan had more miles of paved roads per square kilometer than any other county in the nation. Dongguan was also one of the first Chinese counties to establish a computerized telephone system, which connects it directly with seventeen countries and regions in the world. A total of 13,231 telephones have been installed to cover all townships and villages in Dongguan, of which 8,756 phones, or 20 percent of all installations in China, can dial direct to other countries.[31] The transport capacity of ports and harbors and the generation of electric power have also been increased substantially during the 1980s. The creation of such a good infrastructure has significantly reduced transactional costs for investors and, therefore, underpinned the rapid inflow of overseas investment.

Finally, the availability of cheap labor and land is another important factor that has helped attract Hong Kong manufacturing to move into Dongguan. In the early 1980s, Dongguan was a county where labor and land could be obtained easily and cheaply. A worker employed by an export-processing firm was usually paid a monthly wage of from 150 to 200 yuan, which was about one-tenth of what a Hong Kong worker could make. Although Chinese workers may not be as skillful as their Hong Kong counterparts in certain aspects of industrial production, the low wage rate remains attractive to Hong Kong manufacturers, especially to those who are engaged in highly intensive–intensive industries such as toys and electronics. Over the years since 1979, the increase of employment opportunities has resulted in a tendency toward rising intensive costs. This tendency, however, has been balanced by an inflow of new workers from less-developed interior provinces who will accept low wages. Consequently, low intensive costs in Dongguan remain a significant factor that continues to attract manufacturing from Hong Kong and overseas.

Characteristics of the Export Processing Industry

As the export processing industry continues to grow, it is becoming one of the most dynamic economic sectors in transforming the regional economy of Dongguan. By the end of 1990, more than 70 percent of Dongguan's industrial intensive force was engaged in export processing. The continuous expansion of the export processing industry, the mainstay of Dongguan's industrial development, has led the local economy to enter a new stage of accelerated growth and restructuring. It has also effectively altered the economic landscape of Dongguan and created some distinct spatial patterns associated with industrial production, migration, and land use. As the transformation of the space economy of Dongguan was to a great extent fueled by the relocation of manufacturing from Hong Kong, to understand the dynamics of these structural and spatial changes will require an analysis of the nature and spatial characteristics of the flourishing export processing activities.

For Hong Kong manufacturers, relocating their workshops from Hong Kong to Dongguan was primarily to tap the existing pool of low-priced inexperienced labor. It is, therefore, not surprising to find that the industries that have been developed are simple, unsophisticated, small-scale, and intensive–intensive. In the main, export processing in Dongguan has centered around four sectors: textile, apparel, toys, and electronics. The type of production varies considerably from the processing of toys, assembling of simple radios, sewing of shirts or blouses, to the making of plastic bags, incense, firecrackers, candles, candy and chocolate, and other food products. However, the procedures of production are invariably simple and repetitive, needing a considerable amount of time and intensive effort but little skill. The development of these simple intensive–intensive industries has significant implications for changes in employment structure and migration as it opens up opportunities for those surplus rural laborers who are eager to enter factories but have little experience or skill in manufacturing.

As processing activities are technologically unsophisticated, many factories that have been set up are relatively small in size. Most of them do not require heavy machinery. Some were converted from the dining halls of former communes or brigades. As production expands, buildings of two or three stories are constructed containing several large rooms which accommodate fifty to a hundred desks, one for each worker. Thus a typical factory may employ several dozen to a hundred workers, which is considered small by Chinese standards. A 1991 survey sampling 2,931 joint ventures and compensational trade enterprises in Dongguan revealed that the average number of workers in each factory was 147 for joint ventures and 105 for the processing of imported materials or compensation trade factories.[32] Some workshops in the countryside were so small that they had only a dozen workers on their payrolls. The fact that the export processing industry is composed of numerous small workshops without a single major plant has been vividly described by the local people as "a spread of numerous stars in the sky without a large shining moon in the center" (mantian xingdou queshao yilun mingyue).

Another feature of Dongguan's export processing industry, closely related to the previous ones, is that the concentration of factories is not in a few large urban centers but is widely scattered throughout the countryside. Since the scale of production is small and the processing procedure is simple, factories in Dongguan do not necessarily have to be located in the large urban centers, where technical experts or other high-ranking social services are easily accessible. Rather, existing personal kinship ties, the improved transport and electric power infrastructure, an abundant supply of cheap surplus rural laborers and land space, and a less regulated environment in the countryside have all combined to attract investment and manufacturing activities away from Hong Kong to the rural townships and villages. This distinct feature is evident from an official survey conducted at the end of 1987, which revealed that Dongguan's export processing factories were predominantly located in the townships and villages of the countryside. Among the 2,500 factories established for the processing of imported materials or compensation trade, 1,591 were found in rural townships and villages. They accounted for 63.64 percent of the total number of export processing firms, 72.52 percent of all processing fees received from Hong Kong and overseas, and 87.91 percent of the total construction area of all factories set up for the processing industry.[33]

Consequences of Export Industrial Development

With the distinct features concerning the nature, size, and spatial distribution of the export processing industry identified, it is now possible to analyze the structural and spatial consequences of this externally driven industrial development. The most significant outcome of the flourishing of labor-intensive export processing activities has been a disproportionate increase in employment and production in the manufacturing sector and the subsequent restructuring of the local economy. When Dongguan was first opened up to foreign investment in the late 1970s, its economy was predominantly agricultural, with two-thirds of its population working in the fields at a subsistence level.

The rapid expansion of the export processing industry since 1978 has greatly increased the pace of manufacturing development. Between the years of 1978 and 1991, an estimated 380,000 jobs were created by the export processing industry and absorbed both local rural laborers, who were released from agricultural production, and immigrants, who moved in from other less developed areas.[34] Consequently, the labor force in the secondary sector, primarily manufacturing, has expanded at 10.45 percent per annum since 1978, with its share of the total labor force increasing from 16.85 percent in 1978 to 40.64 percent in 1990.[35] At the same time, the number of those engaged in agricultural production and other primary activities was reduced and their share of the total labor force dropped substantially from 71.57 percent in 1978 to 36.15 percent in 1990. The production of the local economy exhibited a pattern of restructuring similar to that of the labor force. The contribution of manufacturing to total output rose from 42.06 percent in 1978 to 66.20 percent in 1990, while the share of the agricultural sector declined from 39.40 percent to only 19 percent in the same period.[36]

In addition to economic restructuring, the development of the export processing industry has contributed to an accelerated growth of the local economy and helped to raise personal income for the general population. During the years from 1980 to 1990, the production of industrial and agricultural output, of which the export processing industry was a main part, recorded a growth rate of 23 percent per annum, which was significantly higher than the regional average of the Pearl River Delta. The export processing fees received by Dongguan increased from 2.34 million U.S. dollars in 1979 to 163 million U.S. dollars in 1990, which represented an annual growth rate of 53.5 percent.[37] Per capita income rose substantially from 193 yuan to 1,359 yuan for peasants and from 547 yuan to 3,552 yuan for salaried workers in the twelve years between 1978 and 1990.[38] This extraordinary process of economic structural change and accelerated growth since the late 1970s has been unprecedented in Dongguan's history and was clearly fueled by the inflow of capital and manufacturing facilities from Hong Kong.

An interesting phenomenon that has been especially evident in Dongguan as a result of export industrial development is the increasing participation of women in manufacturing. Since export production is predominantly labor intensive in nature, its rapid expansion has created employment opportunities for women who are generally considered by manufacturers to be nimbler than men in doing such jobs as making toys, sewing apparel, or processing electronic products. A growing number of women have joined this army of factory workers and are playing a major role in industrialization. It was reported in 1989 that among the 166,000 workers employed by export processing firms, 130,000 were women, accounting for 78 percent of the total work force.[39] In many workshops, workers are almost entirely female with only a few men being responsible for repairing machinery, factory security, loading and unloading finished products or imported materials, and managerial work. Most female workers are young, with an average age under twenty-five years. Some of them have begun to earn incomes equivalent to men's.

Women's participation in manufacturing production has undoubtedly raised their economic and social status, but it has also placed them in a confined environment in which they are asked to work repetitively on the same single piece at a desk for long hours in order to get pay on a piece-work basis. For those who are already married, factory work and household affairs form an almost unbearable burden. For those who are young, entering the factory at an early age means that there will be little chance for them to receive necessary education and, therefore, few alternatives for making career choices or finding advancement. The intrusion of global market forces from Hong Kong has thus pushed Chinese women who might have been housewives or college girls to take part in the process of the new international division of labor.

Another distinct demographic feature that characterizes the recent development of Dongguan is the rapid growth of immigration, which is also a direct outcome of flourishing export processing activities. By the mid-1980s, the rapid expansion of the intensive–intensive processing industry had exhausted the local supply of intensive labor and created a large demand for outside workers. With the relaxation of government control on migration, which took effect in 1984, intensive labor began to flow in from other less-developed counties of Guangdong and interior provinces. Since the mid-1980s, immigration of outside intensive labor has grown substantially at 43 percent per annum. By the end of 1995, the number of "outside intensive" labor (*wailai laogong*) had reached 1.42 million, which almost equaled the local population.[40] Considering that outside laborers have an employment rate of 98.39 percent, which is higher than that of local laborers (76.02 percent),[41] it can be argued that immigrants have actually run more than half of the local economy. This is especially evident in the manufacturing sector, where 63 percent of its total intensive force was from outside. In some areas such as Changan Town at the border with Shenzhen, the number of migrants reached 91,000 in 1992, which was almost four times the local population.

By far, the vast majority of migrants to Dongguan were engaged in manufacturing production, particularly in export processing. Statistical data have shown that 76 percent of the total outside labor force, or 1.08 million out of 1.42 million, were found in the manufacturing sector.[42] Of all factory jobs created by the export processing industry from 1979 through 1990, 85 percent were taken by migrants from outside.[43] Many migrants to Dongguan are young girls aged between eighteen and twenty-five years, who are frequently referred to by the local people as "working girls" (*da gong mei*) or "girls from outside" (*wai lai mei*).[44] They usually live in a dormitory room shared by eight to twelve persons near the factory where they work and they pay rent or a "managerial fee" (*guanli fei*) to local officials who are responsible for the construction and maintenance of both the factory and the dormitory buildings. The money they save is sent back via banks or postal offices to their relatives in poor interior areas. As a result, those townships that have a large number of outside workers tend to have a disproportionately large number of banks and post offices. In Changan Town, for instance, the main street of the town, several hundred meters long, has fourteen banks, which are open from 8 A.M. to 9 P.M. to serve outsiders who want to deposit or mail their savings to their hometowns. Some of these outsiders work in Dongguan for several years until they earn enough money to go home. Others stay for a prolonged period of time. A few have married local residents or set up their own businesses. The penetration of global market forces through Hong Kong into Dongguan has thus not only promoted the participation of local peasants and women in manufacturing production but also effectively drawn the young and cheap labor of China's interiors into the theater of mass production and global capitalism.

The rapid growth of export production and its subsequent economic and demographic changes highlighted above have manifestations in physical space. With a locational focus in the countryside, the development of the export processing industry has inevitably resulted in a process of land use transformation, whereby much farmland has been turned over for the construction and expansion of factories. Data obtained from the Agricultural Department of Dongguan reveal that in the years from 1978 through 1988, a total of 18,585 *mu,* or 3,061 acres, of farmland was transformed into industrial land use, mostly for the building of export factories, workshops, and industrial districts.[45] Consequently, per capita cultivated land dropped substantially from 1.06 *mu* in 1978 to 0.67 *mu* in 1990.

Many small workshops and factories developed in the early 1980s were scattered over the rural townships and villages. As production expanded, local officials began to realize that such a spatial arrangement made it difficult to provide electricity, water, and sewage disposal facilities. A new type of industrial land use has since gradually emerged, covering a sizable scale of land area and located at the outskirts of towns or villages along trunk roads. By the end 1987, a total of 119 such industrial zones had emerged. In Changan Town where fieldwork for this study was conducted, an industrial zone covering an area of 198 *mu,* or 32.6 acres, was developed jointly by the local government and several Hong Kong companies. It absorbed a total investment of 236.50 million Hong Kong dollars (US$30.32 million) and accommodated over a thousand employees working on the spinning, weaving, and dying of textile materials for Hong Kong manufacturers.

Most of the export processing factories, either built separately or in groups, are located in the vicinity of the headquarters of former communes and brigades. Their development and continuous expansion have greatly fostered the industrialization of land in the countryside and created a distinct type of land use characterized by a mixture of farmland, factories, and housing for peasants. Such a process of industrialization did not, however, force those farmers who lost their land to move into the city. Instead, by creating factory jobs in the countryside, the growth of the processing industry has been able to allow peasants to "enter the factory but not the city" or "leave the soil but not the village." Between the years of 1978 and 1987, for instance, an estimated 154,000 people, most of them surplus rural laborers, joined the industrial labor force of Dongguan. Among these new workers, only 34,000 or 22 percent went into factories in towns. The other 120,000 new workers or 78 percent entered factories and workshops in the countryside. Clearly, most of those farmers who were released from traditional agricultural production have acquired factory jobs near their villages without moving into cities and towns. In a similar manner, the magnitude of land use change in the rural areas has been actually much greater than in the city. It was reported that the conversion of land from cropland to construction sites increased at an astonishing rate of 968.9 percent between the years of 1988 and 1993 while the expansion of urban built-up areas only rose by 13.7 percent for the same period.[46] Export industrial development, with its locational focus in the countryside, has undoubtedly contributed to shaping this spatial pattern wherein the transformation of population and land in the countryside has been greater than that in the city.

Social and Cultural Change

The influence of Hong Kong has gone beyond the economic sphere and provoked significant social changes within the townships and villages of Dongguan. With its frontier location and excellent connections with Hong Kong, Dongguan is one of the first among the cities and counties of the delta that has felt the strong "south wind" from Hong Kong, which brings the air of capitalism into socialist territory. As a special identity of Dongguan, the development of an export processing industry since 1978 has ushered in new production systems, new management styles, and a new job attitude. In the processing plants subcontracted from Hong Kong manufacturers, there is no promise of job security, rewards are tied to the amount of work finished, time requirements are rigid, and pressure on workers to keep a quick working pace is high. For those who were used to the socialist production system under which job security or "iron bowl" is guaranteed and by which equity is achieved at the cost of efficiency, to work in such a Hong Kong subcontract factory or joint venture means fundamental changes in job attitude, value judgments, and working behavior. Doing a factory job is no longer considered to be fulfilling the glorious socialist obligation of "serving the people" but a way of earning a living for personal gain. As there is nothing that can be counted on, people have become more independent, efficient, and sensitive to changes in their living environment. In the meantime, loneliness, frustration, and depression over not being able to keep up with the working pace or to realize personal ambition have become increasingly noticeable in the local community.

Visitors from Hong Kong to Dongguan doing business or seeing relatives have often brought with them ideas, information, and different lifestyles. Since its opening up in 1979, Dongguan has been visited more frequently than ever before by relatives from Hong Kong. In 1990, for instance, 262,586 visitors entered Dongguan from Hong Kong either for business or family affairs.[47] These visitors always brought information and materials into Dongguan, allowing their countrymen to share the Hong Kong consumerist vision of modernity. In the early 1980s, when modern consumer goods such as TVs, VCRs, and refrigerators were still rarely seen elsewhere in the nation, Dongguan had already started to receive a variety of gifts from Hong Kong kinfolk, including washing machines, TV sets, VCRs, hi-fi stereos, motorcycles, and fashionable clothes. Over the years, Dongguan has received so many consumer goods from Hong Kong that its residents own more color TVs, stereo tape decks, and washing machines than people in other cities and counties of Guangdong. A survey conducted by Guangdong officials in 1990 revealed that town residents in Dongguan owned 112 color TV sets, 102 stereo tape decks, and 94 washing machines per hundred households, all higher rates than the rates among surveyed households in other cities in Guangdong, including Guangzhou, Foshan, Shenzhen, and Zhuhai.[48] As well, the ownership rates of color TVs, motorcycles, refrigerators, and stereo tape decks for the peasant households of Dongguan in 1990 were also significantly higher than the provincial average. Needless to say, these consumer goods have formed a material basis for the imitation of the Hong Kong lifestyle. Modern electronic receivers such as TVs, radios, and VCRs are also important conduits for the penetration of Hong Kong culture into the towns and villages.[49]

The most effective means that has transplanted the Hong Kong model of living to the local people is probably the modern mass communication network that links Hong Kong to almost all Dongguan households. The computerized telephone system, which was installed in 1984 and has rapidly expanded ever since, allows Dongguan's residents to dial direct to their relatives in Hong Kong and overseas for information about the outside world. Electronic conduits such as TV and radio have brought almost all programs broadcast from Hong Kong stations into nearly all local households. For the first time since the founding of the People's Republic, Dongguan's residents are able to receive sounds and images about the lives of their relatives on the other side of the border, a lifestyle which is in sharp contrast to what they have been used to for over thirty years. When the field investigation for this research was conducted in 1992, it was found that many peasants in rural villages were able to watch all sorts of TV programs broadcast from Hong Kong, including many American programs such as *CBS Evening News, 60 Minutes, 20/20,* and *America's Funniest People,* and movies in bilingual (English/Cantonese) form. From TV, radio, and other media, the local people have become increasingly familiar with product brand names and have begun to consume foreign goods such as Colgate toothpaste, Marlboro cigarettes, Nike sneakers, and foreign-made cosmetics. Foreign-made drinks such as Pepsi Cola, Coca Cola, 7–Up, and Maxim coffee, which were never heard of before 1979, have become the most familiar items for daily consumption by the local population. Given sufficient time, a unique culture which blends the local tradition with Hong Kong innovations in dress, speech, music, and lifestyle may well emerge in Dongguan and in other parts of the delta region as well.[50]

Discussion and Conclusion

For over three decades since the founding of the People's Republic, socialist China adopted an inward-looking approach to national and regional development to cope with the hostile international environment. The demise of the radical Maoist regime in the late 1970s, coupled with changes in the global political economy, has enabled China to rejoin the world and find its standing in the theater of flexible capital accumulation. With its proximity to and traditional linkages with Hong Kong, Guangdong Province has moved "one step ahead" of the nation to receive foreign capital and promote manufacturing exports. Its intensified interaction with Hong Kong has resulted in the formation of a distinct economic region in southern China, with Hong Kong acting as a "display window" and the Pearl River Delta as a great manufacturing workshop. The recent downturn of the American economy and the accession of China into the WTO will combine to further stimulate integration of Hong Kong and the Pearl River Delta. Given sufficient time, a distinct "global city region," in which Hong Kong functions as the control and marketing center and the Pearl River Delta as the hinterland, is quickly taking shape.

Regional integration in the Chinese context is a result of interaction between local and global forces. As part of the global processes of flexible accumulation, the relocation of manufacturing from Hong Kong to the Pearl River Delta has been motivated by the economic incentives of reducing labor costs, strengthening industrial competitiveness, and increasing profits. To this end, the case of Hong Kong–Pearl River Delta integration has lent support to the new geography of production, particularly the theories of flexible specialization and spatial division of labor that are developed primarily on the basis of the logic of economic transactions.[51] The imperative of global capitalist accumulation is not, however, an independent force that operates separately from or against local conditions. As the case of Dongguan has illustrated, the establishment of many subcontracting firms is often the result of some particular local relations, such as kinship ties, interpersonal trust, and connections between Hong Kong investors and their local Chinese partners. Such place-specific social relationships do not exist outside the sphere of global economic transactions. Instead, they provide the most effective and secure channel for global capitalism to take root in the socialist territory.[52] This distinct manner of local-global interaction, in which global forces seek protection from some localized social relations, has been one of the most important factors leading the socialist economy to transform gradually rather than abruptly. It also suggests that the Chinese experience contains some special features that may not be adequately accounted for by the prevailing model of local-global interaction, in which global economic transactions are seen as the dominant force and the function of local conditions is often described as secondary, reactive, or resistant to global penetration.[53]

The transformation of the Hong Kong–Pearl River Delta economic region has been facilitated by the deregulation of the socialist state and the dramatic development of the local transportation infrastructure which significantly "compresses" time and space.[54] It is characterized by the vertical disintegration of control and production functions, dominance of small- and medium-sized firms, extensive use of contracted workers including women and immigrants, and the development of inter-firm relations on the basis of proximity and reliability. These features bare striking resemblance to those displayed in the process of transition from the Fordist regime of production to the post-Fordist regime of flexible specialization in North America and Western Europe.[55] However, the Chinese case is distinguished by its engagement in low-tech and intensive–intensive manufacturing, its dual-track mechanisms in which the plan and market sectors coexist, and its reliance on cultural affinity.

Unlike the formation of trading blocs in North America and Europe, the economic integration of Hong Kong and the Pearl River Delta has taken place spontaneously outside the constraints of any political agreements. While the Chinese central state is responsible for making necessary institutional changes, it is the local government that has played an active role in creating an accommodating built environment to attract overseas investors. With the gradual demise of the rigid centrally controlled planning system, a new "bottom-up" development mechanism is taking shape, in which initiatives are made primarily by local governments to solicit foreign and domestic capital, mobilize intensive and land resources, and lead the local economy to enter the orbit of the international division of intensive and global competition. In view of the emergence of this local-driven mechanism, the previous notion of socialist development, which often assumed a powerful socialist central state monopolizing local political and economic affairs, might need fundamental reassessment and modifications.

Manufacturing facilities relocated from Hong Kong to the Pearl River Delta have displayed a dispersed pattern of spatial distribution without high concentration in the primary city.[56] The existence of personal kinship ties, an improved transport and electric power infrastructure, an abundant supply of cheap intensive labor and land space, and the lack of strict regulations on environmental pollution have all made the suburban corridor between Hong Kong and Guangzhou a place no less attractive than a congested large city to multinationals from Hong Kong and overseas. As the case study of Dongguan has revealed, a large majority of the small-scale, intensive–intensive, and technologically unsophisticated processing plants subcontracting for Hong Kong companies have widely spread over the townships and villages of the countryside. Rural industrialization in the region has resulted in a process of spatial transformation, whereby a great number of surplus rural laborers entered factories in the countryside without moving into the city and wherein industrial and agricultural activities stand side by side. The geographic outcome of intense rural-urban interaction in the countryside has been the formation of a distinctive settlement pattern that does not confirm to the classic definition of urban or rural but displays characteristics of both types.[57] The Chinese experience of spatial transformation has thus raised important theoretical questions concerning the adequacy of the conventional wisdom of urban transition which was based on the arbitrary dichotomy of urban and rural settlements and which often assumed population concentration in large cities as an inevitable product of industrialization.

Notes

This research is funded by the Hong Kong Research Grant Council (HKU 7219/00H) and the Committee on Research and Conference Grants of the University of Hong Kong. I wish to thank Alvin So, Yi-min Lin, Graham Johnson, and Alan Smart for their critical comments and suggestions. Any errors remain my sole responsibility.

1. For detailed discussions of the emergence of "global city regions," see Roger Simmonds and Gary Hack, eds., *Global City Regions: Their Emerging Forms* (New York: Spon Press, 2000) and Allen J. Scott, ed., *Global City-Regions: Trends, Theory, Policy* (Oxford: Oxford University Press, 2001).

2. Alvin Y. So and Stephen W. K. Chiu, *East Asia and the World Economy* (Thousand Oaks, Calif.: Sage, 1995); Alvin Y. So, "China Under the Shadow of Asian Financial Crisis: Retreat from Economic and Political Liberation," *Asian Perspective* 23, no. 2 (1999); I.G. Cook, M.A. Doel, and R. Li, eds., *Fragmented Asia: Regional Integration and National Disintegration in Pacific Asia* (London: Avebury, 1996); G.C.S. Lin, "State, Capital, and Space in China in an Age of Volatile Globalization," *Environment and Planning A* 32, no. 3 (2000): 455–471; C.H. Kwan, *Economic Interdependence in the Asia-Pacific Region* (New York: Routledge, 1994).

3. T.G. McGee, "Urbanization in an Era of Volatile Globalization: Policy Problematiques for the Twenty First Century," paper presented at the Workshop on Development Issues in the Twenty First Century organized by the World Bank & German Foundation for International Development, Villa Borsig, Berlin, 1998; D. Forbes, "Regional Integration, Internationalization and the New Geographies of the Pacific Rim," in R.F. Watters and T.G. McGee, eds., *Asia Pacific: New Geographies of the Pacific Rim* (London: Hurst, 1997), pp. 13–28; Y.M. Yeung and F.C. Lo, "Global Restructuring and Emerging Urban Corridors in Pacific Asia," in F.C. Lo and Y.M. Yeung, eds., *Emerging World Cities in Pacific Asia* (Tokyo: United Nations University Press, 1996), pp. 17–47; H.M. Hsiao and A.Y. So "Ascent Through National Integration: The Chinese Triangle of Mainland-Taiwan-Hong Kong," in R.A. Palat, ed., *Pacific Asia and the Future of the World-System* (Westport, Conn.: Greenwood, 1993), pp. 133–150.

4. J.A. Alwin, "North American Geographers and the Pacific Rim: Leaders or Laggards," *Professional Geographer* 44 (1992): 369–376; N. Ginsburg, "Commentary on Alwin's "North American Geographers and the Pacific Rim," *Professional Geographer* 45 (1993): 355–357; P. Gourevitch, "The Pacific Rim: Current Debates," *Annals of the American Academy of Political and Social Science*, no. 505 (1989): 8–23; A. Dirlik, ed., *What Is in a Rim? Critical Perspectives on the Pacific Rim Idea* (Boulder, Colo.: Westview, 1993); R.A. Palat, ed., *Pacific-Asia and the Future of the World-System* (Westport, Conn.: Greenwood, 1993).

5. D. Aikman, *Pacific Rim: Area of Change, Area of Opportunity* (Boston: Little Brown, 1986); S. B. Linder, *The Pacific Century: Economic and Political Consequences of Asian-Pacific Dynamism* (Stanford: Stanford University Press, 1986); G. Segal, *Rethinking the Pacific* (New York: Clarendon, 1990).

6. Alvin Y. So, *Social Change and Development: Modernization, Dependency, and World-systems Theories* (Newbury Park, Calif.: Sage, 1990); C. Dixon, and D. Drakakis-Smith, eds., *Economic and Social Development in Pacific Asia* (New York: Routledge, 1993); G.C.S. Lin, "State-led Dependent Development in the East Asian NIEs: A Case Study of Taiwan," *Western Geography*, no. 4 (1994): 5–28; B. Balassa, *The Newly Industrializing Countries in the World Economy* (New York: Pergamon, 1981); H. Hughes, ed., *Achieving Industrialization in East Asia* (Cambridge, UK: Cambridge University Press, 1988); K. Ohmae, "The Rise of the Region State," *Foreign Affairs* 72, no. 2 (1993): 78–87; K. Ohmae, *The End of the Nation State: The Rise of Regional Economies* (New York: Free Press, 1995).

7. R.F. Watters and T.G. McGee, eds., *Asia Pacific: New Geographies of the Pacific Rim* (London: Hurst, 1997); X. Chen, "China's Growing Integration with the

Asia-Pacific Economy," in A. Dirlik, ed., *What Is in a Rim? Critical Perspectives on the Pacific Rim Idea* (Boulder, Colo.: Westview, 1993), pp. 89–119; G.C.S. Lin, "Changing Theoretical Perspectives on Urbanization in Asian Developing Countries," *Third World Planning Review* 16, no. 1 (1994): 1–23; M. Thant, M. Tang, and H. Kakazu, eds., *Growth Triangle in Asia* (Hong Kong: Oxford University Press, 1994).

8. Reginald Y.W. Kwok and Alvin Y. So, eds., *The Hong Kong-Guangdong Link: Partnership in Flux* (New York: M.E. Sharpe, 1995); Ezra Vogel, *One Step Ahead in China: Guangdong Under Reform* (Cambridge, Mass.: Harvard University Press, 1989); Yun Wing Sung, *The China-Hong Kong Connection: The Key to China's Open Door Policy* (Cambridge, UK: Cambridge University Press, 1991).

9. A.G. Walder, "China's Transitional Economy: Interpreting its Significance," *China Quarterly*, no. 144 (1995): 963–979; G.C.S. Lin, "State Policy and Spatial Restructuring in Post-reform China, 1978–95," *International Journal of Urban and Regional Research* 23, no. 4 (1999): 670–696.

10. Nicholas R. Lardy, *China's Entry into the World Economy* (Lanham, Md.: University Press of America, 1987); A.G.O. Yeh and X. Xu, "Globalization and the Urban System in China," in Fu-Chen Lo and Yue-man Yeung, eds., *Emerging World Cities in Pacific Asia* (Tokyo: United Nations University Press, 1996), pp. 219–267; George C.S. Lin, *Red Capitalism in South China: Growth and Development of the Pearl River Delta* (Vancouver: UBC Press, 1997).

11. Yue-man Yeung and Xuwei Hu, eds., *China's Coastal Cities* (Honolulu: University of Hawaii Press, 1992); C.P. Lo, "Recent Spatial Restructuring in Zhujiang Delta, South China: A Study of Socialist Regional Development Strategy," *Annals of the Association of American Geographers* 79, no. 2 (1989): 293–308; C.C. Fan, "The Origins and Patterns of Regional Uneven Development in Post-Mao China," *Annals of the Association of American Geographers* 85, no. 3 (1995): 421–449; Greg Veeck, ed., *The Uneven Landscape: Geographical Studies in Post-Reform China* (Baton Rouge, La.: Geoscience Publication, 1991).

12. L.J.C. Ma and G.C.S. Lin, "Development of Towns in China: A Case Study of Guangdong Province," *Population and Development Review* 19, no. 3 (1993): 583–606; Y.M. Yeung and D.K.Y. Chu, *Guangdong* (Hong Kong: Chinese University Press, 1992).

13. P.T. Cheung, "The Case of Guangdong in Central-Provincial Relations," in H. Jia and Z.M. Lin, eds., *Changing Central-Local Relations in China* (Boulder, Colo.: Westview, 1994), pp. 207–238; G.E. Johnson and Y.F. Woon, "Rural Development Patterns in Post-Reform China: The Pearl River Delta Region in the 1990s," *Development and Change* 28, no.4 (1997): 731–751; Lin, "State Policy and Spatial Restructuring in Post-Reform China."

14. A.G.O. Yeh, "Economic Restructuring and Land Use Planning in Hong Kong," *Land Use Policy* 14, no. 1 (1997): 25–39; I. Eng, "Flexible Production in Late Industrialization: The Case of Hong Kong," *Economic Geography* 73, no. 1 (1997): 26–43; C.P. Lo, *Hong Kong* (London: Belhaven, 1992); V.F.S. Sit, "Hong Kong's New Industrial Partnership with the Pearl River Delta," *Asian Geographer* 8, nos. 1 and 2 (1989): 103–115; B. Taylor and R.Y.W. Kwok, "From Export Center to World City: Planning for the Transformation of Hong Kong," *Journal of the American Planning Association* 55 (1989): 309–322.

15. Chen, "China's Growing Integration with the Asia-Pacific Economy," p. 100.

16. John T. Thoburn et al., *Foreign Investment in China Under the Open Policy* (Hong Kong: Gower Publishing, 1990); Ezra Vogel, *One Step Ahead in China: Guangdong Under Reform* (Cambridge, Mass.: Harvard University Press, 1989).

17. China, State Statistical Bureau, *Zhongguo tongji nianjian 2000* (China Statistical Yearbook 2000) (Beijing: China Statistical Press, 2000), pp. 604–609.

18. Kwok and So, *Hong Kong-Guangdong Link*; Sung, *The China-Hong Kong Connection*; G.E. Johnson, "The Political Economy of Chinese Urbanization: Guangdong and the Pearl River Delta Region," in G. Guldin, ed., *Urbanizing China* (Westport, Conn.: Greenwood, 1992), pp. 185–220; G. Guldin, "Towards a Greater Guangzhou: Hong Kong's Sociocultural Impact on the Pearl River Delta and Beyond," paper presented at the Workshop on Hong Kong-Guangdong Integration, Vancouver, Canada, University of British Columbia, 1992.

19. Sit, "Hong Kong's New Industrial Partnership with the Pearl River Delta"; C.K. Leung, "Personal Contacts, Subcontracting Linkages, and Development in the Hong Kong-Zhujiang Delta Region," *Annals of the Association of American Geographers* 83, no. 2 (1993): 272–302; C.K. Leung, "Foreign Manufacturing Investment and Regional Industrial Growth in Guangdong Province, China," *Environment and Planning A* 28 (1996): 513–536; J. Smart and A. Smart, "Personal Relations and Divergent Economies: A Case Study of Hong Kong Investment in China," *International Journal of Urban and Regional Research* 15, no. 2 (1991): 216–233; Thoburn et al., *Foreign Investment in China Under the Open Policy*.

20. Alan Smart, "Flexible Accumulation Across the Hong Kong Border: Petty Capitalists as Pioneers of Globalized Accumulation," *Urban Anthropology* 28, no. 3–4 (1999): 373–406; Josephine Smart, "The Global Economy and South China Development in Post-1978 China: Relevance and Limitations of the Flexible Accumulation Approach," *Urban Anthropology* 28, no. 3–4 (1999): 407–445; Mee Kam Ng and Wing-Shing Tang, "Urban System Planning in China: A Case Study of the Pearl River Delta," *Urban Geography* 20, no. 7 (1999): 591–616.

21. Guangdong Land Development Bureau, *Guangdongsheng guotu ziyuan* (Land Resources of Guangdong Province) (Guangzhou: Internal document, 1986), pp. 369–370.

22. Dongguan Statistical Bureau, *Dongguan tongji nianjian (1978–1990)* (Statistical Yearbook of Dongguan [1978–1990]) (Dongguan: Internal document, 1991), pp. 14 and 104.

23. G.C.S. Lin, interviews conducted in Dongguan during September 12–October 10, 1992.

24. Dongguan Statistical Bureau, *Dongguan tongji nianjian (1996)* (Statistical Yearbook of Dongguan [1996]) (Dongguan: Internal document, 1996), pp. 401–405.

25. CCP Team (Chinese Communist Party, Central Committee Special Investigation Team), *Dongguan shinian* (Dongguan's Ten Years) (Shanghai: People's Publishing House of Shanghai, 1989), p. 6.

26. Guangdong Statistical Bureau, *Guangdongsheng duiwai jingji maoyi luyou tongji ziliao* (Statistical Information on Foreign Trade and Tourism for Guangdong Province) (Guangzhou: Internal publication, 1991), p. 357.

27. Hong Kong Federation of Hong Kong Industries, *Hong Kong's Industrial Investment in the Pearl River Delta* (Hong Kong: Federation of Hong Kong Industries, 1992), p. 13.

28. G.C.S. Lin, interviews conducted in Dongguan during September 12–October 10, 1992.

29. Vogel, *One Step Ahead in China*, p. 176.

30. G.C.S. Lin, interviews conducted in Dongguan during September 12–October 10, 1992.

31. CCP Team, *Dongguan shinian*, pp. 7, 34, and 37.

32. P. Lu, "Zhujiang Sanjiaozhou-Xianggang jingji jishu hezuo de huigu yu qianzhan" (A Retrospect and Prospect on Economic and Technological Cooperation Between the Zhujiang Delta and Hong Kong), in Research Centre for Economic Development and Management of the Zhujiang Delta, ed., *Zhujiang sanjiaozhou jingji fazhan huigu yu qianzhan* (Economic Development in the Zhujiang Delta: Retrospect and Prospect) (Guangzhou: Zhongshan University Press, 1992), p. 146.

33. CCP Team, *Dongguan shinian*, p. 32.

34. *Asia-Pacific Economic Daily*, August 2, 1992.

35. Dongguan Statistical Bureau, *Dongguan tongji nianjian (1978–1990)* (Statistical Yearbook of Dongguan [1978–1990]) (Dongguan: Internal document, 1991), p. 6.

36. Ibid., p. 20.

37. Guangdong Statistical Bureau, *Guangdongsheng xianqu guomin jingji tongji ziliao (1980–1990)* (National Economic Statistical Data for Cities and Counties of Guangdong Province [1980–1990]) (Guangzhou: Internal publication, 1991), pp. 238–241, 357.

38. Ibid., pp. 238–241.

39. CCP Team, *Dongguan shinian*, p. 159.

40. Dongguan Statistical Bureau, *Dongguan tongji nianjian (1996)* (Statistical Yearbook of Dongguan [1996]) (Dongguan: Internal document, 1996), p. 100.

41. *Asia-Pacific Economic Daily*, August 2, 1992.

42. Dongguan Statistical Bureau, *Dongguan tongji nianjian (1996)* (Statistical Yearbook of Dongguan [1996]) (Dongguan: Internal document, 1996), p. 100.

43. *Asia-Pacific Economic Daily*, August 2, 1992.

44. Y.F. Woon, "Filial or Rebellious Daughters? Dagongmei in the Pearl River Delta Region, South China in the 1990s," *Asian and Pacific Migration Journal* 9, no. 2 (2000): 137–169.

45. H.S. Huang, ed., *Dongguan nongye jingji* (Dongguan's Agricultural Economy) (Guangzhou: People's Publishing House of Guangdong, 1991), p. 79.

46. A.G.O. Yeh and X. Li, "Urban Growth Management in the Pearl River Delta: An Integrated Remote Sensing and GIS Approach," *ITC Journal (Bulletin de l'ITC)*, no. 1 (1996): 81.

47. Guangdong Statistical Bureau, *Guangdongsheng duiwai jingji maoyi luyou tongji ziliao* (Statistical Information on Foreign Trade and Tourism for Guangdong Province) (Guangzhou: Internal publication, 1991), p. 271.

48. Guangdong Statistical Bureau, *Guangdong tongji nianjian* (Statistical Yearbook of Guangdong) (Beijing: China Statistical Press, 1991), pp. 370–371.

49. G. Guldin, "Towards a Greater Guangzhou: Hong Kong's Sociocultural Impact on the Pearl River Delta and Beyond," paper presented at the Workshop on Hong Kong-Guangdong Integration, Vancouver, Canada, University of British Columbia, 1992.

50. Ibid.

51. David Harvey, *The Condition of Postmodernity: An Enquiry into the Origins of Cultural Change* (Oxford: Blackwell, 1989); Doreen B. Massey, *Spatial Division of Labour: Social Structures and the Geography of Production* (London: Macmillan, 1984); A.J. Scott, "The Roepke Lecture in Economic Geography: The Collective Order of Flexible Production Agglomerations: Lessons for Local Economic Development Policy and Strategic Choice," *Economic Geography* 68, no. 3 (1992): 219–233.

52. C.K. Leung, "Personal Contacts, Subcontracting Linkages, and Development in the Hong Kong-Zhujiang Delta Region," *Annals of the Association of American Geographers* 83, no. 2 (1993): 272–302; A. Smart, "The Emergence of Local Capitalisms in China: Overseas Chinese Investment and Patterns of Development," in S.M. Li and W.S. Tang, eds., *China's Regions, Polity, & Economy* (Hong Kong: Chinese University Press, 2000), pp.65–96.

53. R.A. Beauregard, "Theorizing the Global-local Connection," in P.L. Know and P.J. Taylor, eds., *World Cities in a World-System* (Cambridge, UK: Cambridge University Press, 1995), pp. 232–248; Lawrence A. Brown, *Place, Migration and Development in the Third World* (New York: Routledge, 1990).

54. Harvey, *The Condition of Postmodernity*.

55. Scott, "The Roepke Lecture in Economic Geography."

56. V.F.S. Sit and C. Yang, "Foreign-Investment-induced Exo-Urbanization in the Pearl River Delta, China," *Urban Studies* 34, no. 4 (1997): 647–677; George C.S. Lin, *Red Capitalism in South China* (Vancouver, Canada: University of British Columbia Press, 1997); C.K. Leung, "Foreign Manufacturing Investment and Regional Industrial Growth in Guangdong Province, China," *Environment and Planning A* 28 (1996): 513–536.

57. T.G. McGee, "The Emergence of Desakota Regions in Asia: Expanding a Hypothesis," in N. Ginsburg, B. Koppel, and T.G. McGee, eds., *The Extended Metropolis: Settlement Transition in Asia* (Honolulu: University of Hawaii Press, 1991), pp. 3–25; Norton Ginsburg, *The Urban Transition: Reflections on the American and Asian Experiences* (Hong Kong: Chinese University Press, 1990); G.C.S. Lin, "Evolving Spatial Form of Urban-Rural Interaction in the Pearl River Delta, China," *Professional Geographer* 53, no. 1 (2001): 56–70; G.C.S. Lin, "Metropolitan Development in a Transitional Socialist Economy: Spatial Restructuring in the Pearl River Delta, China," *Urban Studies* 38, no. 3 (2001): 383–406.

Part II

Transformations

5

Migration in China in the Reform Era

Characteristics, Consequences, and Implications

Kam Wing Chan

Introduction

One major consequence of the economic reforms in China has been a dramatic rise in population mobility. "Outside labor" is now a visible and important part of the economy of large cities and coastal export-processing centers. Equally visible is the urban construction boom and the accompanying residential mobility as urbanites increase their housing consumption. The significance of social and economic transformation brought forth by changes in mobility in the last two decades is sometimes equated with the introduction of the momentous household responsibility system and the development of rural enterprises. Population mobility will continue to be important in the coming years as China becomes more open and as the economic structure shifts. The accession to the World Trade Organization (WTO) will only accentuate this process of change. The migration issue is also closely tied to the labor/unemployment issue, and both issues are attracting much current policy concern.

A number of factors have contributed to the surge in population mobility. At the root is the hidden surplus rural labor unleashed by the decollectivization program in the late 1970s and early 1980s. At the same time, rapid expansion of the urban and export-processing sectors has generated demand for tens of millions of low-skill jobs. Such a synergy in supply and demand was made possible by the concurrent relaxation of migratory controls and the development of urban food and labor markets. As migration started to be more prevalent, many migrants have also developed support networks, which in turn make migration easier. Urban residents have also moved a lot more than before, largely for better jobs and housing. Demand for housing has fed suburbanization of cities. These mobility changes are the focus of this chapter. It presents an overview of internal migration in China based on a synthesis of a large amount of materials and available information. The chapter first reviews the institutions controlling migration and then examines the migratory patterns, focusing on recent patterns and characteristics. The last part looks at the consequences of migration and explores major policy implications.

The *Hukou* System and Migration

In China, migration has been an area of heavy state control in the past and active regulation at present. The *hukou* (household registration) system affects migration in many important ways. People wanting to change residence are required by law to obtain permission from the public security authorities. A change in residence is deemed official and approved only when it is accompanied by a transfer of one's *hukou* to the destination. The transfer confers legal residency rights and, most importantly, eligibility for urban jobs and benefits. Such a change is granted only when certain limited conditions are met, especially when the move serves the state's interests defined in various policies, such as state recruitments and transfers of personnel.[1] In essence, the *hukou* system in the pre-reform era functioned as a *de facto* internal passport mechanism. While approvals for migration because of marriage or for seeking support from a family member within the rural areas or within the same level of urban centers were often granted, rural to urban migration was strictly regulated and suppressed in the 1960s and 1970s. In those days, most of this type of migration was reserved for bringing in the necessary labor force in support of state-initiated programs. An approval for self-initiated relocation to a city from the countryside was only a dream for ordinary peasants. Even today, when peasants can travel to many places, getting a registration to be a full-status urban resident in a medium-sized or large city is still largely beyond their reach.

Given the centrality of the *hukou* system in Chinese society, understandingly, it is essential to classify migrants based on whether or not local *hukou* is conferred in migration. Hence, two categories of migrants are differentiated: migration with local (*hukou*) residency rights (hereafter, *hukou* migration); and migration without *hukou* residency rights (non-*hukou* migration). Officially, only *hukou* migration is considered as *qianyi* ("migration"). Anything else is merely *renkou liudong* (population movement or "floating"), implying a low degree of expected permanence: the transients are not supposed to (and are legally not entitled to) stay at the destination permanently. Therefore, they are often termed "temporary" migrants. They are not the *de jure* residents, despite the fact that many of the non-*hukou* migrants may have been at the destination for years. "Rural migrant labor" (*mingong*) is a large component of the non-*hukou* migrant population. On the other hand, *hukou* migration is endowed with state resources and often called "planned" migration (*jihua qianyi*). The floating population is a "self-flowing population" (*ziliu renkou*) whose mobility takes place outside the state plans. From a government administrative point of view, the *hukou* and non-*hukou* differentiation is the most important. For other (statistical and scholarly) purposes, the criteria for defining a migrant are also determined by the geographic boundary a person has to cross, and the minimum duration one has to stay (at the destination or away from the origin).[2] What stands out in China's recent mobility surges is not only that these are large numbers of migrants, but also that a great portion of them are "long-term" circulating labor moving between urban centers and villages. These continuing perennial massive waves of "short-term" peasant migrant laborers in the urban areas, however, pose a host of issues and problems, some similar and some different to those posed by the "permanent" migrant laborers from the countryside. In studying migration in present-day China, one needs to have a framework that encompasses this special but popular form of mobility in the country.

Salient Features of Recent Migration

Types of Migrants and Sizes

Table 5.1 presents a relatively comprehensive set of major migration series I have recently assembled. The definitional complexities have been treated elsewhere[3] and will not be repeated here. The annual volume of *hukou* migrants remained quite stable, between 16 and 20 million in the 1980s and 1990s, the two decades for which data are available. This reflects strong government intervention in this area of *hukou* migration crossing city, town, and township boundaries through mechanisms such as a quota system. In fact, *hukou* migration appears to be declining slightly, possibly due to the decline in importance of the *hukou* system in general. On the other hand, there is a general rising trend in the size of the non-*hukou* migrant population from the early 1980s to the mid-1990s, as shown by the various pertinent figures assembled in Table 5.1. For instance, the size of the floating population stock started to grow rapidly in the mid-1980s to about 70 million in 1988, then dropped somewhat from 1989 to 1991 owing to an economic austerity program, but regained momentum around 1992 through probably 1997, reaching about 100 million. Similar upward trends are seen from other non-*hukou* population figures with long enough temporal coverage.

The rising trend appears to have been arrested in the second half of the

Table 5.1

Major Aggregate Migration Figures, 1982–1999 (in millions)

	Hukou migrants (yearly flow figures) reported by the MPS	Non-*hukou* migrants (stock figures)				
		"Temporary population"			"Rural migrant labor"	
		"Floating population" ("accepted" estimates)	National censuses/SSB population surveys		Estimates based on MOA annual surveys	Estimates based on SSB annual rural household surveys
Geographic boundary	City, town, or township	City, town, or township	Township or urban subdistrict	County or city	Township	Township
Minimum length of stay	No minimum	Usually 1–3 days	6 months	3 months or one year (see below)	Regularly engaged in work outside townships	Those who work outside the township, excluding those away from home for 6 months or more and those employed in TVEs
Series	A	B	C	D	E	F
1982	17.30	30				
1985	19.69	40				
1987	19.73			6.6 (1 year) 15.2* (6 months)		
1988	19.92	70				
1990	19.24			21.6 (1 year)		15.57

Year				(6 months)	
1991					15.80
1992	18.70	60–70			18.28
1993	18.19				34.48
1994	19.49	80	49.7	64.3	39.38
1995	18.46		29.1**		30.27
1996	17.51		60.0	68.4	39.84
1997	17.85	100	61.8	62.6	42.13
1998	17.13		62.4		49.15
1999	16.87	100	63.7		

Source: Compiled by the author from various sources. For details see Kam Wing Chan, "Painting a Portrait of the Elephant: Migration in China," unpublished paper, 2001.

*The geographic boundary is based on city, county, or town.

**The geographic boundary is based on county-level units.

Note: MPS = Ministry of Public Security; SSB = State Statistical Bureau; MOA = Ministry of Agriculture; TVEs = township and village enterprises

1990s, as the latest available data indicate. The magnitude of stock of the temporary population (Series C) between 1996 and 1999 only inched up slightly; in fact, there was even a drop in the rural migrant labor stock in Series E between 1996 and 1997. It is believed that this slowdown in rural outflow was related to the sluggish performance of the urban economy, job competition from laid-off workers of urban state-owned enterprises (SOEs), and increasingly protectionist policies used by local governments against recruitment of outsiders, at least between 1996 and 1999.[4]

How does the Chinese situation compare internationally? Based on the common index of annual "total amount of moving," I estimate that the average annual flow volume for the late 1990s was close to 70 million.[5] This translates into an annual mobility rate, or the percent of the population that changed usual residence in one year, of about 6 percent for China. A rough estimate indicates that China's migration rate has increased at a rapid pace and has doubled from about 2 percent to 3 percent in 1977.[6] The major factors of change are the surge in non-*hukou* migration and intra-urban residential mobility. If we consider those two components as largely market-driven migration, then we can argue that the market has now prevailed in generating population geographic mobility in China. Still, although China's current rate is low by international standards, it is about the same as that of the low mobility Western countries (typically 6 percent to 7 percent in countries such as Ireland, Belgium, or the Netherlands).[7] It is far below the rates for high mobility Western countries, such as the United States and Canada (around 16 percent to 19 percent). China's rate is also lower than that of Taiwan in 1970 and 1971 (10 percent), but is slightly higher than that of the USSR in the 1980s[8] and much higher than the 1.5 percent for India.[9] The annual volume of Chinese internal migration (70 million) is actually larger than that of the United States,[10] which has a similar size in area. In this sense, the "migration density" in China is actually higher than that of the United States, the most mobile large nation based on conventional measurements.

It is important to note that the comparisons thus far still have not taken into account the large volume of short-term circulation in China, much of which is not captured in this type of conventional migration accounting based on a certain extended period of stay to define a migrant (for example, a six-month stay for qualifying as "temporary population" in Table 5.1). But short-term circulation is not a trivial part of China's mobility. Because of the circularity of rural labor, the 40 to 60 million rural migrant labor stock over a period of fifteen years can translate easily into 100 to 150 million peasants engaged in work outside the home township at one time or another in that period. This means that some 40 percent of the rural labor force was drawn into the migration circuit outside the home township in the recent two decades.

Table 5.2

Migrants by Educational Attainment (%)

Educational level	National population 1990 (Age 6+)	1990 census		Rural migrant labor	
		Hukou migrants	Non-hukou migrants	Ji'nan survey 1995	MOA national survey 1993
College	1.6	22.2	2.2		
Technical middle	1.7	11.3	1.9	12.1	9.8
Senior middle	7.3	13.6	9.6		
Junior middle	26.5	26.3	43.2	71.0	54.1
Primary	42.3	20.5	30.8	16.0	31.6
No or little education	20.6	5.6	11.2	0.9	3.8

Source: Kam Wing Chan, "Internal Migration in China: A Dualistic Approach," in Frank Pieke and Hein Mallee, eds., *Internal and International Migration: Chinese Perspectives* (Richmond, Surrey: Curzon Press, 1999), 49–72.
Note: MOA=Ministry of Agriculture.

Social and Economic Characteristics of Migrants

Migration is selective in many respects such as age. Age is mainly related to life cycle events that generate adjustments in the place of residence. Starting a job, changing jobs until one settles on a career, getting married, and going away to college are all closely connected with migration and, moreover, concentrated in the age of young adulthood. The age structure of Chinese migrants is fairly typical of a migrant population. Rural migrant labor, as expected, is more concentrated in the most economically active age group, particularly between the age of 15 to 34.[11] The 1990 census figures show that male migrants slightly outnumbered the female migrants. Male predominance is more obvious in labor migration in general. This is especially pronounced in some rural migrant labor populations, where male migrants outnumber females by 3 to 1.[12] This, however, masks some notable regional exceptions such as Guangdong, where migrants from the countryside are predominantly female.[13] Marriage migrants, however, are almost exclusively females.[14]

Overall, migrants and rural migrant workers are better educated than the average population (Table 5.2). This is partly an effect of the age of the migrants (young adults tend to be better educated than old adults). Despite the general similarity of the age structure between *hukou* and non-*hukou* migrants, there is a clear polarization of the two groups in educational attainment. *Hukou* migrants are disproportionately highly educated (senior–middle-school level

Table 5.3

Migrant Workers by Occupation (%)

	Urban employment 1990	1985–1990	
		Hukou migrants	Non-hukou migrants
Professional and technical	14.0	21.0	3.3
Administrative and managerial	4.9	3.6	1.2
Clerical	5.6	7.8	1.5
Sales	8.1	4.2	10.3
Service	6.9	4.6	9.6
Industrial workers	38.1	31.9	18.3
Farm workers	22.5	26.8	55.7
Unclassifiable	0.2	–	–
	100.0	100.0	100.0

Source: Kam Wing Chan, "Internal Migration in China: A Dualistic Approach," in Frank Pieke and Hein Mallee, eds., *Internal and International Migration: Chinese Perspectives* (Richmond, Surrey: Curzon Press, 1999), 49–72.

and up), while non-*hukou* migrants and rural migrant labor are heavily concentrated in the educational levels of junior-middle and primary school. The most pronounced disparity, which clearly attests to the highly selective nature of the skills of the *hukou* migration, is seen in the college-educated cohort. While only less than 2 percent of the nation's population aged six years and above had a college level education in 1990, close to one-quarter of the *hukou* migrants were college graduates! Despite the lower educational level of rural migrant workers compared to *hukou* migrants, the former is nevertheless better educated than the average rural population. More than half of the rural migrant workers has at least junior middle education. Those who are better educated and have special vocational skills also tend to have a higher propensity to leave, a situation closely related to the nature of the urban labor market. By contrast, those with no or little formal education have a very low out-migration rate.[15]

Table 5.3 reveals the occupational and sectoral similarities and contrasts between *hukou* and non-*hukou* migrants. It is clear that the composition of occupations of *hukou* migrants (predominantly with urban destinations except marriage migration) broadly resembles that of the urban population as a whole; actually, they are significantly overrepresented in professional and technical positions. In contrast, 95 percent of the non-*hukou* migrants had employment at the clerical level or lower. Common jobs were manufacturing frontline workers, construction workers, nannies, and sales and service workers.[16] There are a lot of self-employed craftsmen and small vendors. In fact, self-employment has become a more favored sector for more entrepreneurial rural migrants for good reasons.[17] The large number of farm workers among *hukou* migrants largely reflects rural-rural marriage migration of women.

Among the urban migrants without *hukou*, a handful might have been able to make it and moved upward via connections or entrepreneurship, but the great majority stays at the margin of the society.[18] The non-*hukou* urban migrants are often shut out of more desirable urban positions and have to take up the "3D" (demanding, dangerous, and dirty) jobs. In short, a dual urban social structure has emerged: on the one side those for whom jobs, housing, education, subsidized food, and medical care are an entitlement, and on the other, those who must scramble for those goods or even do without them.[19] The occupational composition in Table 5.3 clearly reflects the polarities in the social and economic status based on the *hukou* divide. In many ways, this dualism is parallel to the formal/informal sectoral dualism elsewhere in the developing world and the local/foreign (and illegal) labor dichotomy in many developed countries

Geography of Migration

Significant disparities in wages and living standards between the urban and rural sectors and between the coastal and inland regions underlie the peasant migratory flows in the reform era. Rural migrant labor moves across different geographic scales to benefit from these income differentials: some to nearby towns outside the villages, others across thousands of miles to big cities on the coast. Figure 5.1 shows only the largest flows crossing provincial boundaries from 1990 through 1995 based on the 1995 One Percent National Population Sample data. The geographic pattern is broadly similar to that between 1985 and 1990.[20] Guangdong continued to be the largest importer of migrants from outside, estimated to be at 1.9 million, followed by Jiangsu (0.97 million) and the two metropolises, Shanghai (0.72 million) and Beijing (0.69 million). On the "supply" side, Sichuan continued to be the largest "exporter" of migrants (1.45 million), followed by Anhui and Henan (each 0.74 million).[21] A useful finer differentiation of the interprovincial migration patterns by *hukou* status based on 1990 census micro data shows that there are considerable deviations of the *hukou* migrants from the above geographic pattern of long distance migration.[22] While the non-*hukou* streams are mostly moving for jobs and are predominantly from the interior to the coast, crossing thousands of miles to converge at major economic hubs like the Pearl River Delta (Guangdong) and major coastal metropolises, most out-of-province *hukou* migratory streams are generally quite

Figure 5.1   **The Largest Thirty Inter-provincial Migration Streams, 1990–1995**

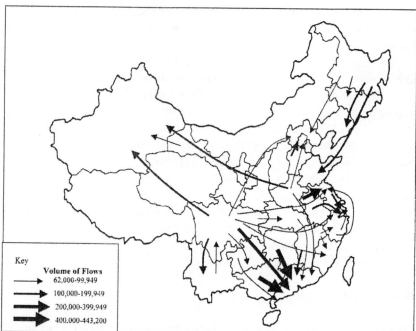

Source: National Population Sample Survey Office, *1995 quanguo 1% renkou chouyang diaocha ziliao* (Data on 1995 National 1 Percent Population Sample Survey) (Beijing: Zhongguo Tongji Chubanshe, 1997).

"conservative," over shorter distances than the non-*hukou* migration.[23] They appeared to have preferred nearby provinces whose culture, languages, and environment were likely to be similar, and, presumably, easier to adapt to.[24] Another characteristic of *hukou* migratory streams at the upper end is the prevalence of two-way flows for some provinces. There were significant exchanges between many pairs of adjacent provinces, both of similar (e.g. Sichuan and Yunnan) and different (e.g. Jiangsu and Anhui) economic levels.

Inter-provincial flows are but a small part of the overall internal migration picture. Going down to finer geographic scales, data from various national surveys of rural migrant labor, while less systematic and with a greater sampling error (because of the smaller samples), provide some very comprehensive information on the geography of the rural migrant labor. According to a study undertaken in 1993 and 1994, the size of the stock of rural migrant labor (those who participated in "outside" work, including seasonal labor) at the end of 1993 and in early 1994 reached 51 million, accounting for about one-eighth (12.5 percent) of the country's rural labor force (Table 5.4). The

Table 5.4

Composition of Rural Migrant Labor, 1993

Region	Total rural labor (1,000)	Out-migration rate (%)	No. of migrants (1,000)	%	Geographic distribution (%)		
					Within counties	Within provinces	Toward urban centers
East	154,505.9	8.5	13,133	25.6	28.4	66.3	82.0
Central	143,295.6	15.9	22,784	44.4	40.6	70.4	83.3
West	113,755.6	13.5	15,357	30.0	37.0	76.4	66.5
Total	411,557.0	12.5	51,274	100	36.4	71.1	77.9

Source: Fan Li, "The Size, Geographical Distribution and Other Characteristics of Outgoing Labor," *Zhongguo Nongcun Jingji* (Chinese Rural Economy), no. 9 (1994): 31–35.

Notes:

Rural migrant labor refers to rural labor who had been outside the townships for work in 1993.

Regional classification:

East = Heilongjiang, Jilin, Liaoning, Beijing, Tianjin, Hebei, Shandong, Jiangsu, Shanghai, Zhejiang, Fujian, Guangdong, Guangxi, and Hainan.

Central = Nei Menggu, Shanxi, Henan, Anhui, Hubei, Hunan, and Jiangxi.

West = Xinjiang, Qinghai, Gansu, Ningxia, Shaanxi, Sichuan, Guizhou, Yunnan, and Tibet.

flow was predominantly toward the urban areas (77.9 percent). The Central region was the largest source of rural migrant labor, having the highest labor out-migration rate (15.9 percent) and volume (22.8 million), followed by the West region (13.5 percent and 15.4 million). The East region had the lowest rate (8.5 percent, about half that of the Central region) and the smallest volume. Because of the large size of the labor force (population) in the Central provinces, this region accounted for 44 percent of the estimated total outflows. The low rate of out-migration in the East region is attributed to the high level of development of rural enterprises in many villages and townships, which absorbed local and nearby rural labor. This is not true for either the Central or West regions. Over a third of the rural labor force migrated within counties (36 percent) and, expectedly, a greater percentage within the migrants' own provinces (71 percent).

Another interesting trend that has been recently noticed, based on additional information contained in a 1998 survey, is that while the size of the rural migrant labor stock was about the same (about 50 million) in 1993 and 1998, these workers had moved to more distant destinations in 1998 (Figure 5.2). There was a drastic increase in the number of rural labor migrants crossing *both* provincial and regional boundaries. In 1998, this group of very-long–distance migrants ("from a different region") accounted for 31 percent of the entire rural labor migrant stock, compared to only 18 percent in 1993. Detailed regional breakdowns in Table 5.5 show that the Central region has further consolidated its role as the largest exporter of rural migrant labor crossing provincial boundaries (55 percent in 1998 compared to 46 percent in 1993), and that the East region is the destination of the vast majority of inter-provincial rural migrant labor (having increased from 70 percent to 83 percent). Inter-provincial rural migrant labor generated in and from the West region (the region with the lowest per capita income) has witnessed the most rapid increase, with its share rising from about one-quarter to one-third in just five years. In absolute terms, the size almost doubled from 7 million in 1993 to 13 million in 1998. While going to the East region had been popular for out-of-province rural labor migrants in the Central region throughout the 1990s, those in the West region only caught up with this in large numbers in the second half of the 1990s. In 1993, about half of the migrants from the West region moved to the East region. In 1998 this percentage rose to an overwhelming level (79 percent). Moving to the East region allows migrants to maximize the largest possible geographic wage disparities,[25] and more and more peasants in the poorest provinces are getting this message and taking action.

Figure 5.2   **Origins of Rural Migrant Labor, 1993 and 1998**

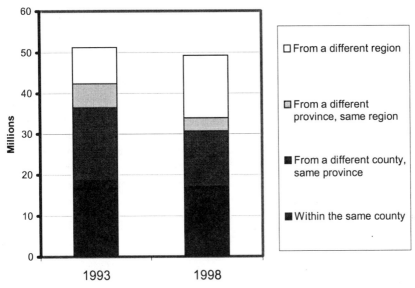

Source: Based on Kam Wing Chan, "Painting a Portrait of the Elephant: Migration in China," unpublished paper, 2001.

Table 5.5

Percentage of the Rural Migrant Labor Population from a Different Province, 1993 and 1998

Percentage share	Origins			
	East	Central	West	All regions
1993 (total stock = 28.9 million)				
Regional share	29.9	45.6	24.5	100
Destinations				
East	71.4	79.2	52.2	70.3
Central	21.8	18.9	9.4	17.4
West	6.8	1.9	38.4	12.3
Column total	100.0	100.0	100.0	100.0
1998 (total stock = 37.8 million)				
Regional share	11.0	55.0	34.0	100.0
Destinations				
East	72.7	87.3	79.4	83.0
Central	18.2	9.1	5.9	9.0
West	9.1	3.6	14.7	8.0
Column total	100.0	100.0	100.0	100.0

Source: Kam Wing Chan, "Painting a Portrait of the Elephant: Migration in China," unpublished paper, 2001.

Note: Regional classification is explained in Table 5.4.

Social and Economic Consequences

It is clear that economic development in the reform era in China is intimately linked with migration. From an individual's perspective, migration is often driven by a desire to improve one's livelihood through taking advantage of the wage differentials in different locales. At the macro level, migration is a redistribution of labor that helps balance regional labor supply and demand. It has been well established in the literature that migration can ameliorate or perpetuate sectoral and regional disparities and can have many consequences requiring policy attention. Historical experience suggests that modern economic development took place with massive intersectoral migration, often among regions, especially in the early stages of industrialization, as the geographical distribution of labor adjusts to the structural shifts in the economy.[26]

The Impact of Migrants on Urban Centers

The vast pools of rural migrant labor provide a plentiful supply of cheap labor in sustaining China's urban economic boom in the reform era. This labor force is also flexible, able, and willing to move quickly into new growth areas. It has eased the tightness of the labor supply in low-skilled urban occupations and in many ways made up for the structural labor shortages in cities, which are caused by shifts in occupational preferences of urban workers, because low-skilled, "dirty" jobs were eschewed by urban job-seekers, especially in the 1980s and the early 1990s. Some estimates suggest that the full cost of hiring an outside (non-*hukou*) worker is only about one-quarter that of a local worker.[27] Also, outside workers are willing to work not only for less and for long hours, but also often under unsafe conditions with minimal protection. Even with increasing protectionist measures in many cities, outside migrants today still fill many low-skilled positions in both the service sector (as nannies, restaurant attendants, and sanitary workers) and industrial sector (such as factory frontline positions in textiles, chemicals, construction, and mining). Rural migrant labor is also engaged in self-employed small businesses. For example, they are traders, artisans, shoe repairers, tailors, and furniture-makers in cities and some less commercially developed provinces. The increasing supply of labor from outside has also fostered the development of an urban labor market. Because of the large numbers of non-*hukou* entrants into the urban low-skilled occupations, the competitive pressure is highest in that sector. In the Pearl River Delta, where the industrial labor market in the nonstate sector is most developed, recruitment of workers, both for factory frontline positions and technical and managerial positions, is largely decided by market forces. There is an increasing convergence in the wage rates among low-skilled outside workers in different regions and gradual development of a national labor market at the lower ends of the skill hierarchy.

While the economic contributions by migrant labor to the urban sector are unequivocal, the massive influx of newcomers has also posed some problems to large cities where the migrant masses congregate. The problem urban residents have complained about most is the rise in criminal and illicit activities. It is widely believed, and portrayed in the media, that the deteriorating urban public order is connected with the increasing presence of transients from the rural areas. Police figures cited by Li and Hu,[28] for example, show a rising proportion of transients in police arrests. It is also common to find police statistics showing that the floating population accounts for more than half of the crimes in some locales and as high as 90 percent in Shenzhen.[29] It is probable that transients have a higher crime rate, especially because they are concentrated in the demographic group (young male) most apt to commit crimes. Some of them can become understandably desperate when they exhaust their meager resources before they find a job. It is equally true that the media image of masses of jobless peasants roaming from one city to another and participating in illicit activities is grossly exaggerated, fed by the common xenophobic attitude of the natives and the easy tendency to scapegoat transients from poor areas.[30] While crimes committed by rural migrants might make headlines, the reality is that the overwhelming majority of the rural migrant workers are living quietly and working painstakingly in factories and on construction sites rather than causing a menace to law and order.[31]

Another issue that has raised public concern is the pressure the floating population has put on urban services and infrastructure. Under the current system, however, many of the urban "public" services, especially public housing, hospitals, and schools, are highly excludable against outsiders. Access to those services still depends on the possession of the urban *hukou*, and they are for most part allocated by one's work unit. For this reason, the inflow of population into the cities did not make any substantial difference to the congestion of these services in the last fifteen years.[32] Many in the floating population simply do without these services, or get them from private sources—of course, usually at extraordinary high prices. On nonexcludable or less excludable public goods and services such as public transportation, piped water, electricity, and waste disposal, the story varies. Undoubtedly, floaters, given their number in many big cities, consume a large amount of those public goods and have strained many of the already inadequate municipal services, though it must be pointed out on a per capita basis, these newcomers generally consume less than the urban average because of their lower purchasing power and accessibility to those services. Solinger argues that the increased consumption of at least two public goods, water and urban transport, is either low enough in rivalry or high enough in elasticity as not to present a genuine problem of supply to the existing urban residents.[33] The real problem appears to stem from the fact that most of these urban public goods are subsidized and any increased consumption poses an extra budgetary burden on local governments, most of which are already under heavy fiscal pressure caused by the transition to a market system.

The biggest strain migrants have put on the infrastructure, and truly at times stretched it to the breaking point, is the pressure on the already seriously clogged rail systems during certain peak times. The pressure is very acute during the Spring Festival period every year when most migrants customarily return to their home villages to spend the time with their families.[34] This generates a traffic load, often ten or twenty times the normal capacity. It is estimated that the rail systems in the 1994 Spring Festival interlude handled about 185 million passenger trips. This includes 35 million out-of-province journeys, 60 percent of which were made by rural migrant workers.[35] The government was caught off-guard in 1992 by the greatly expanded demand for transport caused by a sudden spurt in mobility as peasant migrants moved more and over longer distances. The inability of the transportation systems to ship all the passengers and the extremely congested rail systems caused not only chaos and frustrations but also many injuries and small riots that threatened public order. In recent years, measures taken to damper the demand for travel during the Spring Festival period have yielded some positive effect, but the problem of moving hundreds of millions of passengers within a short period of time continues to be a perennial challenge.[36]

Largely because of the existing *hukou* system and other associated institutions and attitudes, new migrants in cities are easily marginalized. The situation these Chinese newcomers face is comparable to the experiences of ethnic minorities and immigrants in cities elsewhere. Except for those working in factories with provided housing, migrants have to find accommodations in the still rudimentary urban housing market. One of the results has been the establishment of "migrant villages" based on village houses or land rented at the urban fringes. These migrant communities are places where new migrants from the same native place, speaking the same dialect, congregate. This is a self-help mechanism, as well as a natural outcome of non-*hukou* migration, most of which is connected by social networks based on native place. Migrant villages are often without proper infrastructure services and may present a menace to public health. In the second half of the 1990s, as migrants become more established, many family members also arrived in the cities. Providing affordable schooling for migrants' children has now become a major issue of concern among the migrant communities in Beijing and Shanghai.[37]

The Impact of Migrants on Rural Areas

Peasant labor migrates primarily for economic reasons, especially to improve family incomes. Remittances thus become a major contribution by these outside workers to their families back home. The State Statistical Bureau estimates that the average wages of rural migrant workers in cities in 1997 was ¥5,642 per year.[38] After housing and meal expenses, the average net income per peasant migrant worker is about ¥300 per month. This is about three to four times the normal average rural income. Other studies have also indicated that about 50 percent to 60 percent of their incomes is remitted back home. If we use the 60 million figure for the number of rural migrant workers and the remittance figure of ¥3,000 per year,[39] this will yield ¥180 billion a year, or roughly an equivalent of 15 percent of China's agricultural sector's GDP.[40] As the origins of the migrants are not evenly distributed in the country, the impact of remittances is more pronounced in places with higher percentages of out-migrants (such as in inland provinces). It is estimated that rural migrants remitted a total of ¥7.5 billion in 1994 to their hometowns in Anhui, or an equivalence of 25 percent of the GDP generated by agriculture in that province or about the same as the total wage bill of all the township and village enterprises in the province.[41] Funan County in the province sent out 110,000 peasant laborers and brought in ¥200 million per year in the early 1990s. This amount was about the same as the total industrial output value of the county.[42]

Working in the cities is also an important opportunity for many peasants to learn about the modern world and skills. This is particularly crucial to the rural population, especially after being isolated for more than two decades under the suffocating policy of rural-urban segmentation in the pre-reform era. Combined with the circularity of movements, these positive effects (along with some less desirable ones, of course) are readily transmitted to the countryside. Because of policy discrimination, most rural migrants cannot settle permanently in the urban destination and have to engage in seasonal migration or eventually return to their home villages. The circularity of movements has generated a reverse flow of not only wealth (remittances) but also progressive attitudes and modern, technical skills to the peripheral areas. Many returnees continue to find work in the nonagricultural sector. It is not uncommon for them to use the savings, skills, and business contacts they bring back to start up or invest in small businesses. In Moxian County, Anhui, for example, 57 percent of all the 21,000 rural enterprises in the county were set up by return migrants.[43] A similar case can also be made for returnees in Fuyang Prefecture in the same province.[44] It is very likely that the exposure to the outside world and especially nonagricultural skills can have more of a lasting impact on the local development of rural communities than the remittances can.[45]

The rural outflows have reduced the population pressures on land in the sending villages. This is especially obvious as most rural migrant labor is from regions of very high population density and from households with very small farms.[46] Out-migration is arguably an effective and cheap way to siphon off surplus rural labor and ease pressure on local land and resources, in addition to providing a valuable source of income through remittances or temporary wage earnings. On the other hand, rural out-migration can also drain away young adults and the educated from the farm sector, leading to an aging of the rural labor force. So far, it appears that the overall impact of out-migration on agriculture is probably quite small. First, the percentage of the rural outflows is still small, averaging about 12 percent to 14 percent of the rural labor force. Secondly, about 60 percent of these outflows are seasonal, meaning that they still participate one way or the other (part-time) in farm work, especially during the peak labor demand season. Thirdly, the loss of the physical labor due to migration can be generally replaced by other family labor or contracted labor from outside (as in the case of Guangdong). Of course, for some households, the greater reliance on outside work (remittances) has meant less attention to agriculture.[47] This is partly a natural process of labor adjustment as the country industrializes—as those who can do better in nonfarm jobs gradually move out of agriculture. In some instances, the total withdrawal of households from agriculture (by leasing out their land) has actually helped greater specialization in agriculture and enhanced economies of scale. The moves enable small farms to merge into larger ones. The real damage to agriculture comes from those who continue to hang on to valuable farmland but only farm halfheartedly. The economic and policy uncertainties faced by migrant workers in the urban areas have fostered an attitude of using farmland more as a fall-back security than farming it productively. The more important concern with the loss of more educated and young rural workers is the longer-term impact on the modernization of the rural sector. The aging of the farm labor force will retard the rate of technological modernization in the rural sector. However, in many regions, this is offset by the cash brought in by migrant workers, which allows those working on the farm to purchase fertilizers and other needed modern inputs (such as better seeds) for farming. One study in Sichuan shows that about one-third of the remittances from rural migrant workers was used for agricultural production. Families with migrant workers tend to use more modern inputs in farming than those without migrant labor.[48] It has also been argued that out-migration raises the rural labor costs and hence increases the rate of return of capital. This might induce more capital inflow to the farm sector, a crucial aspect of modernization of Chinese agriculture.[49] Of course, the incentives to invest in the farm sector in China are influenced more fundamentally by government policies than by any other factor.

Absolute poverty in China is almost entirely restricted to resource-constrained remote upland areas, though there is also a growing urban poor, mainly of the unemployed, in recent years. Almost all of the counties with poverty face extremely scarce arable land and rapidly degrading environmental resources.[50] Because of their remote and upland locations, they are often shut off from the outside world. In short, "geography" contributes a large part to the poverty. In the absence of massive capital investment, further expansion of farm or off-farm opportunities in these regions is severely limited. The only option for increasing incomes and lessening the population pressure on the environment is to seek farm and off-farm jobs outside.[51] Generally, those rural areas with the poorest residents have not been as active in taking part in this process, but there is a great potential to realize benefits via this route. Some evidence presented earlier (Table 5.5) shows that in the 1990s, increasingly more peasants in the poorest Western provinces moved longer distances (crossing many provinces to the coastal provinces) to seek better-paid jobs, very much following the footsteps of migrants in the middle-income Central provinces. If this "diffusion" of migration continues, it is likely that the poorest will be drawn into migration more and benefit from it in the future.

Implications for China's Development and Policy

In the last few years, China's economic growth has been hampered by a lack of internal demand, which is partly caused by the stagnation of rural incomes. In fact, most low-income farm households in 1999 and 2000 experienced real income declines. Stagnation of rural incomes is related to the inadequate supply of gainful employment for the growing rural labor force.[52] The Chinese countryside contains an enormous surplus labor, which was estimated at 160 million for the early 1990s. A significant portion of the labor redundancy in the rural sector exists in the form of underemployment. Although various kinds of nonfarm activities (mainly rural enterprises) in the rural sector created about 77 million jobs in the period between 1984 and 1994, the size of absorption was offset roughly by the size of the new additional labor supply due to natural increases (87 million in the same period).[53] A real reduction in the size of the rural surplus labor was only possible when rural migrant labor was absorbed by the urban sector. Taking this factor into account, approximately 90 million people in the countryside currently need jobs.[54] Shukai Zhao has estimated that the rural labor force will continue to grow at a rate of about 5 to 6 million per year in the coming ten years.[55]

Further expansion of the employment absorption capacity of the rural sector has become very limited. Indeed, agricultural employment since 1992 has experienced an absolute decline almost every year. Technological improvements in the agricultural sector will further dampen the demand for labor. Township and village enterprise (TVE) employment also stagnated in the second half of the 1990s (it peaked at 135 million in 1996 but decreased to 125 million in 1998). It appears that TVE employment may further expand in the coming years, but at a very slow rate (about 2 to 3 million a year), and it is unlikely that it will repeat the rapid employment expansion seen in the second half of the 1980s and first half of the 1990s.[56] Because of the accession to the WTO, it is expected that China will lose about another 2 to 3 million jobs in agriculture as a result of the competition from imported farm products. It is also likely that farming will be increasingly perceived as a "dead-end" job by rural youths entering the labor force. In other words, many rural youths will simply not consider a job on the farm regardless.[57] As a result, while the average annual natural growth of the rural labor force[58] is estimated to be about 9 million in the next five years,[59] the actual number of those wanting to find jobs in the non-agricultural/urban sector is far larger.

On the urban side, employment will be a serious problem in the coming years, since, in addition to the existing large urban unemployment,[60] about another 10 million SOE workers are expected to be laid off in the next five years.[61] The employment situation China will face in the coming several years will be difficult, as the net labor supply will outstrip the demand, and the urban sector does not have the capacity to accommodate more labor transfer from the rural areas. The situation, however, may be changed around 2006 or 2007 as the size of the urban labor force begins to decline, creating some room for rural migrant labor.[62] This demand will be much greater if rural migrant labor is more freely allowed to replace some of the existing less productive urban workers when an integrated rural and urban labor market is established in China.

Another potential source of new jobs in the near future lies in the tertiary sector, especially in smaller (county-level) cities and towns. It has been observed that the agglomeration effect and service multiplier effect of the TVEs in China have not been brought into full play due to their generally dispersed locations and localized orientations.[63] A modest relocation of these rural enterprises to nearby urban centers will boost the growth of the tertiary sector in these centers and generate jobs for rural migrant labor. With a larger tertiary sector, these smaller urban centers can also help to generate growth in agriculture by functioning as service points for agriculture and the rural population. Indeed, in the last two years, these urban centers have become more popular destinations of rural migrant labor.[64]

Furthermore, there is a great potential in using labor migration (including organized export of labor and resettlement) to combat poverty, especially in remote and resource-constrained regions. This will represent a shift from China's conventional approach, which places emphasis on developing the local economy.[65] As pointed out before, the rate of migration is still quite low among the poorest group in the rural sector and in high-poverty regions (such as in the West region). Lower education levels, lack of relevant contacts, and lack of monetary resources to pay for transportation are barriers to exploring outside nonfarm opportunities. Measures can be designed to help the rural poor overcome these major short-term and long-term mobility obstacles. These may include offering low-interest migration loans and encouraging labor recruitment agencies to go to these counties, as well as more long-term investment in education.

Given the above considerations, China should focus more on creating gainful employment, together with labor market reforms, as a major policy in the years to come. When there is economic growth and when there are expanded resources generated from growth, it is easier to reform and dismantle labor migration restriction measures. Such a policy will include an industrial strategy that is built on the right input mix that reflects China's comparative advantage (plentiful labor).[66] Understandably, further reforms and rural-urban integration of labor markets are going to lead to dismissals of unproductive state workers concentrated in certain age cohorts (middle-aged) and industries (traditional producer industries). Layoffs carry the risk of triggering urban political turmoil. To mitigate these social and political dangers and resistance to the market reforms, the government should consider compensating those who lose out in this transition, so that the urban workers can accept a more open and competitive labor market. This approach is probably a more acceptable and realistic way in the current Chinese context, as the recent reforms in China are bound to produce gainers and losers. In longer terms, a comprehensive safety net for workers has to be built.

There are some short-term merits in keeping migrant labor flexible ("floating") without permanent urban citizenship, as outlined before. However, a more stable migrant labor force is economically more efficient, especially as migrant workers gain skills and experience and move up to skilled occupations.[67] With a view toward equity and sociopolitical stability considerations, there are significant advantages in assimilating internal migrants and making them equal members of the urban community. Breaking down labor market barriers and allowing freer migration within the country are strategies for China's economic growth and long-term stability. Some advances have been made in the last two years in liberalizing the urban *hukou* system.[68] Totally dismantling the migration restriction policies is a complex task, as it affects the interests of many social groups and different levels of governments differently. Careful phasing in of the liberalizing measures is important, so that migration to cities becomes manageable, even in the short run. In specific terms, it appears that the government can expand the current "blue-stamp" *hukou,* as a preparatory urban *hukou* to full urban citizenship,[69] to include migrant workers in skilled occupations, and gradually further expand it to benefit all migrant workers who have secured urban jobs (or set up businesses) for an extended period (say, three years). Access to basic education (primary and secondary schools) and housing are two major obstacles in preventing permanent settlement of many relatively established rural migrant workers in the cities. Therefore, developing affordable, low-cost social facilities for migrants should become a priority for the receiving regions. As migrant labor has already become an inseparable part of the labor force in many large cities, local governments should be able to see the long-term advantages and importance of providing them with social facilities instead of leaving them out.

Notes

Material for this chapter draws from work supported by the National Science Foundation under Grant No. 9618385 and the World Bank.

1. Tiejun Cheng and Mark Selden, "The Origins and Social Consequences of China's *Hukou* System," *China Quarterly,* no.139 (1994): 644–668. Kam Wing Chan and Li Zhang, "The *Hukou* System and Rural-urban Migration: Processes and Changes," *China Quarterly,* no. 160 (1999): 818–855. Hein Mallee, "China's Household Registration System under Reform," *Development and Change* 26, no. 1 (1995): 1–29.

2. These are criteria used by many studies internationally; see Ronald Skeldon, *Population Mobility in Developing Countries* (London: Belhaven Press, 1990).

3. Kam Wing Chan, "Painting a Portrait of the Elephant: Migration in China," unpublished paper, 2001.

4. Shukai Zhao, "The Mobility of Rural Migrants: New Stage and New Issues," in *1998: Zhongguo shehui xingshi fenxi yu yuce* (1998: Analysis and Forecast of the Social Situation of China) (Beijing: Shehui Wenxian Chubanshe, 1998), 76–89. Cai Fang and Kam Wing Chan, "The Political Economy of Urban Protectionist Employment Policies in China," *Working Paper Series,* no. 2 (2000), Chinese Academy of Social Sciences, Institute of Population Studies.

5. Chan, "Painting a Portrait of the Elephant."

6. Ibid.

7. See Larry Long, "Residential Mobility Differences Among Developed Countries," *International Regional Science Review* 14, no. 2 (1991): 133–147.

8. Ibid.

9. Based on India's 1981 census; see Ronald Skeldon, "On Migration Patterns in India During the 1970s," *Population and Development Review* 12, no. 4 (1986): 759–779.

10. It is estimated that about 43 million Americans changed residence in the year ending March 1998. See U.S. Census Bureau, *Geographical Mobility: Population Characteristics (March 1997 to March 1998)* (Washington D.C., 2000).

11. Kam Wing Chan, "Internal Migration in China: A Dualistic Approach," in Frank Pieke and Hein Mallee, eds., *Internal and International Migration: Chinese Perspectives* (Richmond, Surrey: Curzon Press, 1999), 49–72.

12. Ibid.

13. See, for instance, Alvin Chin-hung So, "Rural-urban Migration in China: A Study of Migrant Workers in Shunde City," *Research Paper,* no.17 (1995), Department of Geography, University of Sussex.

14. Cindy Fan and Youqin Huang, "Waves of Rural Brides: Female Migration in China," *Annals of the Association of American Geographers* 88, no.2 (1998): 277–251.

15. Fan Li and Xiaoyun Han, "Waichu dagong renyuande nianling jiegou he wenhua goucheng" (The Educational Composition and Age Structure of Outgoing Workers), *Zhongguo nongcun jingji* (Chinese Rural Economy), no.8 (1994): 10–14.

16. Yunyan Yang, *Zhongguo renkou qianyi yu fazhande changqi zhanlue* (Internal Migration and Long-term Development Strategy of China) (Wuhan: Wuhan Chubanshe, 1994).

17. Qiming Liu and Kam Wing Chan, "Rural-urban Migration Process in China: Job Search, Wage Determinants and Occupational Attainment," *Seattle Population Research Center Working Paper,* no. 99–16 (1999).

18. Dorothy Solinger, *Contesting Citizenship in Urban China* (Berkeley: University of California Press, 1999).

19. Ibid.

20. Chan, "Internal Migration in China."

21. National Population Sample Survey Office (NPSSO), *1995 quanguo 1% renkou chouyang diaocha ziliao* (Data on 1995 National 1 Percent Population Sample Survey) (Beijing: Zhongguo Tongji Chubanshe, 1997).

22. Kam Wing Chan, Ta Liu, and Yunyan Yang, "*Hukou* and Non-*hukou* Migration: Comparisons and Contrasts," *International Journal of Population Geography* 5, no. 6 (1999): 425–448.

23. Except for return migratory streams such as those coming out of Xinjiang and Heilongjiang.

24. See also Jinghong Ding, "Zhongguo renkou shengji qingyide yuanyin bieliuchang tezheng tanxi" (An Analysis of Inter-Provincial Migratory Streams in China by Reason), *Renkou yanjiu* (Population Research) 18, no.1 (1994): 14–21.

25. Cai Fang, "Spatial Patterns of Migration under China's Reform Period," *Asian and Pacific Migration Journal* 8, no. 3 (1998): 313–327.

26. W.A. Lewis, "Economic Development with Unlimited Supplies of Labour," *The Manchester School of Economic and Social Studies* (May 1954): 131–191.

27. Min Zhao, "A Study of Outside Labor in Some Enterprises in Shanghai," *Zhongguo renkou kexue* (Chinese Population Science), no. 3 (1995).

28. Mengbai Li and Yin Hu, *Liudong renkou dui dachengshi fazhande yingxiang ji duice* (Impact of the Floating Population on the Development of Large Cities and Recommended Policy) (Beijing: Jingji Ribao Chubanshe, 1991).

29. *SingTao Daily,* July 2, 1995, A5.

30. Dorothy Solinger, "The Floating Population in the Cities: Chances for Assimilation?" in Deborah Davis et al., eds., *Urban Spaces: Autonomy and Community in Contemporary China* (Cambridge: Woodrow Wilson Center Press and Cambridge University Press, 1995), 113–139; Christopher Smith, "Migration as an Agent of Change in Contemporary China," *Chinese Environment and Development* 7, no.1 and 2 (1996): 14–55; Shukai Zhao, "Delinquent Behaviours and Public Management," in Hong Ma and Mengkui Wang, eds., *Zhongguo fazhan yanyiu 2000* (Development Studies in China, 2000) (Beijing: Zhongguo Fazhan Chubanshe, 2000), 467–479.

31. A study in Guangzhou, a major city with a high crime rate, shows that even if all

the criminals arrested were assumed to be rural migrant labor, this number would represent merely 2.5 percent of the total size of the rural migrant labor in the city. See Xiaomin Liu, "On the Flows of Peasant Labor to Guangdong," *Shehui yanjiu* (Sociological Studies), no. 4 (1995).

32. Solinger, *Contesting Citizenship in Urban China.*

33. Ibid.

34. Linda Wong, "China's Urban Migrants: The Public Policy Challenge," *Pacific Affairs* 67, no. 3 (1994): 335–356.

35. Jun Yang and Jinhai Wang, "Moving to a More Organized Wave of Peasant Workers," *Gongren ribao* (Workers Daily), January 25, 1995.

36. According to Agence France-Presse, officials expected 1.5 billion trips to be made during the Lunar New Year interlude (see *South China Morning Post,* Internet edition, February 3, 1999).

37. James Irwin, "China's Migrant Children Fall Through the Cracks," *The UNESCO Courier,* September 2000, 13–14.

38. *SingTao Daily,* July 25, 1998, A5.

39. This figure (¥2,800) is very close to the average annual remittance of Sichuan rural migrant workers in 1997 (*SingTao Daily,* January 29, 1998, A7). Sichuan's migrant workers are arguably the most "representative" nationally, given their size and geographical distribution. It is estimated that elsewhere in Dongguan, the average annual remittance by migrant workers reached ¥7,800 in 1998 (*SingTao Daily,* January 14, 1999, A7). Of course, Dongguan is one of the areas with the highest average incomes for migrant workers partly because it includes a sizable entertainment sector (night clubs) staffed by migrant women.

40. State Statistical Bureau, *Zhongguo tongji nianjian 1998* (Statistical Yearbook of China 1998) (Beijing: Zhongguo Tongji Chubanshe, 1998), p. 55.

41. Anhui Province Policy Analysis Office, "On Survey of Rural Labor Outflows and Policy Recommendations," *Zhongguo nongcun jingji* (Chinese Rural Economy), no.1 (1994): 53–57. State Statistical Bureau, *Zhongguo tongji nianjian 1995* (Statistical Yearbook of China 1995) (Beijing: Zhongguo Tongji Chubanshe, 1995).

42. Xiaoguang Wang, "Changes in Rural Economic Structure and Model Options," *Nongye jingji wenti* (Agricultural Economies and Problems), no. 7 (1994).

43. Anhui Province Policy Analysis Office, "On Survey of Rural Labor Outflows and Policy Recommendations."

44. Dewen Qin, "Survey and Reconsideration of Return Flows of Rural Labor in Fuyang Prefecture," *Zhongguo nongcun jingji* (Chinese Rural Economy), no. 4 (1994): 11–14.

45. Zhongdong Ma, "Urban Labor-force Experience as a Determinant of Rural Occupation Change: Evidence from Recent Urban-rural Return Migration in China," *Environment and Planning A* 33 (2001): 237–255.

46. Xiaohui Zhang et al., "1994: Nongcun laodongli kuaquyude shezheng miaoshu" (1994: An Empirical Description of the Inter-Regional Flows of Rural Labor), *Zhanlüe yu guanli* (Strategy and Management), no. 6 (1995): 26–34.

47. Project Group, "Labor Transfer and Population Migration in Hunan," *Shehuixue* (Sociological Studies), no. 3 (1995): 71–82.

48. Ministry of Agriculture Project Group, "Empirical Studies of the Impact of Rural Labor Outflows on Agriculture," *Zhongguo nongcun jingji* (Chinese Rural Economy), no. 8 (1996): 12–18.

49. See *Far Eastern Economic Review,* November 16, 1995, 88–96.

50. World Bank, *China: Strategies for Reducing Poverty in the 1990s* (Washington, D.C.: World Bank, 1992).

51. Maolin Zhang and Zhiliang Zhang, "A Comprehensive Evaluation of the Resettlement Process in Poverty Alleviation," *Zhongguo renkou kexue* (Chinese Population Science), no. 5 (1995): 26–34. World Bank, *China: Strategies for Reducing Poverty in the 1990s*.

52. Shukai Zhao, "Confronting Challenges of Chinese Farmers," paper presented at University of Washington, Seattle, October 11, 2001.

53. Computed from State Statistical Bureau. *Zhongguo tongji nianjian 1995*, p. 330.

54. Estimate by Lanrui Feng cited by Zhiyuan Cui, "Economic Reform and the Political System," paper presented at Jackson School of International Studies, University of Washington, Seattle, February 10, 2000.

55. Zhao, "Confronting Challenges of Chinese Farmers."

56. Du Ying et al., "Analysis of Demand of Employment of Rural Labor Force in China in the Early 21st Century," paper presented at the Seminar on Rural Employment Promotion Policy, Beijing, January 2000.

57. Zhao, "The Mobility of Rural Migrants: New Stage and New Issues."

58. This refers to the balance of the number of new entrants and the number of those leaving (mostly old workers) the labor force in the rural sector.

59. Du et al., "Analysis of Demand of Employment of Rural Labor Force in China in the Early 21st Century."

60. The real rate of urban unemployment is estimated by Angang Hu to have been at 8 percent in 1999 (cited in Cui, "Economic Reform and the Political System").

61. Du et al., "Analysis of Demand of Employment of Rural Labor Force in China in the Early 21st Century."

62. Du et al. estimate that this may be in the range of about 7 to 8 million jobs a year. Ibid.

63. Dening Cheng and Zhang Deng, "The Road to Agglomeration in Urban Centers for Township Enterprises is a Rocky One" (in Chinese), *China Reform*, no.8 (1998): 16–18.

64. Jianjing Liu, "Employment and Mobility of Rural Labor Force in China," paper presented at the Seminar on Rural Employment Promotion Policy, Beijing, January 2000.

65. See State Council's White Paper, *Poverty Alleviation and Development in Rural China*, reported in *SingTao Daily*, October 15, 2001, A9.

66. Gary Jefferson and Thomas Rawski, "Unemployment, Underemployment, and Employment Policy in China's Cities," *Modern China* 18, no. 1 (1992): 42–71.

67. For some international experience, see John Knight and R.H. Sabot, "From Migrants to Proletarians: Employment Experience, Mobility and Wages in Tanzania," *Oxford Bulletin of Economics and Statistics* 44, no. 3 (1982): 199–226.

68. See *SingTao Daily*, August 30, 2001, A7. Also Chaolin Gu and Kam Wing Chan, "Gradually Opening the *Hukou* System in Large Cities," *Chengshi fazhan yanjiu* (Urban Development Studies) 8, no. 6 (2002): 25–33.

69. See Gu and Chan, "Gradually Opening the *Hukou* System in Large Cities," for a discussion on "blue-stamp" *hukou*.

6

Social Transformations, Civil Society, and Taiwanese Business in Fujian

Hsin-Huang Michael Hsiao

Since 1978, under the "Deng Doctrine" of "Four Modernizations," market forces have been brought back into socialist China, with an open-door policy to attract foreign investments. As a result, coastal China entered a new development era in the 1980s, and Fujian has been a part of this unfolding drama ever since.

Over the past twenty years, Fujian Province under the open-door policy has registered an impressive record of economic growth in comparison with other inland provinces. From 1980 to 1999, Fujian's agricultural, forestry, and fishery products increased from 4.5 to 101.1 billion yuan; industrial products grew even greater, from 8.2 to 478.8 billion yuan; and the total electricity generated increased from 4.95 to 35.6 billion megawatt hours. On the other hand, the residents' year-end savings deposits also jumped from 1.2 to 173.9 billion yuan while the total retail value of consumer goods registered more than a thirtyfold increase, from 4.55 to 124.6 billion yuan.

Fujian's development has several distinctive characteristics. First, Fujian has experienced slow growth in comparison with Guangdong. The macroeconomic statistics clearly show that Fujian's rapid growth began in the late 1980s and early 1990s. In other words, Fujian has been a latecomer in the dynamic southern Chinese growth triangle by taking a catch-up strategy for industrialization.

Second, such a catch-up industrialization strategy finally boosted Fujian's industrial output per capita to exceed that of the national average in 1992. In the mid-1990s, this statistic had grown to 1.5 times the national average. Fujian's success can be marked by its industrialization efforts since the 1990s, as its total industrial output grew nine times between the period of 1990 and

1999 while nonagricultural output grew more than four times in the same period. The changes in the relative importance of different types of enterprises also reflect the major forces behind Fujian's industrialization in recent years. It appears that the township enterprises, backed by local authorities and operated jointly by the emerging private and the joint-venture businesses have become the most dynamic sector, while the state enterprises have been losing ground over the years.

Third, Fujian's industrial development since the 1990s has moved significantly toward an extroversion of the economic structure in which imports and exports have greatly expanded. In 1988, the ratio of export value to gross national product (GNP) in Fujian had already exceeded the national average, and in 1994 the ratio was 41 percent for Fujian and only 22.4 percent for the nation. Between 1994 and 1998, the cumulative export value was US$83.5 billion, an average increase of 14.3 percent. In 1998, Fujian ranked the top fifth export province of the nation. The statistics in 1995 demonstrated that Fujian outperformed the national average with 35.6 percent to 21.7 percent, respectively. The major items of Fujian's exports are light industrial goods and textiles.

Finally, accompanying the active exports was the increasing foreign investment. Direct investments into Fujian from abroad in 1980 were about US$3.6 million; in 1990, 1995, and 1999, the FDI amounts were US$117 million, US$4.02 billion, and US$4.02 billion, respectively. From the period 1979 through 1999 as a whole, a total of more than US$22 billion foreign investment was utilized, and that accounted for more than 50 percent of Fujian's overall fixed asset investment in the same period.[1]

Among the foreign investors, ethnic Chinese businesses outside China have always played a very important role. For example, in the early 1980s, ethnic Chinese investors from Southeast Asia (Philippines, Thailand, Malaysia, Singapore, and Indonesia) were the major sources of foreign capital in Fujian. Singapore developed close economic and investment ties with Fujian after Lee Kuan Yew's visit to Fujian in 1980. Many major Southeast Asian Chinese business groups with Fujian origins, such as Tan Yu and Lucio C. Tan of the Philippines, Liem Sioe Liong (Sudono Salim) of Indonesia, and Robert Kuok of Malaysia, have made substantial investments in Fujian since the 1980s.

But, since the mid-1980s, investments from Hong Kong, Macau, and Taiwan began to take the lead. Taiwan's capital has been registered under Hong Kong/Macau over the years, but Taiwan investment to Fujian has been even greater than that from Hong Kong and Macau. From 1985 through 1995, among all foreign direct investments, Taiwan, Hong Kong, and Macau capital has always ranked at the top, followed by the United States and Europe,

Southeast Asia, and Japan. The investments from Southeast Asia declined significantly over the whole period, from 45.7 percent in 1980, dropping to only 13.1 percent in 1985, to merely 1.6 percent in 1990. Yet, later, investments increased to 13.9 percent in 1995, but then dropped to 7.8 percent in 1999. Japanese investment also followed a similar declining trend, with its ratio dropping from 18.6 percent in 1980 to 12.5 percent in 1985 and then to around 2 percent in the first half of the 1990s.

In contrast, direct investments from the United States and Europe increased significantly over the past twenty years. They accounted for only 3.1 percent in 1980, but increased to 14.0 percent in 1985. They then jumped to 40.2 percent and 32.9 percent in 1990 and 1995, respectively. Similarly, foreign investments from Taiwan, Hong Kong, and Macau increased substantially, and they surpassed other origins of foreign capital. Although they contributed 32.6 percent of Fujian's total foreign investment in 1980, their contribution increased to 60.4 percent in 1985, 56.1 percent in 1990, 50.7 percent in 1995, and 60.6 percent in 1999. Overall, it can be said that Fujian's economic development was made possible largely because of the ethnic Chinese capital from Southeast Asia, Hong Kong, Macau, and Taiwan since the 1980s.

Ethnic Chinese and Taiwanese Capital in Fujian's Economic Reform

Like Guangdong, Fujian has long been one of the major sources of Chinese emigrants. It is estimated that there are about 8 million Chinese with Fujian origins who reside outside of Fujian (exclusive of Taiwan), and 80 percent of these Fujianese descendants are currently in Southeast Asia. Though these former Fujian emigrants have been naturalized to become citizens in the Southeast Asian countries, they have kept close social and economic ties with their hometowns in Fujian. The overseas connection has not only provided economic remittances to Fujian, but also given Fujian an opportunity to develop external linkages to the outside world. From 1950 to the outbreak of the Cultural Revolution, overseas Fujian Chinese consistently invested in Fujian, amounting to an estimated 80 million yuan of investment. However, after the outbreak of the Cultural Revolution in 1966, investment from Fujian emigrants was terminated for twelve years. It was only in 1978 when China began its open-door policy that this overseas connection was resumed.

The Fujian provincial government took advantage of this policy change and set up a Fujian investment company in 1979 to attract foreign investment. In 1980 Min-Hua Inc. (Overseas Fujian Chinese Company) began its practice in Hong Kong, with an aim to attract those overseas Fujian businessmen to invest in Fujian. The contributions made by Fujian Chinese businesses in Southeast Asia, Hong Kong, and Macau to Fujian's economic development since the 1980s can be demonstrated in the following ways.

Through personal and kin connections, many overseas businessmen have helped develop the growth of village-township enterprises (VTEs) since the early 1980s. The VTEs were transformed from the people's commune and production brigade enterprises during the pre-reform era through privatization and subcontraction mechanisms. The investment from overseas Fujian-origin businesses was timely and critical to meet the need for capital formation in those emerging VTEs in Fujian in the 1980s. In addition to capital contributions, the overseas Fujian Chinese businesses also donated necessary production equipment to Fujian's VTEs. By 1991, 6,000 sets of small-scale production facilities (each valued below 100 thousand yuan) had been received from abroad. In agricultural businesses alone, more than 700 kinds of new products were introduced into Fujian.

Moreover, the overseas Fujian Chinese have invested a significant amount in the various forms of enterprises (the so-called san-zi enterprises: sole ownership, joint venture, and technical cooperation) and made direct contributions to Fujian's industrial development. For example, in Shishi of southern Fujian, 80 percent of the families had overseas relatives. As a result, although Shishi had a population of less than 100 thousand in 1992, there were 3,800 VTEs, 440 san-zi enterprises, more than 200 private-owned businesses, and 7,000 shops of various sizes.[2]

The total industrial output of the san-zi enterprises has increased rapidly since the 1990s, from 10.01 billion yuan in 1990 to 32.85 billion yuan in 1993 and to 85.99 billion yuan in 1996, which accounted for 18.48 percent, 24.13 percent, and 31.63 percent of Fujian's overall industrial output in those three respective years. In other words, enterprises with overseas capital produced more industrial output value than state-owned enterprises and self-employed business units in 1996. Furthermore, in 1996, almost 30 percent of Fujian's taxes was generated from those foreign-invested enterprises, greater than that from those collective-owned enterprises.[3] By the end of 1999, there was a total of 17,965 registered foreign-invested businesses in Fujian, of which 11,184 (62.3 percent) were solely owned by foreign capital.[4]

Overseas capital further opened the previously closed Fujian economy to the world market. Through the inflow of overseas capital and the setting up of various enterprises with external investment, Fujian was incorporated into the global division of labor with the timely use of its abundant labor surplus and cheap labor costs. Hence, the labor intensive manufacturing sector of the world economy soon found a new production base in Fujian, and Fujian also found economic opportunities in the global capitalist system.

The expanding outward-looking economy also accelerated the development of the other inward-looking economies in Fujian. After the 1990s, Xiamen, Quanzhou, Zhangzhou, and Fuzhou became the four cities in Fujian that had a large concentration of foreign capital. Fujian also witnessed the growth of many prosperous towns in areas away from the coast and not necessarily engaged in the export economy. One type was the induced suburban development where surrounding towns and villages of those major cities were given the opportunity to grow commercially and fulfill the needs of expanding urban consumption. The other type was the so-called local resource development centers, where local natural resources were finally utilized for actual production, with the help of external investment. The examples for the former are Taisan near Fuzhou, Nanping near Quanzhou, and Zhisan near Zhangzhou. The examples for the latter are Gutian (cement production) and Chizau (ceramic making).

Furthermore, overseas Chinese investment at the early stage of the economic reform functioned as a model to attract more ethnic Chinese business from Southeast Asia, Hong Kong, and even Taiwan to enter Fujian. It is important to note that overseas Chinese investors showed many Taiwanese businessmen the best way to invest in Fujian, thus helping the Taiwanese businessmen to overcome their fear of the long-lasting political tension between Taiwan and China. Thereafter, Taiwanese businessmen were inspired to invest in Fujian despite the KMT state's prohibition policy at that time. The early move of overseas Chinese investment also served as a mediator linking Taiwan capital with the so-called regional Chinese business network in a joint effort to invest in Fujian. Therefore, in the mid-1980s, it was not easy to make a distinction among capital from Taiwan, Hong Kong, or overseas Chinese originating from Southeast Asia or North America.

As early as 1981, the Fujian provincial government begun to launch plans to attract Taiwan capital and investment. In October of that year, Fujian's Federation of Industry and Commerce (Gongshanglian) issued an invitation letter to many business leaders of Taiwan to come to Fujian for business cooperation talks. The Aviation Bureau and the Civil Aviation Bureau also began preparations for possible direct air transport in 1981. But, the response from Taiwan business circles was not enthusiastic at all at the beginning. Lack of trust and great suspicion toward China and the fear of being prosecuted by Taiwan's government were the reasons behind the Taiwanese businessmen's hesitation. The first Taiwanese direct investment case finally took place in 1983, according to Fujian's official record. Up to 1987, a total of fifty-eight cases were registered with the sum of US$40 million, with the majority registered under the names of Hong Kong companies or foreign companies.

The year 1987 marked the beginning of the rapid entry of Taiwanese businesses into Fujian. In July, the Taiwan authorities relaxed control over foreign currency transfers; in November, home visits for mainlanders in Taiwan were allowed, leading to an acceleration of a new wave of civilian contacts with China. With these new policies, many businessmen from Taiwan went to Fujian to explore business opportunities under the guise of visiting relatives, attending family reunions, or tourism. The "mainland investment fever" was then made public. The most noticeable example was the Fujian business exploration tour organized by a sizable group of Taiwanese shoe-manufacturing businessmen in 1989. After that visit, Taiwan's shoe-making industry was relocated to Fujian on a massive scale. With the influx of Taiwanese investment in the shoe industry, Fujian became the shoe empire of Asia within a very short time. According to 1992 data, out of Fujian's top VTEs, eight were in the shoe-making business. The output of shoe production jumped to 320 million pairs in 1994 from 33 million pairs in 1990, and the export value of sport shoes alone rapidly increased to US$100 million in 1993 from US$3.63 million in 1989.

Similarly, the expansion and growth of the garment, umbrella, and electric appliance industries were also very impressive due to the inflow of Taiwan capital and plant transplantation. Fujian's ratio of export value to national GNP exceeded the national average for the first time since 1988; and that could be attributed to the crucial Taiwan factor. In short, it was the Taiwan factor that further successfully transformed Fujian's economic structure into an outward-looking economy.

The speed of the increase of Taiwanese investment in Fujian was very impressive. Between 1988 and 1989, 400 Taiwanese companies were approved to invest in Fujian with a total investment of US$680 million. There were another 700 businesses from Taiwan that invested US$870 million in 1990 and 1991. In the succeeding years, the growth of Taiwan investment in Fujian was even more substantial. In 1993 alone, 1,010 Taiwan-capital–financed businesses were established, investing more than US$1.5 billion. By 1995, 4,427 Taiwanese enterprises operated in Fujian, with a total approved investment of over US$6.8 billion. In an account by Fujian bankers and economic experts in July 1997, Fujian was reported to have attracted more than 4,900 Taiwanese enterprises, with the total realized investment exceeding US$6.9 billion. Between 1997 and 2000, Taiwanese investment added another US$1 billion. Moreover, Taiwan capital has greatly diversified, ranging from small-scale, labor-intensive manufacturing to capital-intensive, heavy, and high-tech industries. Arguably, Taiwan capital further transformed and upgraded Fujian's industrial structure and its course of development. According to a Fujian government official's private statement in 2001, Taiwan is a necessary linkage for Fujian to develop into China's southeastern regional center.[5]

What is striking about the rapid inflow of Taiwan capital into Fujian are the dense networks among Taiwanese entrepreneurs in their investment pattern. One of the consequences has been the spatial concentration of Taiwanese investment, starting with one or a few companies that apply for permission to develop land and set up plants and then attract chains of other businesses to move in through personal connections or networks. Therefore, the concentration of businesses of the same sector can be found in one locality.

The other significant characteristic of Taiwan business in Fujian has been the diversification of investment and the shift from manufacturing to high-tech industries. For example, Formosa Plastics once intended to invest in a large-scale oil refinery plant in the Hai-chan Development Area near Xiamen. Although the plan was later stopped by Taiwan's authorities, Formosa Plastics still intended to invest in a power plant in Zhangzhou. A high-tech industrial park near Fuzhou was developed by a Taiwanese personal-computer company and its subsidiaries. Taiwan's Zhonghua Motor Company also established a joint venture, Dong-Nan Motor Co., with China's Fuzhou Motor Co., a state-owned enterprise in the mid-1990s. Also, a new automobile industrial zone was set up by Zhonghua Motor Co. and twenty-seven other Taiwanese automobile parts plants.

Taiwanese businesses also began to invest in real estate and tourism in Fujian in the 1990s. The Meizhou Recreational Economic Area of Putian in 1991 and Fuzhou's Olympic City and Wuyishan Recreational Area in 1993 are examples. In addition to investing in real estate development projects in Fujian, Taiwanese enterprises also participated in local government-sponsored urban renewal construction projects, and one-third of Fuzhou's renewal projects were contracted to Taiwanese firms.

Like Guangdong, Fujian's industrial development has a lot to do with the direct foreign investment, of which Taiwan capital has played a critical role. In 1992, among the top five provinces and cities with the greatest inflow of foreign investment, Fujian ranked number two (only after Guangdong) in terms of average value of foreign investment per capita. The figures were US$45.7 and $56.7 per capita, respectively. Since 1995, due to the rise of Shanghai, Fujian's foreign investment value per capita dropped to number three with Guangdong as number two, though its foreign investment per capita had, in fact, increased three times at US$124.4. Even official Fujian documents have openly stated that due to the use of foreign capital and its job creating effect, Fujian's per capita income in the national ranking had risen to number six in 2000, from twenty-second in 1980.

Fujian's Social Transformation

Since 1978, South China has also experienced unprecedented changes brought about by the economic reforms. Of course, Fujian is no exception, especially considering its location in the coastal development area and the impressive industrial changes contributed by Taiwan businesses. Three aspects of social transformation in Fujian are most noticeable.

The first is the change from single-dimensional vertical integration to pluralistic horizontal integration affecting the structuring of society. Before 1978, China's society was structured by a top-down centralized chain of command from the party hierarchy to each *danwei* (work unit) and down to the family and the individual. The *danwei* was the only intermediary organization between the state and the individual. Individuals were highly dependent on the *danwei* they belonged to, and the *danwei* was totally subordinated to the party-state. The social fabric was completely dominated by the above vertical and hierarchical organizational forces, and no horizontal linkages were allowed among individuals, families, or *danwei*.

What has emerged after the 1980s is a new kind of *danwei* that has no direct command–obedience relations with the party-state hierarchy, such as the foreign capital–invested *san-zi* enterprises, the larger private businesses (*siying qiye*), and the smaller self-employed business operators (*getihu*). A significant result has been the rise of a new category of individuals who have little direct power relations with the old *danwei,* such as those private business owners, employers, operators, and the employees and labor working for foreign and private enterprises.

By 1996, about 760,000 individuals were employed in those *san-zi* enterprises, accounting for 21.6 percent of Fujian's total employees and 5 percent of the total working individuals. Also, there were 686,000 self-employed business operators accounting for 4.5 percent of Fujian's total working population. In other words, in late 1990s, about 1.5 million working individuals (less than 10 percent) in Fujian were currently not controlled by the old *danwei*. By 2000, more than one-fourth of Fujian employment was created by foreign investment. The relative autonomy enjoyed by the above mentioned new organizations and individuals was much greater than before.

The pluralistic organizations have also extended the horizon of the "intermediary" structures of Fujian society between the party-state and the families and individuals. What further signifies the social transformation taking place in Fujian and many other coastal provinces is the rise of many new functional specific associations (*xiehui*) constituted of those increasingly "autonomous" social organizations or individuals. They include the Self-Employed Laborers Association (Geti laodongzhe xiehui), the Private Enterprises Association (Siying qiye xiehui), the Enterprise Owners Civic Associations (Qiyejia gonghui), and the Local Federations of Industry and Commerce (Gongshanglian). All these have expanded horizontal linkages and alliances among different societal units and individuals.[6] Overall, the expansion of the intermediary structures has relaxed the commanding control of the party-state and even challenged for the first time the base of tight vertical integration.

The second aspect of social transformation is found in the shift of the societal character of Fujian from relative isolation to integration with the outside world under the globalization process. Such globalization was started by the economic forces of foreign investment, and then it penetrated many other social and cultural realms in Fujian society. The gap between Fujian and the rest of the world is gradually narrowing. Among the sources of foreign capital, Taiwan and Hong Kong direct investment, accompanied by entrepreneurial and managerial know-how, has played an accelerating role in bringing about fundamental social and cultural changes.

The third transformation is a combination of the above two aspects which awaits closer observation, that is, the consequential political change from authoritarianism to democracy. The rise of more and more autonomous horizontal intermediary social groups and organizations has induced the economic growth and the emerging open character of a society in closer contact with the outside world under global democratization. It is only natural to foresee a possible transformation in Fujian's political life. Such social changes should then raise the critical issue, that is, to what extent state-society relations have fundamentally changed and whether or not civil society exists in today's Fujian.

The preliminary assessments of many observers have suggested that, in comparison with two other Chinese societies like Taiwan and Hong Kong, a free and autonomous civil society as such does not exist in today's Fujian. But it does not mean that the conditions for creating an array of more or less autonomous civil society institutions are completely absent in Fujian. The economic reforms have undoubtedly resulted in the creation of a new market system and the strengthening of many new and semi-autonomous social groups and institutions under less pervasive state influence. It may not be unsound to assert that some conditions for the making of civil society institutions in Fujian have emerged in a nascent form. The prospective agents for making such nascent civil society possible are the opportunities for free assembly of horizontal associations among emerging private enterprises, the intellectuals, and the students.

In short, macroeconomic reform policies since the 1980s have already provided political and economic space for the nascent civil society elements in Fujian to develop and to expand. The increasingly pluralistic ideas and the mushrooming of different forms of autonomous and semi-autonomous grassroots social and economic groups in Fujian's various prosperous cities and townships may be capable of providing the basis for the development of many regional-sector–based civil society forces. And such nascent civil society formation in Fujian has, in one way or another, a lot to do with the capital globalization forces that have directly accelerated Fujian's economic reform.

However, one should be aware of the fact that the civil society (or the social forces) phenomenon is still very much in a weak and even fragile position. Its political future is still heavily dependent on the tolerance of the Beijing regime. Its institutionalization with some legal protection also remains problematic. However, as long as the open-door reforms are continued and the cleavages between the political center and economic regions and local governance widen, the prospective civil society forces are likely to strengthen and consolidate in various selected regions and localities such as Fujian.[7]

The Nascent Civil Society in Fujian

Fujian is thus far qualified to be a rapidly developing and prosperous province located at China's gateway to the outside world. The following preliminary assessments of the potential for developing a nascent civil society in Fujian focus on two related aspects. First, the relative autonomy of two prospective civil society constituents, that is, private business and the intellectuals, and their relations with the state, will be examined. The underlying assumption is that emerging horizontal social groups like private businesses and their associations and the intellectuals are in a good position to develop into civil social forces vis-à-vis the state. The limited role of Taiwanese capital in its relations with the above two possible civil society constituents also will be examined.

Second, two other related contexts in which the development of civil society is shaped, that is, the rising autonomy of local government vis-à-vis the central government and the increasing unequal development and class conflicts, will be considered. The issue to be examined is that, under the above specific contexts, the possible development of Fujian's civil society will inevitably be affected. Similarly, the extent to which Taiwan capital has contributed to the above two aspects of the emerging social and political change will then be assessed.

Private Business and the Emergence of Civil Society

One of the most noticeable structural changes in China after eighteen years of economic reform has been the rebirth of the "private" business sector. In

1953, right after the communist takeover, there were still 8.98 million employees in the private sector. However, by 1956, the private business sector was almost eliminated, as private sector employment dropped to only 160,000 and the private merchants and business class became the targets of severe attacks during various mass movements.

Since 1980, the open-door economic policy has made the reemergence of private businesses inevitable, making them the primary force behind China's capitalist transformation. If we define a small self-employed business operator (*getihu*) as a business unit hiring seven or less workers and define a larger private business (*siying qiye*) as a business unit hiring more than seven employees, then they, together with joint-venture businesses (*sanzi qiye*), constitute China's current private sector and are responsible for the increasing industrial output as a percentage of the overall total national product. It was 0.5 percent in 1980, 3.1 percent in 1985, and quickly increased to 10 percent in 1990. The importance of private business in Fujian's economy is even greater. The relative contribution of the private sector to Fujian's overall industrial output since 1980 has been very impressive. It contributed only 0.03 percent in 1980. But it increased to 8.1 percent in 1985, 24.9 percent in 1990, and to more than 50 percent in 1995. If we consider the nonstate sector as a whole (that includes the township and village enterprises), then the private and semi-private business sector's contribution to Fujian's industrial product in 1995 could be as high as 83 percent.

Compared to China's overall level, Fujian is undoubtedly one of the few provinces where private business has been playing a vital role under economic and societal changes. The reemergence of private business in Fujian in a sense indicates one significant transformation of Fujian's social structure, that is, the rise of new classes that are not directly dominated by the socialist state. Two such new classes are in formation, the working class in the private business sector and the small and large private business owners. For these two emerging classes, the business owner class is of particular significance to the possible formation of Fujian's civil society. How to identify those mushrooming private business owners in class terms is still not an easy task. However, these newly emergent private business owners, who are both the result and the movers of the state's changing economic policies, adhere to some class traits similar to those of the middle class in the enterprise sector as characterized in the middle-class literature.

First, they are no longer under the "absolute" economic and political control and command of the communist state in Beijing. They do enjoy a relative autonomy provided by the rise of market forces since China adopted the market economy for its national development path in the 1980s. Second, they have begun to think of their own "class interests" by making demands on and negotiating with different layers of the state bureaucracy and even have succeeded in opening new political channels for voicing their interests. The various business associations at both national and local levels have been considered to be legitimate bodies in the eyes of state officials. The private businessmen and their representatives do have access to different levels of the policy-making process. The Chinese state has publicly stated that it intends to use those business associations as "bridges" between state and society. In short, the significance of the rise of the private businessmen and their respective associations should not be underestimated in any serious assessment of the making of civil society in China.

Some Chinese and foreign observers have contended that the failure of the 1989 pro-democracy student movement was largely due to the lack of backup from the weak private business sector and the inadequate influence of the middle class in China.[8] The democratic role of the rising business class in China's future course of political change has been explicitly suggested. Though the political role of the rising business class, as such, is not the immediate concern here, the social and political inclination of the private businessmen in relation to China's current political development deserves careful attention and clarification. In the midst of the pro-democracy movement event in 1989, Wank interviewed Xiamen businessmen as to how they viewed the students' protests in Beijing and at Xiamen University. To Wank's surprise, most of his business respondents revealed uneasiness toward the student movement. Only two of the twenty-nine entrepreneurs with whom he spoke admitted having taken part in some kind of supportive actions. Their common reaction to the student movement was that the students demanded too much and too quickly, and that they supported political changes under an orderly reform (*gaige*) rather than those political changes imposed by popular pressures in a potentially chaotic transformation (*gaizao*). They worried that the student protests would result in a state crackdown that would disrupt their bureaucratic connections that ensured their protection and profits.

This is particularly true for those entrepreneurs owning larger private firms. They even suspected the anti-corruption and anti-nepotism platform advocated by the student activists. They argued that anti-corruption measures would not in the end affect the largest transgressors and the entrepreneurial offspring of the high-level power elite, but they could fall hardest on businessmen at the local levels like themselves who lacked high-level patrons to shield them. The Xiamen businesspeople's conservative political attitudes toward the pro-democracy movement led by students cautions that the rising middle class in Fujian may not be the ideal agent for China's future democratic reform and for the forging of a viable social force vis-à-vis state power.

The assertion of Xiamen's business political mentality made by Wank has its insight.[9] But the conservatism expressed by the entrepreneurs at the time of political chaos and uncertainty can also be interpreted as an act of self-protection and a common behavioral pattern for any business to play it safe and not directly express political views in public. The inner motivation behind the overt expressed conservatism should be considered as well, since private business was still at its formative phase. It would be unrealistic to expect any openly expressed political activism or radicalism from the infant business class in China. That might also explain why in the same study Wank found that the Xiamen entrepreneurs showed a weak attachment to the Civic Association of Private Industry and Commerce (Xiamen shi siying gongshang gonghui) and its political fate. The real issue lies in the changing and uncertain business and state (bureaucratic power) relations. The alliance of the private business class with the state is very much viewed as necessary to protect its existence and even to promote its collective interests.

The alliance of the new business class with the local state and bureaucratic power can be seen as a pragmatic political tactic of survival and self-protection, considering the fact that in the past, the state bureaucracy had completely controlled the economy. The autonomous space that private business has enjoyed for its further development was "given" and "handed down" from the state, and private business must recognize its political limit at the present. The political survival pragmatism of business cannot be simply dismissed all together. In other words, the private business class in Fujian cannot afford to adopt a "detachment" or "avoidance" approach in dealing with the state bureaucracy and for its development, the only viable approach is to develop an "alliance" with the state, especially with the local state. Whether such a strategy of mutual penetration and mutual support is a conscious collusion between private business and the state as termed by Solinger,[10] or merely a reflection of "communist neo-authoritarianism" as pointed out by Walder,[11] remains to be examined. But it is true that the expansion of private businesses and the market economy and their relative autonomy cannot be taken too far to maintain that they have already empowered civil society at the expense of the state or as a definite sign of the force of institutionalized civil society.[12]

Another line of analyzing the rise of private businesses and the associations which represent them is related to the emergence of a new kind of "corporatism." The state has recognized the new business class as a social force and employed institutional arrangements to bring about new business associations under the rubric of corporatism, so the state will not quickly lose control over the business class. The essence of such a corporatist structure is that the state still holds the power to rule and to approve which interest associations are to be established. From time to time, tension occurs between the state bureaucracy and the business associations when the latter move one step further to "avoid" the state's oversight. Indeed, the All-China Federation of Industry and Commerce has taken a deliberate strategy to establish other "independent" associations under its umbrella in order to avoid direct intervention from the state.

In Fujian and Guangdong, the Federation has established local chambers of commerce (*shang hui*) as a way to secure greater independence from the central and local state for themselves and for their constituency.[13] The state is not unaware of the intention behind the move made by the business class. And when a business association like the Federation has moved too far from the state's oversight, the state will put a brake on the formation of new local associations. The corporatist rule spells out that only one association can be recognized as representing a given social sector in one administrative unit, a common practice that Taiwan experienced under its past authoritarian rule. That is exactly what Wank discovered in Xiamen; when the Federation's local Chambers of Commerce further sponsored the founding of a new local association for private entrepreneurs, the Xiamen Civic Association of Private Industry and Commerce (Siying gongshang gonghui), the city bureaucracy moved to suppress the Civic Association. The forming of the new association for Xiamen's private entrepreneurs was viewed as a direct challenge to the City Bureau of Industry and Commerce since the Bureau has already established a Self-Employed Laborers' Association (Geti laodongzhe xiehui) under its supervision. This suppression by the Xiamen city bureaucracy illustrates aptly the kind of tension that existed between the business class and the state.

However, the story does not end with the state suppression. The responding moves made by the Xiamen Chamber of Commerce were of more significance to the current assessment of the business class as a potential strategic base for developing autonomous civil society institutions in Fujian. After a decision from the central state supporting the city bureau to cease the operation of the new Civic Association, the Xiamen Chamber of Commerce then moved to accept private firms as its constituency into various new sector-specific trade associations (*tongye hui*) also organized by the local chambers. What has happened is that both the state and the private business class and its civil society associations have actively engaged in the inevitable tension management under the emerging "new corporatism."

On the one hand, the state uses the corporatist structures for monitoring the private business class by establishing certain designated business associations, such as the above-mentioned Self-Employed Laborers' Association, under its tutelage. As Nevitt also found in Tianjin, this local state bureaucracy—

backed small entrepreneurs' association has been firmly under the control of the local state. It is more interested in controlling the small business class than in pursuing its economic or political interests.[14]

On the other hand, this new "corporatist mode" also has provided more open social and political space for the private business class to develop into other more autonomous civil society constituencies, as long as they do not contest the imposing corporatist rule. The Federation and its local chambers have done exactly that by going around the rule while still expanding their constituencies. Unlike the farmers and industrial workers in the nonstate sector who were excluded from gaining access to the emerging corporatist structures, the private business class holds a much better strategic position in the formation of a nascent civil society in Fujian.

What role has Taiwanese capital played in the formation of a nascent corporatist civil society in Fujian? Although Taiwanese businesses have been active and even successful in developing an alliance with Fujian's local state and its officials, and although they also helped the Fujian local state to gain greater autonomy vis-à-vis Beijing's central government, they have not yet become involved in any substantial way in the organization and the activities of those horizontal enterprise associations which held negotiations with the local state.[15] The Taiwanese businessmen in Fujian have been more or less acting as "outsiders" to many of the local chambers of commerce. The political sensitivity faced by many Taiwanese businesses in Fujian is certainly the major consideration for them to keep out of all possible trouble. For Taiwanese business investors, to protect one's own business with private efforts and interpersonal connections and without engaging in any collective action seems to be the best and the safest survival strategy.[16] Their relations with the local private business class and small self-employed operators have been quite limited to economic and business affairs. Therefore, while Taiwan capital has been a part of Fujian's corporatist rule, there is a missing link between Taiwan capital and the collective bargaining effort made by the local Fujian business class with the local state.

The Intellectuals, the New Middle Class, and the Emergence of Civil Society

In two interesting studies, the social and political attitudes of different classes or occupations are analyzed. Drawing from a national sample, Feng (1995) compared the levels of economic and political satisfaction among workers, small entrepreneurs, members of the business managerial class, and professionals.[17] Among the four classes, the small entrepreneurs expressed the highest satisfaction with the current economic and political conditions, followed by the workers. The managerial class and professionals in both private business and public sectors revealed the highest discontent, particularly the professional class; of the professionals interviewed, 27 percent and 44 percent openly expressed their discontent toward the political and economic status quo, respectively. Also, according to educational differences, the higher educated groups (high school and college and above) were inclined to reveal their dissatisfaction. In this study, the term "intellectuals" was not used, but the managerial and professional classes can be viewed as representing the intellectuals or the new middle class, whose members hold white collar managerial and professional jobs and have higher education backgrounds. The findings depict that the intellectuals are more inclined to openly express their views as they become dissatisfied with the current development of the society. By comparison, small entrepreneurs can be seen as the beneficiaries of the ongoing economic transformation, and they tend to be more conservative.

Min's study in Beijing further illustrates the contrast between the "maintaining status quo" mentality and the "opt for change" attitudes held by the small business class, workers, farmers, and intellectuals. The intellectuals, though they admitted the current political situation to be stable, were most inclined to request reforms in the political system and openly demand democracy for China, and they advocated that the government should not interfere in private life. They were also, among the four classes under investigation, most likely to contest the view that there is no need of change in life under the current conditions.[18] Min's finding concerning the liberal attitudes of the intellectuals was further confirmed by Chu (1993) in his research on the differences in attitudes toward the government depending on educational level.[19] Chu concluded that the higher the level of education, the more demand for public participation in political and decision-making processes. The more highly educated groups also revealed the need to limit private business and for economic liberalization to be managed as well.

The intellectuals or the new middle class, as summarized from the above two studies, are more inclined to express a higher level of political liberalism in that the state is viewed to be held accountable and democratic reform is demanded. But at the same time, the intellectuals and the new middle class are more concerned with the social consequences of the rapid growth of the private economy. Such anxiety was also reflected in their attitude that private business needs to be limited.

The existing political and economic attitudinal inconsistency between the intellectuals and the growing small business class can easily turn into a social base of class conflict between the new middle class (represented by the managerial and professional classes) and the old middle class (represented by the small entrepreneurs and small employers). As Fujian has developed into an economy of many vibrant small entrepreneurs and sizable private business owners, the possibility of witnessing growing class conflict is not ungrounded.

Moreover, the inherent political liberalism held by the intellectuals and the new middle class does have a significant implication for forging a potential civil society force in Fujian in the years to come. Though the new middle class in Fujian as a whole is not expected to develop any expressive pro-democracy civic organization that demands overt political change, it is possible that the intellectuals and new middle class could exert their individual influence to bring about gradual change in their workplaces and the communities from below. Such gradual institutional change potentials might exist in the existing various social organizations standing between the family and the state where the intellectuals and new middle class hold management positions.

In other words, the potentials of the intellectuals and the new middle class for civil society formation are to be examined in the existing and newly formed intermediary structures like schools, religious organizations, media, welfare and charitable organizations, women's groups, consumer and environmental organizations, and other cultural institutions. The formation of civil society, however, will be gradual, because the state at the central and local alike is still in place in many of the so-called nongovernmental social organizations listed above, as those intermediary institutions have limited economic resources at present. They cannot act in the way the business class has for their corporatist associations in gaining more autonomy in one way or the other.

Finally, possibilities for forging a viable civil society force will take a slow and long route to come to fruition, as the size of the new middle class in today's Fujian is still not significant in comparison with the small business owners, workers, and farmers. In 1994, in Fujian, there were 450,000 professionals in the state-run enterprises, accounting for only 1.4 percent of the total population. The 11,000 research and development personnel in the government only accounted for 0.034 percent of Fujian's population. There were only 8,000 teachers and professors employed in higher educational institutions, about 0.026 percent of Fujian's overall society. It is not only the relative small size of these white collar professionals in Fujian that will delay the social transformation needed for the creation of a civil society force; the long-lasting discrimination against the "brain" in favor of the "physical" (the upside down of the brain and body, *nao ti dao gua*) is another detrimental factor that will constrain the social and political power of the intellectuals and the new middle class.

The Taiwanese businessmen in Fujian, along with many other Taiwan investors in the rest of China, hold a general view that China's social and political conditions will maintain the status quo. Among the Taiwanese investors interviewed, more than 70 percent expressed such an expectation. It is interesting to point out that while only 10 percent feared that the political situation might become more unstable, more than 20 percent worried that the society might become more chaotic in the near future. With such concern and worry, most Taiwanese business owners in Fujian have been very cautious in dealing with management-labor problems in that they tend to be conservative. According to a survey in Xiamen, Taiwanese businesses were criticized from time to time by the local people for having caused many labor disputes, such as long working hours, a bad working environment, inadequate welfare facilities and provision, unreasonable salary differentials and bonuses, undelivered salaries to workers, an unsatisfactory managerial style, and control over unions.[20]

They are conservative in dealing with their own internal management-labor issues; they are even more hesitant in expressing views on Fujian's social reform issues. They are not in any position to encourage or assist the local intellectuals and new middle class to gain more autonomy vis-à-vis the state. There is no clear evidence that Taiwan capital in Fujian has ever made a conscious attempt to develop direct or close contact with Fujian's various intellectuals, professionals, and other intermediary institutions.

The Rising Local State Power and the Nascent Civil Society

Following Guangdong and a few pioneering other outward-looking provinces, Fujian in the 1990s actively began to enlist investment from Taiwan and other foreign capital. From the provincial level down to the municipalities, counties, townships, and villages, all local government bureaucracies have been active in providing special incentives to investors from abroad, especially from Taiwan. Xiamen and Fuzhou have improved their port facilities and opened dozens of "development zones" to woo Taiwanese investors. Some of these were approved by the central government, but others were simply the local governments' own decisions. Unlike Guangdong's linkage to Hong Kong, Fujian's local governments did not maintain an office in Taiwan to provide assistance to Taiwanese investors in their areas due to the existing political tension across the Straits. But the various local state bureaucracies have indeed extended their administrative power in relation to the central government because of their extensive economic ties with Taiwan investment. Many Fujian officials have openly admitted that Taiwanese investment is indispensable to the success of Fujian's economy. It is not an exaggeration to say that the external economic ties with Taiwan have accounted for the growing autonomy of local state power, an unprecedented new political phenomenon.

Meanwhile, the economic decentralization policy also weakens the macroeconomic control of the central government over the provinces. This was accompanied by the increase in fiscal conflict and debates over specific development projects. Though Fujian was not much of a target of attack from the conservatives in the central government on ideological grounds, several incidents did occur when the central state considered Fujian's local economic development to be "overheated" and some decisions to be "illegal."

As Long (1994) has documented, Fujian was a target of criticism from the central state in its campaign to close down those unauthorized development zones in July–September 1993.[21] That was part of the central state's effort to cool down Fujian's "dangerously overheated economy," attacking irresponsible bank lending as the cause of an inflated property market from which Fujian had suffered. Such a "semi-austerity" policy was received with complaints and denials from the local officials in Xiamen and Fuzhou and the private business community. They argued that rapid growth in Fujian was led by increases in exports and foreign investment, and it should be allowed. Furthermore, they denied that the alleged "overheating" was a problem in their prosperous cities. The reform initiative made by Quanzhou municipal government to save forty-one nearly bankrupted state enterprises by bringing in Hong Kong business groups' investment also aroused the anger of the central government. The central state officials accused Quanzhou of selling the state enterprises too cheaply and even laying off numerous employees and workers. The Quanzhou officials defended their policy on the grounds of economic necessity.

Another conflict between the central and local states was caused by the announcement in December 1993 by the central government that Fujian's share of the total national tax revenue would be increased from 38 percent to 60 percent over a period of several years. Though the actual impact of such a new fiscal policy reform has not been felt because the time frame for implementation was not precisely determined and a proposal for restructuring the whole tax system was being examined, the tension between Fujian and Beijing is expected to continue, and the conflict is likely to be a prolonged one. Long has correctly pointed out the continuing policy tension between Fujian and Beijing will be an almost structural one, since Fujian sees many opportunities for desirable rapid growth, while Beijing wants to moderate growth nationally and is extremely concerned about stability.

The social base of the local state's increasing autonomy vis-à-vis the central state has a lot to do with the emerging market forces generated from and booming in various developing localities. The economic reforms have indeed created new opportunities and incentives for the local bureaucracy to increase local autonomy and to develop local resources to ensure that end. As analyzed above, private business has reached the point that it can develop a critical developmental coalition with the local state. The local state has even exploited and taken advantage of the rising private business interests and turned the new situations to fulfill its own institutional needs. The local state has actually served as a new patron to those private businesses and their associations. The power of the local bureaucracy is buttressed by the emergence of private business at a time when central state control recedes.

As Wank (1995) has discussed, through discretionary control over regulatory levers and resource allocations, local officials can realize income from private enterprises and reduce their dependence on the central state. It is particularly the case for Fujian, since Fujian was assigned by Beijing the special mission of engaging in the united front with Taiwan. Fujian was then given special privileges and decentralized executive decision power in order to flexibly fulfill its designated task to attract Taiwan capital. For example, Fujian gained its power to legislate from the central government, and in 1994, the Xiamen Special Economic Area was granted independent power to rule special laws concerning economic and trade affairs in relation to Taiwanese investment. The Taiwanese businesspeople in Xiamen are even given the political right to take part in politics to elect and to be elected into the People's Congress.

How should we analyze the increasing local state power in the context of the current economic transformation and future prospects for civil society in Fujian? So far, private business and its business associations are the only possible social entities that could be evolving into what could be identified as part of a civil society; the intellectuals and the new middle class have not appeared to possess such institutional capacity. It is also evident that the emerging developmental alliance between business and the local state has, to a great extent, contributed to the increasing autonomy of the local state vis-à-vis the central state. Furthermore, such an alliance between the local state and certain other businesses might have also protected and enhanced the collective interests of the actors involved in facing the central state's intervention. It does not mean that other social sectors or classes outside the interest block would benefit as well.[22] Neither does it entail the increasing autonomy of civil society vis-à-vis the state.[23]

The observations made by Nevitt (1996) and Chamberlain (1994) on the alliance of business associations with the local state and its implication for civil society prospects are quite instructive.[24] They both have contested the applicability of the Western conception of the antagonistic relationship between civil society and the state to the Chinese reality that is still undergoing changes. To modify Nevitt's and Chamberlain's general propositions, they could be rephrased to hypothesize that in today's Fujian context a civil society may not develop separate from and in opposition to the "local state" but rather in the niches and spaces that the "central state" has unintentionally left open. And it will grow in response to opportunities deliberately engineered or accidentally created by the already opened space in the alliance between private business and the "local state."

Still, in the foreseeable future, such a civil society force may make demands upon the "local state," not necessarily to undermine or weaken it but to constrain its conduct in some circumstances and even to endorse and support it in others. It is therefore plausible to witness that, in Fujian, a prospective civil society and the local state may develop in a "symbiotic tension" involving "mutual exploitation and support" as Nevitt has observed. And Taiwan capital, taking all things into consideration, indeed has already been involved in such a newly emerging political economic structure in Fujian.

Increasing Social Inequality and the Future Development of Civil Society

It is more and more evident that, under the economic transformation and increasing prosperity in Fujian, even farmers wish to leave the farming sector and work for small private enterprises. In a survey conducted in Shanghang, 54 percent of the farmers interviewed expressed their intention to work at the *geti* enterprises, and 41 percent said their ideal occupation was to become a private business owner.[25] The 1994 Gini coefficient for China's income inequality was 0.37, much greater than 0.19 in 1986. The income gap in Chinese society has been widening over the years during the economic reforms. The income inequality for the countryside was much more acute; the Gini coefficient was 0.41. In other words, social inequality in the countryside has been more serious than that in the townships and cities.

The social inequality among different income households and that between rural and urban areas has become an increasingly serious social problem for China. Fujian's situation is quite similar to that of China as a whole. Starting in 1992, there has been a deteriorating trend of a widening gap between rich and poor in townships and cities. In 1992, the rate of increase in the discrepancy between the highest one-seventh households in terms of income and the poorest one-seventh was 26.8 percent, using 1991 as a base. In 1994 the rate of increase jumped to 31.9 percent. If one looks at the income gap in absolute terms, it is more alarming. In 1995 the average households' income for the richest one-seventh was 8,986 yuan, while the poorest households had only 2,641 yuan; the gap was 6,345, almost double the figure in 1992 (3,231 yuan).

In other words, in the prosperous townships and cities, the income inequality between the poor and the rich has been increasing along with the rise of the market economy. When turning to the countryside, the prospect is worse. The surprising contrast is found that among the top five provinces attracting the largest foreign investment, Fujian ranked at the bottom in social welfare provisions to the farming population, outperformed by other prosperous coastal provinces such as Jiangsu, Liaoning, Shandong, and Guangdong. The average rural social welfare fund available to each farming population was only 0.49 yuan in 1993, and 0.74 yuan in 1995. Guangdong ranked the highest in this regard; the per capita fund for its farmers was 4.31 yuan in 1993 and 9.51 yuan in 1995. The national average was greater than that in Fujian for both 1993 and 1995, 2.69 yuan and 4.04 yuan, respectively.

Regardless of what reasons might be behind such low rural social welfare funds available for Fujian farmers, the contrast between the rapid industrialization and the poor performance of social welfare for the farmers is a clear indication of the worsening social inequality in Fujian. The pro-industrial ideology of Fujian's current economic development path has already been associated with a rural-urban cleavage and an income gap. Considering that the poor farmers and the lower-income industrial workers cannot organize into any visible civil society force in exerting political pressure on the state, and the unlikely alliance between these two underprivileged classes with the private business and the new middle class, the worsening social inequality may present a structural obstacle to the formation of a healthy civil society in Fujian in the future. In this regard, Taiwan capital, along with other foreign investment, may somehow indirectly be responsible for the worsening social inequality and potential social conflict in Fujian under the given pro-industrial policy upheld by Fujian's provincial state.

Conclusion

The economic and social transformation in Fujian since the late 1980s has been very impressive. The reform initiative from the central state set the tone for Fujian to enter the era of the market economy and industrial growth. The ethnic Chinese investment in Fujian has been the most crucial agent in bringing about structural changes in Fujian. Taiwanese capital was and still is the major driving force behind Fujian's economic transformation. Based on a study of Taiwanese investors in Xiamen, Wu estimated that the average number of workers employed in Taiwanese-invested firms was 152.[26] By the end of 2000, there were more than 4,500 Taiwanese business establishments in Fujian. That means more than about 600,000 work opportunities have been created in Fujian as a result of the direct investment from Taiwanese businesses, a clear indication of the economic impact of the Taiwan factor on Fujian's development. In this regard, Taiwan capital is quite crucial to Fujian's economic success. As pointed out earlier, by the late 1990s, Fujian-Taiwan trade had already reached US$17 billion, and realized FDI from Taiwan was US$7 billion. Despite a decline of Taiwan investment during 1996 and 1998, from 2001 forward, as a result of the "little direct shipment link" between Taiwan and Fujian and the expected accession of Taiwan and China into the WTO, Fujian, especially Xiamen, has once again become a new attraction for Taiwanese business.

The existence of Taiwanese factories and firms and the frequent social contact between Taiwanese visitors and Fujianese residents would also have a great impact on social and cultural lives in Fujian. In 1993, an incredible 3.48 million cross-Straits trips by Taiwanese to Fujian were recorded, and among them one-third went to Xiamen. In Fujian, Taiwanese visitors were more visible than residents from Hong Kong and Macau. Due to this high intensity of social contacts between Taiwanese and Fujian residents in Fujian, popular culture from Taiwan was widespread in every corner of Fujian's townships and cities. Pop songs, fiction, MTV, videos, and commercials for Taiwanese consumer goods and products were rapidly entering Fujian's cultural markets. Many of Fujian's streets, shops, restaurants, cinemas, and MTVs were named after places in Taiwan. That even forced the Fujian authorities to ban the use of Taiwanese names for commercial establishments. To many residents of Fujian, Taiwan lifestyles might represent a model of the modernized version of Fujian's future, as nearly 70 percent of the Taiwanese are of Fujian origin.

There are also negative aspects to the influx of Taiwanese elements as perceived by many Fujian residents. Wu's study also detected that 50 percent of the Xiamen residents interviewed were dissatisfied with the image that Taiwanese business owners have presented to them, higher than the positive responses. Corroborating this negative image, the Taiwanese businessmen (49 percent) said that they were not satisfied with their own social images. Similar surveys conducted in four major cities in China on the youths' perception of Taiwanese businessmen and visitors also found that while the Taiwanese were perceived to be rich, open, and industrious, they were also perceived prone to "going through the back door,"sneaky, back-door goers, and sometimes mean to other people. Therefore, the social and cultural image of Taiwan as represented mostly by the businesspeople and the casual tourists has been a mixed one.

The social and political transformations of Taiwan as manifested in the democratization and the rise of civil society in changing the state and society relations have not been adequately and correctly appreciated by the ordinary people of Fujian. And, therefore, the Taiwan factor has been demonstrated partially and even distortedly by only the presence of Taiwanese capital. The popular culture has not directly contributed to the formation and development of Fujian's civil society. Nevertheless, the Taiwan experience as perceived and acknowledged by the intellectuals who have contacts with information from Taiwan and even followed the democratic progress of Taiwan might be, in longer terms, considered to be something valuable for Fujian's intellectuals to learn for their participation in various civil society activities.

In conclusion, the prospect for civil society in Fujian remains to be examined in the context of the nature and configurations of local state power and the possible alliance of formative civil forces inside Fujian. The "Taiwan factor" as represented mostly by Taiwanese capital, though indispensable to Fujian's ascent to a southern China's edge, has a limited role to play in further facilitating the rise of civil society in Fujian in the near future.

Notes

1. *Fujian Statistical Yearbook* (1995, 1997, 2000).
2. *Fa-Zi Daily News*, January 27, 1993.
3. *Fujian Statistical Yearbook*, 1997.
4. *Fujian Statistical Yearbook*, 2000.
5. *Global Views Monthly*, December 2001.
6. Ying Wang, Xiaoye Zhe, and Bingyao Sun, *The Intermediary Level of Chinese Society: Reform and China's Associational Organizations* (in Chinese) (Beijing: Zhongguo Fazhan Chubanshe, 1993); Jonathan Unger, "Bridges: Private Business, the Chinese Government, and the Rise of New Associations" (unpublished manuscript, 1996).
7. David S.G. Goodman and Gerald Segal, eds., *China Deconstructs: Politics, Trade and Regionalism* (London: Routledge, 1994).
8. Zhau-Zhi Su, Kang-Mien Mai, and Xiao-Min Xiao, "The Developmental Trend of Civic Society in China" (in Chinese), in Zhou Xueguang, ed., *The State and Society Relations in Contemporary China* (Taipei: Guiguan Books, 1992); Jean-Pierre Cabestan, "The Future of Mainland China's Political Reform in View of Taiwan's Democratic Experience," Chinese trans., *Journal of Social Science* 6, no. 2 (1991): 120–135.
9. David L. Wank, "Private Business, Bureaucracy, and Political Alliance in a Chinese City," *Australian Journal of Chinese Affairs*, no. 33 (1995): 55–71.
10. Dorothy Solinger, "Urban Entrepreneurs and the State: The Merge of State and Society," in Arthur L. Rosenbaum, ed., *State and Society in China: The Consequences of Reform* (Boulder, Colo.: Westview Press, 1992), pp. 121–141.
11. Andrew Walder, "The Political Sociology of the Beijing Upheaval of 1989," *Problems of Communism* 38, no. 5 (1989): 30–40.

12. Arthur L. Rosenbaum, ed., *State and Society in China: The Consequences of Reform* (Boulder, Colo.: Westview Press, 1992).

13. Jonathan Unger and Anita Chan, "China, Corporatism, and the East Asian Model," *Australian Journal of Chinese Affairs*, no. 33 (1995): 29–53.

14. Christopher Earle Nevitt, "Private Business Associations in China: Evidence of Civil Society or Local State Power?" *China Journal*, no. 36 (1996): 25–43.

15. You-tien Hsing, "A New Pattern of Foreign Direct Investment: Taiwanese Guerrilla Investors and Local Chinese Bureaucrats in the Pearl River Delta," *Taiwan: A Radical Journal in Social Science*, no. 23 (1996): 159–182.

16. National Federation of Industries (NFI), *The Views of the Taiwanese Business-men on the Straits Relations and Mainland's Domestic Market: A Survey Report* (NFI, 1997).

17. Bo-Lin Feng, "Study of the Social Mentality Under Market Economy" (in Chinese), *Sociology Research*, no. 2 (1995).

18. Qi Min, *Chinese Political Culture* (in Chinese) (Kunming: Yunnan People's Publishers, 1989).

19. Chien Chu, *Observation on the Current Cultural Perceptions in Mainland China* (in Chinese) (Taipei: Council on Mainland Affairs, Executive Yuan of ROC, 1993).

20. An-Chia Wu, *The Influences of Taiwanese Investment on Mainland China: A Case Study of Xiamen Special Economic Area* (Taipei: Council on Mainland Affairs, Executive Yuan of ROC, 1996).

21. Simon Long, "Regionalism in Fujian," in David S.G. Goodman and Gerald Segal, eds., *China Deconstructs*, pp. 202–223.

22. Sarah Pfitner, "One Step Ahead or One Step Outside: State and Society in Guangdong," paper presented at the conference on China's Provinces in Reform, Suzhou University, China, October 23–27 (1995).

23. Wank, "Private Business, Bureaucracy, and Political Alliance."

24. Heath B. Chamberlain, "Coming to Terms with Civil Society," *Australian Journal of Chinese Affairs*, no. 31 (January 1994): 113–117.

25. Weizhi Ding, ed., *Shang-Hang, Fujian* (in Chinese) (Beijing: Chinese Encyclopedia Publication Company, 1994).

26. Wu, *The Influences of Taiwanese Investment on Mainland China*.

7

The Outsider Within and the Insider Without

A Case Study of Chinese Women's Political Participation

Ping-Chun Hsiung

Introduction

Women's political participation has been recognized internationally as an important measure of the status of women in any particular country. In China, concerns over women's political participation caught national attention when the percentage of women cadres in national, provincial, and local party/government offices dropped to an all-time low in the 1980s. While the Chinese Communist Party (CCP) state has implemented various measures to address the situation, and has been eager to broadcast any tangible improvement since the 1980s, gender politics surrounding Chinese women's political participation remains under-explored.

This chapter examines Chinese women's political participation as it is experienced and articulated by professional women. While the term "outsider within" points to their outsider's status in a male-dominated system, the term "insider without" acknowledges their relative lack of political and social resources *within* the state apparatus in comparison to their male counterparts. I draw upon the reflections and narratives of professional women to show how they make sense politically of the contrast between their everyday working experience and the CCP's official rhetoric on gender equality. By conceptualizing the political arena as an engendered site of discontent, I examine how women professionals came to challenge the gender system in post-Mao China, and what forces have sustained these women in times of uncertainty and defeat. My analysis indicates that their lived experiences, together with the legacy of Chinese women's liberation, have laid the foundation for an oppositional, engendered identity. By focusing on gender politics at the everyday level, this study presents a nuanced approach to women's discontent and activism that goes beyond the existing literature on women's political participation in contemporary China. It contributes to recent scholarship on the emergence of civil society in China in general and women's organizing in particular.

To set the stage, I first compare and contrast sinologists' perception of Chinese women and their relations with the CCP state, with the increasing dynamism of women's activism in post-Mao China. I then draw upon women's experiences, and their articulation of these experiences, to show how they perceive the CCP state and its rhetoric on gender equality. The professional women's notion of self-realization and selflessness is conceptualized to illuminate the meaning of, and the driving force behind, their effort to establish careers in a male-dominated society. Their construction of an engendered, oppositional identity is seen both as an indication of collective consciousness and as the outcome of gender politics at the everyday level.

To assess the attitudes of professional women in China, I conducted thirty in-depth interviews in two provinces, one coastal and one inland, between February and July 1998.[1] The interviewees were those who, at the time of the interview, worked at various levels in the Party or government or were employees of the Women's Federation (hereafter, Federation). The interviews were arranged by provincial and city-level federation staff. To a certain extent, I believe the women who were currently holding Party or government office were selected to be interviewed as exemplars of success.[2] Other interviews with professionals of the Federation were arranged more by virtue of individual availability and through personal or professional networks. Most of them were conducted one-on-one. A few were in focus groups. Table 7.1 provides a summary of the informants.

The interview itself was loosely structured to cover the individual woman's background, marriage and family, career path, and working experiences. All the interviews were tape-recorded and transcribed, with special care taken to ensure confidentiality.[3] This study employs an ethnographic approach and examines a small number of professional women. It does not attempt to test any specific theories. Instead, the personal narratives are used to shed light on the meanings that Chinese women attribute to their professional careers. The analysis of these narratives is situated in the larger context of discursive politics in post-Mao China, which sees women and the state renegotiating their relationship.

Women, the State, and Women's Political Participation

Over the last decades, sinologists have upheld a one-dimensional portrayal of the CCP state and its relations with Chinese women. In the late 1960s and

Table 7.1

An Overview of the Informants

Position	Administrative level	Type of interview	Total number of informants
Mayor	County	Individual	2
Deputy mayor	County	Individual	2
Party secretary	Township	Individual	1
Party deputy secretary	Township	Individual	1
Deputy chair of the public health department	County	Individual	1
Principal of the women's cadres school	City	Individual	1
Police officer	City	Individual	1
Chairs of the propaganda department at the Federation	Province	Group	6
Staff of the Federation	Township	Group	4
Heads of five neighborhood committees	Community	Group	6
Head of a neighborhood committee	Community	Individual	1
Staff of the Federation, workers' union, and township enterprises	Township	Group	4
Total number of interviews			30

1970s, the proletarian revolution led by the CCP state was said to have liberated the Chinese woman.[4] A decade later, cynicism and criticism had replaced this positive appraisal. Now, the notion of socialist patriarchy is employed to portray the CCP state as having betrayed its commitment to women's emancipation.[5] In general, these pioneering studies assumed that the CCP state enjoys an absolute, invasive, and effective power to either liberate or to repress Chinese women, and that Chinese women have played limited roles in the process. Although recent studies have adopted a more sophisticated model, a one-dimensional approach continues to be invoked.[6] This is especially evident in debates surrounding the United Nation's Fourth World Conference on Women (FWCW) held in Beijing in 1995, when Western feminist/activist groups categorized the CCP state as an authoritarian regime that persistently violated women's rights.[7] This undifferentiated conceptualization of the CCP in relation to women's emancipation entirely ignored the increasing dynamism of women's activism in post-Mao China.

Since the mid-1980s, Chinese women intellectuals and professionals have engaged in public debates, extensive research, and practical actions to redress both the unresolved issues in the CCP's Marxist approach toward women's emancipation and numerous problems that have emerged in the course of China's market reform.[8] The Federation's internal discussion, for example, covers topics such as how to redefine its relationship with the CCP state and to incorporate the concerns of ordinary women into its core agenda. The Federation has also responded to emerging concerns over divorce, discrimination in hiring and housing, women's unemployment, and the commodification of women.[9] Initiatives centered on women's interests have flourished since the mid-1990s, when financial resources and political legitimacy became available as a result of China's hosting of the FWCW.[10] Over the last few years, newly established legal services, hot lines, and other community groups have gradually created a web of professional networks essential for community organizing and grassroots mobilization. Individual activists taking part in the initiatives have drawn upon both official and nonofficial resources, and their affiliation has cut across the conventional boundaries between governmental and nongovernmental organizations. While such developments further suggest that the CCP state should no longer be conceptualized as a static, homogeneous entity, recent research on women-centered activism also indicates that it is not adequate to cast the Chinese woman either as passive victim or as autonomous agent.[11] To appreciate women's multifaceted activism, I believe, an empirically grounded approach is needed to examine how cracks are seized, subjective positions are formed, and daily struggles are carried out under the CCP regime.

This research aims to examine how trials and triumphs are defined and articulated by women professionals in the political arena. It also seeks to expand the existing literature on Chinese women's political participation. Earlier studies have mainly drawn on statistics to illustrate that Chinese women are subordinated in the political arena as much as in other areas. For example, women are two times less likely than their male counterparts to be Party members and they only constitute 6 to 15 percent of the payroll in the Party, government, and mass organizations at all levels.[12] The ratio gets worse as one moves up the hierarchical power structure, even though, in comparison with the capitalist states, China fares rather well in including women in the political leadership.[13]

Various efforts have been made to identify the causes of Chinese women's persistent subordination, and the negative effects of the recent economic reform on women's political participation.[14] The statistics provide a general overview of the situation of women in the political arena, but we know very little about how those women get to where they are. Nor do statistics tell us what political participation means to the women themselves. By treating women professionals as a homogeneous group, they also fail to acknowledge tension and conflict among women of various sociopolitical strata. Besides, an exclusive emphasis on statistical sources implies that a numerical shift is all that is required to reform a bureaucratic system that is said to be indifferent, if not detrimental, to women's welfare.

To go beyond the sheer numerical paradigm implied in statistical documentation, I adopt an empirically based and institutionally grounded approach toward gender politics and Chinese women's political participation. I unmask the state entity by showing how professional women within its apparatuses have come to decode the official rhetoric on gender equality in the post-Mao era. Inspired by many recent initiatives taken by local women activists, I draw upon women professionals' narratives to show that the political arena provides a platform for the professional woman to realize her individual professional dreams.[15] These narratives also echo the discontent of other groups in the post-Mao era. I show that a woman professional's desire for self-realization is interlocked with her yearning for collective, group emancipation. Together, these aspirations form an oppositional, engendered identity that inspires the everyday activism of women professionals. Their engendered oppositional identity not only grows out of their current status as outsiders within and insiders without. It is also connected to the unique historiography of Chinese women's emancipation.

Seeing Through the Official Rhetoric

Women cadres who eventually develop a political career often have worked at several levels of the Federation. Therefore, their experiences can tell us much about the Federation. As a mass organization with an estimated thirty thousand employees nationwide, the Federation provides its staff, most of them women, with opportunities to gain professional skills and experiences. It is also the Federation's mandate to encourage its cadres, and other professional women, to join the CCP state apparatus. However, structurally speaking, it is impossible for the Federation to function as a forceful advocate for women's political participation. Nor have that many professional women been able to use the Federation as a stepping-stone for a political career outside of it. Historically speaking, the Federation has had an ambivalent and ever-changing relationship with the CCP state. Mandated both to follow the directives of the CCP and to represent women's interests, the Federation is never free to advocate women's causes that would compromise its Party function.[16] Second, although the Federation can support women professionals through nomination or recommendation, the Party-controlled mechanism grants the personnel department of the CCP the ultimate authority to decide who gets promoted, nominated, and/or elected.[17] Thus, while many women professionals believe that the Federation has to bear some blame for not working hard enough to promote women cadres, it is obvious to them that the power rests in the hands of the male leaders. These power holders are known to have no trouble praising federation cadres for their commitment, contribution, and hard work, but have rarely backed up such appraisals with solid support when it comes to promotion or election. One Federation cadre puts it vividly:

> [Male leaders] often say, "You Federation people are very active" or "The federation's cadres are great" or "The Federation's work has been outstanding in recent years" or "Compared to other provincial federations, your [name of local] provincial Federation is very good." They praise you in these ways. But they won't consider you when it comes to promoting or electing female cadres. (#98042305)

Such an experience is crystallized in the cynicism of a slang expression that is quite popular among Federation cadres: "Entering [the Federation] with black hair and leaving [the Federation] with gray hair." The saying not only speaks volumes for their frustrations, but also describes the ultimate fate of many women cadres who spend their entire career in the Federation without advancing to more prestigious posts.

The career advancement of professional women is particularly hindered by the CCP's ideological premise that articulates their presence in terms of *representation,* rather than *participation.* That is, upon nomination or election, an ideal woman candidate is expected to be able to simultaneously represent multiple groups, for example, the intellectuals, minorities, the working class, the constituency of the democratic parties, and other under-represented groups. This reduces the number of potential candidates because relatively few women wear multiple hats.

Such systemic obstacles are compounded by a political culture in the post-Mao era that perceives and treats women professionals as sex objects.[18] Although professional women have stepped into the political arena for decades, they have yet to acquire a stable, professional identity. A woman professional can easily be cast as a seductive, sexual object that makes her interaction with male colleagues problematic, if not outright dangerous. The following sentiments expressed by a mayor highlight the gender politics that surround the relationship between men and women in the workplace:

> When two male cadres work well together, people consider that to be normal. If they don't work well together, others will say that there is a conflict between them. That's all people will say about it. However, if it were to involve a man and a woman cadre, the comments will be totally different. When they work well together, people will say, "Hey, who knows what's between them. Nobody can really tell." Motivated by feelings of jealousy or revenge, many use gender to attack your character. You often hear re-

marks such as, "How is it possible for a man and woman to work so well together?" or "What kind of relationship is it between these two anyway?" What kind of relationship? Working relationship! [Spoken in indignation]. But people always put a distorted spin on things. If the two don't work well together, the woman is to blame. People say something like, "Wherever there is a woman, there is trouble." When there is conflict in a team consisting of men and women cadres, people won't say that the team isn't united. They say, "Wherever there are women, there are fights." All the blame and problems are attributed to the women cadres. Under such circumstances, I think it's not easy to be a women cadre and it is even more difficult to be a successful woman cadre (#98062613).

This narrative illustrates that without a publicly accepted professional identity, a woman cadre in the political arena faces a no-win situation. She is turned into a sex object when a collegial male/female working relationship is cast as a surreptitious courtship encounter. Moreover, when there is a professional conflict, "the woman" is made the scapegoat. In neither case does a female worker's achieved status as a professional woman exempt her from being objectified.

In the current climate, where the men often network while indulging in heavy drinking, smoking, and, occasionally, recourse to prostitutes, women professionals find it impossible to accumulate political resources through networking activities. To avoid gossip, a woman professional must also refrain from cultivating mentoring relationships with the men in power. Thus, when it comes to promotion and nomination, it is extremely unlikely, though not impossible, for a woman professional to get unconditional backing from her superior, a man in most cases. A woman county mayor believes that she has been sidestepped many times because she lacks the open, unconditional backing of her superior:

When it comes to nominating women cadres, the male leader always has some reservations, being afraid that others might gossip, "Why is he supporting this woman cadre? Is there any liaison or other type of relationship between the two?" Sometimes people ask questions such as, "Are they relatives?" or "Are they classmates?" Such questions are easy to deal with. But there are times when people suspect that you have bribed him, or that you two have a liaison. These are the external constraints to women comrades' growth and success [in the political arena]. For men, this would never be a problem. No matter how close two men become, nobody is going to raise their eyebrows. In theory, we have equality between men and women. In practice, equality can't be achieved by shallow words. . . . Throughout my career, I have experienced a lot. I have gone through many setbacks. Yes, quite a few setbacks. . . . I rarely disclose this to others. Why is it that for so many times I have been recommended but then sidestepped? My experiences are examples of not having fair competition in an equitable environment. Whenever there was even just a tiny bit of disagreement [about my nomination], the discussion stopped right there. The possibility of my candidacy was terminated with no further question asked. If I had been a man, it would have been different. If I'm qualified, I'm qualified. But because I was a woman, no one was willing to stand up for me. (#98051817)

Because women in general, and women professionals in particular, are now being cast as sex objects, a professional endorsement from a male superior can easily be interpreted as an act of infatuated favoritism. In this context, many Chinese women professionals welcome the CCP's stipulation that a specific percentage of women cadres must be elected to local offices. Although some have charged that such quotas give women "special treatment," or prolong their "subordinate status," many more women professionals consider the stipulation "very decisive" to their career development.[19] As one Federation department chair put it, "In China, only when there is a mandate handed down from the top is there a guarantee at the lower levels" (#98042320). When reflecting upon her own experiences, a newly elected woman mayor at the county level explains how affirmative action has buttressed her career: "With personal dedication, and the government's policy, you'll be easily promoted from the rank and file. Without the policy, even if you're qualified, it won't happen" (#98051108).

Living through the official rhetoric on equality between men and women implies that a woman professional would eventually come to see the gap between the official claim for its unwavering commitment to gender equality and the various institutionalized obstacles professional women actually encounter. As women professionals reflect upon their own career paths, they often resort to engendered lenses to make sense of their personal experiences and the world they are in. In our interviews, individual women professionals either began or concluded a detailed description of their experiences or observations with statements such as, "This is still a male-centered system," "The ultimate truth about the system is that it is dominated by men," and "It is men who are withholding the power." They also use statements such as, "In theory, gender equality exists. But in practice, it takes more than written words" to articulate overt and covert forms of discrimination within the state apparatus.

Although these statements embody an essentialist assumption, they are very different from the abstract categories such as "feudalism" or "capitalism" that are often used in the official rhetoric as explanations of persistent gender inequality. By juxtaposing their observed reality against the official rhetoric, women professionals testify to an unregimented position vis-à-vis the CCP state. Rather than submissively subscribing to the official categories as the sources of their grievances, they point to the systemic impediments within the state apparatuses. By directing their criticism to the norms and practices of a male-centered power structure, the women professionals represent a subversive voice from within. This suggests that the CCP state is no longer a static, homogeneous entity that upholds a unanimous position on gender issues. Professional women's narratives indicate that gender identity is a significant element of their perception of political participation. This is especially evident when women professionals talk about how they were inspired to embark on a professional career in the first place and what has sustained them as they fought their uphill battles.

The Formation of an Oppositional, Engendered, Identity

When talking about their work and careers, women cadres convey a clear sense of commitment and dedication. At various stages of their careers, they invest a huge amount of effort and thought into their work. To establish their presence, many women professionals put in extra hours at work and/or in private study. Stories of arriving earlier and leaving later are typical. Once on the job, it is not that unusual for a woman professional to make extraordinary moves to prove herself. For example, a woman officer at the city level asked for additional assignments in her new post. Another woman, a deputy mayor, insisted on inspecting a fire site while she was ill and had an intravenous drip on her arm. The woman president of a school for women cadres took only one day off after her abortion. Attending meetings all day on her return, she couldn't even stand straight by evening. "I didn't know how to protect myself. When I worked, I put my life on the line," she stated. Many women professionals endure a profound sense of loss and guilt because they are compelled to be absentee mothers.[20]

Such extraordinary measures bear witness to women professionals' deliberate efforts to either override systemic sexism, or to attract long overdue attention in a male-dominated political system. Nevertheless, they are also offshoots of China's mass line policy that encourages individuals, especially those of disadvantaged backgrounds, to earn their places through personal dedication and merit.[21] In this light, these unusual moves are not merely reactive strategies. Instead, they exemplify a subjective endeavor of *Ziwo Shixian* (self-realization), a term used by many women to articulate the meanings of their professional careers. For many women cadres, especially those of peasant background, having a professional career has been a childhood dream. For example, since she was little, the chairperson of a provincial Federation said that she had aspired to be the woman leader of her natal village. The woman county mayor, as the youngest in a peasant family of five daughters, swore to bring pride to her family, so that the villagers would no longer laugh at her parents for not having a son. A Party secretary from a peasant background wanted to have a life different from her sisters-in-law. With only two years of formal education, she has "grabbed every opportunity to learn" throughout her professional life. In her own words, "I have been carrying within me the curiosity of that little kid outside of the classroom window."

> Although I was in school for only two years, I have been very interested in learning. The poor kids usually work very hard. At age nine, I spun at nights, and was asked to cut and gather grasses for the pigs during the days. I would cut the grasses really fast and run to school whenever I got a chance. Other kids sat in the classroom and I stood outside the window to listen. They had books. I didn't. With a stick, I copied all the strokes and characters the teacher had put on the board onto the ground. I appreciated any learning opportunities. There were kids who fell asleep in the classroom. I didn't know what sleepiness was like. All I could think of was to steal every chance to learn. The teacher came to notice me because once he had asked the class to recite a text. Standing outside the classroom, underneath the windows, I was too short to see his gesture to have the kids stop. So I continued reciting the text loudly. The teacher came out to see who it was reciting the text so well. Early on in my life, I developed the habit of reading and learning on my own. I wanted to be different from my sisters-in-law, even though my mother was more concerned about the farm work she had assigned to me. To this day, regardless of my busy schedule, I still read a great deal every night. I guess I have been carrying within me the curiosity of that little kid outside of the classroom window. (#98061011)

When reflecting upon events pivotal to their careers, many women professionals reveal a diligent, uncompromising drive. The following examples illustrate how this subjective perception is articulated in relation to two individual women's professional endeavors and objectives in life:

> I'm the kind of person who is very committed to whatever I do. I'm unwilling to be inferior, fall behind, get criticized by my superior, or have others dissatisfied with my work. No matter what I do, I do my best. So, no matter where I go, my superiors have always been rather pleased with me. They like me and appreciate my ability. (#98021920)

For a month, I hid in a high school to prepare for the college entrance examinations. I studied day and night and eventually got the highest marks of the entire province.[22] Many of my colleagues failed. As I have said earlier, whenever I am given a chance, I never let it slide away. . . . Whenever there is a chance, I'll fully utilize it to make it meaningful. I'm not interested in political in-fighting. Nor do I use personal contacts or networks to get ahead. I feel I have my own vision about life. I have my own purposes in life, even though this way of thinking may not be appropriate in other's eyes. (#98032705)

Thus, the political arena can be a platform for women cadres to confront the stereotypical notions about women and their place in the larger society. As she moves up the career ladder, the successful professional woman continues to encounter male provocation. This is especially true when she takes up a leadership position that requires many men to take orders from her. For example, a woman county mayor recalled that when she was nominated, a furious male deputy mayor blazed, "Damn it. I have worked for so many years. Now here comes a woman to give me orders. It shames me to death." Recounting this incident, she commented:

Men have real trouble working under a woman. A male deputy mayor would accept a male mayor as his boss, because they're both men. When he is under a woman's leadership, he would feel, "How can I be led by a woman?" or "You're just a woman, how can you lead me?" I would say, "I'm a woman. Why can't I lead you? I must lead you and lead you well."

The statement, "I'm a woman. Why can't I lead you? I must lead you and lead you well," inserts a subjective voice that reveals a woman professional's resolve to be an engendered leader. As a whole, the narrative records the continuous, conscious effort women professionals apply in their efforts to define an identity that reconciles their womanhood with achieved professional status. In this light, developing a professional career is a deliberate undertaking to realize personal worth.

The superior stamina and personal determination revealed in the narratives take on additional symbolic meanings when a woman professional becomes either the first woman in a local community to reach that administrative level, and/or a the first woman to hold that position. The woman who had sworn to bring pride to her family eventually became the first woman in her village to be a county mayor, the first woman mayor of that county, and the first woman mayor of that entire municipal unit. Her voice trembled when she said that the villagers now complimented her as "the pride of the village." She recalled what had happened at the inauguration:

"You're the first woman county mayor in [X] city's history. We believe in you. You have to excel on our behalf, for the sake of women and for the sake of [X] city." Our [male] provincial Party secretary at the inauguration made these comments. There were twenty-four county Party secretaries. All of them were men. People applauded and roared with loud laughter. Everyone there turned his or her gaze on me. Although I didn't show it, I told myself that now the Party had put its trust in me, I needed to be confident and determined. After the ceremony, many women cadres, directors, and high-ranking officers came to me. No matter if they had known me or not, they said ":xxx Go ahead. Strive to excel on our behalf. Don't let women down," "There is no way that women can only be the deputy mayor but not the mayor. We're behind you"; "We're so proud of you. Who says a woman can only be the deputy mayor!" So many people came to me after the ceremony. I was very encouraged and touched. (#98032012)

Although the appointment came only after years of persevering struggle and hard work, she nevertheless observed meanings beyond her personal fulfillment:

Although this position is not really very prestigious in [X], there has never been a woman [in this position] before.[23] I feel whether or not I perform well is no longer my own business. Not just my personal reputation is at stake. What I do is related to the issue of women's political participation, an indication of whether or not women can really handle power. So, this is related to the entire society, the entire Party, and each administrative level's attitudes toward women's political participation. Besides, it challenges Chinese feudal tradition of a thousand years that men work outside and women stay at home. So, I feel the meaning of whether or not I perform well is now beyond myself as an individual, my personal worth, and my own efforts at self-realization. (#98032014)

By setting new precedents, the woman professional attempts to rewrite the generic, derogatory category, "woman," to accord with her personal trials and triumphs. In this light, the self-realization that individual women professionals attain through political participation acquires additional political significance. The self-realization of the Chinese woman professional is transmuted into *Wuwo* (no individual independent existence; selflessness) or *Wangwo* (oblivious self-existence; self-forgetfulness).

The notion of selflessness and self-forgetfulness is used by women professionals themselves to characterize their commitment and devotion toward a larger cause, that is, women's emancipation, and it has been the driving force behind many local initiatives. A woman township Party deputy secretary, who has initiated a number of projects on women's health in rural China, reflects upon her recent work:

> Now, whatever I do, I don't do it to get the superior's attention. I don't do it for any of the superiors. I want to contribute to our society. Last time at the women's workshop, I said that if I were to work for personal gain, I'm sure that with my ability, it's absolutely impossible for me to get this meager salary. But I'm putting my effort to push for equality between men and women of the whole society. I'm fighting for the entire group. I feel my contribution is worthwhile. From this viewpoint, I can find peace in my heart. Otherwise, there is no way that this little money can pay for my shouting, running around, and hard work. With the current serious emphasis on money-worship, what are we for? That's why I have said that I don't care about the monetary return. (#98012809)

Although the official rhetoric on equality between men and women grants individual women legitimacy for their initiatives, the statement, "I don't do it for any of the superiors," indicates that in everyday activism, women not only have to take the causes into their own hands. They also need to be able to rise above the system once they find themselves a niche within it. It is the selfless passion to contribute to the welfare of the society in general, and to improve women's status in particular that has inspired individual professional women to surmount the immediate bureaucratic barriers. The spirit of self-forgetfulness also makes it possible for individual women to adopt a broader outlook and rise above the materialism that pervades the current market economy.

In the early twentieth century, concern about the collective well-being of Chinese women constituted an important impulse for activism and nationalism among Chinese intellectuals, both male and female.[24] This discourse is now employed to sustain and advance gender-specific causes. As a deputy mayor at the county level puts it:

> Without joining the struggles, fights, and devotion of previous generations that have continuously pushed for equality between men and women, how much longer are we willing to wait? China is a country evolved from feudal tradition, with feudal prejudice going very deep. It is also a huge country. Without the effort of us, the women, and if we were simply to rely upon the guys to liberate us, how long would we have to wait? From this standpoint, I feel my effort is worthwhile. The previous generations have sacrificed so much. We should make some sacrifices as well. (#98050603)

Here, the sense of pushing forward a yet-to-be-realized mission is articulated in a historical continuum that links the present to the previous and future generations of women. The statement, "[if] we were simply to rely upon the guys to liberate us, how long would we have to wait," reveals a blatant gender focus. Its claim to a women-centered approach presents an alternative vision to the top-down hegemony that the CCP state continues to uphold. The critical, reflective, voice speaks about the practical, painstaking work needed to realize women's emancipation. This is very different from the official rhetoric where women's emancipation remains abstract and su-perficial. And the selfless/self-forgetful image projects a historical, collec-tive self that obliges every woman to fight against gender inequality.

The simultaneous, interwoven nature of individual self-realization and the notion of selflessness/self-forgetfulness embedded in the Chinese woman's collective being enables Chinese women professionals to withstand, and rise above, the difficulties, grief, and hardship they encounter in a male-centered and male-dominated professional world. The following two narratives speak eloquently about this:

> When I sometimes feel that it isn't worth it to endure so much hardship and grief, I come to think about the suffering and hardship of numerous women in the past. Can we go back? No, there is no going-back. Otherwise, what's going to happen to our daughters? For this [reason] and [so that] more people . . . enjoy happiness, I have to excel. It depends on each one of us, and the effort of our generation, to liberate women cadres from the tradi-tional forces, get them out of their subordinate position, and shape them into confident, independent individuals who will no longer be overshad-owed and disdained. Think about those women leaders before us. They put their lives on the line and left their families behind. What were they fight-ing about? Having their struggles in mind, the obstacles we're facing are minimal. (#98021703)

> Although the Federation is a place with neither power nor money, I dedicate myself to its mission with neither shame nor regret. Why? I think the Federa-tion is a place to toughen individuals. . . . I came to the provincial Federation and was involved in writing the history of women cadres in the Shaan-Gan-Ning area. Can you imagine a national women's movement without the women cadres of the Shaan-Gan-Ning area? So, the women cadres of the Shaan-Gan-Ning area inspire us. I interview them. [During the war,] they hid in the bushes during the day and emerged at night to cook for the soldiers. . . . Their lived experiences touch me deeply. So, even though I have no money, nor power, and I keep a meager life-style, I feel I'm very rich spiritually. Yes, this is how I feel. Three key perspectives, i.e., cosmology, philosophy of life, and value system, sustain me throughout my career to endure years of diffi-culties and hardship. Although there have been moments of dissatisfaction, it's only a very brief moment. After that, I rise above it. (#98042311)

A number of themes essential to the formation of women professionals' oppositional, engendered identity emerge from these two excerpts. First of all, oral histories and memory have been identified as significant in the creation of oppositional agency in Third World women's writings.[25] In politics, as well as in any other professions, simply being a woman is not sufficient for an individual to assume an oppositional engendered identity. For those who adopt such a stance, collective, historical memory supplies the necessary impulse. By comparing the struggles of the revolutionary vanguard, who put their lives on the line, with their own everyday struggle and personal grief, some women professionals in contemporary China are able to gain a wider perspective and renew their strength.

Second, the *funu* discourse is not a static entity as has been assumed in Barlow's analysis.[26] Although it embodies the CCP's commanding role in liberating woman, it also encodes women revolutionaries' biographies. While the Chinese government continues to uphold its claim that the proletarian revolution led by the CCP has liberated Chinese women from a feudal, imperialistic past, alternative positions have emerged in recent years.[27] Instead of subscribing to a self-congratulatory, Party-centered telling of history about women's emancipation, the narratives present a woman-centered historiography. In such an alternative account, the history of women's collective selves includes the sacrifices of individual women revolutionaries. And the torch is now carried on by another generation of women. The process of re-remembering and re-presenting a woman-centered historiography runs parallel with the efforts of some community women to organize initiatives in the post-Mao era. Clearly, Chinese women have come to assume central roles in women's emancipation.[28]

Third, the political arena is a contested terrain filled with objectified discourse that both incarnates the stereotypical notion of womanhood and includes the combative voices of women who evoke the ideological heritage of the revolutionary vanguard. While the stereotype still portrays women professionals as sex objects, the women themselves are constructing an oppositional, engendered identity to combat this assault. The struggle testifies to the discursive politics surrounding the Chinese woman's subjective position and agency. At the center of the conflict lies the question of how Chinese women professionals define the origins of women's subordination.

Conclusion

In the post-Mao era, the political arena is a site where professional Chinese women experience oppression, exercise resistance, and achieve self-realization. It is a contested terrain between state rhetoric and the women's subjective position. Woman professionals are positioned to constantly negotiate a professional identity against ideology and practices that define their position and write them into sex objects. Their subjective position is to seize the political arena as a platform for self-realization, and for the selfless, self-forgetful cause of women's emancipation. In practice, the real challenge lies in defiance of a male-centered system that has subscribed to equality between men and women in rhetoric, but has become increasingly indifferent to women's actual agenda. Thus, women's activism is as much about their ability to be pragmatic as about their determination or their espousal of feminist ideology.

All the narrators recount incidents of systemic sexism in the nominating process, at elections, and within the working relationship. Amid the ample incidents of injustice, however, the narratives attest to the persistent, conscious battles carried out by individual women professionals. The official gender discourse during the Cultural Revolution, which centered on an androgynous model of women's emancipation, is now being rewritten with new meanings. The revised historiography is filled with images of revolutionary vanguards, and underlies a collective, woman-centered agenda that inspires women's activism within the state apparatuses. In contemporary China, the struggle of women professionals toward self-realization is immersed in, and merges with, a sense of historical mission that was ignited at the turn of the century, but is only superficial in current CCP rhetoric. As outsiders within and insiders without, Chinese women professionals are subjected to systemic discrimination, but have operated as active agents in defiance of such discrimination.

In a broader context, the experiences of women professionals in the political arena show that the official rhetoric on gender equality remains shallow and superficial when it comes to day-to-day realities. Idiomatic terms such as "a thousand years of feudal tradition," "dramatic social changes," or "influences of the market economy," are too abstract to explain away the systemic obstacles women professionals encounter. Nor are they useful as sociological concepts in understanding the engendered world. More studies based upon ethnographic research are needed to deconstruct these terms. Critical analysis of the micro-politics surrounding the political participation of women professionals would also help in the articulation of practical solutions. To make the system accountable, certain kinds of built-in mechanisms are needed. These would not only support individual women professionals in their daily struggles, but also would begin to address systemic discrimination at the institutional level.

Notes

I appreciate detailed comments from Alvin So. Even though I have not incorporated all his comments, they helped me to clarify my thinking and strengthen my arguments. Joan Campbell's editorial assistance has improved the presentation of this chapter.

1. This chapter is part of a larger project that studies the nature and institutional basis of women's activism in contemporary China. At a later stage, additional data from newspapers, women's magazines, and historical documents will be used to systematically compare and contrast women's experiences with the state rhetoric.

2. In view of the official desire for positive publicity, I was not surprised that the interviewees selected were examples of success. But I was rather surprised by the degree to which these women were willing to express their discontent with their engendered experiences. As a rule, I did not have any personal contact or relationship with the interviewees before or after I interviewed them, and how they answered my questions during the interview was completely up to them. In one particular incident, I interviewed a county mayor the night before an annual regional meeting of the Federation. The next morning, she became somewhat worried about what she had said late the previous night. We talked for quite some time. Among other things, I spoke of the measures I would be taking to ensure confidentiality. Eventually, she was reassured when she realized that my research would only be written up in English.

3. To ensure confidentiality, I have not used the names of the interviewees. The cities they referred to are indicated by X. The transcribed excerpts are referenced by an eight-digit figure, such as #98041105. The first six digits indicate the year, month, and date of the interview, and the last two digits refer to the page number of the transcript.

4. See Elizabeth Croll, *Women in Rural Development: The People's Republic of China* (Geneva: ILO, 1979); Delia Davin, *Woman-Work: Women and the Party in Revolutionary China* (Oxford: Clarendon Press, 1976); Marilyn B. Young, eds., *Women in China: Studies in Social Change and Feminism* (Ann Arbor: University of Michigan, 1973).

5. See Phyllis Andors, *The Unfinished Liberation of Chinese Women: 1949–1980* (Bloomington: Indiana University Press, 1983); Kay Ann Johnson, *Women, the Family and Peasant Revolution in China* (Chicago: University of Chicago Press, 1983); Margery Wolf, *Revolution Postponed: Women in Contemporary China* (Stanford, Calif.: Stanford University Press, 1985).

6. See Christina K. Gilmartin, Gail Hershatter, Lisa Rofel, and Tyrene White, eds., *Engendering China: Women, Culture, and the State* (Cambridge, Mass.: Harvard University Press, 1994); Zheng Wang, *Women in the Chinese Enlightenment: Oral and Textual Histories* (Berkeley: University of California Press, 1999).

7. Ping-Chun Hsiung and Yuling R. Wong, "*Jie Gui*—Connecting the Tracks: Chinese Women's Activism Surrounding the 1995 World Conference on Women in Beijing," *Gender and History* 10, no. 3 (November 1998): 470–498.

8. See Ping-Chun Hsiung, "The Women's Studies Movement in China in the 1980s and 1990s," in G. Peterson, R. Hayhoe, and Y. Lu, eds., *Education, Culture, and Identity in 20th Century China* (Ann Arbor: University of Michigan Press, 2001), pp. 430–450; Xiaojiang Li, "Economic Reform and the Awakening of Chinese Women's Collective Consciousness," in Christina K. Gilmartin et al., eds., *Engendering China*, pp. 360–384; Naihua Zhang and Xu Wu, "Discovering the Positive Within the Negative: The Women's Federation in a Changing China," in A. Basu, ed., *The Challenge of Local Feminisms: Women's Movement in a Global Perspective* (Boulder, Colo.: Westview Press, 1995), pp. 25–57.

9. See Yihong Jin, "The All China Women's Federation: Challenges and Trends," in Ping-Chun Hsiung, Maria Jaschok, Cecilia Milwertz, eds., *Chinese Women Organizing: Cadres, Feminists, Muslims, Queers* (Oxford, UK: Berg Publishing, 2001);

Yanqiu Guo and Yuan Feng, *Shuishi bawang shuishi ji* (Who Is the Subject, Who Is the Object) (Beijing: Zhongguo Funu Chubanshe, 2001).

10. See Bonhong Liu, "Zhongren shichai huoyangao" (With More People Collecting the Firewood, the Fire Prolific) in *Funu yanjiu luncong* (Women's Research Tribune) 1 (1996): 14–19; Zheng Wang, "Maoism, Feminism, and the UN Conference on Women: Women's Studies Research in Contemporary China," *Journal of Women's History* 8, no. 4 (1997): 126–152; Naihua Zhang, "Looking at the World Through Women's Eyes: Beijing Conference and Beyond," paper presented at the Fourteenth World Congress of Sociology, Montreal, Canada, 1998.

11. See Elizabeth J. Perry and Mark Selden, eds., *Chinese Society: Change, Conflict and Resistance* (London and New York: Routledge, 2000); Ping-Chun Hsiung et al., *Chinese Women Organizing*.

12. Elizabeth Croll, *Changing Identities of Chinese Women: Rhetoric, Experience and Self-perception in Twentieth Century China* (Hong Kong, London, and Atlantic Highlands, N.J.: Hong Kong University Press and Zed Books, 1995); Tamara Jacka, *Women's Work in Rural China: Change and Continuity in an Era of Reform* (Cambridge, UK: Cambridge University Press, 1997); Martin K. Whyte and William L. Parish, *Urban Life in Contemporary China* (Chicago: University of Chicago Press, 1984).

13. See Whyte and Parish, *Urban Life in Contemporary China*, p. 211.

14. Jacka, *Women's Work in Rural China*; Ellen Judd, *Gender and Power in Rural North China* (Stanford, Calif.: Stanford University Press, 1994).

15. Reports on organizing initiatives by women in contemporary China indicate that the impetus generally comes from rather small groups of highly committed individuals who are inspired to challenge the system. See Ping-Chun Hsiung, "Transformation, Subversion, and Feminist Activism: Report on the Workshops of a Development Project, Xian, China," *Bulletin of Concerned Asian Scholars* 31, no. 3 (1999): 47–51. Cecilia Milwertz, "The Political Power of Activist Commitment—Process and Impact," paper presented at the Women Organizing in China Workshop, Copenhagen, Nordic Institute of Asian Studies, 2000.

16. Recent studies have only begun to unpack gender politics within the CCP state and its intertwined relationship with the Federation. For example, Christina K. Gilmartin provides a detailed analysis of gender politics of the CCP in the 1920s. See Christina K. Gilmartin, *Engendering the Chinese Revolution: Radical Women, Communist Politics, and Mass Movements in the 1920s* (Berkeley: University of California Press, 1995). Naihua Zhang traces the continuously negotiated relationship between the Women's Federation and the CCP over the last decades. See Naihua Zhang, "Looking at the World through Women's Eyes: The Beijing Conference and Beyond," paper presented at the Fourteenth World Congress of Sociology, Montreal, Canada, 1998. Yihong Jin discusses how, in recent years, a local Federation was told not to press for female migrant workers' rights because, according to the Party official, "local industry is going through a tough time" (Hsiung et al., eds., *Chinese Women Organizing*). The statement about such an ever-changing relationship made by a high-ranking Federation official in a personal conversation is particularly revealing. Commenting on the lack of a permanent commitment by the CCP to the Women's Federation, she asserted, "To the CCP, the Federation is a high class prostitute. When it sleeps with you, it spoils you. When it doesn't need you, you're out of the window."

17. The ultimate authority of the Party is entrenched in the system. For example, Federation cadres at various levels, like other state employees, are often approached

to attend professional training workshops that provide updates on policy, administrative skills, or the latest political campaign. While workshops organized by the Federation are for everyone in the designated unit, the ones organized by the Party are only for the selected few who have been chosen as candidates for the next round of promotion. Those few are referred to as the *"zhuzi peiyang duixiang"* (targeted individuals for indoctrination) by the personnel department of the Party (see Yihong Jin, "The All China Women's Federation: Challenges and Trends").

18. The predicament of women professionals in the Maoist era was a denial of their engendered selves. See Mayfair Mei-Hui Yang, "Introduction," in Mayfair Mei-Hui Yang, ed., *Spaces of Their Own* (Minneapolis: University of Minnesota Press, 1999). Many women professionals who grew up in the Maoist era spoke about having never experienced any overt gender discrimination. One of the key ways in which Chinese women intellectuals and activists depart from the official stand on women's liberation is in their emphasis on the biological differences between men and women. See Hsiung, "The Women's Studies Movement in China in the 1980s and 1990s."

19. Xiaojiang Li, "Economic Reform and the Awakening of Chinese Women's Collective Consciousness."

20. With the current system, having a career means that a woman professional has to devote much of her time during her primary childbearing years to additional career training. Moreover, to avoid nepotism, the current system also posts individual professionals to an administrative unit that is geographically far away from their home base. In most cases, it forces them to leave their children behind to be attended by relatives or other family members. Many mothers end up seeing their children only a few times a year, over several years. A woman county deputy mayor recalls her two-year study at a city cadre school: "While enduring the excruciating pain of separation from my one-year-old daughter, I wished the study could instantly make up for the missed opportunity caused by the ten-year disaster [the Cultural Revolution]." After paying for her meals and books, she sent the rest of her meager allowance home for infant formula. At the same time, she writes, "I had to bear the pain of engorgement. Every time I released my milk, I was in tears and calling my daughter in my heart." Quoted by Linfang Lei, *Yongbao qingchun zuiqiu zhuoyue* (Retaining Youthfulness, Pursuing Excellence), in X. Wong and J. Wong, eds., *Dangqixia de fengcai* (Elegant Poise under the Party's Flag) (Xian: Shaanxi Renmin Chubanshe, 1997), p. 418.

21. The CCP's mass line policy in political participation allows individuals from the disadvantaged categories to rise above their desperate backgrounds through personal dedication and merit. M. Sheridan examines how this policy enabled some women to become "labor models" in the 1970s. See M. Sheridan, "Young Women Leaders in China," *Signs* 2, no. 1 (Autumn 1976): 59–88. In the reform era, the emulation campaigns that promoted various "models" and "advanced elements" have gradually lost their significance in mass education. However, there are still ample examples of individuals of disadvantaged backgrounds earning promising political/public positions through hard work.

22. After the Cultural Revolution, entry exams were held at various levels for the sent-down youth to access the higher education system. Professionals whose formal education was interrupted by the Cultural Revolution studied for these exams in hopes of getting into university.

23. That particular county is considered as the least desirable one in the entire municipal unit because it is located in a remote mountainous area with few resources and little economic potential. I have noted that many women professionals are as-

signed to similar undesirable posts. The rationale is to "test their ability," I was told. It will be useful to investigate systematically how such unfavorable conditions may have, in fact, unfairly disadvantaged the woman professional.

24. Wang, *Women in the Chinese Enlightenment.*

25. See Chandra T. Mohanty, Ann Russo, and Lourdes Torres, eds., *Third World Women and the Politics of Feminism* (Bloomington and Indianapolis: Indiana University Press, 1991).

26. Tani Barlow, "Politics and Protocols of *Funu*: (Un)making National Woman," in Gilmartin et al., eds., *Engendering China*, pp. 339–359.

27. According to the CCP state, Chinese women now enjoy an unprecedented high status "which had remained unattainable in Chinese society over millennia." PRC, *The White Paper: The Situation of Chinese Women* (Beijing: Information Office of the State Council, 1994), p. 1. For typical examples of the state's rhetoric, see PRC, *The White Paper.*

28. One of the themes at the workshop, "Women Organizing in China," held at Oxford University in June 1999, was how Chinese women have come to take leadership roles in many local initiatives in post-Mao China. For the workshop report, see citd.scar.utoronto.ca/PCHsiung/WomenOrganizing.html

Part III

Challenges

8

Assessment of the Current State of China's Economic Reforms

Carsten A. Holz and Tian Zhu

Introduction

The World Bank in its *World Development Report 1996* outlined three challenges for countries in economic transition: (1) liberalization, stabilization, and growth; (2) property rights and enterprise reform; and (3) social policies that address the ill effects of transition on particular groups.[1] China scores highly on liberalization, stabilization, and growth, the core reform package. By the mid-1990s China's economy had largely been liberalized: China's economy enjoyed mostly market-determined prices, current account convertibility, falling import tariffs with few remaining export controls, free entry to many sectors, a rapidly growing private sector, and a sharply reduced number of state monopolies. The most recent period of overheating with a short inflationary bout (1993 to 1994) ended in a soft landing, and real economic growth throughout the reform period averaged 9.5 percent per annum. The first item in the World Bank's list of challenges for transition economies thus no longer poses a challenge to China.

The progress of enterprise and property rights reform, however, has been slow, focusing on the establishment of a "modern enterprise system" in large and medium-sized state-owned enterprises (SOEs), rather than on privatization. This need not be a reform deficit. The literature on transition has increasingly come to view competition (an outcome of liberalization) to be much more important than privatization. McMillan and Naughton a decade ago maintained that "privatization is not crucial, competition is" (p. 132).[2] Rawski in 1999 concluded that economists overstate the importance of ownership, and that privatization is not a magic potion for prosperity.[3] For Stiglitz, "the contrasting experiences of China and Russia suggest that, if

183

one has to make a choice, competition may be more important than private property, especially the form of ersatz privatizations that actually occurred. It is competition that provides the driving force for greater efficiency and lower prices. But competition is also an important part of corporate governance: It is the absence of competition that creates rents that so often get diverted to inefficient uses" (p. 10).[4]

Yet limited progress in enterprise and property rights reform can pose serious hazards. Thus, for example, widespread price liberalization in combination with a continued soft budget constraint for SOEs implies that SOEs compete on price irrespective of their profitability.[5] But profitability is an issue not only in SOEs. The fact is that China in the 1990s experienced the development of three financial crises: bad loans in the state banks, losses in the SOEs, and government budget deficits. In an economy of incomplete enterprise and property rights reform, these three financial crises are intricately linked.[6] For example, social security payments could be made either by SOEs or through the government budget. If they are made by an SOE, they reduce SOE profits; if they are financed through the government budget, they increase the budget deficit. SOE wage payments could either reduce SOE profits, or increase state bank (all too often bad) loans. Infrastructure projects could either be financed through government budget appropriations, increasing the budget deficit, or through state-ordained low-interest loans from the state banks, reducing bank profits. Conclusions on the financial health of the government, the state banks, or the SOEs individually thus appear meaningless. The extent of bad loans, SOE losses, and fiscal shortfalls reflect little more than a political decision on where within the state sector to place the financial deficit attributable only to the state sector as a whole.[7]

Only when the government began to address the financial crises in the state sector did social security reform, the third challenge on the World Bank's list, become acute, especially the urban aspect of social security reform. The social security reform in progress in China in the second half of the 1990s is so closely related to SOE reform that it is less of a separate challenge than part of the overall state sector financial crisis.

This chapter assesses the current state of China's economic reforms. We view the financial crises in the state sector as the currently most pressing issue on the reform agenda; these financial crises are directly related to incomplete enterprise and property rights reforms. The chapter proceeds by first taking stock of the current extent of the financial crises. The development of China's economy hinges largely on how these financial pressures are resolved. Then current policy measures for state banks, SOEs, and the state budget are presented and evaluated. The issue of property rights reform is then revisited, and conclusions are drawn concerning reform.

Extent of Financial Deficits

State Banks

By the mid-1990s, estimates of the bad loans by the state banks ranged from 20 percent to about 50 percent. The 20 percent estimate of bad debts tended to cover only nonperforming loans (*daizhi daikuan*) and loan losses (*daizhang daikuan*), while the higher estimate usually included overdue loans (*yuqi daikuan*).[8] In 1995 an economist at the Central Party School suggested that "according to today's most conservative estimate," the share of nonperforming loans and unpaid interest in all bank loans is about 25 percent; "some scholars even think this figure to be around 47 percent."[9] Foreign credit rating agencies usually give higher figures. For example, Moody's offered an estimate for end-1996 of 35 percent to 70 percent.[10]

The four state commercial banks, that is, the Industrial and Commercial Bank of China (ICBC), the Agricultural Bank of China (ABC), the Bank of China (BoC), and the Construction Bank of China (CBC) account for approximately 75 percent of all loans in China.[11] For the mid-1990s, Xia estimated that some 40 percent of their total assets were "unhealthy assets" (*buliang zichan*).[12] In 1999, the four state commercial banks each established an "asset management company" (AMC) to take over the commercial bank's bad loans. By the end of 2000, more than 1,390 billion yuan of bad loans had been transferred to the AMCs, equivalent to 21.12 percent of the four state commercial banks' loans at end-1999.[13] Consequently, bad loan figures for the year 2000 and 2001 are significantly lower than in earlier years. On 1 November 2001, Dai Xianglong, head of the People's Bank of China (PBC), China's central bank, reported that the ratio of bad loans in the four state commercial banks is 26.62 percent, with approximately 7 percent of all loans already categorized as losses.[14] Liu Mingkang, head of the BoC, on 31 October 2001 offered a 28.7 percent bad loan rate for the BoC at the end of 2000 and expressed his confidence that this rate could be reduced by 3 percentage points every year.[15]

The banking system traditionally serves the state-owned sector of the economy: in 1978, 91.06 percent of all loans extended by state banks went to the state sector. Communal or state agriculture received 6.25 percent, and urban collective-owned enterprises 2.69 percent. Even in 2000, the percentage of total loans extended by the state banks going to SOEs was officially still around 80 percent (see Table 8.1). The state banks' performance thus depends largely on the ability and willingness of SOEs to honor their debts.[16]

Table 8.1

State Bank Lending

	1978	1980	1985	1990	1995	1996	1997	1998	1999	2000
Total loans (b yuan)	185.00	241.43	620.62	1,516.66	3,939.36	4,743.47	5,931.75	6,844.21	7,369.58	7,639.375
Growth over previous year (in %)						20.41	25.05	15.38	7.68	3.66
Lending to state-owned enterprises (b yuan)	168.46	215.60	528.79	1,289.82	3,307.66	4,004.66	4,907.67	5,666.75	5,989.05	6,044.784
Growth over previous year (in %)						21.07	22.55	15.47	5.69	9.31
of which: for investment in fixed assets (b yuan)	0.00	5.55	70.53	224.57	1002.56	1,203.42	1,472.46	1,974.43	2,279.17	2,640.609
Growth over previous year in %						20.03	22.36	34.09	15.43	15.86
Share in total lending (in %)										
State-owned enterprises	91.06	89.30	80.90	85.04	83.96	84.42	82.74	82.80	81.27	79.13
Agriculture	6.25	7.29	6.71	6.84	4.88	4.99	5.16	5.17	4.95	3.54
Urban collective-owned enterprises	2.69	3.23	5.00	5.38	2.71	2.53	—	—	—	—
Individual-owned industry and commerce	0	0	0.17	0.10	0.09	0.11	0.27	0.30	0.41	0.46
Foreign-funded enterprises	—	—	—	—	2.28	2.57	2.89	3.25	3.63	3.51
"Others"	0	0.17	2.91	2.63	6.08	5.37	8.93	8.48	9.74	13.36

| Total loans by all financial institutions (in b yuan) | NA | NA | NA | 1,768.07 | 5,053.80 | 6,115.28 | 7,491.41 | 8,652.41 | 9,373.43 | 9,937.107 |
| Share of state banks in total lending (in %) | | | | 85.78 | 77.95 | 77.57 | 79.18 | 79.10 | 78.62 | 76.88 |

Sources: China Financial Statistics 1952–1996 (Beijing: China Fiscal Economy Press, 1997), pp. 12–14; *Financial Yearbook 1997*, pp. 464, 471; *Financial Yearbook 1998*, pp. 508–509; *Financial Yearbook 1999*, pp. 384–385; *Financial Yearbook 2000*, pp. 401–402; *Zhongguo jinrong*, no. 2 (Feb. 2001), pp. 47–48.

State banks comprise the People's Bank of China (until 1983 a commercial as well as central bank, since then a central bank only); the four state commercial banks (Industrial and Commercial Bank of China (since 1985), Agricultural Bank of China (since 1980), Bank of China (since 1980), Construction Bank of China (since 1985), Bank of Communications (since 1990), and the three development banks (State Development Bank, China Import–Export Bank, and Agricultural Development Bank of China) since 1995.

Lending to state-owned enterprises comprises lending to industrial production enterprises, material supply enterprises, commercial enterprises, construction enterprises and lending for investment purposes. Beginning with the 1998 data, "investment in fixed assets loans" have been re-labeled "medium- and long-term loans," while all other loans, apart from a small category of "other loans" are now labeled "short-term loans." "Others" in the table here beginning with the 1998 data comprise the categories "short-term loans —— others" and "other loans." In 1997 the two categories, material supply enterprises and urban collective-owned enterprises, disappeared; loans to the urban collective-owned enterprises are likely to have been included since 1997 in the category lending to industrial production enterprises. Since 1997, loans to state-owned enterprises as reported here thus slightly exaggerate the total volume of lending by state banks to state-owned enterprises.

Lending to agriculture since 1998 is the sum of lending to "agriculture" and (a newly published category) "township and village enterprises."

Lending to agriculture is in part or perhaps even predominantly to state-owned agriculture.

The total loan volume in 1985 is 590.56b yuan in the source, but the individual loan categories add up to 620.62b yuan.

All financial institutions comprise the People's Bank of China, the three development banks, the four state commercial banks, other commercial banks, urban commercial banks, urban credit cooperatives, rural credit cooperatives, post office savings, financial trust and investment companies, finance companies, and financial leasing companies.

State-owned Enterprises

Although state-owned enterprises are spread across all sectors of China's economy, state ownership in the industrial sector usually receives most attention, as few data are available on the other sectors. In 1999, industrial "SOEs and state-controlled shareholding companies" accounted for 56.80 percent of all state equity in state-owned enterprises.[17] Industrial SOEs' financial performance deteriorated sharply over the reform period. Losses of industrial SOEs increased drastically in the late 1980s and continued to rise through 1997. (See Table 8.2.) Nominal profits in 1997 were lower than in 1978. Official "profit" figures equal the profits of profitable enterprises minus the losses of loss-making enterprises; the ratio of profits of profitable enterprises (here called "gross profit") to the losses of loss-making enterprises after 1985 fell to an all-time low in 1997.

Since 1998 the category "SOEs," which prior to 1998 included "pure" SOEs organized in accordance with the 1988 SOE law as well as solely state-invested limited liability companies and state-state joint operations, has been replaced with the category "SOEs and state-controlled shareholding companies." This new category includes all SOEs, all state-controlled shareholding companies (where shareholding companies comprise limited liability companies and stock companies), as well as any state share in any other enterprise or company.[18] A direct comparison between the data since 1998 and pre-1998 data thus is not possible. Nevertheless, the profitability in 1998 of the new category "SOEs and state-controlled shareholding companies" was very similar to the profitability in 1997 of the old SOE category. Following the new classification, profitability improved significantly since 1998. Profits rose in both 1999 and 2000, while losses fell. Gross profits relative to losses by 2000 reached a level three times higher than that in 1998, while profits per equity, the most meaningful indicator of profitability, almost quadrupled. These data suggest a recent improvement in the financial performance of SOEs.

Governments

The fiscal balance deteriorated from a small budget surplus in 1978 to a deficit equivalent to more than 10 percent of expenditures in 1990; from 1995 through 2000, approximately 20 percent of total annual expenditures were financed through borrowing, increasing gradually over time (Table 8.3, pp. 190–91). In 2000, the budget deficit was equivalent to 4.55 percent of the gross domestic product (GDP). Domestic debt grew rapidly from zero in 1978 to a minimum of 9.68 percent of GDP in 2000, the highest level in the reform period so far, but perhaps double that percentage (see notes to Table 8.3, pp. 192–93, on the derivation of the domestic debt, for which no cumulative data are published); foreign debt has was rather constant at about 14 percent of GDP throughout the 1990s.[19]

Over time, an ever-smaller share of government expenditures has been spent on capital construction. The share fell from 40.27 percent in 1978 to 11.99 percent in 2000, with a slight rebound in 1998 through 2000; the share of government expenditures on innovation has always remained around 5 percent. While the government budget deficit thus is rising, in the long run government expenditures on investment, much of it infrastructure investment, are falling. This implies that an ever-larger share of government expenditures—and with revenues in recent years rising relative to GDP—is spent on nonproductive purposes. The budget deficit has come to exceed the sum of capital construction and innovation, suggesting that the government is borrowing not only for infrastructure projects (and thus promoting future growth), but also to finance current consumption.

State Bank Reform

The bad loans of the state banks may be their most visible deficiency. But resolving the bad loan problem by transferring some of the bad loans to AMCs may not be sufficient if the banks continue to incur new bad loans. A second issue therefore is whether banks are adopting professional lending practices, which could limit the occurrence of new bad loans. A third issue is whether banks are achieving a satisfactory level of profitability that allows them in the future to write off the invariably newly incurred bad loans, and to be able to compete with newer and perhaps more capable banks.

Resolving the Bad Loan Problem of the Past

Since 1997, the government has repeatedly injected funds into the state banking system. In 1997, more than 30 billion yuan of budgetary funds were set aside to write off SOE bad debts, presumably old capital construction (fixed-asset) loans. But these funds were equivalent to only 1.94 percent of total investment in fixed-asset loans outstanding at end-1997, while investment in fixed asset loans accounted for only 20.65 percent of all loans extended by state banks.[20] In 1998, the government financed another 40 billion yuan bad debt write-off as well as a conversion of 57.7 billion yuan of outstanding loans into state equity, without specifying the types of loans covered.[21] In 1999, the government financed a further 50 billion yuan bad loan write-off.[22] But apparently much larger write-offs were needed to clean up the banks' balance sheets.

190

Table 8.2

Financial Performance of Industrial SOEs (b yuan unless otherwise noted)

	Profit	Losses	Equity	Debt	Gross profit[a]	Gross profit/ losses	Profit / equity (in %)	Leve- rage[b]	LAR[c] (in %)
1978	50.880	4.206	NA	NA	55.09	13.10	NA	NA	[~10%]
1980	58.540	3.430	NA	NA	61.97	18.07	NA	NA	NA
1985	73.820	3.244	NA	NA	77.06	23.76	NA	NA	NA
1990	38.811	34.876	NA	NA	73.69	2.11	NA	NA	NA
1995	66.560	63.957	1,623.009	3,124.197	130.52	2.04	4.10	1.92	65.81
1996	41.264	79.068	1,840.618	3,435.085	120.33	1.52	2.24	1.87	65.11
1997	42.783	83.095	2,046.904	3,863.857	125.88	1.51	2.09	1.89	65.37
1998[d]	52.514	102.33–	2,675.922	4,815.705	154.84	1.51	1.96	1.80	64.28
1999[d]	99.786	85.14–	3,056.688	4,990.481	184.93	2.17	3.26	1.63	62.02
2000[d]	240.833	61.577	3,271.481	5,130.013	302.41	4.91	7.36	1.57	61.06

Sources:

Profit (lirun zong'e): 1978–1997: Statistical Yearbook 1998, p. 461; 1998: Statistical Yearbook 2000, p. 417; 2000: Statistical Yearbook 2001, p. 413.

Losses of loss-making enterprises (kuisun qiye kuisun zong'e): 1978–1997: Statistical Yearbook 1998, p. 461; 1998: Statistical Abstract 1999 (Beijing: Zhongguo Tongji Chubanshe, 2000), p. 108; 1999: Statistical Abstract 2000, p. 113; 2000: Statistical Abstract 2001, p. 125. Data from the Statistical Abstract are preliminary data; final data for the years when the Statistical Abstract is used are not available.

Equity and debt (where debt is derived as total assets minus equity): 1995: Statistical Yearbook 1996, pp. 410, 416; 1996: Statistical Yearbook 1997, pp. 425–426; 1997: Statistical Yearbook 1998, pp. 445–446; 1998: Statistical Yearbook 1999, pp. 433–434; 1999: Statistical Yearbook 2000, pp. 415–416; 2000: Statistical Yearbook 2001, pp. 411–412.

a"Profit" is the profit of profitable enterprises minus the losses of loss-making enterprises. Gross profit is the profit of profitable enterprises, (or "profit" plus "losses").

bLeverage equals debt divided by equity.

cLAR (liability-asset ratio) equals liabilities divided by total assets (that is, liabilities divided by "liabilities plus equity").

dSince 1998 the category "SOEs," which included ("pure") SOEs organized in accordance with the 1988 SOE law, solely state-invested limited liability companies, and state-state joint operations, has been replaced with the category "SOEs and state-controlled shareholding companies" (where shareholding companies comprise limited liability companies and stock companies). The new category includes all pure SOEs, all state-controlled shareholding companies, as well as any state share in any other enterprise or company. For details, see C. Holz and Y. Lin, "Pitfalls of China's Industrial Statistics: Inconsistencies and Specification Problems," *China Review* 1, no. 2 (Fall 2001): 29–71. In the year 2000, the gross output value of the category "SOEs and state-controlled shareholding companies" exceeded the gross output value of the pure SOEs, that is, enterprises organized as "state-owned enterprises" in accordance with the 1988 law on state-owned enterprises, by 101.20 percent, and it exceeded the gross output value of the "SOE" category as defined in the statistics prior to 1998 by 62.89 percent (calculations based on *Statistical Yearbook 2001*, pp. 401, 410). All data refer to industrial state-owned enterprises with independent accounting systems. In 1997, these accounted for 95.97 percent of gross output value of all state-owned industrial enterprises (*Statistical Yearbook 1998*, pp. 433, 454); the percentage is similar throughout the reform period.

Table 8.3

Government Budget (all data are in percent)

	Deficit in % of expenditures[a]	In % of expenditures:[a] Capital construction	In % of expenditures:[a] Innovation[b]	In percent of gross domestic product: Revenues	In percent of gross domestic product: Deficit	In percent of gross domestic product: Domestic debt[c] (minimum)	In percent of gross domestic product: Foreign debt[d]
1978	-0.91	40.27	5.64	31.24	-0.28	0.00	0.00
1980	7.75	27.55	6.40	25.67	2.16	0.00	NA
1985	1.91	27.13	5.06	22.36	0.43	2.65	5.19
1990	10.28	16.72	4.70	15.84	1.81	2.22	13.55
1995	19.00	10.24	6.42	10.67	2.50	3.40	15.22
1996	20.28	9.77	5.63	10.91	2.78	3.79	14.24
1997	22.42	9.14	5.77	11.62	3.36	4.25	14.58
1998	24.90	10.55	4.88	12.61	4.18	5.29	15.43
1999	24.20	14.02	5.07	13.94	4.45	7.38	15.32
2000	23.31	11.99	4.95	14.98	4.55	9.68	13.49

Sources: Statistical Yearbook 1993, p. 228; *Statistical Yearbook 1996*, p. 245; *Statistical Yearbook 2001*, pp. 49, 245, 249, 250, 256. Exchange rate data for 1985: *Financial Yearbook 1986*, p. II–39; 1990: *Financial Yearbook 1991*, p. 92; 1995–1998: *PBC Quarterly Statistical Bulletin* 20, no. 4 (2000), p. 35; 1999: *Financial Yearbook 2000*, p. 397.

[a]Expenditure data in this table comprise the official expenditure figures plus debt-related payments (interest payments, repayment of principal); the latter are not included in the official expenditure figures.

[b]Innovation denotes "innovation funds plus science and technology promotion funds."

[c]In the absence of any data on the (cumulative) balance of domestic debt, minimum domestic debt data are obtained by subtracting the sum of annual "repayment of domestic debt and payment of interest on domestic debts" from the sum of annual domestic debt incurred. If interest payments were zero, the resulting figure would reflect the actual balance of domestic debt. Since some of the "repayment of domestic debt and payment of interest on domestic debts" was expended on interest rather than on the repayment of the principal, the actual (cumulative) balance of domestic debt is larger. *Xinbao*, 30 October 2001, p. 13, gives total domestic debt at end-2000 as equivalent to 15.3 percent of GDP (no source given).

[d]The data on the balance of foreign debt are in USD; for exchange rate into RMB the average annual exchange rate was used (for the year 2000 only monthly data are available, and therefore the 1999 average annual exchange rate, which is very similar to the monthly rates in 2000, was also applied to the year 2000).

In 1999, the four state banks each set up an AMC to which they subsequently transferred some of their bad loans at face value.[23] Each of the AMCs received 10 billion yuan of government start-up capital as well as an unknown volume of loans from the PBC, but otherwise relied on bonds issued to primarily the state banks and guaranteed by the central government to finance the purchase in 2000 of 1.39 trillion yuan of bad loans from the four state commercial banks. Of this total volume, approximately 460 billion yuan were accounted for by a formal debt-equity swap of loans into equity to 601 mostly large SOEs.[24]

The bad loans acquired by the AMCs from the four state commercial banks fall into three categories: (1) loans extended before 1995 which by the end of 1998 had been overdue for more than one year, (2) all loan losses as of September 1999, and (3) loans issued after 1995 that "need" to be turned into equity, with approval of the State Council (SC); in addition, some bad loans of the State Development Bank (SDB) were also acquired by the AMCs. The State Economic and Trade Commission (SETC) chose the enterprises to take part in the debt-equity swap, and then recommended them to the AMCs. The AMCs were to conduct their own evaluations before deciding whether to acquire the bad loans and to turn them into equity. Five basic requirements for enterprises to take part in the debt-equity swap included such criteria as "sales potential" for the enterprises' products and a strong management team.[25]

Lending Decisions

In the early 1980s the government, while gradually abandoning production planning, maintained strict control over most bank lending. Loans for investment in fixed assets were typically initiated by government ministries on behalf of their enterprises and required approval by the State (Development and) Planning Commission (SDPC) in the case of capital construction loans, and by the State Economic (and Trade) Commission (SETC) in the case of loans for technological updating and transformation; once approved, the required loan for the project would enter the credit plan and the bank would extend the loan. Other earmarked (policy) loan categories included, for example, loans for agricultural procurement or loans to enterprises in designated poverty areas.[26] For short-term loans (working capital loans) the four state commercial banks faced aggregate lending limits within which they were expected to largely reach their own lending decisions. But lending authority on short-term loans was often usurped by local governments. Bank managers felt secure in lending to SOEs as governments would always support their enterprises.

Banks, presumably under pressure from governments, extended various types of nonearmarked quasi-policy loans fully aware that repayment would be highly unlikely. Examples of such "short-term" policy loans are the "stability and unity" (*anding tuanjie*) loans of 1989 and 1990, the loans for increasing inventories at SOEs of the early 1990s (loans that remain on the books but on which no interest is charged), the "turn losses into profit" (*niukui zengying*) loans of more recent years, and the special loans extended by the Industrial and Commercial Bank of China since 1994 to pay a basic living allowance to employees of money-losing SOEs.[27]

Since the beginning of 1998 the "mandatory" credit plan with its aggregate lending limits and quotas for earmarked loans has supposedly softened into an "indicative" credit plan. Within the lending limits imposed by the credit plan (submitted by the PBC to the SC for approval), bank branches now are to make their own lending decisions except in a few, specifically identified, cases.[28] Bank managers making their own lending decisions then can be held accountable for the quality of their loans. The transfer of old bad loans to the AMCs in 1999 and 2000 represented an attempt to create a clean balance sheet from which the state commercial banks would start out anew with purely commercial lending.

Yet informal pressure on banks to lend to government-identified projects and SOEs remains high. For example, a central bank circular of mid-1998 to all development banks, the state commercial banks, and all other commercial banks asked these banks to increase their lending in order for the economy to achieve the 8 percent growth target.[29] The circular provided numerous "guidelines" on which banks should lend and requested a response from banks specifying their efforts to increase lending; only in a final paragraph were bank managers briefly reminded that they are now fully responsible for their lending. One particular pressure point is the "closed-circuit" loans (*fengbi daikuan*) that banks are to extend to promising production activities in otherwise poorly performing SOEs. These promising production activities are identified by the SETC and then supposedly independently assessed by the bank. Loans are to be used for the specific purpose only, and the enterprise, under the watchful eyes of the SETC, should feel particularly obliged to make timely interest payments and to return the principal.

Profitability

In order for the state commercial banks to become viable independent economic entities in the long run, they need to achieve a minimum level of profitability. Figure 8.1 shows that the conditions for profitability have never been better than in the years since 1996. The government-determined interest

Figure 8.1 **Absolute Difference between Credit and Deposit Interest Rates**

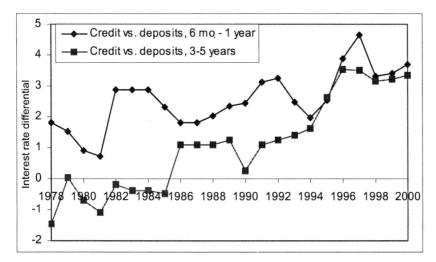

Sources: Various issues of *Financial Yearbook* and *PBC Quarterly Statistical Bulletin.*
If interest rates changed during the year, the annual mean was calculated by weighting
each interest rate with the number of days it was in effect.

rate differential between credit and deposit rates has been at or above 3 percent since 1996, up from between 0 and 2 percent in most previous years.
Interest income and interest expenses account for approximately 90 percent
of total income and costs of the four state commercial banks. A wider margin
thus offers an important chance to improve profitability.

Bank balance sheet and profit and loss account conventions have undergone numerous changes over time, and time series data thus are not perfectly
comparable. Still, some conclusions on overall trends are possible. Profitability, as measured by profit relative to equity, has been on a continuous
decline since 1985. (For the data see Table 8.4.) The decline may have stopped
in 1998; a recapitalization of the four state commercial banks in 1998 approximately doubled their equity, and thus profitability necessarily fell. But
the profitability rates in 1999 were up for the first time. The available information on bank profit and loss accounts is insufficient to draw conclusions
on whether banks are currently actively writing off bad loans. The average
return on equity for the four state commercial banks of 2.72 percent in 1999
is still abominably low; yet if banks were indeed writing off 2 percent to 3
percent of all loans every year, as they are supposed to, this would represent
a cost equivalent to approximately 25 percent of equity. In other words, the
absence of such a write-off would yield a rather high rate of profitability of

Table 8.4

Profitability and Efficiency of Four State Commercial Banks

	1985	1990	1991	1992	1993	1994	1995	1996	1997	1998	1999
Profit/equity (in %)											
ICBC	31.52	23.95	35.01	31.05	11.82	4.84	5.04	6.17	3.15	1.88	2.27
ABC			4.97	4.64	8.67	2.61	10.55	11.10	1.98	-0.68	-0.26
BoC	19.74	14.40	15.59	16.18	14.17	14.83	10.95	14.63	6.70	2.52	2.96
CBC	6.85	5.94	5.42	10.88	7.48	7.12	15.43	10.63	3.79	1.64	6.89
All four		17.24	16.72	17.15	11.41	8.01	9.52	10.31	4.23	1.38	2.72
Profit/assets (in %)											
ICBC	2.16	1.41	1.43	1.13	0.42	0.16	0.15	0.16	0.10	0.11	0.12
ABC	0.49	0.24	0.23	0.18	0.26	0.09	0.35	0.32	0.05	-0.05	-0.02
BoC	0.71	0.72	0.75	0.72	0.57	0.66	0.52	0.55	0.26	0.14	0.17
CBC	0.75	0.37	0.28	0.49	0.24	0.20	0.36	0.23	0.11	0.09	0.33
All four	1.17	0.81	0.78	0.70	0.40	0.28	0.32	0.31	0.14	0.08	0.15
Branches											
ICBC	21,552	30,798	30,834	31,495	34,002	37,039	38,583	38,219	41,990	39,986	36,908
ABC	32,624	55,410	55,614	56,417	58,964	63,816	67,092	65,870	63,676	58,466	56,539
BoC	320	1,483	8,362	1,352	9,886	12,630	13,637	13,863	15,251	15,227	14,368
CBC	2,720	31,595	27,021	29,159	30,530	33,398	35,895	35,118	32,788	30,470	27,889
All four	57,216	119,286	121,831	118,423	133,382	146,883	155,207	153,070	153,705	144,149	135,704

Employees (in thousands)											
ICBC	405	492	505	525	555	562	570	566	559	567	540
ABC	373	468	484	503	536	553	565	539	537	524	539
BoC	19	73	88	118	156	187	196	199	200	198	198
CBC	60	217	239	274	307	322	357	384	383	379	324
All four	857	1,250	1,315	1,421	1,554	1,624	1,687	1,687	1,679	1,668	1,601
Loans/employee (m yuan at 1999 GDP price level)											
ICBC	1.89	2.55	2.70	2.81	2.77	2.62	2.65	3.06	3.40	3.92	4.49
ABC	1.17	1.47	1.62	1.72	1.68	1.21	1.24	1.60	1.81	2.62	2.95
BoC	13.15	8.26	8.07	6.67	5.35	5.36	4.99	5.14	5.53	6.50	6.91
CBC	2.39	1.62	1.86	1.99	2.07	1.99	2.22	2.50	2.78	3.25	3.70
All four	1.85	2.32	2.50	2.59	2.52	2.33	2.36	2.71	3.00	3.66	4.11

Sources: Various issues of *Financial Yearbook.*

Value data may not be fully consistent over time. For example, assets of the ICBC fell drastically in 1997, while those of the CBC fell in 1996. Equity approximately doubled in all four state commercial banks in 1998. The definition of profit may have changed over time. Profit includes income tax, but is net of business taxes and surcharges. The number of branches of the BoC in 1985, 1990, and 1992 is out of line with the number of branches in other years by a factor of almost ten.

about 25 percent. If such large write-offs were to occur, the actually reported profit bears little relationship to current-year operations.[30]

Banks have also begun to streamline their operations (Table 8.4). In 1996, the ABC and the CBC began a process of reducing the number of branches, with the ICBC and BoC starting the same process in 1998. By 1999, the CBC had proceeded furthest, with a 22.30 percent reduction in branches compared to 1995, the year with the maximum number of branches. Similarly, while the number of bank employees almost doubled between 1985 and 1995, there have been only small reductions in employees since the mid-1990s; the bank with the most drastic reductions is again the CBC with a 15.44 percent reduction in 1999 compared to 1996. A given number of employees furthermore handle an ever-increasing volume of loans; this is true even if the inflationary element in the growth of loans is considered. The improvement in lending per employee was most significant in the second half of the 1990s.

Implications

The transfer of bad loans to the AMCs, the formal independence in most lending decisions, the turning point in profitability in 1998 and 1999, and the rapid streamlining of bank operations in recent years all augur well for the future of the four state commercial banks. Yet the break with the past is not absolute. It is hard to gauge the extent of informal pressure on the state banks to lend to certain projects or enterprises. The 1998 PBC circular in no ambiguous terms urging banks to lend appears to be squaring a circle when it also states briefly at the end that bank managers are now fully responsible for their lending. The four state commercial banks still extend earmarked (policy) loans, although presumably on a smaller scale. Who is responsible for these loans should they not be repaid is unclear.

The transfer of some of the bad loans from the four state commercial banks to the AMCs in 1999 and 2000 created a potential moral hazard problem for the future. Dai Xianglong, the head of the central bank, has tried to limit the damage by repeatedly talking about this transfer as being the very last "free meal." Yet with the four state commercial banks still under pressure to lend for policy purposes and the continuing practice of earmarked loans, another free meal a few years down the road should be as justifiable as the 1999 and 2000 bail-outs, and managers of the four state commercial banks thus may not believe Dai's assertions. Any doubt about the center's commitment to a hard budget constraint will imply not only the extension of quasi-policy loans and other high-risk loans, but also sub-standard monitoring and less than sincere efforts in recovering loans.

Even if the center's commitment to no further financial support for bad loans were credible, it is questionable whether the numerous branch managers of the four state commercial banks are fully qualified to make sound lending decisions. Commercial banking may take more than a few years to take root. Even if bank management were sufficiently qualified, a developing and transitional economy with a rapidly changing regulatory environment may by its very nature imply a high default rate on loans. The spread between lending and deposit rates thus may have to be even higher than it is today.

Three examples of transition and development aspects are the following. First, bank managers have to work with highly inaccurate enterprise balance sheets and profit-and-loss accounts, circumstances that will only improve as the accounting profession matures and the application of accounting rules becomes more rigorous. Second, China's legal framework is weak at best. According to a report issued by the PBC on 16 March 2001 on enterprises dodging their liabilities to banks, by the year 2000, 32,140 enterprises had used some form of organizational change to illegally escape debts of 18.51 billion yuan to the four state commercial banks and the Bank of Communications (about 3 percent of these banks' total assets).[31] The report, among others, blames government interference in court decisions, and the limited enforceability of court decisions; in one specifically listed instance, a company officially sealed by court order nevertheless managed to sell all its physical assets, apparently with impunity. According to a nationwide survey of 145 of the 1,520 enterprises that were declared bankrupt between 1993 and 1995, the average loan repayment rate of the 101 enterprises that had completed bankruptcy procedures by the survey date was only 9.2 percent.[32]

Third, it is not only the SOEs which do not repay their loans. For example, from the beginning of 1996 through August 1997 the ABC in Zhejiang Province sued 2,800 private enterprises for the repayment of total loans worth 950 million yuan; it won all cases but was able to collect only 164 million yuan (17 percent of the outstanding amount), and in going to court incurred costs of 17.09 million yuan.[33] Assuming that the ABC sued as soon as it became obvious that the enterprises would not be willing or able to repay the loan, the 17 percent recovery rate suggests abnormal problems in enforcing court orders.

Finally, even if bank managers were allowed to make their own lending decisions, if they were furthermore highly qualified and were not to face a moral hazard problem, and if the transitional and development aspects of China's economy were of little or no importance for bank loan quality, the four state commercial banks still face the challenging task of reducing the remaining share of accumulated bad loans, which currently stands at about

26.62 percent of total loans. The target annual reduction rate of 2 to 3 percentage points appears highly ambitious, especially since it is to be maintained over several years.

SOE Reform

The role of industrial SOEs in the pre-reform economy accounts for many of the difficulties SOEs, banks, and government budgets experience today. First, in the pre-reform economy the government "taxed" agriculture through mandatory agricultural procurement at low prices. Low food prices allowed low wages in urban industry. At relatively high prices of industrial products, the result was a large volume of profit in state industry. This profit was handed over to the government and constituted the main source of government revenues. Virtually all SOE investment and the largest part of SOE working capital in return were appropriated through the government budget. Second, China's industrial structure since 1949 favored capital-intensive heavy industry in an attempt to support national defense and to catch up with developed countries. Industrial production was organized in SOEs located in urban areas; the SOEs provided extensive employment opportunities and a cradle-to-grave social security system to their workers.[34]

These historical facts have two implications. First, on the financial side, with the government no longer providing free budget appropriations, SOEs had to increasingly rely on bank loans as their only source of external funding. This led to a rapid increase in the liability ratio; with little increase in equity, profit *ceteris paribus* stagnates or grows only slowly. Second, the economic reforms revealed the distorted structure of industry and excess employment in industrial SOEs. SOEs across all industrial sectors have a higher capital intensity than non-SOEs; furthermore, since SOEs were originally established following planning objectives rather than as guided by market forces, numerous SOEs face the challenge of phasing out unprofitable production lines and reducing employment.[35]

In order to resolve these problems, the First Plenum of the Fifteenth Chinese Communist Party Central Committee (CCPCC) at its meeting on 19 September 1997 initiated a three-year reform program for industrial SOEs. It comprised two major objectives: most large and medium-sized SOEs were to adopt the modern enterprise system, and most loss-making large and medium-sized SOEs were to "escape their difficulties" (*tuokun*).[36] The government bureaucracy subsequently worked out individual reform measures. On 22 September 1999 the Fourth Plenum of the Fifteenth CCPCC confirmed the various reform measures under way with a comprehensive SOE reform decision.

1998–2000 Reform Program for Industrial SOEs

Adoption of the modern enterprise system for large and medium-sized SOEs is part of an overall strategy of "seizing the big ones and letting go of the small ones" (*zhuada fangxiao*).[37] In 1997, the 14,923 large and medium-sized industrial SOEs accounted for only 20.06 percent of all industrial SOEs, but for 85.43 percent of industrial SOE added value; the 4,800 large industrial SOEs alone accounted for 70.08 percent of industrial added value (calculations based on Table 8.5). The concentration of most value-added in a relatively small number of industrial SOEs thus facilitates reform. Furthermore, in 1997 the largest industrial SOEs were already the most profitable.

The modern enterprise system encompasses four elements, "clearly allocated property rights, clear rights and responsibilities, separation of government and enterprise, and scientific management."[38] The SETC on 28 September 2000 issued a long document outlining the various aspects of the modern enterprise system.[39] The "clear allocation of property rights" implies the gradual switch to the company system; the company law formalizes the relationship between owners, management, employees, and a separate supervisory board. No concise three-year targets for the transformation of SOEs and state-controlled enterprises into formal companies were issued in 1998.

By late 2000, 2,919 SOEs and state-controlled enterprises had been selected to become formal companies; this includes the 100 enterprises originally chosen by the SC as trial enterprises, the 514 state key SOEs, and numerous enterprises of importance to provincial economies. Of these 2,919 enterprises, 2,005 had become a formal company by the end of 2000, including 440 of the 514 state key enterprises.[40] Presumably another approximately 12,000 large and medium-sized industrial SOEs and state-controlled enterprises still do not have a legally binding separation of owners, management, and employees, or a separate supervisory board.

The second overall objective, to make most loss-making large and medium-sized SOEs "escape their difficulties," may have been at least partly achieved, if "escaping difficulties" implies turning losses into profit. Thus China in 1997 had 6,599 large and medium-sized loss-making industrial SOEs (with losses of 66.59 billion yuan), but by the end of 2000 the number had been reduced by 4,799.[41] A further 301 SOEs had stopped production.[42] (The data available on the total number of large and medium-sized industrial SOEs, on the number of loss-making large and medium-sized industrial SOEs, and on their losses vary slightly among different sources; see notes to Table 8.5 for more details.) This, however, does not imply that the number of loss-making large and medium-sized industrial SOEs had fallen to 1,499 (6,599 minus 4,799 minus 301). Some formerly profitable SOEs had in the meantime

Table 8.5

Industrial SOEs, 1997–2000

	1997[a]				Large + medium	1998[b] Total	1999[b] Total	2000[b] Total
	Total	Large	Medium	Small				
Number of money-losing enterprises	74,388	4,800	10,123	59,465	14,923[e]	64,737	61,301	53,489
Value-added (b yuan)	919.293	644.256	141.131	133.906	785.387	1,107.690	1,213.241	1,377.768
Assets (b yuan)	5,910.761	3,976.009	1,024.866	909.886	5,000.875	7,491.627	8,047.169	8,401.494
Equity (b yuan)	2,046.904	1,527.357	277.968	241.579	1,805.325	2,675.922	3,056.688	3,271.481
Profit (b yuan)	42.783	63.188	−10.328	−10.077	52.86	52.514	99.786	240.833
Profit/equity (in %)	2.09	4.14	−3.72	−4.17	2.93	1.96	3.26	7.36
Losses (b yuan)	83.095					102.33	85.14	61.577
Staff and workers[c] (m)	40.40					27.21	24.12	20.96
Average annual employment[d] (m)	38.9375						33.95	29.95

Sources:
Unless otherwise noted, 1997 data are from the *Statistical Yearbook 1998*, pp. 448–51; 1998 data from the *Statistical Yearbook 1999*, pp. 432–435; 1999 data from the *Statistical Yearbook 2000*, pp. 424–427; 2000 data from the *Statistical Yearbook 2001*, pp. 420–423.

Losses of money-making enterprises: 1978–1997: *Statistical Yearbook 1998*, p. 461; 1998: *Statistical Abstract 1999*, p. 108; 1999: *Statistical Abstract 2000*, p. 113; 2000: *Statistical Abstract 2001*, p. 125. Data from the *Statistical Abstract* are preliminary data; final data for the years when the *Statistical Abstract* is used are not available.

Staff and workers: *Statistical Yearbook 2001*, p. 402.

Average annual employment 1997: *Zhongguo gongye jingji tongji nianjian 1998* (China Industrial Statistical Yearbook) (Beijing: Zhongguo Tongji Chubanshe, 1998), p. 81.

Labor productivity (used to calculate average annual employment in 1999 and 2000): *Statistical Yearbook 2000*, p. 429; *Statistical Yearbook 2001*, p. 425.

Number of loss-making large and medium-sized industrial SOEs in 1997: "Zhongguo gan sannian gong ke guoqi tuokun guan" (China Puts Three Years of Effort into Making SOEs Pass the Grade), 13 March 1998, in *China Infobank*.

ᵃSOEs in 1997 comprise ("pure") SOEs organized in accordance with the 1988 SOE law, solely state-invested limited liability companies, and state-state joint operations.

ᵇSOEs in 1998 through 2000 are "SOEs and state-controlled shareholding companies," comprising all pure SOEs, all state-controlled shareholding companies, as well as any state share in any other enterprise or company.

ᶜThe number of staff and workers in "state-owned industry" is reported in the industry section of the *Statistical Yearbook*, but separately from the output and financial data; presumably these data across all years (1997–2000) cover only the pure SOEs, solely state-invested limited liability companies, and state-state joint operations. These employment data are highly likely to be collected separately from the output and financial data.

ᵈAverage annual employment data for 1999 and 2000 are calculated by dividing value-added by "labor productivity"; labor productivity is defined as value-added per average annual total number of employees (*zongye renyuan*). The 1997 value is "average annual staff and workers." State-owned enterprises should by definition only employ "staff and workers," and thus the distinction between staff and workers (1997) and (total) "employment" (1999 and 2000) should be irrelevant. Labor productivity is reported by enterprises together with the output and financial data, and the implicit employment data thus are likely to be highly accurate.

ᵉSOE Escape Difficulties Research Group (Guoqi tuokun yanjiu keti zu), "Guoyou dazhong xing kuisun qiye: Sannian tuokun?" (Can the Large and Medium-sized SOEs Escape their Difficulties in Three Years' Time?), *Zhongguo tongji*, no. 7 (1999), pp. 35–36, offers a number of 16,879 large and medium-sized industrial SOEs in 1997, of which 6,599 were loss-making with total losses of 66.58b yuan.

begun to operate at a loss, so that by the end of 2000 altogether 3,634 large and medium-sized industrial SOEs were running losses of 41.76 billion yuan.[43] Thus the number of large and medium-sized loss-making industrial SOEs, as well as the volume of losses, were reduced by only about 40 percent between the end of 1997 and the end of 2000.

Furthermore, according to a SETC research report, 70 percent of the rise in profit across all industrial SOEs is due to improvements in the macroeconomic environment and state policies, rather than to better performance originating in the enterprises.[44] Indeed, similar efforts to turn losses into profit had failed in 1996, even though responsibility for achieving concise targets had been assigned to the government administrative leadership in charge of each industrial SOE (with target fulfillment becoming part of the cadre evaluation), and SOE management and employees were promised bonuses and threatened with penalties.[45]

While the central government concentrated its SOE reform efforts on large and medium-sized SOEs, reform of small SOEs—predominantly owned by local governments and in 1997 accounting for barely 15 percent of industrial SOE value-added—was left to the local governments. Governments across China began to experiment with selling SOEs to the employees (the "stock co-operative" system), merging SOEs, folding small SOEs into larger ones, removing profitable production processes into new SOEs while letting the old ones go bankrupt, leasing of assets, outright sale of SOEs, encouragement of joint ventures with foreign enterprises, and bankruptcy.[46] Some localities began to privatize with such fervor that the SETC on 11 February 1999 issued strict guidelines on privatization. Data on industrial SOEs according to size are not available for the years 1998 through 2000.[47] But with the number of large and medium-sized industrial SOEs in the three-year period at most reduced by 1,415 (see below), the number of small industrial SOEs must have fallen by one-third between 1997 and 2000. The remaining small industrial SOEs in 2000 turned a small aggregate profit of 4.81 billion yuan (compared to a total profit of all industrial SOEs of 240.833 billion yuan), the first aggregate profit of small industrial SOEs after six years of losses.[48]

A further slogan that became prominent at the beginning of the three-year reform program was "three reforms and one enhancement" (*sangai yi jiaqiang*), namely reducing employment in SOEs while trying to create re-employment opportunities, increasing the equity of SOEs relative to debt, letting some SOEs go bankrupt or merging them with other enterprises, and enhancing enterprise management.[49] While concrete measures for enhancing enterprise management were neither issued nor published, the three proposed reforms took on concrete shape.

Dismissal of SOE Staff and Workers

A three-year target for reduction in SOE employment appears to have never been issued. For 1998 the target was 2 million. The textile sector as one of the prime loss-making sectors became the key reform sector in 1998.[50] Employment was to be cut by 600,000, and 4.8 million "backward" cotton spindles were to be finally taken out of production (out of a total of approximately 40 million), after similar efforts since 1991 had largely failed. By the end of 1999, SOEs in the textile sector had completed the reform process with a total reduction in workers of 1.2 million and a 10 million reduction in spindles.[51]

Overall, SOE employment across all sectors is reported to have fallen by 21 million over the three-year period.[52] Employment in industrial SOEs following the pre-1998 definition of SOEs (focusing only on the pure SOEs, solely state-owned limited liability companies, and state-state joint operations) fell from 40.40 million in 1997 to 27.21 million in 1998 and 20.96 million in 2000 (Table 8.5). However, these data are of only limited use. The employment definition changed in 1998 to include only those staff and workers actually on their post (i.e., the definition now excludes those staff and workers still employed by the enterprise but no longer working in the enterprise). Furthermore, some of the reduction could be due to SOEs turning into state-controlled limited liability companies or stock companies. Employment data on the all-comprehensive category SOEs (post-1998 definition) in 1999 and 2000 (Table 8.5) suggest that the above data for at least 1998 through 2000 present a somewhat reliable picture, with their implicit reduction by 6.25 million workers, or approximately 25 percent of the 1998 total.

The large-scale reduction in SOE employment and thus the surge in urban unemployment required drastic measures to create re-employment opportunities and to support the long-term unemployed. The CCPCC itself on 9 June 1998 laid the groundwork.[53] Dismissed regular (originally permanent) workers of SOEs are to enter a "re-employment service center" (*zai jiuye fuwu zhongxin*), usually located within the SOE, for a period of three years. During these three years the center helps find re-employment, and during the period of unemployment it pays a "basic living allowance" (*jiben shenghuo fei*) as well as the laid-off workers' pension contribution, medical insurance, and unemployment insurance. After three years, the relationship between the SOE and its former workers is severed and the former worker receives regular unemployment insurance payments or social relief support.

The three-year SOE reform program was in part preceded and in part accompanied by a complete overhaul of the social security system. Traditionally, all social security tasks were concentrated within an SOE. Reform required these tasks to be shifted to an enterprise-external institution. This led to the establishment of a provincial-level pension system beginning in 1997, a new urban medical insurance system in 1998, and an unemployment insurance system in 1999. But the implementation of these social security reforms has been less than satisfactory.

Thus, despite the elaborate arrangements on pension payments and the basic living allowance for laid-off workers of SOEs, in practice, many retirees and laid-off workers appear not to receive what they have been promised. A SC circular of 28 May 2000 urges local governments to make up any shortfall in funding for these two purposes through additional budget allocations.[54] But, at the same time, the circular creates a major moral hazard problem in that it promises financial help for "Central and Western regions and the old industrial bases if they are truly in fiscal difficulties." Local governments thus may prefer to delay appropriations for social security purposes in the hope that the central government will be forced to help by reports of large shortfalls in local government budgets, or reports of impending social unrest due to unpaid pensions and basic living allowances. But SOEs, on the other hand, may also have few incentives to pay into social security funds if the local or central government can be forced to contribute a larger share by the enterprise pretending to be too financially weak to fulfill its obligations.

For example, by late 1999, enterprises nationwide owed the pension insurance system 38.3 billion yuan, equivalent to 15.82 percent of all nationwide 1999 pension payments (presumably including those not actually made but only promised, and presumably including those in enterprises and administrative units).[55] The social security system in Liaoning Province, an old industrial base, appears badly underfunded, despite central government injections of 120 million yuan, and SOEs are apparently holding back from dismissing even more workers due to the lack of funding for basic living allowances, while banks are reported to be pressured into extending loans simply to keep some SOEs alive.[56] In June 2001, the SC decreed the sale of state shares in listed companies with the proceeds to be used to finance social security schemes. But after a sharp drop in the stock market, the sales were halted in October 2001.

SOE Finances

One effect of the economic reforms was the increasing indebtedness of SOEs, as the state budget no longer provided all investment funds nor working capital. (Government funding constitutes equity.) By the mid-1990s, industrial SOEs' average liability-asset ratio had reached about 65 percent (Table 8.2). The CCPCC in its reform decision of 22 September 1999 perceived this ratio as too high and therefore detrimental to reaching the objective of SOE reform —presumably the objective referred to is the reduction in losses, as a reduction in debt leads to smaller interest payments and thus a larger residual profit. The CCPCC SOE reform decision elaborated on a number of measures to reduce the indebtedness of SOEs. These included raising equity through land sales, listing on the stock market, or turning loans into equity. Debt relative to equity was to be reduced by banks writing off some loans of merged or bankrupt enterprises, and by keeping interest rates on loans low. Large SOEs could also diversify their debt by issuing bonds. By the year 2000 the liability-asset ratio of (the newly defined and most comprehensive group of) industrial SOEs fell back to close to 60 percent.

As yet the most incisive measure was the debt-equity swap for large and medium-sized industrial SOEs in 2000. This swap at 460 billion yuan is equivalent to more than 5 percent of total industrial SOE assets in 2000, and thus reduced the liability-asset ratio by five percentage points. In addition, assuming a loan interest rate of 8 percent, the debt-equity swap yields a reduction in interest payments and thus an automatic increase in profits of 36.8 billion yuan in the year 2000 (and every year thereafter); this amounts to more than one-quarter of the increase in industrial SOE profits in 2000. But profit in itself appears to be the wrong indicator. If the average return on equity were equal to the interest rate, then a debt-equity swap will leave the rate of profitability unchanged; as profit rises, so does equity correspondingly. It is only when the average return on equity is below the interest rate that a debt-equity swap *ceteris paribus* yields an improvement in the rate of profitability. The significant rise in the rate of profitability of industrial SOEs in the year 2000 from a very low level in 1998 or 1999 suggests that the debt-equity swap may have helped improve profitability, but it cannot account for all of the improvement.

SOE Bankruptcy

According to the 1986 trial bankruptcy law, an SOE can be declared bankrupt if it cannot repay its debt.[57] However, many insolvent SOEs are being kept alive because creditors (mainly the state banks) do not initiate bankruptcy proceedings, or the government invokes an escape clause contained in Article 3 of the bankruptcy law. According to this clause, bankruptcy cannot be declared—even should the creditor desire so—if the SOE is of utmost importance to the national economy and the relevant government departments support it financially or take other measures to help clear debts due.

For most part, SOE bankruptcy proceeds according to plan. Already in the early 1990s the central government established a leading group for "nationwide enterprise merger or bankruptcy and the re-employment of staff and workers" with its office at the SETC. This leading group draws up an annual plan for the merger or bankruptcy of industrial SOEs subordinate to central, provincial, and municipal governments in as of today 111 trial cities for the "perfection of the capital structure"; these 111 trial cities cover virtually all significant urban areas in China. Similar leading groups, for local coordination, were established in these cities and on the provincial level.

It is unclear according to which criteria candidates for bankruptcy are chosen and what limits the overall number of candidates each year. One determining factor for the overall number appears to be the ability of banks to write off bad loans. Thus the SC annually determines what amount of bad loans banks are allowed to write off (using their own profit), and the national leading group then allocates this amount to the individual provinces. A second key concern is securing funding for the laid-off workers. The re-employment service centers are to receive funding equivalent to 3 years' worth of average wages, and these needs take precedence over all other claims on the enterprise. (Even the holder of a land mortgage comes second to employees.)[58]

The national leading group between 1996 and 2000 approved (planned) the merger or bankruptcy of 5,335 industrial SOEs, which required writing off 208.64 billion yuan of bank loans (principal and interest due). In the three-year SOE reform period, 2,334 of these mergers or bankruptcies occurred (with 148.66 billion yuan of bank loans written off). Of the 6,599 large and medium-sized money-losing industrial SOEs in 1997, 1,415 were merged, entered bankruptcy proceedings, or were closed by the year 2000.[59]

Implications

The three-year SOE reform program with the various accompanying measures clearly improved aggregate SOE finances. Yet SOE reform appears far from complete. The 2001 annual plan talks of "further deepening SOE reform" with much of the same as before.[60]

That less than one-quarter of all large and medium-sized industrial SOEs have been turned into formal companies suggests that property rights in most large and medium-sized industrial SOEs may still only be vaguely defined, with perhaps little distinction between ownership and management, and without a formal supervisory institution. The fact that the number of large and medium-sized money-losing industrial SOEs and the volume of their losses have only declined by about 40 percent between 1998 and 2000 suggests that many SOEs are still not economically viable.

The textile sector, after half a decade of unsuccessful reforms, in 1998 and 1999 turned into a model success story. But this success came at a significant cost to the government budget. Thus for every reduction in 10,000 spindles, the government paid a subsidy of 3 million yuan (half borne by the central government, and half borne by local governments);[61] in addition, the enterprise received 2 million yuan in five-to-seven-year bank loans with interest payments subsidized by the local government. (These funds were to be used for the development of new products, the development of tertiary sector activities, and for payments to laid-off employees.) Textile SOEs became prime candidates for inclusion in the bankruptcy plan with its government-approved bank write-offs of bad loans; they were allowed to sell their administratively allocated land use rights; and they received a special 11 percent tax rebate on exports.[62]

Perhaps the aggregate losses of industrial SOEs would have fallen further if enterprises had been able to shed more labor. A deputy head of the SETC in late 2000, based on the 10 million reduction in employment achieved by mid-2000, felt that SOEs were still overstaffed by as much as one-third of their workforce.[63] But the dismissal of excess staff and workers was limited by the ability to find re-employment for laid-off workers and by the financial health of the social security system. Exhortations to find re-employment for at least half of all currently laid-off workers suggest a success rate below 50 percent.[64] Reports from different localities suggest that the social security system by 2001 was stressed to the breaking point. On the other hand, some of the shortfalls could well reflect continued bargaining between the central government, local governments, and enterprises. The latter two, after all, have incentives to under-fulfill their social security obligations, given that the central government has been willing in the past to make up for shortfalls in social security funding.

As in the case of the textile sector reform, social security reform appears dominated by shifting financial burdens from enterprises to government budgets. Industrial SOEs would have had smaller losses had they been able to dismiss more workers. They would have been able to dismiss more workers, if the government had made a larger contribution to the social security system. The same principle is at work in the debt-equity swaps and the bankruptcy plan. Enterprises are freed of some of the recurrent interest burden by shifting nonperforming loans and interest due to the AMCs (and thus the central government). Bankruptcy proceedings appear limited by nonperforming loans and interest due banks being able to be written off (with the volume limit for write-offs determined by the SC, as is the interest spread that determines the volume of potential bank profits and thus the banks' ability to write off loans).

Shifting financial burdens from enterprises to banks and the state budget may make sense if the financial burdens are historical remnants with the reasons for their creation no longer relevant in the future. The dismissal of excess labor, for example, may fall into this category. On the other hand, it is questionable whether some of the bad loans of the SOEs are not the result of recurrent poor performance, and debt forgiveness and debt-equity swaps thus yield only a temporary respite.

Fiscal Burden

Although government debt has been rising rapidly over the past few years, at about 25 percent to 30 percent of GDP, it still appears relatively small. However, given the small size of the government's revenue share in GDP, this debt is formidable. In European Union countries, government debt is equivalent to close to 60 percent of GDP, while the government revenue share of GDP is between 30 percent and 40 percent. In China, government debt equivalent to 25 percent to 30 percent of GDP contrasts with the government's revenue share of GDP of 15 percent. At first sight, the government debt burden in China thus appears comparable to that of European Union countries. However, this debt does not yet include the various unrealized liabilities the Chinese government faces. It is the government which ultimately has to pay for the financial deficits in the financial sector and in SOEs.

By guaranteeing the bonds issued by the AMCs the Finance Ministry has already accepted final responsibility for perhaps close to half of all bad loans. If AMCs were able to recover approximately 25 percent of their loan portfolio (and had no operating costs and did not need to pay interest on the bonds they issued), then the central government still would have to cover a financial deficit in the banking system of 1,002.5 billion yuan (1,390 billion * 0.75–40 billion AMC starting capital), an amount equivalent to 74.84 percent of total budget revenues in the year 2000, or equivalent to 11.21 percent of GDP.[65] If the state commercial banks were unable to write off their remaining stock of bad loans over the next few years, this amount could double. This brings China's actual government debt into the range of 40 percent to 50 percent of GDP.

Similarly, total pension payments to retired staff and workers in 2000 amounted to 273.33 billion yuan, equivalent to 20.41 percent of government revenues or 3.06 percent of GDP; over the past decade, pension payments have been growing at a rate of 21.30 percent per year, compared to nominal GDP growth of 17.03 percent per year.[66] The government may have to shoulder an increasing share of this increasing burden. Health insurance, basic living allowances for laid-off SOE staff and workers, and unemployment insurance are not even yet considered, let alone any future rural social security measures.

Yet the cloud also has a silver lining. To the extent that the government had to rely on bonds to finance the various measures taken during the three-year SOE reform program, it was able to issue long-term debt at rather low interest rates of 2 percent to 3 percent. Second, government revenues as a share of GDP have been rising continuously from a low of 10.67 percent in 1995 to 14.98 percent in 2000 (Table 8.3), and if the eclectic data made available during 2001 are reliable, they will continue to rise. Since the minimum income level to be eligible for income taxes is fixed at a nominal 800 yuan per month, an increasing number of households are beginning to pay taxes; as paying income taxes gradually turns into a nationwide institution, a new and reliable source of government revenues is being established. Third, the central government has been able to claim an increasing share of total government revenues, rising from a low of 20 percent to 30 percent prior to 1994 to 55.7 percent in 1994, then falling back several percentage points to 48.9 percent in 1997, but rising again to 52.2 percent in 2000.[67] Being able to claim an increasing share of total government revenues allows redistribution to the neediest localities, such as those where employment is concentrated in quasi-bankrupt SOEs.

Property Rights Reform

The various measures to reform state banks and SOEs are short on property rights reform. The state banks have undergone no property rights reform whatsoever, with currently only speculation about an eventual listing on the stock market. Property rights reform has become a central element in the reform of small SOEs—which in 1997 accounted for barely 15 percent of industrial SOE added value—but has reached no more than one-quarter of the large and medium-sized SOEs, and only in the form of the adoption of the company system.[68]

Concern about property rights issues centers on the "agency problem."[69] In the case of China's state banks and SOEs, the agency problem is a three-tiered one. Focusing on SOEs, first, the government (or Chinese Communist Party) acts as agent on behalf of the people, the presumably ultimate owners of state assets, in formulating broad objectives for SOEs. Second, government bureaucrats act as agents on behalf of the government in guiding their enterprises. Third, enterprise managers act as agents on behalf of government bureaucrats in managing the enterprises. Thus any profit maximization objective that the owners (the people) may have is likely to arrive at the manager in a highly adulterated form. The government may be concerned about objectives that the owners are potentially less concerned about, such as the continued primacy of the Chinese Communist Party. Government bureaucrats may engage in departmental or private rent seeking.

Even if the government adopted broad economic objectives that the public might agree to, formal mechanisms for ensuring implementation are present only in companies established in accordance with the company law. Most of China's industrial SOEs still lack rigorous control mechanisms, if not proper incentive mechanisms. Instead, they at best operate under the traditional Maoist development strategy with its stress on the ideologically committed communist man as the "fountain of tremendous energy and consciousness."[70]

And yet, at this stage of economic development and transition, limited property rights reform may be inevitable, given the various institutional constraints. If state banks and SOEs were to switch to pure profit maximization overnight, China's economy may well collapse in the short run. A fair share of China's core industrial enterprises would enter bankruptcy proceedings, with numerous, mainly forward linkages causing disruptions across the whole economy. Courts would not be ready to deal with the onslaught of bankruptcies. The social security system could not handle the wave of newly unemployed. Bankers would not know to whom they could lend in a rapidly changing environment, with their rights in bankruptcy proceedings seriously curtailed in favor of the employees. If the public loses trust in the state banks, bank runs may ensue.

Most industrial SOE added value is produced in large enterprises with relatively high capital intensity. Many of these enterprises have large positive externalities through research and development and learning by doing and their impact on the development of local infrastructure.[71] Private entrepreneurs focusing on profitability might choose to eschew these industries if they cannot internalize a significant share of the positive externalities. Furthermore, private entrepreneurs may only now, with the latest capital market developments, come into a position where they can possibly finance large-scale, capital-intensive production.

The development of China's industrial SOEs matches well-accepted development patterns, with the central government providing a big push in core industries that then have numerous forward (and sometimes backward) linkages. These are then taken up by smaller, local SOEs, or enterprises in other ownership forms. It is only now, after two decades of reform and development and declining catch-up effects, that the developmental role of the Chinese government may be receding, or shifting domestically from the more developed coastal regions to less developed Central and Western China.

The Tenth Five-Year Plan (2001–2010) presents an advanced stage of government development policy by clearly delineating the scope of state ownership in industry.[72] The plan distinguishes between five groups of industrial sectors. (1) Military-industry remains overwhelmingly state-controlled. (2) In public goods industries and services as well as in natural monopolies, the state holds a controlling stake. (3) In industries of great economic importance for the "strength of the nation," such as the petroleum industry, car production, telecommunications, machine building, and high technology industries, state "backbone" enterprises continue to hold a dominant position. (4) In key high technology areas, the state adopts a driving function; it need not control related production, but must provide financing and support basic and applied research. (5) In "ordinary," competitive sectors, the existing SOEs should focus on improving efficiency, with large enterprises adopting the company system and small and medium-sized enterprises undertaking various property rights reforms; enterprises not in state ownership and foreign enterprises are invited to participate in the SOE restructuring.

Hopes have been pinned on ownership diversification through listing on the stock market. Xu and Wang found that the performance of firms listed on the Shanghai and Shenzhen stock markets was positively correlated with the fraction of legal person shares, suggesting that legal persons may exert a positive influence on performance through effective monitoring of enterprise management.[73] The fraction of state shares had an ambiguous or negative effect on performance, while ownership concentration had a positive effect. Wang, Xu, and Zhu in a study including more recent data did not look at the impact of legal persons' share but found that ownership concentration did not significantly affect performance.[74] Neither did the fraction of state shares affect performance. While these findings do not necessarily reject the hypothesis that some form of privatization via the stock market may be beneficial to enterprise performance, at least they give reason to pause and reflect.

In a 1998 random sample of large and medium-sized industrial SOEs that had run losses two years in a row, the "responsible" persons in 758 (of 950 sampled enterprises) answered, among others, a closed question as to the three main reasons for the losses. Out of the nine possible answers (which included "others" as a possible answer), "administrative interference" was the answer least frequently chosen as the prime cause of the losses. (For six SOEs, it was the most important reason, for eighteen SOEs, the second-most important reason, and for sixteen SOEs the third-most important reason.) The three top reasons were a lack of funds, faltering sales, and the social burden. While the survey results may not be perfectly objective, they still suggest a potential for further reform that need not necessarily be linked to property rights reform.[75]

Conclusions

We started with what we viewed as the key issues after two decades of economic reform in China today, namely the financial crises in the state banks, the SOEs, and the government. We then proceeded to investigate the reform measures taken to address these issues (with a focus on the state banks and the SOEs), and assessed whether the individual reform measures successfully addressed the three financial crises. The Chinese government has indeed been very active in addressing the three financial crises over the past three to four years, with mixed but promising results. In the process of assessing the success of the reform measures, we also learned about the complexities of the problems, including in some instances how far the implementation of individual reform measures impinges (usually negatively) on the implementation of other reform measures.

We finally turned to the one element in the World Bank's recipe for transition on which China has scored low, namely property rights reform. The need for property rights reform, the speed at which it is implemented, and its timing within the overall transition process have all been debated in the literature. Property rights reform would in theory improve the profitability of the (surviving) state banks and SOEs. Yet given the complexities and interdependencies of the problems China currently faces, the short-run costs of rapid property rights reform may simply be unacceptably high to the Chinese leadership. Since China's transition path is not so much different from well-accepted development strategies of other East Asian countries, perhaps China is doing just fine the way it is proceeding right now.

China could easily complete the process of economic transition to a largely market-oriented economy by privatizing the state banks or by insisting on truly commercial lending decisions by all state banks, and imposing a hard budget constraint on them. This would bankrupt many SOEs, overwhelm the state budget with social security tasks, and thus force the government on a general retreat from productive activities, which it can no longer subsidize, and in theory create a clean slate from which the market economy can take off.

This assumes, among others, that (1) bank managers are highly qualified and able to make purely commercial lending decisions, (2) China's economic development and transition has no extraordinary impact on loan quality, or interest rates are freed and can fully reflect the differing risks of borrowers, even if that means average annual real lending rates between 20 percent and 50 percent and thus the end of aggregate economic growth, and (3) banks can write off at least one-quarter of their loan portfolio (which is currently bad). It also assumes that (4) the current state of SOE finances reflects their future viability and growth opportunities rather than historical liabilities accumulated in a nonmarket environment, (5) China's social overhead capital, including infrastructure, is already highly advanced, or a significant share of the positive externalities of such investments can easily be internalized, (6) entrepreneurs stand ready and are qualified to run large-scale production activities that involve hundreds of thousands of employees, and employees are ready for their enterprise to be taken over by private capital even if it may mean that their own jobs will be cut and the social security net is as yet insufficient to support them, and (7) private entrepreneurs complete the catching-up process as directed by the invisible hand, and are maintaining the research and development departments necessary to build up a long-run substantial industrial base.

The lesson Mao taught when attempting to create a "clean slate" on which to spell out the new Communist China may have been well learnt. Western observers all too often appear ignorant of the many ways their governments interfere in and direct Western "market" economies; they also appear to live in blissful oblivion of the fact that today's market economies had a fair number of state-owned enterprises in their earlier phases of development, and that the quite successful Asian newly industrializing countries (NICs) achieved their catching up with major state ownership across the economy. How much state ownership is right appears a question of degree. The cost-benefit analysis for state ownership in economic development needs to be redone continuously.

Some reform measures are in the long run more promising than others. Three types of measures can be distinguished: the shifting of financial holes from one agent to another without real effect; one-off reforms that improve the performance of an agent forever, but stop short of moving the agent to a production frontier that incorporates different options for institutional arrangements; and systemic reforms that improve the functioning of the system and move potential production to the highest possible production frontier. Thus a recapitalization of the state banks, as happened in 1998, cost the government budget 270 billion yuan, but has little real effect. It is largely a cosmetic measure that makes the state banks look better. One-off reforms with fixed effects include the dismissal of excess labor, or access to new external funds through listing on the stock market. Systemic reforms include the introduction of the company system, the debt-equity swaps if they lead to an eventual increase in external control, and measures that clearly demarcate responsibilities and rights, such as the introduction of a functioning enterprise-external, urban social security system (which truly transfers the authority to hire and fire to the enterprise manager). Systemic reforms are rarely "hard" reforms in the sense that today the old system applies, and tomorrow the new system applies. Thus, the control mechanisms embedded in the formal company system are not immediately fully applied, but are likely to be in the future when the rules and the reasoning behind the rules have become common knowledge.

A factor that should not be underestimated is the importance of continued economic growth. At an 8 percent growth rate, things double every nine years.

Or, the other way round, if the amount of bad loans can be held constant by avoiding the creation of new bad loans, bad loans as a share of GDP or government revenues halve within nine years. Over a period of two decades, the current stock of bad loans turns virtually irrelevant. The same principle holds for employment. As China's population stabilizes, any extensive growth immediately reduces the number of unemployed; if industrial output doubles (over nine years) and if all this growth were extensive, employment would double. In practice, SOEs are likely to still be overstaffed today, and not all growth will be extensive, but the speed of China's economic growth creates a significant potential for job creation (or further reduction in SOE employment). Rapid economic growth in China also means that the SOE share in GDP will continue to decline, as most of the growth occurs in the nonstate sector. The issue of property rights reform for existing SOEs becomes less relevant every year.

This does not mean that economic reform in China is all downhill from now on. Economic growth will slow if only for the simple reason that population growth is slowing. Accession into the WTO will bring new challenges (but also opportunities). Reports on a "chaotic market order" with illegal fees, corruption, counterfeiting, local protectionism, and a gray area of banking abound, with repeated instructions by the SC for remedial action. A rural social security net will have to be established. But these are not so much signs of a need for "faster" reform or "more market" than of a need for better institutions. Institution building takes time.

Notes

1. World Bank, *World Development Report 1996: From Plan to Market* (New York: Oxford University Press, 1996).

2. J. McMillan and B. Naughton, "How to Reform a Planned Economy: Lessons From China," *Oxford Review of Economic Policy* 8, no. 1 (Spring 1992): 130–143. R. Smyth, "Property Rights in China's Economic Reforms," *Communist and Post-Communist Studies* 34, no. 3 (September 1998): 235–248, after analyzing the role of property rights in China's agriculture, nonstate sector, and state-owned sector, concludes that there are viable alternatives to private property rights in economic transition.

3. T.G. Rawski, "Reforming China's Economy: What Have We Learned?" *China Journal*, no. 41 (January 1999): 139–156.

4. J. Stiglitz, "Quis Custodiet Ipsos Custodes?" *Challenge* 42, no. 6 (November/December 1999): 26–67 (obtained via PROQUEST, with pages numbered 1 through 20).

5. The soft budget constraint is a concept first proposed by Janos Kornai in his analysis of centrally planned economies. See Janos Kornai, *Economics of Shortage* (Amsterdam: North-Holland, 1980). It refers to seemingly unprofitable enterprises being bailed out by the government or the enterprises' creditors.

6. The PRC's financial institutions are virtually all state-owned. The term "state

banks" technically excludes the local state-owned banks such as provincial development banks and municipal commercial banks, the rural credit cooperatives (which are
controlled by the central bank), the nationwide "other" commercial banks (which are
either owned by state-owned entities or indirectly controlled by the central government),
and a few other negligibly small financial institutions. Also see notes to Table 8.1.

7. C. Holz and T. Zhu, "Banking and Enterprise Reform in the People's Republic
of China After the Asian Financial Crisis: An Appraisal," *Asian Development Review*
18, no. 1 (2000): 73–93. For more details see C. Holz, "Economic Reforms and State
Sector Bankruptcy in China," *China Quarterly*, no. 166 (June 2001): 342–367, who
constructs a consolidated balance sheet for the state sector in total (government, SOEs,
and state banks) to determine the overall financial health of the state sector. The ratio
of state net worth to state assets has declined from approximately 90 percent in 1978
to approximately 20 percent in 1997. The state sector thus has become a very large net
debtor to domestic households. If the bad loans of the banking system were to be
written off against state net worth in the state sector balance sheet, the state sector
would be bankrupt.

8. Y.S. Chen and M. Cong, "Guanyu fangfan he huajie jinrong fengxian de fenxi"
(An Analysis on Preventing and Resolving Financial Risk), *Jingji yanjiu cankao* (Economic Research Reference), no. 101 (1997), pp. 2–6. Loans are categorized as overdue if they have not been repaid by the due date. They automatically turn into
nonperforming loans after two years. Overdue loans also turn into nonperforming
loans within the two-year period, if the borrowing unit has already stopped production on an investment project or terminated its business. Nonperforming loans finally
turn into loan losses if one of several conditions is met, such as enterprise bankruptcy.
PBC, 28 June 1996, "Daikuan tongze" (General Credit Rules), in *Jinrong guizhang
zhidu xuanbian*, vol. 1 (Selected Financial Rules and Regulations) (Beijing: Zhongguo
Jinrong Chubanshe, 1996), pp. 20–33. For more details on the "quality" of bad loans
in China, see C. Holz, "China's Bad Loan Problem," Working Papers in the Social
Sciences, no. 44, Hong Kong University of Science and Technology (1998).

9. T.Y. Zhou, "Yinhang daizhang he huaizhang shi daozhi shehui dongdang de
yinhua" (Loan Losses and Bad Accounts: Hidden Dangers to Social Stability), *Jinrong
cankao* (Financial Reference), no. 1 (January 1995), pp. 1–3.

10. *Xinbao* (Hong Kong Economic Journal), 30 July 1998, p. 2.

11. The figure is for the year 2000; see *People's Bank of China Quarterly Statistical Bulletin* 21, no. 1 (2001): 18, 24.

12. D. Xia, "Guanyu Zhongguo jingji zhuangui shiqi guoyou yinhang buliang
zhaiquan wenti de yanjiu" (A Study of the Unhealthy Loan Problem of State Banks
During China's Economic Transition), *Guanli shijie* (The World of Management), no.
6 (November 1996): 40–47. Technically, unhealthy *assets* need not all be unhealthy
loans. Yet with the state commercial banks prohibited from holding enterprise stocks
or bonds, their assets consist primarily of loans and some (secure) government bonds.

13. *Zhongguo jinrong nianjian 2000* (Almanac of China's Finance and Banking
2000) (Beijing: China Statistical Press, 2001), pp. 443–444 (hereafter abbreviated
as *Financial Yearbook 2000* and similarly for other years). *Xinbao*, 2 November
2001, p. 14.

14. *Xinbao*, 2 November 2001, p. 14. This statement retrospectively invalidates
earlier claims by Dai Xianglong that the four state commercial banks' unhealthy loan
ratio in early 1998—prior to the establishment of the AMCs—was about 20 percent,
with 6 percent to 8 percent unrecoverable. (See *Ming Pao*, 22 April 1998, p. 4, or

another quote by Dai Xianglong in *Ming Pao* of 17 January 1998, p. 7, with a bad debt ratio of 25 percent.)

15. *Xinbao*, 1 November 2001, p. 3. The PRC's ratio of bad loans compares to a 30 percent bad loan ratio for Mexico at the peak of its bad loan problem. In the aftermath of the Asian financial crisis the share of nonperforming loans in Thailand reached 38.7 percent (*The Economist*, 18 March 2000); similar ratios are likely to have been reached in Indonesia, Korea, and Malaysia (*The Economist*, 17 October 1998).

16. The figure derived from the official statistics is likely to be imprecise. A report in the *Financial Yearbook 2000*, pp. 585–587, suggests that the classification used in the official statistics is misleading. According to this source, in 1998 shareholding companies that were not state-controlled (where "state-controlled" is not defined), together with collective-owned enterprises, foreign-invested enterprises, private enterprises, and individual-owned enterprises (*getihu*) accounted for 42 percent of all loans extended by all financial institutions; if off-balance sheet lending and lending to these enterprises via SOEs is considered, this share could even be 50 percent to 60 percent. For the four state commercial banks, the share of lending to these enterprises in 1998 was 32.8 percent, which would imply that 67.2 percent of their lending was to SOEs.

17. *Zhongguo tongji nianjian 2000* (China Statistical Yearbook 2000) (Beijing: Zhongguo Tongji Chubanshe, 2001), p. 416 (in the following abbreviated as *Statistical Yearbook 2000* and similarly for other years). *Zhongguo kuaiji nianjian 2000* (Accounting Yearbook of China 2000) (Beijing: Zhongguo Caizheng Zazhishe, 2000), p. 690. The data may not be perfectly comparable, for example, not all industrial "SOEs and state-controlled shareholding companies" given in the first source may be included in the total given in the second source, but the data give at least a rough idea of the state share. In terms of employment, state industry in 1999 accounted for only 32.07 percent of total employment in state-owned units. The second-largest state employer was education, culture, and media at 17.19 percent, the third-largest government and Party agencies and social organizations at 13.00 percent (*Statistical Yearbook 2000*, pp. 126–127).

18. For details see C. Holz and Y. Lin, "Pitfalls of China's Industrial Statistics: Inconsistencies and Specification Problems," *China Review* 1, no. 2 (Fall 2001): 29–71.

19. An article in *Xinbao*, 30 October 2001, p. 13, gives a cumulative figure of government domestic debt equivalent to 15.3 percent of GDP (presumably for the year 2000), without offering a source.

20. *China News Digest*, e-mail newsletter also available at: www.cnd.org/CND-Global/, "Government Said to Write Off Bad Debts for State-Owned Firms," 17 October 1997, Global News, no. GL97–142. *Statistical Yearbook 1998*, p. 668.

21. *TCFA Update* (an e-mail newsletter), no. 7 (December 1998). The National People's Congress Standing Committee in 1998 also recapitalized the four state commercial banks to enable them to meet the 8 percent risk-weighted equity-asset ratio specified in the Commercial Bank Law of 1995 (and recommended by the Bank for International Settlements). After the minimum reserve requirement was lowered, on 18 August 1998, the four state commercial banks used their now excess reserves at the People's Bank of China to purchase 270 billion yuan of special thirty-year interest-bearing bonds. The Finance Ministry then recapitalized the banks by returning the 270 billion yuan. Although the recapitalization was undertaken to meet international capital requirement standards, it also increased the banks' net worth and thus provided a cushion for writing off bad debts.

22. "Zhongguo gan san nian gong ke guoqi tuokun guan" (China Puts Three Years

of Effort into Making SOEs Pass the Grade), 13 March 1998, in *China Infobank* (Internet database).

23. The four AMCs are the Xinda (Cinda) AMC, which took over the bad loans of the CBC, the Dongfang AMC (for the BoC), the Changcheng AMC (for the ABC), and the Huarong AMC (for the ICBC).

24. Y.T. Wang, "SOEs' Profits Increased by 70 percent Last Year and the Amount of Debt-for-Equity Swaps Has Reached 459.6 Billion Yuan," *Renmin ribao* (People's Daily), 26 January 2000, p. 2.

25. *Financial Yearbook 2000*, pp. 15–16 and SC, "Guanyu jinrong zichan guanli gongsi tiaoli" (Stipulation on the AMCs), 20 November 2000, in *China Infobank*. If the AMC agreed to the debt-equity swap, then the State Economic and Trade Commission as well as the Finance Ministry and the PBC conducted one further audit before recommending the debt-equity swap to the SC for approval.

26. Data on the extent of "policy" loans are not publicly available. G. Xiao, *Chanquan yu Zhongguo de jingji gaige* (Property Rights and China's Economic Reforms) (Beijing: China Social Science Press, 1997), p. 374, offers some estimates for the year 1991: formal policy loans, that is, loans on which the bank has no decision-making power, accounted for 58.0 percent of CBC lending, 51.2 percent of ABC lending, 66.6 percent of BoC lending, and 17.9 percent of ICBC lending. For details on the credit plan system up through the beginning of the 1990s, see C. Holz, *The Role of Central Banking in China's Economic Reforms* (Ithaca, N.Y.: Cornell East Asia Program, 1992).

27. S.T. Hu and H.L. Wang, "Lishui diqu yinhang buliang zichan chuzhi yu zhuanhua wenti tansuo" (An Exploration of How to Handle and Transform the Problem of Unhealthy Bank Assets in Lishui Municipality), *Jinrong cankao*, no. 3 (March 1998), pp. 28–31. ICBC, 13 June 1994, "Guanyu dangqian de guoyou gongye kuisun qiye fafang jiben zhuanxiang daikuan de guanli banfa" (Administrative Measures for Special Loans to Presently Loss-Making Industrial SOEs), in *Jinrong guizhang zhidu xuanbian*, vol. 1 (1994), pp. 297–299.

28. ICBC, 6 July 1998, "Zhongguo gongshang yinhang xiangmu xindaibu guanyu dui yuan guding zichan zhuanxiang daikuan shishi guodu guanli youguan wenti de tongzhi" (ICBC Project Loan Department Circular on Some Issues in the Transitional Administration of Originally Earmarked Loans for Investment in Fixed Assets), in *Jinrong guizhang zhidu xuanbian*, vol. 1 (1998), pp. 927–928, categorically (somewhat belatedly) ends the practice of earmarked investment in fixed assets loans. However, the circular is riddled with transition arrangements and vague exceptions (such as for infrastructure loans where government departments still play a major role); the State Council has the authority to earmark loans any time. For the ABC, earmarked loans continue to be regular fare for numerous small-scale projects from grain and cotton procurement to poverty alleviation. (See, for example, the credit regulation ABC, 2 April 1998, "Zhongguo nongye yinhang xindai jihua guanli banfa" [Agricultural Bank of China Credit Plan Administration Measures], in *Jinrong guizhang zhidu xuanbian*, vol. 2 [1998], pp. 26–30). Agricultural procurement loans (a formal policy loan category) have largely been shifted to the Agricultural Development Bank, while the SDB is responsible for most infrastructure loans and other (policy-oriented) investment in fixed-asset loans. In the case of capital construction loans, the SDPC recommends projects to the SDB and orders a project appraisal from the China International Engineering Consulting Company; the SDB supposedly has the right to reject the project. (SDB, 29 Dec. 1998, "Guojia kaifa yinhang jiben jianshe daikuan

xiangmu shuangxian xuanju guanli zanxing banfa" [Temporary Measures on the Twin Selection and Administration of SDB Capital Construction Loan Projects], in *Jinrong guizhang zhidu xuanbian*, vol. 1 [1998], pp. 399–401.)

29. PBC, 26 May 1998, "Guanyu gaijin jinrong fuwu, zhichi guomin jingji fazhan de zhidao yijian" (Guiding Suggestions on Improving Financial Services and Supporting the State Economy), in *Jinrong guizhang zhidu xuanbian*, vol. 1 (1998), pp. 240–246.

30. Dai Xianglong reports that the PBC has set a target for the state commercial banks to reduce unhealthy assets by 2 to 3 percentage points per year (*Xinbao*, 2 November 2001, p. 14). Part of the reduction is financed directly with the fixed 2.5 percent annual return on 720 billion yuan of ten-year tax-free government-guaranteed AMC bonds that the four state commercial banks are holding in exchange for some of the bad loans handed over to the AMCs. With equity equivalent to approximately 6 percent of assets, writing off 1.5 percent of assets (or close to 3 percent of loans) requires an extra return on equity of 25 percent.

31. PBC, 16 March 2001, "Guanyu qiye taofei jinrong zhaiwu youguan qingkuang de baogao" (Report on Enterprises Dodging Their Debts to Financial Institutions), transmitted by the SC Office, *Shaanxi zhengbao* (Shaanxi Bulletin), no. 18 (2001), pp. 16–18.

32. *Financial Yearbook 1997*, p. 285.

33. *Financial Yearbook 2000*, p. 587.

34. During the period of the Third Front Construction in the late 1960s and early 1970s, some coastal and border region industrial SOEs were relocated to the interior "Third Front" in order to protect them from any foreign attack, and new investment during this period similarly focused on the Third Front. Due to their remote location and outdated capital stock, these enterprises tend to be among the worst-performing enterprises today.

35. C. Holz, "Long Live China's State-owned Enterprises: Deflating the Myth of Poor Financial Performance," *Journal of Asian Economics*, fall 2002. On the distorted industrial structure, also see J.Y. Lin, F. Cai, and Z. Li, *State-owned Enterprise Reform in China* (Hong Kong: Chinese University Press, 2001), section 5.1.

36. SETC, 28 Nov. 1997, "Guojia jingmaowei fu zhuren Chen Qingtai tan guoyou qiye zenyang sannian zouchu kunjing" (SETC Deputy Head Chen Qingtai Talks About How the SOEs Can Leave Their Difficulties Behind Within Three Years), in *China Infobank*. Zhu Rongji in a visit to Liaoning Province on 18–24 July 1997 may have been the first to set the three-year deadline. (Chinese Academy of Social Sciences Economic Research Institute, *Zhongguo gaige kaifang yilai jingji dashiji yao 1978– 1998* [Compendium of Major Economic Events Since the Beginning of the Reforms 1978–1998] [Beijing: Jingji Kexue Chubanshe, 2000], p. 933). A single document explicitly listing all specific targets of the three-year reform program does not exist. Specific targets are scattered across numerous government and ministerial circulars.

37. T. Zhu, "China's Corporatization Drive: An Evaluation and Policy Implications," *Contemporary Economic Policy* 17, no. 4 (1999): 530–539.

38. CCPCC, 22 September 1999, "Zhonggong zhongyang guanyu guoyou qiye gaige he fazhan ruogan zhongda wenti de jueding" (CCPCC Decision on Some Important Issues in the Reform of SOEs), in *China Infobank*.

39. SETC, 28 September 2000, "Guoyou dazhong xing qiye jianli xiandai qiye zhidu he jiaqiang guanli jiben guifan (shixing)" (Trial Basic Standards for the Establishment of the Modern Enterprise System and for Strengthening Administration in Large and Medium SOEs), transmitted by the SC Office, in *China Infobank*.

40. "Zhongguo guojia jingmaowei shenhua guoyou qiye gaige yanjiuzu" (SETC Research Group on Deepening SOE Reform), 25 June 2001, in *China Infobank*. An earlier article reported that 430 of the 514 key SOEs and state-controlled enterprises had been turned into companies, but of these 430 only 282 had become limited liability companies or stock companies; this seems to imply that "solely state-owned limited liability companies" are not regarded as "limited liability companies," and thus 148 key SOEs and state-controlled enterprises had undergone relatively little change. "Zhongguo guoqi gaige yu tuokun sannian mubiao jiben shixian" (China's Targets for SOE Reform and the Three-Year Reversal of Difficulties Have Basically Been Achieved), 8 January 2001, in *China Infobank*.

41. "Guojia jingmaowei yanjiu baogao biaoming: Zhongguo you san da yinsu cu guoyou qiye sannian tuokun" (SETC Research Report Shows That Three Big Factors Allowed SOEs to Escape Their Difficulties in Three Years), 25 June 2001, in *China Infobank*.

42. X. Yu, "Liu wen guoqi" (Six Questions on the SOEs), *Zhongguo tongji* (China Statistics), no. 7 (July 2001), pp. 19–21. This source claims a reduction in the number of large and medium-sized money-losing industrial SOEs of 4,800 rather than 4,799.

43. Ibid.

44. "Guojia jingmaowei yanjiu baogao" (25 June 2001).

45. SETC, 24 July 1996, "Guanyu jianli qiye niukui zengying gongzuo mubiao zerenzhi yijian" (Suggestions on Establishing Targets for Enterprises to Turn Losses into Profit), issued by SETC, Finance Ministry, PBC, and State Statistical Bureau, approved by SC, in *China Infobank*.

46. H. Fan, "Guoyou xiao qiye gaige: Jinzhan yu wenti" (Reform of Small SOEs: Progress and Problems), *Jingji yanyiu cankao*, no. 13 (7 February 1997), pp. 33–38.

47. SETC, 11 Feb. 1999, "Guanyu chushou guoyou xiaoxing qiye zhong ruogan wenti yijian de tongzhi" (Suggestions Regarding Some Issues in the Sale of Small SOEs), *Zhonghua renmin gongheguo guowuyuan gongbao*, no. 9 (7 April 1999), pp. 297–301.

48. T. Zhang, "Jinyibu shenhua guoyou qiye gaige de ruogan sikao" (Some Thoughts on Further Deepening the SOE Reform), *Jingji yanjiu cankao*, no. 52 (13 July 2001), pp. 2–5.

49. SETC, 28 November 1997, "Guojia jingmaowei fu zhuren Chen Qingtai tan guoyou qiye zenyang sannian zouchu kunjing" (SETC Deputy Head Chen Qingtai Talks About How the SOEs Can Leave Their Difficulties Behind Within Three Years), in *China Infobank*.

50. See C. Holz, "Identifying the Patterns of Profitability Across Chinese State-owned Enterprises: Which Industrial State-owned Enterprises in China Are Profitable?" *Journal of Asian Business* 17, no. 2 (2001): 33–62, for details on the profit and loss pattern across sectors.

51. "1998 nian Zhongguo guoyou qiye gaige zhanwang" (Outlook for SOE Reform in 1998), 8 January 1998, in *China Infobank*. China Textile Association (Zhongguo fangzhi zonghui), 5 March 1998, "Quanguo yasuo taotai 1000 wan luohou mianfang ding he fenliu anzhi zhigong guihua shishi yijian" (Suggestions on Implementing the Outline of Nationwide Reducing and Replacing 10 Million Backward Cotton Spindles and Dismissing and Re-employing Staff and Workers), issued in cooperation with the SETC and the SDPC, in *China Infobank*. China in 1991 had 41.92 million cotton spindles, of which about 10 million were "backward." Beginning in 1992, the government issued a special plan to update spindle technology and to take 5 million backward spindles out of production. In 1994 provinces were reminded of this 5 million

spindle reduction target and a new target of a reduction by 10 million spindles to be achieved by 1998 was issued. Between 1992 and 1996, only 4.65 million spindles were taken out of production, with a further 1.06 million expected to have been taken out of production by the end of 1998. But at the same time (presumably between 1992 and 1996), 4.44 million new spindles were added, so that the total by the end of 1996 was 41.71 million spindles.

52. "Zhongguo guoyou qiye gaige yu tuokun sannian mubiao de yi jiben shixian" (The Objectives of China's SOE Reform and Three-Year Program to Escape Difficulties Have Already Been Basically Achieved), 20 June 2001, in *China Infobank*. A figure for total employment in all SOEs is not available. Employment in all state-owned units (including, for example, government and Party organizations as well as health care) at the end of 2000 was 78.78 million, down from 107.66 million at the end of 1997 (*Statistical Yearbook 2001*, pp. 118f.). As far as any reduction in government employees is concerned, many of these employees may have been shunted off into semi-independent economic entities.

53. CCPCC, 9 June 1998, "Guanyu qieshi zuohao guoyou qiye xiagang zhigong jiben shenghuo baozhang he zai jiuye gongzuo de tongzhi" (On Conscientiously Providing a Basic Living Guarantee to Laid-off Staff and Workers and Creating Re-employment Work), issued in cooperation with the SC, in *China Infobank*.

54. SC, 28 May 2000, "Guanyu qieshi zuohao qiye lituixiu renyuan jiben yanglao jin anshi zu'e fafang he guoyou qiye xiagang zhigong jiben shenghuo baozhang gongzuo de tongzhi" (On Conscientiously Making Timely and Full Basic Pension Payments and Guaranteeing a Basic Living Allowance for Laid-off Workers of SOEs), in *China Infobank*.

55. Labor and Social Security Ministry (Laodong he shehui baozhang bu), 25 November 1999, "Guanyu qingli shouhui qiye qianjiao shehui baoxianfei youguan wenti" (On Problems Related to the Collection of Overdue Enterprise Social Security Contributions), in *China Infobank*. *Statistical Yearbook 2000*, p. 765.

56. On Liaoning Province see the *Asian Wall Street Journal*, 6 November 2001, p. 1.

57. National People's Congress, 2 December 1986, "Zhonghua renmin gongheguo qiye pochanfa (shixing)" (Trial PRC Bankruptcy Law), in *China Infobank*.

58. For details on the bankruptcy plan see SC, 2 March 1997, "Guanyu zai ruogan chengshi shixing guoyou qiye jianbing pochan he zhigong zai jiuye youguan wenti de buchong tongzhi" (Supplementary Circular on SOE Mergers and Bankruptcy and Staff and Worker Re-employment in Certain Cities), in *China Infobank*.

59. "Zhongguo guojia jingmaowei shenhua guoyou qiye gaige yanjiuzu" (SETC Research Group on Deepening SOE Reform), 25 June 2001, in *China Infobank*.

60. National People's Congress, 15 March 2001, "Guanyu 2000 nian guomin jingji he shehui fazhan jihua zhixing qingkuang yu 2001 nian guomin jingji he shehui fazhan jihua de jueyi" (Decision on the Implementation of the Year 2000 National Economic and Social Development Plan and on the Year 2001 National Economic and Social Development Plan), *Zhonghua renmin gongheguo guowuyuan gongbao*, no. 13 (10 May 2000), pp. 14–25.

61. The 3 million yuan government subsidy for each reduction in 10,000 spindles amounts to a 3 billion yuan subsidy for the overall reduction by 10 million spindles. This subsidy of 3 billion yuan compares to the total profits of all textile SOEs of 3.194 billion yuan in 2000 (*Statistical Yearbook 2001*, p. 423).

62. SC, 27 February 1998, "Guanyu fangzhi gongye shenhua gaige tiaozheng jiegou jiekun niukui gongzuo youguan wenti de tongzhi" (On Some Issues in Strengthening

the Reform of the Textile Industry, Adjusting the Structure, Resolving the Problems and Turning Losses into Profits), in *China Infobank.*

63. *Xinbao*, 30 August 2000, p. 9.

64. CCPCC, 9 June 1998.

65. *Statistical Yearbook* 2001, pp. 49, 245. A recovery rate of 25 percent is suggested by the first results of AMCs in collecting debts and selling SOE equity (*Xinbao*, 30 November 2001, p. 4, and 6 December 2001, p. 7); if the AMCs are handling their most promising assets first, this recovery rate will fall in the future.

66. *Statistical Yearbook 2001*, pp. 49, 245, 770.

67. *Statistical Yearbook 2001*, p. 257.

68. Y. Lin and T. Zhu, "Ownership Restructuring in Chinese State Industry: An Analysis of Evidence on Initial Organizational Changes," *China Quarterly*, no. 166 (June 2001): 305–341.

69. The principal-agent, or corporate governance issue, refers to how one can ensure that managers of the firm act in the interests of the "owners" (the shareholders), or, following the "multiple principal agent theory," in the interests of all stakeholders. (Stiglitz, "Quis Custodiet Ipsos Custodes?"). On Kit Tam, *The Development of Corporate Governance in China* (Cheltenham, UK: Edward Elgar, 1999), in the second chapter provides numerous competing definitions of corporate governance, including corporate governance as understood by Chinese authors. Tam's favored interpretation is a broad definition as "the processes and mechanisms for ensuring that a company performs in a responsible, responsive and pro-active way in the interests of its stakeholders" (p. 18).

70. Alexander Eckstein, "Development Strategies and Policies in Contemporary China," chapter 2 in Alexander Eckstein, ed., *China's Economic Revolution* (Cambridge: Cambridge University Press, 1977), pp. 31–65.

71. For example, of the 520 state key industrial enterprises (of which 514 are state key SOEs), 423 had established a formal "technology development center" (*jishu kaifa zhongxin*) by late 2000. The enterprises are expected to expend an amount equivalent to 3–5 percent of their sales revenue on research and development. (SETC, 1 September 2000, "Guanyu jiaqiang guoyou zhongdian qiye jishu zhongxin jianshe gongzuo de yijian" [Suggestions on Establishing Technology Centers in State-owned Key Enterprises], in *China Infobank.*) Many township and village enterprises and other collective-owned enterprises have in their early phases relied on employees of SOEs for advice in setting up and maintaining their production lines.

72. SETC, October 2001, "'Shiwu' gongye jiegou tiaozheng guihua gangyao" (Outline of the Adjustment in the Industrial Structure During the Tenth Five-Year Plan), in *China Infobank.*

73. X. Xu and Y. Wang, "Ownership Structure, Corporate Governance, and Corporate Performance: The Case of Chinese Stock Companies," Policy Research Working Paper, no. 1794, World Bank Economic Development Institute (June 1997).

74. X. Wang, L.C. Xu, and T. Zhu, "Is Public Listing a Way Out for State-Owned Enterprises? The Case of China," Mimeo (December 2001).

75. On the survey see "Zhongguo guoyou kuisun qiye fuzeren ruhe kandai kuisun wenti" (How Do the Responsible Persons in Loss-Making SOEs View the Losses), 13 May 1998, in *China Infobank.* The question reported here was only one among several, and the survey and its interpretation appear highly professional. The author(s) do not dwell on the administrative interference issue. The article does not state who organized the survey; given its scope and quality, perhaps it was organized by the SETC.

9

Chinese Nationalism

The Precedence of Community and Identity over Individual Rights

Suzanne Ogden

Certain communities, such as religious or ideological communities, and even nations, have as one of their first principles that the preservation of community, community values, and identity takes precedence over individual rights. To summarize the communitarian argument of Amitai Etzioni (one made in essence long ago by Jean-Jacques Rousseau), for communities and nations to remain cohesive, community morality and well-being, not individual morality and well-being, must define virtues. Etzioni challenges the perspective of liberals, libertarians, and even "laissez-faire conservatives," who argue that the individual, not the community, should be deciding what is best. They see community morality as a threat to democratic values because it is based on majoritarian, not individual, values. Once a community determines what its values are, they believe "these will be used to suppress dissent and minorities, to violate individual and civil rights. . . ." By contrast, communitarians believe that even though most democracies are based on majority rule, they are nevertheless concerned that minority and individual rights and values be respected. (This was especially true for the United States, a country founded by dissenters who wanted to escape dogma.)[1]

Making a case in opposition to such liberals as Michael Novak and Sidney Hook, Etzioni argues for the need to find and institutionalize shared communitarian morals and values; for without them, a government is far more likely to rely on coercion. "Once [communitarian] virtues are eroded, social and civil order must, by default, rest more and more on government regulation, controls, and police force."[2] Indeed, this is precisely the problem China's leaders are confronting as they face the collapse of those communitarian values fostered by Marxism-Leninism-Mao Zedong Thought and the replacement of a social structure based on collective units that supported those values. Below the national level of discourse, community has, broadly speaking, been based on the work units and living units (often one and the same) in the cities. In the countryside, community was based on agricultural collectives; but after the dismantling of the communal system in 1984, it was based on village culture, which has tended to be dominated by one or a few family clans. Before the reform period that began in 1979, these hundreds of thousands of collective units were knitted together by socialist policies and dogma; but they were also bound together by a national communism that was rooted in a strong commitment to the Chinese state and nation—not to China's old, feudal culture, but to China as a strong and independent country able to stand up against potential invaders and bullies. With liberalizing economic reforms that encourage and even force people to leave their homes to find work elsewhere, work units in the cities and collectives in the countryside no longer serve as the building block of community. As a result, communitarian values must find other societal frameworks if they are to survive.

Individual Rights and the Nation-state

In the twentieth century, when China's national dignity was challenged by other countries, the people usually rallied behind their government, and even accepted restrictions on their individual rights in the name of the greater good of the society.[3] Indeed, neither individual rights nor one-man-one-vote nor equality has had deep philosophical roots in China. For over 2,000 years, China had accepted a system that emphasized the strict ordering of interpersonal relationships according to Confucian hierarchical standards, in which subordinates were required to do the bidding of their superiors. China's Confucian heritage shaped the belief that the common people had no role to play in governing unless the emperor lost his Heavenly Mandate and that officials were to be obeyed and feared, not voted in and out of office. So the Chinese did not easily grasp the Western democratic notion of governance by the people. The psychological need of the Chinese people to have China recognized as an equal among all nations has seemed to take precedence over a demand for individual freedom. Nationalism has been a collective seeking of recognition and face, and an individual's value has been derived from the value of the collectivity. For this reason, the Chinese people seem to have been more willing to make sacrifices for the strength of the national community than for their own individual freedom. As Gan Yang has noted, since the beginning of the twentieth century, "the Chinese have repeatedly yielded individual independence and personal freedom to the nation's independence and self-determination."[4]

Thus, although Sun Yatsen, the "father" of the Chinese Revolution of 1911, argued for the support of the "Three Principles" of democracy, nationalism, and the "people's livelihood," the core of the inspiration for the revolutionary overthrow of the Manchu (Qing) Dynasty was nationalism, not a desire to establish democracy or individual freedom. For Sun Yatsen, individual rights were never important. Later, he even "dismissed them as inappropriate for China."[5] Although Sun Yatsen conceptualized democratic government as government responsive to the will of the people, he did not envision it as giving the people the right to weaken effective centralized authority. Given the pressing demands China faced, the government could not permit the people to interfere with the administration of the state, as happened in Western liberal democracies. This interpretation of democratic government fit the existing conception of the role of the government in China. Whether imperial, republican, or communist, the Chinese seemed bound by their history and culture to favor a powerful elitist government at the expense of popular democratic rule and individual rights. The chaos suffered when China was under less than authoritarian rule has, to this day, confirmed for many Chinese the correctness of this view.

Sun interpreted the European dismissal of China as "a sheet of loose sand" to mean that the Chinese people had "excessive individual freedom." Unlike the Europeans who, Sun averred, made revolution because they lacked freedom, the Chinese needed to make revolution in order to *end* excessive individual freedom and bind them together so that they could resist foreign oppression. He concluded by asking what the relationship was between the slogan of the French Revolution, "liberty, equality, and fraternity," and the slogan for the Chinese revolution, "nationalism, democracy, and the people's livelihood":

> Our nationalism could, in my opinion, be said to be equivalent to their freedom, because to realize nationalism is precisely to fight for our nation's freedom. . . . How should we apply the word freedom today? If it were applied to the individual, we would turn into "a sheet of loose sand." *It is therefore imperative to apply the word freedom, not to the individual, but to the nation. The individual should not have too much freedom, but the nation must have complete freedom. . . . To achieve this goal, however, we must all sacrifice our [individual] freedom.*[6]

Similarly, the May Fourth Movement and the New Culture Movement of the 1920s reflected a desire to end China's humiliation at the hands of other powers and a search for national strength. Mr. Science and Mr. Democracy were part of the inspiration of this search to make China rich and powerful, but the demand for individual rights took a back seat.

China's nationalism has above all, then, been directed toward shoring up China's national dignity, with a gain in dignity for the individual largely a spin-off from an enhanced national dignity. Individual rights were rationalized as a way of strengthening the nation.[7] In fact, not only China's broad masses, but also its intellectuals and political leaders, have *craved* recognition of China's greatness—far more than they seem to have craved individual rights. In the nineteenth and twentieth centuries, China's well-educated intellectuals were still dedicated to the traditional model of a strong state. As a result, "Chinese liberals fell into the trap of nationalism and brought tragedy upon themselves by abandoning their beliefs in liberalism for the sake of national salvation or national construction."[8]

Since the Chinese Communist Party (CCP) gained power in 1949, the Chinese people have appeared genuinely angry with the West (and Japan), which they see as having repeatedly tried to thwart China from becoming a great power, infringing on China's sovereign rights, and even trying to take away Chinese territory:

- from the 1950s to 1971 by excluding China from participation in the world community and international trade through policies of "isolation and containment";
- since 1989, by using the issue of human rights as a pretext for threatening the end of China's most-favored-nation trade status (normal trade status), denying China the right to host the year 2000 Olympics, and blocking China's entry into the World Trade Organization for years;
- by accusing China of "stealing" U.S. nuclear secrets and making illegal contributions to the U.S. Democratic Party in the 1996 elections;
- by continuing U.S. military support to Taiwan and the sending of two U.S. aircraft carriers to the Taiwan Strait in 1996;
- by Japan permitting the repair of a lighthouse on one of the Diaoyu/Ryuku Islands in 1996, thereby seeming to renew Japan's challenge to Chinese claims of sovereignty;
- by NATO's bombing of the Chinese Embassy in Belgrade, Yugoslavia in May 1999 during the war over Kosovo;[9]
- by U.S. air surveillance of China, which led to the crash of a Chinese jet and an emergency landing of the U.S. plane on the island of Hainan; and
- by the U.S. consideration of building a theater missile defense that might include Taiwan, as well as a national missile defense that would deny China a second strike capability.

All these events and policies fuel the view in China that its security and greatness are under threat today, just as it has been so much of the time in the past 150 years. Because China's nationalism today is propelled by a sense that the West is out to harm China, much of the nationalism is anti-Western in tone.[10] Thus, although there was significant public support in China's cities for the Tiananmen demonstrators' basic demands in 1989, a shift in sentiments occurred in the following years. Many dissidents, as well as the general public, while still angered by party-state corruption, and disapproving of the use of force to end the demonstrations, nevertheless came to support the government's view that, first, the demonstrations were endangering China's unity and stability; and second, that the West had supported these demonstrations for just this reason.[11] In response to the question (in 1988), "What is the most important criterion for evaluating whether a country is well-managed," and (in 1990), "What is the most important criterion for judging whether a state is doing well," Chinese urban youth (whether before or after the Tiananmen demonstrations of 1989) ranked "social stability and justice" (1988) and "social stability" (1990) as the most important, with support for greater democracy or the protection of individual rights much less important. Support for "a powerful country" and "high international status" also outranked interest in individual rights. The rankings were:

1988

1. social stability and justice;
2. a high standard of living;
3. a powerful country;
4. high international status;
5. full protection of freedom and individual rights;
6. have a sort of concept of universal harmony;
7. a low polarization of wealth;
8. a society's wealth and power is collectively developed.

1990

1. social stability;
2. strong economy;
3. high standard of living;
4. collective beliefs;
5. high degree of democracy.[12]

In another study of several large cities, the concern for social stability shot up from ranking seventh in 1993 to ranking first in 1995.[13] In a 1994 study of urban residents, respondents again considered social stability the most important condition to be hoped for from reforms (76.9 percent). Respondents felt it was even more important than that the reforms should lead to increased income (68.5 percent); and far more important than that they should raise social status (33.9 percent), have the right to know how the state's decisions are made (33.4 percent), or gain the right to have a say in public affairs (25.3 percent).[14] A 1995 study on the relationship between state, collective, and individual interests indicated that the vast majority of Chinese surveyed (70.9 percent) believe "individual interests should follow the interests of the party and country," an increase of 10 percent over 1994.[15]

Although scholars do publish articles challenging the perspective that the collective rights of a society or nation are of a higher order than individual rights,[16] the themes of national unity and nationalism are still paramount. Further, the people believe the government has been particularly successful in gaining respect for China as a state. For example, in a 1994 survey, when asked to evaluate progress in every aspect of the society, economy, and politics, the respondents ranked the government as most successful at "maintaining unity of the motherland" and "progress in foreign relations."[17]

Although many Chinese may truly dislike their government, they seem to overwhelmingly support the Chinese government when it is able to make the case that China is a nation under threat. This support comes from a deep love of China as a nation and a culture, something the people want protected; but it has also been built on a carefully constructed history that portrays China as the "victim" of other states, a history familiar to every person schooled in China. In this context, United States pressure to promote democratization and improve human rights has come to be viewed by a growing number of Chinese as a mere pretext for interfering in China's affairs and containing China's greatness.[18] Nor has any amount of evidence and protestation on the part of the U.S. government been able to convince the Chinese government, or its people, that the bombing of the Chinese embassy was accidental.[19] One poll indicated that 90 percent of respondents in Beijing, Shanghai, and Guangzhou thought the attack was intentional.[20] Chinese appear to assume that the motive was to destabilize China and to stop China from becoming a great power.

Of course, the regime wants the support of the Chinese people for the stance it takes in foreign affairs. At the same time, it has been mindful of not letting nationalism get out of hand by becoming a force propelling Chinese foreign policy. That is, the regime has wanted to use patriotic nationalism to hold China together, not to rationalize a militant nationalism abroad; but keeping nationalism in check has at times been a challenging task. China's leaders seem to believe that the best approach is to build a strong sense of national cohesiveness based on cultural values, socialist morality, and economic progress rather than a nationalism based primarily on hostility toward the outside world.

Traditional Culture and National Identity

In addition to threats from the outside world, China faces other challenges that threaten its sense of community. These challenges are generated by internal institutional changes and social and economic liberalization, as well as the invasive and destabilizing forces of capitalism, individualism, commercialism, and modernization. The search for communitarian values to replace the collectivist values of communism has led to official support for nationalism, patriotism, and the re-invention of Chinese popular culture. Many Chinese intellectuals do not believe Chinese traditional culture can serve as the foundation for a strong national identity, but others advocate a return to Confucian morality as the basis for China's nationalism because it "enables individuals to overcome their excessive individualism and contribute more to the nation as a whole. This is where the meaning of [the] Confucian ethic *tianxia weigong* (the whole world as one community) lies.[21] In 1992, China's cultural nationalists (sometimes referred to as "neoconservatives") published a document stating that Marxism-Leninism had become ineffective "in mobilizing loyalty and legitimating the state. It was necessary to develop a new ideological vision that drew selectively from China's culture." They argued that China needed to become a powerful state, and that, at this point in history, communist ideology was useless for this purpose. Only nationalism could play this role.[22] As for the trade-off between a strong state and less democracy that this could entail, even those same intellectuals who demonstrated in Tiananmen Square in 1989, but today "almost blindly" support the CCP, would describe themselves as "patriots first and democrats second."[23]

Many ordinary Chinese people have tried to fill the vacuum created by the demise of collective social virtues and a disintegrating sense of community with religion. Unlike nationalism, the re-emergence of religion is not the result of a state-directed policy; yet ironically, religion—and especially religious cults—has flourished since the 1990s precisely because of the state's efforts to draw upon the great traditions of ancient and imperial China as an antidote for the wholesale Westernization and rejection of the Chinese past that had dominated the 1980s. Unexpectedly, the search for the Chinese "essence" *(guoqing)*, instead of remaining confined to the great Confucian homilies and traditions, led to the revival of traditional popular culture. The result was the emergence of cultural nationalism in the form of popular cults, among which were a host of *qigong* cults.[24]

Outside of China, the best known of these cults is the Falungong (Wheel of Law), which was founded in 1992. It is a good example of an effort to reassert traditional collective social virtues in China, including as it does a broad mix of traditional populist values: Buddhism, Taoism, magic, popular science, meditation, and breathing exercises (generally known as *qigong*). It is particularly appealing to those who have suffered from some of the negative effects of capitalism and commercialism in China, or who are ill. Still, some Chinese worry that the sect could destabilize China and should be banned; for, although perhaps more benign than many of the charletans around in China taking people's money, Falungong leaders have made claims to extraordinary spiritual powers, and predicted the end of the world, as well as a horrible death for anyone who does not belong to Falungong. This has made some Chinese anxious and fearful, and they are inclined to believe the government's claims that many have suffered ill health and even death from following the sect's practices.[25] Thus, what may be an effort to develop new community values for one group of people may be perceived by the nonbelieving community as quite destabilizing and even anticommunity. The latter tend to understand the government's crackdown on the Falungong sect not as a deprivation of individual rights, but rather as a policy that will help maintain China's unity, stability, and national strength.

The Chinese government has tried to revive Chinese culture as part of its effort to confront a "fever" for Western ideas, but its overall goal was to use culture to bolster the power of (cultural) nationalism, which it chose to fill the vacuum caused by the collapse of communist values. The government hoped to carefully circumscribe the dimensions that this nationalism assumed in China, but the people embraced it more passionately than anticipated. Indeed, although the government wants to use nationalism to serve its own interest, it has had a difficult time harnessing its public expression. Many observers believe, in fact, that a highly nationalistic Chinese people (and the younger ranks of the People's Liberation Army) have had to be held back by a more rational, pragmatic, and cautious government. They believe that if President Jiang Zemin had been *voted* into power, he would have had to take more forceful actions to recover Taiwan in order to satisfy the demands of the electorate; and that if Taiwan were successfully to declare independence, the Chinese people would want to overthrow the Chinese Communist Party regime. In their view, it is only because Jiang is not democratically elected that he can be unresponsive to popular nationalism. His militant rhetoric over Taiwan may thus be viewed as a mere sop to the Chinese people and the military, a substitute for real action. Evidence supporting this view is that, beginning in March 2000, when Taiwan was holding elections, the government refused to approve any application from students for demonstration permits to march against Taiwan independence.[26] In addition, on May 19,

2000, the Chinese government also issued an order to university students not to demonstrate regardless of what Taiwan's newly elected president, Chen Shuibian, said in his inaugural speech the next day concerning Taiwan's relationship with the mainland.[27] Similarly, the Chinese government was exceedingly reluctant to get drawn into a dispute with the Japanese over the Diaoyu (Ryuku) Islands in the fall of 1996. During this period of heightened tension when I was working in Beijing, students were quarantined to their dormitories on the anniversary of one of the significant events of the Sino-Japanese War. The students' nationalism was clearly far in advance of the Chinese government's own willingness to take action. As Jianwei Wang puts it, "[T]he surge of nationalism is largely a spontaneous phenomenon reflecting the change of China's international position. To a large extent, it is transgenerational and transnational, as well as transideological. It is shared by Chinese overseas, including many who are strongly antiregime and anticommunist ... [and] cannot easily be explained by government manipulation."[28]

Thus, it would be wrong to conclude that nationalism had to be whipped up by the Chinese government. Nationalism cuts both ways, however, and the government knows well that excessive nationalism might not only undercut the Chinese Communist Party's ability to rule but also "disrupt China's paramount foreign policy objective of creating a long-term peaceful environment for its modernization program."[29] The state's concern is reflected in its rejection of more radical nationalism, such as that advocated by He Xin[30] and the authors of *The China that Can Say No*,[31] as well as in its efforts to control anti-Japanese sentiment. Indeed, the mainland's response to the Japanese provocation over the Diaoyu Islands (noted above) was far more restrained than in Taiwan and Hong Kong. The government's concern that nationalism had to be controlled was also evident in its efforts to restrain anti-Americanism in the aftermath of the NATO bombing of the Chinese Embassy in Yugoslavia. "Every Chinese could tell you that if the government had not taken measures early enough to dredge the emotions among the masses, the American embassy and consulates could have been burned to the ground and diplomats killed."[32] Chinese students in Beijing cried out "Blood for blood!" Most seemed to feel that China had been insulted and offended by the attack, and apart from demanding an apology and compensation, wanted militarization and revenge. Almost all expressed intense nationalism and interpreted the bombing as an effort to victimize China.[33]

The Chinese nationalism that has been spurred on by what are perceived as "anti-China" policies from abroad explains why even China's dissidents, such as those who participated in the 1989 Tiananmen Square demonstrations, overwhelmingly take the government's side in defending China's claims to Taiwan and Tibet, their extraordinary pleasure in Hong Kong's return to

Beijing's rule in 1997,[34] and their anger at what they interpret as the West's support for Japan's military expansion and containment of China, including U.S. consideration of plans to build a "theater missile defense" in Northeast Asia that would protect Japan, and possibly Taiwan, from attack. The West's support of the Dalai Lama's request for greater autonomy for Tibet, its continued sale of weapons to Taiwan, its pressure for a more democratic Hong Kong, and its rationalization of its involvement in a war in Yugoslavia as protecting the "human rights" of the Kosovars against the actions of the Serbian government—all suggest to the Chinese people that Western governments are interfering, or preparing to interfere, in what are legitimately China's own affairs. Protecting and advancing China's national dignity in the face of such onslaughts still seem to take precedence for the Chinese people over protecting and advancing their own rights.[35]

China's intellectuals have expressed remarkably diverse opinions in the debates now raging over nationalism, modernization, external threats to China, and China's position within the international system. Ironically, many of those Chinese intellectuals advocating cultural nationalism received their training in the West. They have used the intellectual tools of the West, including " postcolonialism, postmodernism, post-Marxism, and Orientalism to attack Western culture." To wit, they "have chosen as their weapons the language, concepts, and style of Western discourses," with the result that their own discourses on nationalism are so full of Western jargon that anyone unfamiliar with it would find it difficult to comprehend "these erudite exponents of Chinese nationalistic writings."[36] The following lists only a few of the more widely debated issues among the diverse intellectual groupings in China, from leftists and neo-leftists to liberals, conservatives, and cultural nationalists.[37]

- Nationalism motivated by external threats to China;
- Appropriate symbols for China's new nationalism;
- The effect of China's traditional culture and a culturally fueled nationalism on efforts to democratize;
- China's ties with the international system and the degree to which it should accept established international norms and rules that were made largely without China's participation;[38]
- The degree to which the state should relinquish Chinese traditions and "Chineseness" and accept more "universal" values such as those prevalent in the West;[39]
- The degree to which Westernization-oriented government policies should guide China's domestic development.[40]
- The role of ideology in maintaining national identity;

- The relationship between Confucian-based ethnic nationalism and modern nationalism;
- The superiority of Chinese civilization, and whether a "patriot" must support China's traditional cultural values and oppose Western liberalization;
- The tensions between national identity and internationalization, and between a national cultural identity and cultural invasion from abroad;[41]
- Samuel Huntington's portrayal of the post–Cold War period and future conflicts.[42]

As for Huntington, the arguments among Chinese intellectuals over the contrary ideas of Huntington and Francis Fukuyama[43] engendered a debate even more rowdy than the intellectual debate their ideas generated in the West. An increasingly large number of China's intellectuals have come to the conclusion that ideology has, in the post–Cold War period, been replaced by a desire on the part of individual nation-states to enhance their own national identity and interests. Confrontations will thus arise "between different nation-states, understood as cultures, but under the banner of nationalism."[44]

Education and Nationalism

Among the world's nations today, China is unusual in the degree to which it presses the theme of national unity and national dignity. And it does so successfully. Throughout the period of communist rule, the state has made "love of the motherland" and an emphasis on doing what is good for the country a paramount theme in school education. In primary school, children are taught to "love the motherland"; in secondary school, to "love socialism." Students are urged to study hard, work hard, and keep in good health so that *China* will have international respect and never again be disparaged as the "sick man of Asia." The CCP leadership has emphasized the physical and spiritual health of its people for the purpose of making the Chinese state strong. The same themes appear in the press, and even in business negotiations with foreigners.[45]

The success of China's efforts to inculcate patriotism is palpable, whether it is a little ten-year-old girl on the street who looks up at a foreigner and blurts out, "You foreigners used to look down on us. Now China is strong, and you must respect us"[46] to polls that indicate that what most pleases Chinese people is the fact that China has international respect and stature. In a 1994 study of urban residents, out of a choice of eighteen conditions of life that pleased or displeased the respondents, they took most satisfaction in China's international status (63.5 percent).[47] To be a "patriot" in today's China means, then, to support the national community and its goals, notably, national unification, economic growth, and political stability.[48]

These themes need not be viewed as reflecting a conscious effort to deny individuals their rights, but rather, a sincere and profound anxiety about the victimization of a weak and divided China. Unquestionably, China's long history of fragmentation and of imperialists taking advantage of China's weakness has spurred on China's efforts to inculcate patriotism and its attendant nationalism. In the wake of the demonstrations in Tiananmen Square in 1989, however, China's leaders believed that the antidote to the fragmenting forces created by China's "open door" policy and economic liberalization was to pull China back into a collective community working for common goals. In hopes of instilling a greater commitment to the state, it required first year university students to undergo military training. Beginning in 1992, China's government widened its patriotic education campaign beyond primary and secondary schools to include universities. In 1994, when it abolished the national exam on Marxism, it substituted courses on patriotic education in high schools and colleges. In the "I am Chinese" program in universities, students were taught to be proud of being Chinese because of the great things China, and the Chinese Communist Party, had done. The Chinese Communist Party leadership was legitimate not because of its communist ideals and ideology, but because of its *patriotism* as it struggled for China's national independence.[49] In some circles, the nationalism generated by the patriotic education campaign was so intense that it came to be considered "unpatriotic" to discuss individual rights and democracy. The 1994 document, "Outlines for Patriotic Education," offered guidelines for teaching about patriotism that included both cultural and political messages: the official party line and Deng Xiaoping's theory of "socialism with Chinese characteristics" were the guiding principle; the purpose of patriotic education was socialist modernization and the peaceful reunification of China, as well as to "rejuvenate China's national spirit" and "reconstruct the sense of national esteem and dignity." The key points in the curriculum included a study of Chinese history, especially about the CCP's rise to power, and the incompatibility of China's special characteristics with Western values. Overall, the patriotic education campaign was linked to morality, which focused on socialist values.[50] As Jonathan Unger has so aptly noted, Chinese patriotism is an "admixture of political nationalism, ethnic Han identity, and a culturalist pride that is observed in allusions to Chinese civilization as a point of self-identity."[51]

On the other hand, it must be noted that the patriotic nationalism that emerged after the crackdown on Tiananmen Square demonstrators in 1989 was not entirely a response to victimization from other countries. Although foreign involvement with the 1989 demonstrators and the many external challenges to the Chinese state enhanced nationalist appeals after 1989, the regime (and even many intellectuals who had participated in the Tiananmen demonstrations) also used patriotism instrumentally to justify rejection of sudden democratization in China, because it might lead to national disintegration, as it had in Eastern Europe and the republics of the former Soviet Union. Thus patriotic nationalism has been used to create a sense of community as part of an effort to shore up the legitimacy of the regime.[52]

Nevertheless, the government has successfully pressed the paramount importance of China's national dignity and national territorial integrity. (The public tends to believe China's media coverage of international affairs, Taiwan, and Tibet far more than its coverage of domestic affairs.) For example, according to polls done in Chinese cities by the Lingdian (Horizon) Company and other survey institutes in 1994 and 1995, the public agreed strongly with the government's stance on a variety of policies that advanced China's "open door" policy, such as China's bid for hosting the Olympic Games, admission to WTO, and hosting the United Nations' Women's Congress in 1995.[53] The public also broadly supported Beijing's policies on the return of Hong Kong to Chinese sovereignty, its policies toward Taiwan, and its position on relations with the United States. In a poll conducted in 1996, respondents stated that the Chinese government should use domestic public opinion as a sort of political force to support its international policies.[54]

Surveys have also measured nationalism as what might be called a loyalty to the state, that is, a commitment to the community which is held together by the state. For example, in a survey done in Beijing in 1991 and repeated in 1995,

- Over 70 percent "strongly disagreed" or "mostly disagreed" with the statement, "If the state disappoints me, I have no obligation to do anything for the state."
- More than 80 percent "strongly agreed" or "mostly agreed" with the statement, "Even if the state wrongs me, I still must respect the state."[55]

Similarly, in another poll (1988), youth were asked to respond to such statements as,

- "Even though humble, I dare not forget to love the state [the motherland]."[56]
- "An individual's affairs are minor, no matter how big [no matter how important to the individual]; the state's affairs are big, no matter how small [no matter how insignificant they are to the individual]."[57]

These are, incidentally, not the sorts of questions which would probably even cross the minds of most survey researchers in Western liberal democratic countries; but they reflect a very "Chinese" way of thinking about their commitment to the nation-state.

Cultural Openness, Pluralism, and the Threat to Community

Is China's opening up to the world of ideas outside leading to a potentially fragmenting pluralism? Is participation in the international community itself a threat to China's identity as a nation-state? How open should China be to the emergence of a pluralism which could threaten national unity? Will the adoption of an "international" perspective by its citizens challenge the idea of China as a *national* community? Can the support for individual rights, in the form of liberalism, which prides itself on creating strong communities, also mean the end of community?

Francis Fukuyama, in his commentary on the United States, argues that because it has become unacceptable to believe

> . . . in any *one* doctrine because of an overriding commitment to be open to *all* the world's beliefs and 'value systems,' it should not be surprising that the strength of community life has declined in America. This decline has occurred not *despite* liberal principles, but *because* of them. This suggests that no fundamental strengthening of community life will be possible unless individuals give back certain of their rights to communities, and accept the return of certain historical forms of intolerance.[58]

This is an argument against multiculturalism, a "liberal" doctrine that embraces or at least respects the values of all cultures as equal. Multiculturalism challenges the legitimacy of communities based on distinct values and identities that are interpreted as *superior* to other values. Fukuyama's argument thus makes the case for why China might resist becoming open to those cultural values from abroad that threaten the cohesiveness of a community unified by Chinese cultural values. A communal identity requires distinct values and traditions, a sense of otherness, which set it apart from other communities and make belonging to it worthwhile. If a community accepts the validity of other values as equal, and begins to adopt those values as part of its own identity, it either flourishes as the archetypical liberal community (which in turn rigidly discriminates against those who insist on nonliberal values) or it ceases to exist as a distinct community, the raison d'être for its existence.

The issue is how open China can be to a multiplicity of ideas, without their threatening the maintenance of community, and even redefining what it means to be Chinese.[59] It should not be surprising if China sees the balance differently from the United States, where the battle about how open to be to competing values is hardly over, and where much of the population strongly opposes the liberal values that undergird the pluralism of multiculturalism. Nor is China alone in its concern for maintaining its distinct national identity. European countries have themselves been fighting "spiritual pollution," the same term used by the Chinese to refer to efforts to limit the invasion of foreign cultural values. In Europe, the film, television, and music industries are seen as major instruments in socializing people into their own cultures. Allowing them to fall into foreign hands is considered a serious cultural threat. In 1996, using reasoning and language virtually identical to that used in China, the European Parliament went so far as to pass a resolution limiting the quantity of foreign (i.e., American) television programming in order to protect Europe from "spiritual pollution."[60]

France has tried to control "spiritual pollution" and sustain French national identity by such policies as prohibiting the Anglicization of French and not permitting its North African immigrants to engage in Islamic practices in the schools.[61] Further, France has banned books concerning Islamic fundamentalism on the grounds that they are a threat to the "national interest."[62] France, Great Britain, and Germany have banned the cult of (and free speech about) Scientism, which in Hollywood is considered a religion, not a cult. Both France and Great Britain still debate whether self-censorship by the press is adequate, or whether government legislation on censorship of the press is necessary. Thus, even liberal democratic countries see the opening up to new ideas and new values from other cultures as a potential threat to cultural and community identity.

Within Asia, countries such as Japan and Singapore have also resisted opening up to cultural invasion from abroad. And countries like the United States, Germany, and Singapore have tried to restrict pornography on the Internet, with Singapore adding restrictions on religious information. It is certainly the case that China does not want the Internet used for the purpose of subverting the Chinese state. While some might consider this ludicrously impossible, other states also take measures to control the Internet when they do think it possible. Indeed, the Internet is carefully monitored by the internal security service of every major liberal democratic country; and "information warfare," the stealing and destruction of information on computers through the use of the Internet, is a major concern for all developed states today. American companies rather arbitrarily monitor the e-mail and Internet use of their employees. And in 2000, Great Britain's Parliament passed a law that gives the government wide powers to monitor encrypted e-mail traffic and other coded communications among organizations, individuals, and companies. Malaysia and Singapore already have such laws.[63] So, it is not surprising that China also debates the problems and concerns of liberalization and democratization when interpreted as the right of individuals and organizations to introduce ideas that challenge the values binding the Chinese into a cohesive community or threaten national security.

Globalization, and the erosion of national sovereignty, may also have a corrosive effect on a state's identity. China, like all countries, must decide where to take a stand in this trade-off between communal identity and the universalization of values: Becoming more deeply enmeshed in the international community means the Chinese state will have to relinquish control over many of its community values. China is, in short, facing a number of trade-offs, but its position is hardly unique.

Do the Chinese people support globalization and the potential challenge to Chinese stability and identity that it is bringing? According to a survey of the attitudes of urban residents toward China's "open door policy," there is cautious support for enlarging openness, although the survey tells us little as to whether support is only because respondents see commercial advantage, or for broader reasons.[64] In any event, globalization will undoubtedly affect China's self-perceptions. China's interpretation of its own history and culture has shaped its national myth and profoundly affected its self-perceptions. In this, of course, China is not alone, for "any nation, even the United States, is held together by stronger cultural cement than reason. What appears to be politically rational behavior is actually driven by common stories about the origins and destiny of the nation, about its place within the larger community of nations and within the process of history."[65] Arguably, Chinese identity as a nation, formed in isolation from knowledge of others, was a pseudo identity, one that held up while China was isolated, but could not have withstood the test of time. It is only by seeing themselves in contrast to other nations that the Chinese may, in fact, achieve a new sense of who they are.

What, then, does nationalism and the precedence of community and national identity over individual rights mean for the future of civil society in China? "From a Western perspective, 'communitarian' citizens lack the freedom of will, conditions of trust, and protection of law to act freely as rational individuals. Thus, the basic requisites of civil society are missing. But from a non-Western perspective, one might see this as a slow transition to soft authoritarianism, mediated by the state rather than by civil society. If Japan, Taiwan, and South Korea can make this transition over time, why not assume the same for Chinese citizens?"[66]

The issue for any society is, of course, one of balance: How can communitarian values, especially ones based on patriotism and nationalism, hold a community together, yet adequately protect minority and individual rights? And how can communitarian values also protect pluralistic values, yet not have those values undercut the communitarian values that maintain stability and national unity? Pluralism "provides no moral foundations for community-wide consensus per se, no overarching values and criteria for working up differences other than such mechanical . . . notions as splitting the differences and nose count."[67] Pluralism could, then, significantly challenge the many myths and self-perceptions on which Chinese nationalism and identity as a community is based.

The experiences of post-communist Eastern European states such as Yugoslavia, as well as Russia and the former republics of the USSR, suggest that states have a limited ability to accommodate individualism and pluralism when simultaneously confronted with the fragmenting forces of globalization, modernization, capitalism, and commercialism. It is a formidable achievement to get individuals within a state to curtail the pursuit of their private interests out of concern for the greater public good. The problem remains that an unbridled individualism that loses sight of broader national needs, and a pluralism that merely represents a host of narrowly defined constituencies seeking their own self-interests instead of the public interest, could lead China once again to become a "sheet of loose sand."

Notes

1. Amitai Etzioni, "On the Place of Virtues in a Pluralistic Democracy," in Gary Marks and Larry Diamond, eds., *Reexamining Democracy: Essays in Honor of Seymour Martin Lipset* (London: Sage Publications, 1992), p. 71.

2. Ibid., p. 72.

3. Some of the following commentary originally appeared in Suzanne Ogden, *Inklings of Democracy in China* (Cambridge, Mass.: Harvard University Asia Center, Harvard University Press, 2002) which, in chapters 1–3, presents an expanded analysis of the impact of Chinese history and culture on views of individual rights and the role of the state.

4. Gan Yang, "Build a Country with a United Constitutional Government Rooted in Individual Freedom and Rights," *China Strategic Review* 1, no. 4 (July 5, 1996): 5.

5. Stephen C. Angle and Marina Svensson, eds., "Introduction," in "On Rights and Human Rights: A Contested and Evolving Chinese Discourse, 1900–1949," *Contemporary Chinese Thought* 31, no. 1 (Fall 1999): 6.

6. Sun Yatsen, "Minquan zhuyi" (The Principle of Democracy), lecture given in 1924, reprinted in *Sanmin zhuyi* (The Three People's Principles) (Taipei: Sanmin Press, 1996), pp. 73, 96–98, 100, 101; translated in Angle and Svensson, eds., "On Rights and Human Rights," pp. 66–68. Italics added.

7. During the May Fourth Movement that began in 1919, for example, the emphasis on women's rights, and the development of the *baihua* movement allowed the common person access to literacy by changing the form of writing Chinese from a difficult classical form to a colloquial form.

8. Chongyi Feng, "The Party-state, Liberalism and Social Democracy: The Debate on China's Future," paper presented at a workshop on "Chinese Intellectuals between the State and the Market," Fairbank Center, Harvard University (June 30–July 1, 2001), p. 10.

9. For a collection of translated Chinese writings about the anti-China press in the United States, see Carine Defoort, "Demonizing China: A Critical Analysis of the U.S. Press," *Contemporary Chinese Thought* 30, no. 2 (Winter 1998–99).

10. Geremie R Barmé, "To Screw Foreigners is Patriotic: China's Avant-Garde Nationalists," in Jonathan Unger, ed., *Chinese Nationalism* (Armonk, N.Y.: M.E. Sharpe, 1996), pp. 183–208.

11. Based on discussions with Chinese people during my stay in China in 1996 and 1997, from the Chinese press since 1989, as well as from talking with Chinese students and scholars who have come to the United States and England since 1989.

12. Chinese Academy of Social Sciences, Institute of Sociology, Project Team on the Change of Values of Contemporary Chinese Youth, *Zhongguo qingnian de toushi: Guanyu yidairen de jiazhiguan yanbian yanjiu* (A Perspective on Chinese Youth: Research on One Generation's Changing Values) (Beijing: Beijing Publishing House, 1993), pp. 140–141. In 1988, rural and urban youth were surveyed separately; in 1990, the results were merged.

13. In 1993, the top three concerns were prioritized as "housing reform, anti-corruption, and price reform"; by November 1995, the top three were "social order, inflation, and anti-corruption." Yue Yuan, "Stability, Psychology, and Attitude of the Public in Chinese Cities in 1995–1996," in Liu Jiang, Xueyi Lu, and Weilun Shan, eds., *1995–96 nian Zhongguo shehui xingshi fenxi yu yuce* (Analysis and Predictions of Social Conditions in China, 1995–96) (Beijing: Chinese Academy of Social Sciences Publishing House, 1996), chart, p. 113.

14. State System Reform Commission for Societal Investigation, "The Characteristics of Psychological Changes of Our Nation's Urban Residents and Analysis of Reform and Society Situations—An Analytical Report for 1994 by the State System Reform Commission for Societal Investigation," in *World of Management* (Guanli shijie) (Beijing), no. 4, 1995, pp. 130–136.

15. Jiang et al., *1995–96 nian Zhongguo shehui xingshi fenxi yu yuce*, p. 312. As with most of the surveys, there is no need to accept them at face value if they are overseen by a government research institute such as CASS, but it begs the question of why the Chinese would bother to present a survey with false results on this matter. See Ogden, "Appendix: Value of Surveys Done in China," in *Inklings of Democracy in China.* The real problem with assuming the surveys accurately reflect public opinion is that there is a tendency for respondents (especially youth) in China to say what they think they should say—not because of fear of reprisals, but because they want to think of themselves as "modern." See Yiyun Chen, "Out of the Traditional Halls of Academe: Exploring New Avenues for Research on Women," translated in Christina K. Gilmartin et al., eds., *Engendering China: Women, Culture, and the State* (Cambridge, Mass.: Harvard University Press, 1994), pp. 70–73.

16. For example, one legal scholar argues that according to Marxism, the history of mankind is the history of the development of individuals. Individual activities and development are the basis of society's collective activities and development. Thus, as individuals are the building blocks of society, their rights are basic to the collective rights of society. A communist society will be a collective in which, according to Marx, the free development of each person is the condition for the free development

of the entire society. Buyun Li, "Lun geren renquan yu jiti renquan" (On Individual Human Rights and Collective Human Rights), *Journal of Graduate School of Chinese Academy of Social Sciences* (Beijing), no. 6 (1994), pp. 23, 24. The author goes on to say (p. 25) that not all "individual rights" *(geren quanli)* are "human rights" *(renquan)*. Contracts between individuals, or between an individual and a state enterprise, for example, are not "human rights," but merely individual rights.

17. These were ranked ahead of "strengthening collective authority of the central leadership," "curbing inflation," "combating criminal activities," "fighting corruption," and other items. Jianhua Lu, Guodong Yang, and Qing Tu, "Social Conditions in 1995–1996: Comprehensive Analyses of a Survey of Experts." In Jiang et al., eds., *1995–96 nian Zhongguo shehui xingshi fenxi yu yuce*, p. 37.

18. For how America's "anti-China" policies lead to the United States being the most disliked country in the world among Chinese youth, see "The Vision of the World from the Perspective of Chinese Youth," an influential survey that was conducted in May 1995 and published in *China Youth Daily*. The results of this survey are summarized in Muqun Zhu, "Chinese Nationalism in the Post-Deng Era," *China Strategic Review* 2, no. 2 (March/April 1997): 81–83.

19. Indeed, since the 1999 embassy bombing, it has been difficult to find any person born and raised in China (including those with access to the Internet and CNN news), or Overseas Chinese living in any country, or even those who have lived for years in the United States and have permanent residency who reject the Chinese government's view that the bombing was intentional.

20. See Barrett L. McCormick, "Introduction," in Edward Friedman and Barrett L. McCormick, eds., *What if China Doesn't Democratize?* (Armonk, N.Y.: M.E. Sharpe, 2000), note 3. However, these figures are from China's press.

21. Jun Zhao, "'Tianxia weigong' yu shiji zhijiao de Zhongguo minzu zhuyi" ('The Whole World as One Community' and Chinese Nationalism at the Turn of the Century), *ZLGL*,1 (1996), pp. 1–3; referenced in Yongnian Zheng, *Discovering Chinese Nationalism in China: Modernization, Identity, and International Relations* (Cambridge: Cambridge University Press, 1999), p. 85.

22. Suisheng Zhao, "We Are Patriots First and Democrats Second: The Rise of Chinese Nationalism in the 1990s," in Friedman and McCormick, eds., *What if China Doesn't Democratize?* pp. 3, 22.

23. Samuel Wang, "Teaching Patriotism in China," *China Strategic Review* 1, no. 4 (July 5, 1996): 13.

24. Vivienne Shue, seminar on "Falun Gong," New England China Seminar, Harvard University (December 5, 2000). Shue notes that, although *qigong* cults had already emerged in the 1980s, they became a cultural craze by the 1990s.

25. Discussions with Chinese colleagues, Beijing and Shanghai, fall 1999.

26. "Taiwan Stands Up," *The Economist* (March 25, 2000): 28.

27. Shiping Zheng, discussion, May 2000.

28. Jianwei Wang, "Democratization and China's Nation Building," in Friedman and McCormick, eds., *What if China Doesn't Democratize?* p. 37.

29. Jianwei Wang, "Democratization and China's Nation Building," p.37.

30. The writings of Xin He, a scholar at the Chinese Academy of Social Sciences, are collected in two volumes entitled *Zhonghua fuxing yu shijie weilai* (Renovation of China and the Future of the World) (Chengdu: Sichuan renmin chubanshe, 1996). Zhao, "We Are Patriots First and Democrats Second," p. 33, note 40. See ibid., pp. 30–31 for other intellectuals who were against any kind of Westernization.

31. Qiang Song et al., *Zhongguo keyi shuo bu* (The China That Can Say No) (Beijing: Chinese Commercial Alliance Press, 1996).

32. Wang, "Democratization and China's Nation Building," pp. 37–38.

33. Peter Hays Gries, "Tears of Rage: Chinese Nationalist Reactions to the Belgrade Embassy Bombing," *China Journal*, no. 46 (July 2001): 25–43. Gries based his analysis on 281 letters, poems, and essays sent to *Guangming Daily* after the bombing.

34. A survey done in 1994 and 1995 about the Chinese people's understanding of "the Chinese nation" (*Zhonghua minzu*) indicated that, of 135 respondents, 103 believed that "Every member of each of 56 nationalities is a Chinese national"; 124 believed that "Hong Kong, Taiwan, and Macao are China's inalienable territory"; 113 believed that Ethnic Autonomous Regions at all levels are parts of the People's Republic of China; 127 believed that the government should "oppose every attempt at secession and maintain solidarity of nationality and the country's unity"; and 124 believed that "overall national interests transcend the interests of each component nationality." Jieming Weng, Tiao Zhang, Zhiming An, Ximing Zhang, and Jinghua Liu, eds., *1994–1995 nian Zhongguo fazhan zhuangkuang yu qushi* (Developing Conditions and Trends in China, 1994–95) (Beijing: Chinese Academy of Social Sciences Publishing House, 1995), p. 213. My own conversations with Chinese people in China, England, and the United Sates substantiate these survey results.

35. On a lighter note, in 1997 the Chinese introduced computer games in which China battles against foreign invaders, and made a movie, *The Opium War*, which featured the perfidious British imperialists in China in the 1830s and 1840s.

36. Zhao, "We Are Patriots First and Democrats Second," p. 38.

37. Many of the following topics on nationalism are discussed in Zheng, *Discovering Chinese Nationalism in China*; Gong Nanxiang, "Make Nationalism a Constructive Force for Democratization," *China Strategic Review* 2, no. 2 (March/April 1997): 14–30; Zhu, "Chinese Nationalism in the Post-Deng Era," pp. 57–86. They are also discussed in a special issue of *China Studies* (Zhongguo yanjiu), no. 6, 2000, dedicated to the issue of nationalism. For more about the diversity in perspectives among Chinese intellectuals, see Ogden, *Inklings of Democracy in China*, chapter 8.

38. Shenzhi Li, a well-known liberal intellectual and former vice-chair of the Chinese Academy of Social Sciences, advocates that China accept internationalization and the rules of the international system. He believes an emphasis on Chinese nationalism would harm China. For a list of Li's articles, see Gong, "Make Nationalism a Constructive Force," pp. 25–26, note 1.

39. Xianlin Ji, a well-known liberal Chinese scholar, believes that much can be learned from ancient Chinese culture that would be beneficial to the post-modern world; and that nationalism should be channeled into positive international cultural exchanges (Gong, "Make Nationalism a Constructive Force for Democratization," pp. 26–27, note 2).

40. Xin He, a "conservative" intellectual and neo-nationalist, opposes any form of Westernization (Zhu, "Chinese Nationalism in the Post-Deng Era," pp. 58–59, notes 1–2).

41. Gang Gong, "National Identity and Cultural Resistance: A Commentary on Zhang Chengzhi's Cultural Sociology," *China Studies* (Zhongguo yanjiu), no. 5 (1999): 129–145.

42. Samuel P. Huntington, *The Clash of Civilizations and the Remaking of World Order* (New York: Simon & Schuster, 1996).

43. Francis Fukuyama, *The End of History and the Last Man* (New York: Fre Press, 1992).

44. Zhao, "We Are Patriots First and Democrats Second," p. 34. For Chinese dis cussions of Huntington's and Fukuyama's ideas, see Baoyun Yi, "Minzuzhuyi y xiandai jingji fazhan," *Zhanlue yu guanli,* no. 3 (1994); and Jisi Wang, ed., *Wenmin, yu guoji zhengzhi: Zhongguo xuezhe ping Huntington de wenming chongtulun* (Shang hai: Shanghai Renmin Chubanshe, 1995). Wang Jisi is director of the Institute o American Studies in the Chinese Academy of Social Sciences.

45. The emphasis on what is good for the nation even affects the specifics of busi ness negotiations. For example, in business deals with foreigners to set up joint ven tures, Chinese officials must address the issue of the benefits of such a joint venture t the country as a whole. If only the joint enterprise itself is going to benefit (e.g., b making profits) and the country as a whole will receive no tangible benefit, that is no considered adequate justification, and the project may not be approved by appropriate state agencies unless the principals can make a strong case that the joint venture wil serve the national interest. Conversations with Malcolm Warner, Cambridge Univer sity, May 1996; Also see Malcolm Warner and Hong Ng, *China's Trade Unions and Management* (London: Macmillan, 1997). Of course, it need hardly be said that both Chinese and foreign businessmen often cynically address the issue of what is good fo the country.

46. This author's experience while waiting patiently to cross the street in Shanghai.

47. State System Reform Commission for Societal Investigation, "The Character istics of Psychological Changes of Our Nation's Urban Residents and Analysis of Reform and Society Situations, p. 133.

48. Zheng, *Discovering Chinese Nationalism in China*, pp. 87–110.

49. Zhao, "We Are Patriots First and Democrats Second," pp. 29–30.

50. Wang, "Teaching Patriotism in China," pp. 13–15.

51. Unger, ed., *Chinese Nationalism,* p. xiii.

52. Zhu, "Chinese Nationalism in the Post-Deng Era," pp. 69–70.

53. Victor Yuan (Yue Yuan), "Public Opinion Polling in China: Development and Its Problems," seminar, Fairbank Center for East Asian Research (Harvard Univer sity), September 27, 2000. Yue Yuan is president of the Horizon Company, which is a private survey research company.

54. Yuan, "Stability, Psychology, and Attitude of the Public in Chinese Cities in 1995–1996," p. 122.

55. The polls showed that in both years, 43.7 percent "strongly disagreed" and over 30 percent in both years "mostly disagreed." In 1991, 43.3 percent "strongly agreed" and 40.1 percent "mostly agreed." In 1995, 52.6 percent "strongly agreed" and 30.8 percent "mostly agreed." Lei Fan, "Investigation of Beijing Citizens' Political-Psychological Attitudes in 1995," *Beijing jingji liaowang* (Beijing's Economic Out look), no. 1, 1996, pp. 6–10, in *Renda fuyin ziliao* (Reference Materials Copied and Collected by People's University, Beijing), in the Sociology Section, pp. 3–157.

56. In response, 49.9 percent "supported" and 29.3 percent "supported somewhat" this statement. Chinese Academy of Social Sciences, Institute of Sociology, Project Team on the Change of Values of Contemporary Chinese Youth, p. 69.

57. About 60 percent of urban youth polled and about 70 percent of rural youth polled in 1988 "agreed" or "agreed somewhat." About 68 percent of both rural and urban youth "agreed" or "agreed somewhat" in 1990. Ibid., p. 64.

58. Fukuyama, *The End of History and the Last Man,* p. 326. Italics added.

59. Robert Putnam notes that perhaps America, in its quest for ending discrimination against minorities, women, and others by embracing multiculturalism, has moved to the point where few communities remain to which individuals may belong, or even wish to belong. By erasing difference, there are fewer associations, clubs, societies, or groups to which a person is inclined to belong. All are part of an amorphous whole. Left without communal identity, individuals have become isolated—and lonely. Without a communal identity based on an organizational affiliation, many Americans care about little, to the point that they do not even vote because they lack a strong collective identity with the local community, or the larger polity. Although they may well support associations or lobbies that serve their self-interests (such as economic interest groups and the American Association for Retired People), they belong to few if any communities in which people interact with each other in a personal manner and primarily for the purpose of building social relationships. Robert D. Putnam, *Bowling Alone: The Collapse of American Community* (New York: Simon and Schuster, 2000).

60. I was present at the European Parliament in Strasbourg, France, on February 14, 1996, when this resolution finally came to the floor. I read many of the relevant documents, spoke with members of the European Parliament, and heard the debates. The resemblance to the Chinese discourse on "spiritual pollution" was remarkable.

61. For example, Islamic girls may not wear a veil while in school.

62. *International Herald Tribune*, January 20, 1996.

63. What the law will do is require anyone using the Internet "to turn over the keys to decoding e-mail messages and other data." And, the British government will not have to request a court to determine the legitimacy of any search of such private data, for unlike the United States, "Britain has a tradition of unfettered and often uncontested intrusion by the authorities into citizens' privacy." Sarah Lyall, "British Authorities May Get Wide Powers to Decode E-Mail," *New York Times,* July 19, 2000, A3. Opponents of the bill believe it contravenes basic rights in the European Convention on Human Rights, including the rights to privacy, freedom of expression, and association.

64. The results of this study were: 20.6 percent said "China open to right degree"; 18.9 percent said "inadequately open"; 6.4 percent said "opening of China overdone"; 47.5 percent said "the opening of China is not balanced, with some areas too open and other areas inadequately open; 6.0 percent said "hard to say." See Yuan, "Stability, Psychology, and Attitude of the Public in Chinese Cities in 1995–1996," p. 122. This survey was conducted by the Lingdian ("Horizon") Company and *Beijing Qingnian Bao* (Beijing Youth Post).

65. Richard Madsen, *China and the American Dream* (Berkeley: University of California Press, 1994), p. 81.

66. B. Michael Frolic, "State-Led Civil Society," in Timothy Brook and B. Michael Frolic, eds., *Civil Society in China* (Armonk, N.Y.: M.E. Sharpe, 1997), p. 52.

67. Etzioni, "On the Place of Virtues in a Pluralistic Democracy," pp. 72, 74–75.

$$\text{---- } 10 \text{ ----}$$

Saints and the State

Religious Evolution and Problems of Governance in China

Richard Madsen

Introduction

In a solemn ceremony during the 2000 Jubilee Year, on October 1, the Feast of Saint Teresa of Lisieux, Patroness of Missions, Pope John Paul II canonized 120 Chinese martyrs. The group of newly declared saints included thirty-three foreign missionaries and eighty-seven Chinese, their ages at death ranged from seven to seventy-nine, and they included bishops, priests, nuns, seminarians, and lay people. Although one died as late as 1931, the others had been martyred during the Ming and Qing Dynasties, more than seventy of them during the Boxer Rebellion. It was a joyful event for Chinese Catholics around the world, a public recognition by the universal church that the Chinese church was equal to Catholic communities around the world in the ability to produce men and women of heroic virtue. Fifty-two Chinese cardinals and bishops from Taiwan, Hong Kong, and other parts of the world concelebrated the Papal Mass at St. Peter's Basilica that day. Four thousand Chinese Catholics from around the world attended, including some from mainland China who already happened to be residing in Europe.[1]

But the official reaction in China was bitter indignation. The Party line was set out in a *People's Daily* editorial on October 3. "The People's Republic of China has ushered in its fifty-first birthday. The entire country rejoices with jubilation, and the people of all nationalities throughout the country are celebrating together the great day that symbolizes the day when the Chinese nation thoroughly overturned the three big mountains and truly stood up. However, at St. Peter's Square of the Vatican, a farce was staged, during which some foreign missionaries who had committed ugly and evil crimes in China and their followers were canonized as 'saints.' The Vatican disregarded strong opposition from the Chinese people including the vast numbers of

Catholics, and insisted on engaging in the perverse act of 'canonization,' greatly hurting the feelings of the Chinese nation. It is a severe provocation to the 1.2 billion Chinese people."[2]

This indictment was amplified and given a veneer of scholarship by an accompanying article "Exposing the True Colors of 'Saints.'" The so-called saints, the article by Shi Yan argued, had been either direct agents of foreign imperialism or victims of popular anger against imperialism. Moreover, they were immoral, arrogant people who fully deserved to be punished for their crimes. As illustrations, it cited details of cases of four of the newly canonized foreign missionaries and three Chinese who allegedly stole property, raped women, destroyed families, and abused children—as well as offending local customs and arrogantly insisting that their religion was superior to Chinese traditional beliefs.[3]

Beginning about a week before the canonizations and continuing for about three weeks after, statements were issued by all official organizations whose purview touched upon the issue: the Catholic Patriotic Association, the Chinese Catholic Bishops Conference, the Protestant Three Autonomies Association, the official Buddhist, Taoist, and Islamic associations, the Ministry of Foreign Affairs, the Institute of Religious Studies at the Chinese Academy of Social Sciences, the United Front Work Department, and the Chinese People's Political Consultative Conference. They all said the same thing and often used many of the same words as the *People's Daily* articles.[4]

The outspoken coadjutor bishop of Hong Kong, Bishop Joseph Zen Zekiun, issued a defiant statement denying any factual or moral basis to the official objections to the canonizations. Addressing himself to the Chinese Catholic Patriotic Association and the Chinese Catholic Bishops Conference, he suggested that these bodies were not expressing their own views but simply reflecting the government line: "It would not be surprising, considering previous communist tactics, for the government to put words into the mouths of the bishops." (Actually, under the circumstances, it would be surprising if it did not. Bishop Zen seemed to have lapsed into an uncharacteristic tactfulness here.) He ridiculed the accusation that the martyrs had committed crimes likes robbery and rape. "Before the canonization a thorough investigation was conducted into the background of each martyr. A so-called 'devil's advocate' was appointed to dig out any possible scandal, so there was no way such 'enormous crimes' could pass undetected." He denied that the martyrs were accomplices of the "deplorable historical fact" of imperialism. Contrary to accusations that the canonizations were against the wishes of the church in China, he claimed that at least forty bishops in the mainland had petitioned Rome to carry out the canonizations, in spite of the fact that such contact was forbidden by Beijing. "The canonizations,"

Bishop Zen declared, "have provided a good opportunity for Beijing to paint the Holy See as an enemy of China and thus force the bishops and priests to make a choice between loyalty to the pope and loyalty to their country. This diabolic plan is an attempt to rape the spirit of the bishops and priests. It is the worst kind of persecution."[5]

Understood in its historical context, the canonization controversy is a good opportunity to explore problems of governance that go beyond Beijing's particular conflicts with the Vatican. Far from demonstrating the power of the Chinese state, the event reveals its weakness. Like other struggles with expanding religious communities, Beijing's struggles with the Catholic Church demonstrate a continuing erosion of state power. The erosion, I will argue, is on two levels, structural and moral. The Chinese government no longer has structures of control adequate to make local communities of Catholics consistently behave in ways that support state interests. And, superficial appearances to the contrary, it is losing the ability to represent the national aspirations of many of its people.

From Underground to Unofficial: New Challenges to State Control

Let us first consider the evolution of church-state relations that precipitated the canonization controversy and show how they mark a decline in state capacities for control.

In the first three decades of the People's Republic of China (PRC), most Chinese Catholics nurtured their faith in the "underground"—although they did not necessarily use that term then. They hid their practice from agents of the government and passively resisted any efforts of the government to control them. At the beginnings of the PRC, the Vatican, under the strongly anti-communist Pope Pius XII, forbade Chinese Catholics, under pain of excommunication, to cooperate in any way with the Chinese regime.[6] For its part, the Chinese government attempted to incorporate the church into its system of control by establishing a Catholic Patriotic Association (CPA) which regulated church affairs in cooperation with the government's Religious Affairs Bureau and the Party's United Front Department. Staffed by a small cooperative minority of Catholic clergy and laity, the CPA, like all "mass associations" in China, was meant to be part of a transmission belt between the government and society. To be a member of the CPA, a Catholic had to renounce allegiance to the Vatican, in the name of maintaining the sovereign autonomy of the Chinese church. Bishops and priests who refused to cooperate with this association were imprisoned. Most Catholics considered the demand to sever ties with the Vatican an affront to their identity. Many prominent bishops and priests went to prison rather than submit to the CPA. During the Cultural Revolution, persecution of the church increased and all public religious practice was forbidden, even that which had been sanctioned by the CPA. Catholics carried on their faith in secret. Mothers baptized their children at home and parents quietly passed on the rudiments of doctrine. Sometimes Catholics met furtively in each other's homes to pray. At other times, they mumbled prayers quietly to themselves.[7]

After 1979, in accord with the policy of Reform and Opening, new regulations were established for religious practice. Church buildings were reopened or rebuilt, bishops and priests released from detention, and seminaries and convents reestablished. According to regulations promulgated in 1982, however, Catholics could worship only in venues registered with the government, and registration required approval and supervision by the CPA. The new policies toward religion reduced government interference in theological and liturgical matters, enough so that many Catholics were willing to affiliate themselves with the government-sanctioned system, even though it refused to accept Papal authority over Chinese Catholic religious affairs. Probably most of these Catholics who worshipped in "open" churches did so not because they supported the principles of the CPA, but because the CPA was unable to intrude too deeply into their affairs. Although the CPA claimed authority to choose new bishops of Catholic dioceses independently from the Vatican, many bishops in the open church were in fact quietly receiving "apostolic mandates" of approval from the Holy See. By the mid-1990s, perhaps a third of the bishops in the open churches had received such Vatican approval.[8]

In the meantime, a strong "underground" church had grown up alongside the open churches. The underground churches consisted of Catholics who worshipped in venues that had not received government approval, and they were led by bishops and priests who had not been chosen or authorized by the CPA. Growth in the underground church had been facilitated by secret Vatican regulations issued in 1978 giving underground bishops great discretion in choosing other bishops and training new priests without normal oversight from the Vatican. The underground churches have grown even more rapidly than the open churches. There are now probably about eight million Catholics in the underground churches in addition to the four million registered with the government. Catholics participate in the underground churches for many reasons, related to principle and practicality. Some believe that the underground bishops and priests are of purer faith because they have demonstrated their unequivocal loyalty to the pope. Others participate in underground churches simply because the government has not allowed an open church to be registered in their area.[9]

The government sees the growth of the underground churches—and indeed of any kind of independently organized groups—as a threat to its control, and therefore as a threat to social stability. As a consequence, it has periodically sought to suppress the underground church by jailing its leading bishops and priests, destroying underground places of worship, and subjecting underground Catholics to "reeducation." None of these measures has worked. One important reason is that Chinese Catholics truly believe in the old saying that "the blood of martyrs is the seed of Christians." A recently published "Appeal from the Underground" expresses this well. "Although the underground church is being persecuted and attacked, its ministry continues to prosper. . . . We firmly believe in Jesus' promise: 'The gates of hell will in no way overcome the church founded on the rock.' With the Lord's help we do not fear the powers of evil and persecution, for we know that persecution is a special gift from the Lord. . . .We are honored to share in the Lord's passion."[10]

Because of the ways in which missionaries carried out their evangelization in the late nineteenth and early twentieth centuries, it is common for whole lineages, whole villages, or even in some places, whole counties to be Catholic. Under such circumstances, the practice of religion can become implicated in a wide array of social divisions, such as those between rival lineages or villages. Especially in the rural areas where the great majority of China's Catholics are located, distinctions between underground and open church communities sometimes become intertwined with other social divisions. This increases the intensity of such divisions and sometimes even leads to violence. These problems become exacerbated when there are rivalries between underground and open church bishops in a given diocese and there is no way clearly to determine which bishop should have primary authority.[11]

Because the Vatican does not have diplomatic relations with the PRC it has no way of clearly adjudicating such local conflicts. Nor does it have the regular channels of communication with the Chinese church, whether underground or open, that would enable it to give it guidance on matters of doctrine or liturgy. Particularly because its members are often cut off from the outside world, some parts of the underground church may be in danger of developing unorthodox practices deriving more from Chinese folk religion than from Catholic traditions. For such reasons, the Vatican has been eager to normalize diplomatic relations with China, even though that would mean breaking diplomatic relations with Taiwan. So far, however, the conditions have been impossibly high. In its need to control the church, the Chinese government demands the right to have final say in the selection of bishops.

In the conclusion to the book on *China's Catholics* that I published in 1998, I expressed pessimism that the major conflicts between underground and official Catholic communities could soon be reconciled and that the Vatican and the PRC could normalize relations. Since then, however, the process of reconciliation, or at least accommodation, between the underground and open churches has advanced further than I would have expected, and the Vatican and the PRC have undertaken some serious, if so far unsuccessful, efforts at normalization. These developments constitute the immediate context of the canonization controversy.

In the latter half of the 1990s, there was a rapid increase in the number of open church bishops seeking and receiving Vatican approval of their positions. By the beginning of the new millennium, at least two-thirds (and possibly considerably more) of open church bishops had received "apostolic mandates," and knowledge of this was widely disseminated (mostly informally, by word of mouth, because it could not be officially acknowledged) among the Catholic communities. Thus was removed a major source of conflict between the underground and open churches. Sources of tension remain, since underground and open church divisions sometimes correspond to other forms of social division. But there are now many cases of open and underground church communities not only tolerating one another but actually cooperating, for instance through sharing of church facilities and in carrying out common educational and pastoral programs.[12]

This evolution has been made possible not only by specific ecclesiastical or government policies but by a steady opening of Chinese society. Although suspicious officials still try to regulate contact between church members and outsiders, it is in practice increasingly easy for visitors, especially from Hong Kong and Taiwan, to circulate among Catholic communities. Through such channels of communication, the Vatican can more easily evaluate the cases of particular open church bishops and convey its apostolic mandates. As more bishops receive legitimization from the Vatican, a snowball effect takes place. Those who have not done so have difficulty gaining the respect of their congregants and are thus all the more eager to seek papal approval. Meanwhile, migration of rural people to towns and cities is in some places decreasing the relevance of traditional rivalries between villages and kinship groups that sometimes amplified tensions between underground and open church communities.

Economic development diminishes the scarcities that also fueled such disputes. A major bone of contention has been the ability of some but not other local communities to have the government return church property confiscated during the 1950s and to provide the funds to rebuild churches. According to Anthony Lam, the government has recently been trying its best to "clear its debt" toward religious bodies. "It has managed to settle the disputes with religious bodies on land and real properties. . . . It seems that they do not want to owe the religious bodies anything."[13] At the same time, there is enough money available either through local sources or through foreign donations that underground as well as open church communities are finding it relatively easy to construct their own church facilities.

Finally, a younger generation of Chinese Catholics is no longer so interested in carrying forth the grudges that their elders may have harbored toward rival Catholic communities. With some major sources of conflict diminishing, underground and open church communities are gravitating toward one another.

A black-and-white conflict between open and underground churches is being replaced by shades of gray. Although the terms remain in wide use among Catholics in China, perhaps "open" and "underground" no longer represent the sociological divisions of the Chinese Catholic community. A better pair of Chinese contrast terms might be "official" (*guanfang*) and "unofficial" (*wuguanfang*). As used in modern Chinese parlance, "official" refers to the realm of activity that is publicly recognized and controlled by the state. "Unofficial" refers to a realm of private transactions at least partly independent of state control. In ordinary Chinese speech, "unofficial" has a connotation of "unorthodox" or "deviant," reflecting a political system that denies the legitimacy of any forms of association not under state supervision. But "official" and "unofficial" are not neatly separated. They form a continuum. Most people have to live and work under the supervision of state-controlled organizations, but within those organizations (sometimes in complicity with the organization's leaders) they carry out a great deal of unofficial activity, which sometimes contradicts and subverts the stated purposes of the organization.[14]

Thus, to regulate and supervise Roman Catholics, there are official government regulations for religious activity and officially recognized organizations, like the Catholic Patriotic Association and the Chinese Catholic Bishops Conference. But within this framework, Catholics are developing their own informal rules and unwritten procedures for establishing legitimate authority. As in much of the rest of China, this vigorously developing unofficial sector does not overtly defy government authorities, but it subtly neutralizes them and renders them increasingly irrelevant.

In the unofficial church, people, ideas, and moral rules from the open and underground churches become blended together in new syntheses. And no matter what government officials or leaders of the Catholic Patriotic Association might desire, the religious life of the unofficial church is oriented toward communion with the universal church, under the jurisdiction of the pope.

In the late 1990s, many Catholics outside of China rejoiced in this, because it seemed to be a sign that old divisions between church factions were

▶eing healed and old conflicts with the state rendered irrelevant. Such devel-
▶pments were part of a general efflorescence of unofficial, informal social
▶elations that have been celebrated by foreign observers eager for signs of a
▶eaceful evolution toward a civil society. But dominant factions within the
▶arty apparently took a much less benign view. As they saw it, the flourish-
▶ng of unofficial China was undermining the foundations of their power.

From Unofficial to Underground: Reassertion of Government Control

▶t was under these circumstances that the Vatican and the PRC resumed ne-
▶gotiations in 1999 about normalizing diplomatic relations. In March of 1999,
▶when Jiang Zemin was on a state visit to Italy, the president of Italy passed
▶him a letter from the Vatican expressing a wish for new negotiations. The
Vatican was willing to break its diplomatic relations with Taiwan, even though
this would cause great unhappiness in the church in Taiwan. This was indeed
valuable to the PRC government. The Vatican was the only state in Western
Europe that retained diplomatic relations with Taiwan. Moreover, a Vatican
shift in diplomatic allegiance would likely influence the handful of strongly
Catholic states in Central America that diplomatically recognize Taiwan. In
return for a concession on the Taiwan issue, the Vatican wanted improvement in conditions for religious freedom in the PRC.[15] But the Vatican did
not have to insist on any radical changes in PRC policy toward religion. The
fact of the matter was that, even under restrictive official policies, the Catholic Church was unofficially evolving in what for the Vatican was the right
direction. In China, officials in the Religious Affairs Bureau (recently re-
named the State Administration for Religious Affairs [SARA]) and officials
in the Catholic Patriotic Association reportedly put up some resistance, because Vatican normalization would ultimately diminish some of their power.[16]
The matter was temporarily settled by a document from Jiang Zemin dictating that in this case external affairs, improving the climate for foreign relations, should take precedence over internal affairs, maintaining tight control
over the Catholic Church. Resistance from SARA and the CPA continued,
however, especially from cadres at regional and local levels.[17]

   Then an event occurred that strengthened the hand of SARA and the CPA.
On April 23, 1999, the Falungong staged its large demonstration in front of
Zhongnanhai, and the evolving role of religion in domestic affairs suddenly
seemed more important. At the end of July, the government officially declared the Falungong an evil cult and began a massive campaign to suppress
it. The supposed evils of the Falungong (or at least the threat this rapidly
growing indigenous religious movement may pose to state control over the

population) bolstered the resolve of religious affairs officials to tighten control over all manner of unofficial religious activity, including Catholic activity

In the fall of 1999, Catholic church researchers in Hong Kong obtained parts of "Document 26 Regarding the Strengthening of Catholic Church Work in the New Circumstances," supposedly issued by the Secretariat of Party Central on August 17, 1999. There is some question about the document's authenticity—some have suggested that it was fabricated by church circles in Taiwan to strengthen their argument that the Vatican should not normalize relations with the PRC. However, the PRC government's actions in the second half of 1999 did in fact closely follow the script laid out in Document 26, and there is now a consensus of outside experts on the Catholic Church in China that the document is probably authentic.[18]

According to the document, "The Vatican still plans to use the adjustment in Sino-Vatican relations to negate our policy of running the church independently, and to reestablish control over our country's Catholic Church. . . . The most urgent duty at present is to greatly strengthen the setting up of the Catholic patriotic organizations, to conscientiously give attention to educating and converting the underground Catholic forces, to maintain social stability, and to guarantee that the leadership of our nation's Catholic Church is firmly in the hands of patriotic forces."[19]

To regain control over the Catholic Church, the document prescribed a strengthening of the Catholic Patriotic Association (which in many places had atrophied at the local level). This would require recruiting some additional "politically reliable persons to become involved in the leadership group of the Patriotic Association at the provincial level. . . ."[20] Through this leadership core, the Catholic Patriotic Association could "convert the majority and isolate the minority . . . making the leading authority in our country's Catholic Church to be always in the hands of the patriotic forces."[21] The CPA would refuse to recognize the priestly identity of those priests who refused to cooperate with the government—"no matter whether the Vatican recognizes them, we will not recognize them."[22] The government proposed to "strengthen education . . . and strictly control" such priests and bishops. The laity of the underground church should be subject to increased "guidance and education," so as to "prevent the appearance of religious fervor."[23]

Key to the success of this strategy was the ability to win over the majority. The document recognizes that the "great majority . . . due to their faith, do not agree with the policy of the independent running of the Catholic Church. Only a small minority of them use religious matters to create disturbances and oppose the government."[24] The document seems to hold that the problem of faith that alienates the great majority from official policy might be resolved if the Vatican officially recognized the PRC government (while keep-

ing the troublesome minority sufficiently isolated). In other words, normalization of Vatican–PRC relations could be used as a means to strengthen government control over the church. This was not what the Vatican had in mind.

In the fall of 1999, the government (as specified in Document 26) began
to increase the number and tighten the organization of local Patriotic Associations. For its part, the underground church, in anticipation of normalization, began to consecrate more young bishops who would represent its
viewpoint in the new ecclesiastical order. Vatican negotiators wanted these
bishops officially recognized by the Patriotic Associations. Chinese negotiators refused. Basically the Vatican would agree to normalization only if it
could lead to less—even if slightly less—government control of the Catholic
Church and the PRC would agree only if normalization could lead to more
control. The Vatican had proposed variations on the "Vietnam model" for the
appointment of bishops, in which the government could nominate several
candidates with the final decision made by the Vatican. The PRC, however,
insisted on having the last word on all appointments of bishops.[25] Even as
rumors floated through Hong Kong and Taiwan that the Vatican would normalize relations by the beginning of 2000 (and Pope John Paul II could realize his
aspiration of setting foot on Chinese soil at the beginning of the new millennium), the negotiations were doomed. They fell apart by the end of 1999.

A public sign that the negotiations were over came on January 6, 2000.
On that day, the Feast of the Epiphany, the Catholic Patriotic Association
carried out the consecration of five new bishops, none of them approved by
the Vatican. This event, one of the few church ceremonies widely broadcast
in the official media, was an act of defiance against the Vatican. According
to an editorial in the journal *Tripod,* published by the Holy Spirit Study
Centre in Hong Kong, "For the Church it is nothing less than a tragedy. . . .
From the viewpoint of the Universal Church, these consecrations were ill
conceived. They might not only delay, but even destroy, much if not all of
the mutual trust that had been building up among people of good will on
both sides, and even discourage and alienate those who are sympathetic
towards the open church."[26]

Although it may indeed have been a tragedy for those who hoped for a
normalization of Vatican–PRC relations, the defiant consecration of the new
bishops was by no means a triumph for the Chinese state. The Chinese government was in a bind. The evolution of Catholic communities had created
an unofficial church (blending Catholics from both the open and underground)
that, while no longer confronting the government, threatened to slip out of its
control. In the past, the use of raw force had failed to stop this growth. The
government's best hope was cooptation, "winning over the majority." This
would require the cooperation of none other than the government's old en-

emy, the Vatican. But it could not offer terms the Vatican could accept. The possibilities of cooptation having vanished, the government now had to reassert control through a desperate and probably futile use of blatant force.

The desperation and futility were illustrated by the circumstances of the January 6 episcopal consecration. It turned out that the Catholic Patriotic Association had originally wanted to consecrate twelve bishops (symbolizing the twelve apostles) at the ceremony, but most of its candidates refused. Several of those who did accept did so reluctantly, under great pressure. The very form of the ceremony confirmed that the dependable minority of official church functionaries had become alienated from the broad majority of Catholics. Usually, the consecration of new bishops would have been a joyful event, carried out in a packed church. This time, however, the Beijing Cathedral of the Immaculate Conception (the "Nantang") was over half empty. The seminarians at the Beijing National Seminary refused to attend. (Because of this disobedience, they were later subjected to "political reeducation" and their rector was dismissed.) More government cadres than practicing Catholics occupied the pews. Police surrounded the cathedral.[27] The government had now given up all hope to "win over the majority."

Throughout the rest of 2000, the government increased its heavy hand. It demolished hundreds of nonregistered church buildings, particularly in Fujian and around Wenzhou, stepped up arrests of underground bishops and priests, and established new local branches of the Catholic Patriotic Association.[28] For its part, the Vatican reiterated the section of canon law that mandates automatic excommunication for those who accept episcopal consecration without an apostolic mandate.[29] Meanwhile, in February 2000, Cardinal Sodano, the Vatican's Secretary of State, revealed the existence of a "non-official channel of communication with Beijing,"[30] and Bishop Fu Tieshan, the head of the CPA, said he was optimistic that Vatican–PRC relations could be normalized soon.[31] In May, an open church bishop was consecrated in Shandong with explicit approval of the Vatican. According to the Vatican news agency Fides: ". . . sources in Shanghai say that the government's 'laissez faire' attitude is due to social and economic tensions in China: Beijing wants to avoid further disputes with the Catholic Church and the international community."[32]

All of this formed the immediate backdrop to the canonization controversy. The canonizations had been in the making for a long time. All of the 120 martyrs had received "beatification," the ritual step preliminary to full-fledged canonization, before 1946. Intensive preparations for the final step of canonization would have been conducted for several years before 2000. The Jubilee Year of the millennium was a prime time for conducting such ceremonies. There was no evidence that the canonizations were originally planned as a provocation to the Chinese government, in direct retaliation for the breakdown in negotiations. Before going forward with the canonizations, the Vatican had received the official recommendation of Taiwan's Regional Bishops' Conference (most of whose members are in fact mainlanders), and informal recommendations (because, absent normalization, official communication with the Vatican is forbidden by the Chinese government) from at least forty bishops, both in open and underground churches, from the PRC.

When the canonizations were announced by the Vatican on March 13, 2000, the initial reactions, even from the open church, seemed positive. Bishop Paul Jiang Taoren, the government-recognized bishop of Shijiazhuang, Hebei Province, said that "he was very happy about the canonization, although he admitted he had no prior knowledge about the development. 'It bears great meaning to the church in China,' he said. . . . When asked if the Chinese government will interpret the canonization as a move by the Vatican to interfere in China's internal affairs, Bishop Jiang said that since this is a religious decision and the blesseds were people of the past, the government was unlikely to oppose the move. . . ."[33] In villages where some of the martyrs came from, local Catholics happily went about planning shrines to their new saints— a source of local glory and perhaps tourist revenues.[34]

A day later, however, a spokesperson for the Chinese foreign ministry warned that "We hope that the Vatican will not do anything again that wounds the feelings of the Chinese."[35] The Party line was now set down, but the government was largely silent about the canonizations until September. In mid-September, Cardinal Roger Etchegaray, a high-placed cardinal who has often helped the Vatican carry out unofficial diplomacy, visited China ostensibly to attend an academic conference. At that time he was warned of strong objections to the forthcoming canonizations, which he widely reported, in a tone of some surprise, after leaving China. Interestingly, his interlocutors did not object to canonizations as such—indeed they indicated that they wanted to see Chinese canonized—but they said that canonizations "should be postponed until after normalization for China–Holy See relations."[36]

If the canonizations had taken place after normalization, with at least the appearance of consultation with the government-appointed leaders of the Chinese church, the canonizations might have aided the government's effort to coopt the majority of Catholics. But without normalization the canonization only widened the gulf between most Catholics, who were proud that some of their ancestors had achieved the highest glory possible in the church, and the government-controlled Patriotic Association.

Having lost the capacity to win over the majority, all the government could do was to force a minority of Catholics to demonstrate that loyalty to the government was more important than loyalty to most of their fellow Catholics. The official denunciations of the Chinese martyrs were so crude and so extreme as to have little credibility among people who knew anything about Chinese church history. (It may well be plausible that some of the missionary martyrs were guilty of cultural arrogance. But given the church's scrupulosity about sex, it boggles the mind to think that the Vatican would have approved anyone for canonization if a thorough investigation had turned up any credible suggestions of sexual misconduct.) By demanding that key Catholic officials embrace these criticisms fully, the government separated them from their congregants and enabled them to be all the more blatantly used as instruments of political control, thus eventually creating more religious martyrs who would further inspire Catholics to serve God rather than Caesar.

In the Maoist era, perhaps, such an aggressive assertion of government control over the church could have been seen as a victory for the state against the undisciplined forces of society. But in the present social context, I would argue, such measures are more of a symptom of defeat. The Maoist party-state imposed a net of political organization over all major economic, social, and cultural institutions. The use of overt police power—beatings, imprisonment, executions—was only the culmination of a system that bound citizens into place through a wide range of economic, social, and political pressures, enforced through work units, residential neighborhoods, and people's communes from which citizens had few opportunities to exit. However, since the reform era, citizens can increasingly move around, seek independent sources of livelihood, and build networks of social relations beyond the view of official surveillance. Police power stands alone. Now, it does not simply crush those relatively few people who have dared to break free of a tight system of social control. It can only apprehend a few of the many people who are defying or simply ignoring government regulations. In some circumstances the harsh application of police power might intimidate others into compliance. But such attempts to "kill the chicken to scare the monkeys" are especially ineffective toward religious communities that revere martyrdom.

The government is challenged to develop new forms of "soft power" to secure voluntary compliance from a rapidly developing unofficial society that is too large, too flexible, too complicated, and too connected with global networks to be crushed by the traditional instruments of hard power. One form of such soft power could be achieved through cooptation—by proffering sufficient positive incentives to induce natural leaders of important social communities to reliably support most government policies. The government's truculent reaction to the canonization of Chinese saints marked a failure of its strategy to coopt those church leaders who had the respect and allegiance of most Chinese Catholics—a failure in the effort to create forms of soft power sufficient to reliably achieve order and stability in an increasingly fluid society.

Papal Authority Versus Pontifical Nationalism

Besides exposing the government's problems in keeping a portion of its dissatisfied population under control, the canonization controversy exposed difficulties in representing Chinese national aspirations. In response to increasing class, ethnic, and regional tensions and to a crisis of meaning caused by the loss of credibility of communist ideology, the Chinese government has been trying to increase a sense of Chinese nationalism and to portray itself as the only legitimate defender of that nationalism.

The kind of nationalism embraced by the Chinese government is what one might call a "pontifical nationalism." Most Western nation-states were attended by the rise of more "congregational" forms of nationalism in which national consciousness was constructed to an important degree from the bottom up by a variety of cultural and political entrepreneurs and then drawn upon by emerging states to legitimate their power. In the pontifical Chinese version, the only legitimate form of nationalism flows from the top down and the state insists on being the sole arbiter and judge of its content.

Meanwhile, however, Chinese citizens are developing their own versions of national identity. Sometimes, the government-approved version coincides with popular national sentiments—as in the celebrations over gaining the 2008 Olympics. But such popular sentiments can turn against the government's pontifical nationalism. To the extent that ordinary Chinese become united by deep pride in their nation and concern over its future, they could find reasons to turn against a regime that they felt was stifling their potential. This, after all, was one of the main messages of *River Elegy,* the television series that helped catalyze the Tiananmen protests of 1989: the Chinese nation is in decline because of a rigid, authoritarian culture that is manifested in the current government.[37] So to maintain its position as the only legitimate defender of the Chinese nationhood, the government has to keep strict control over the national myth. It has to assert that all of the problems of modern China have been caused by imperialism and to celebrate its record of fighting imperialism. It has to proscribe any accounts of national history that would suggest that any of the serious problems are the result of the moral failings or ineptitude of its own revolutionary heroes. It has to stake its legitimacy to a flat, one-dimensional nationalism. As if to compensate for its loss of control over much of economic, social, and political life, the state has to cling ever more strongly to its control over national symbols.

But there are many subcommunities in China with versions of the national myth different from the official one. Religious communities form a very important type of such communities because the stories they tell themselves about their Chinese identity are stories invested with sacred significance. This is particularly clear in the case of Chinese Catholic communities, which attach a sacred significance to history, but to a history that at crucial points runs counter to the government propagated national myths.

In *China's Catholics,* I described a widely displayed chart that depicts, on one side, a salvation history that runs from Adam and Eve through Jesus to the popes and saints of the church and on the other side, a history of China, which runs from the legendary sage emperors down to the present. At some point the two histories intersect.[38] This sense of history is not just represented in formal church teachings but in informal local histories, such as the legends about the Boxer Rebellion, carried on by word of mouth in the Hebei Catholic villages that I visited, in which Holy Mary appeared to the beleaguered villagers and helped them fight off the Boxers. Such local Catholic histories were in striking contrast to the histories enshrined in nearby Boxer museums which enshrined the official story of the Boxers as an heroic anti-imperialist force and a forerunner of the communist revolution.[39]

From the Catholics' point of view, their particular understanding of history makes them more rather than less fully Chinese. What their stories emphasize is how their religious tradition has become intertwined with Chinese tradition. Their stories about ancestors who heroically resisted the Boxers, for instance, are stories about how deeply their faith became rooted in China— how the power of God became fully visible on Chinese soil and inspired fellow Chinese believers to endure the supreme sacrifice for the sake of the faith. It was precisely because of their pride in Chinese identity that many were delighted that the church had officially recognized the Chinese martyrs as saints.

This pride in Chinese Catholic accomplishments would fit well with a pluralist, bottom-up nationalism, but not with the pontifical nationalism to which the Chinese government is committed. The government might tolerate such unofficial constructions of community identity as long as they remained private. The Vatican's canonization of the Chinese martyrs publicly—and on a global stage—contradicted the official Chinese government verdict on the Boxer Rebellion in particular and the general myth of national victimization by an undifferentiatedly malevolent imperialist West.

The timing of the canonizations exacerbated the conflict. The year 2000 was the hundredth anniversary of the Boxer Rebellion and the PRC was sponsoring large public celebrations of this event, which it officially regarded as a key moment in China's anti-imperialistic struggle. Moreover—in what Cardinal Etchegaray claimed on Vatican TV was "a regrettable mistake, but not an intentional one"[40]—the canonizations were held on October 1, China's own national holiday. Intentionally or not, the canonizations were a direct challenge to the government's claim not only to defend Chinese nationalism, but also to be the sole judge of its content.

The vehemence of the government's reaction probably only widened the gap between the unofficial, Catholic version of national pride and the government's version. The official statements claimed that the canonizations had "hurt the feelings of the Chinese people." They actually exalted the feelings of some Chinese people; the feelings they hurt were those of government cadres who were now going to have an ever harder time keeping China's Catholics in submission. Excessive pontifical authority over religious matters creates its share of problems within the Roman Catholic Church, but the attempt to assert a pontifical authority over national identity in a large, pluralistic society creates even more severe problems for a secular government. By being forced to stridently assert its version of national myth and national identity, the government only increased the diversity of dissent within China about what constitutes the true national heritage and true national pride.

The canonization imbroglio once again demonstrates a dimension of government weakness rather than strength. The government's capacity to give symbolic expression to national aspirations is an important part of its soft power. It becomes even more important as the implements of hard power become less effective. However, the government's insistence on dictating the content of Chinese nationalism can create a backlash of unofficial nationalisms that can work against the government.

Conclusion

The breakdown in progress toward normalization of Sino–Vatican relations was indeed a tragedy for the Chinese church. If normalization could have been achieved on terms acceptable to the Vatican, it would have helped to stabilize the Catholic Church in China, helped to heal some of its divisions, and provided a framework of steady theological and pastoral renewal. Absent normalization, the Chinese Catholic Church will continue to grow in numbers, reconciliation between open and underground factions will continue to take place, and new generations of priests, sisters, and lay workers will continue to be cultivated. But these developments will remain vulnerable to government harassment, and development will proceed in fits and starts, which will bring unnecessary pain to Catholics struggling to be true to their faith.

The focus of this chapter, however, has been on the effects of the standoff between Beijing and Rome on the Chinese regime. If Beijing had succeeded in normalizing its ties with the Vatican and had been able to handle the canonization controversy in a calmer way, this would have been a positive sign of the regime's stability, its capacity to overcome its internal divisions, and its hope for consistent political reform. I have argued that the government's conflicts with the Catholic Church stem from general weaknesses in the government's capacity to create new forms of soft power sufficient to contain a rapidly developing informal, unofficial social realm. The government's leaders seem too insecure to make the political concessions necessary to coopt such developments. However, attempts to suppress are often counterproductive. They succeed only in increasing the level of hostility of some citizens toward the regime, which renders peaceful political reform all the more difficult. Besides revealing weaknesses in governing capacity, the conflicts with the Catholic Church reveal weaknesses in the government's capacity to represent morally a richly pluralistic, evolving national identity.

I have suggested that the problems with the Catholic Church are part of more general problems, especially with emerging religious communities. It might be objected that the government's handling of the Falungong represents a counterexample. The government does indeed seem to have largely crushed the Falungong, at least within its borders.[41] But this required an enormous expenditure of resources. And there are many more religious movements that pose similar challenges to the government's desires for social control. The increased pressure on the Catholic Church within the past two years has been part of a general effort to suppress any forms of religious activity that eluded government control—an effort which has mostly failed. The government has demonstrated the ability to only plug one hole in a very leaky dike.

Coda

On October 24, 2001, at the opening of an international conference commemorating the four hundredth anniversary of the arrival of the great Jesuit missionary Matteo Ricci to Beijing, the pope expressed to the Chinese people "deep sadness for the errors and limits of the past" and asked "the forgiveness and understanding of those who may have felt hurt in some way by such actions on the part of Christians." "It is no secret," he continued, "that the Holy See, in the name of the whole Catholic Church and, I believe, for the benefit of the whole human family, hopes for the opening of some form of dialogue with the Authorities of the People's Republic of China," and "the normalization of relations between the People's Republic of China and the Holy See would undoubtedly have positive repercussions for humanity's progress."[42]

The official Chinese response came from Sun Yuxi, a Chinese foreign ministry spokesman. He said that "the Chinese government acknowledged the expression was made in a positive manner, but regretted the Vatican failed to apologize for the issue of 'canonization' which occurred last year and which deeply hurt the Chinese people." But he also said that "China has always wished to improve relations with the Vatican." Such improvement, however, was dependent on two principles: "1. The Holy See must break relations with Taiwan and recognize the People's Republic of China as the only representative of all China. Taiwan is an inseparable part of Chinese territory. 2. The Vatican must not use religion to interfere in China's internal affairs."[43] The Vatican made it clear that it was willing to accept the first principle but it continues to insist on having the final word on appointment of Chinese bishops. Since the Chinese side believes that this would constitute an interference in its internal affairs, the negotiations for normalization seem stalled at the point that they reached at the end of 1999. But at least the acrimony of the year 2000 has diminished.

Notes

1. *UCANews*, October 2, 2000.
2. *RMRB*, October 3, 2000. Translated by *FBIS*, October 2, 2000.
3. Ibid.
4. *Xinhua, FBIS Daily Report*, September 26 and 29, October 1, 3, 4, 5, 10, and November 29, 2000.
5. *Hong Kong iMail*, October 5, 2000.
6. "In July, 1949, three months before the formation of the [PRC], Rome issued an order to all Catholics to oppose and to boycott any communist influence. [the Vatican internuncio, Archbishop Antonio] Riberi passed this order on to the [bishops] in China. . . . This order forbade any Catholic to join or to sympathize with [the Chinese Communist Party], to publish, to read, to write, or to propagate any communist literature; violation of this order would lead to the termination of receiving the Sacraments and even excommunication. . . . In July 28, 1951, Riberi conveyed the order from Rome which extended the ecclesial punishment even to the parents or guardians of those who had violated the decree issued [in] July 1949; this order also broadened the scope for excommunication." Kim-kwong Chan, *Struggling for Survival: The Catholic Church in China from 1949–1970* (Hong Kong: Christian Study Centre on Religion and Culture, 1992), pp. 8–10.
7. Richard Madsen, *China's Catholics: Tragedy and Hope in an Emerging Civil Society* (Berkeley: University of California Press, 1998), pp. 34–39.
8. Ibid., pp. 41–42.
9. Ibid., pp. 42–45.
10. "John," "An Appeal from the Underground," *Tripod*, 20:117, pp. 16–17.
11. Madsen, *China's Catholics*, pp. 50–75.
12. Jeroom Heyndrickx, "Epiphany 2000: The Beijing-Rome Confrontation," *The Tablet*, January 13, 2000. It is difficult to find published figures on the percentage of open church bishops recognized by the Vatican. Fr. Heyndrickx is a well-informed, well-respected observer of the Catholic Church in China. His estimate that two-thirds of open church bishops have been approved by the Vatican should be taken as a reliable estimate. If anything, the estimates of church people who comment on China from the outside tend to err on the conservative side. There is a fear that estimates of large numbers of Vatican-approved bishops may increase the level of government pressure on the church.

13. Anthony Lam, "The Catholic Church in China: Conflicting Attitudes," *Tripod*, 20:115 (January–February 2000), p. 29.

14. Richard Madsen, *China and the American Dream* (Berkeley: University of California Press, 1994), pp. 202–203. See also Perry Link, Richard Madsen, and Paul G. Pickowicz, eds., *Unofficial China: Popular Culture and Thought in the People's Republic* (Boulder, Colo.: Westview Press, 1989), p. 2.

15. Information from a briefing in Hong Kong in autumn 1999 with someone closely involved with the negotiations.

16. Anthony Lam, "The Catholic Church in China: Conflicting Attitudes" pp. 33–34.

17. *UCANews*.

18. *Tripod*, 20: 116, p. 33.

19. Excerpts from this document are translated in *Tripod*, 20: 116, pp. 33–40. The quote is from p. 33.

20. Ibid., pp. 35–36.

21. Ibid., p. 36.

22. Ibid., p. 38.

23. Ibid., pp. 38–39.

24. Ibid., p. 36.

25. From briefing in Hong Kong, autumn 1999.

26. "Editorial," 20: 115, pp. 3–5.

27. Editorial Staff, "A Turning Point in China-Church Relations: A Commentary," *Tripod*, 22:116, pp. 16–18.

28. See *UCANews*, May 4, 2000; AFP, December 12, 2000.

29. *UCANews*, June 26, 2000, July 12, 2000.

30. *UCANews*, February 16, 2000.

31. *Hongkong Standard*, March 8, 2000.

32. *ZENIT*, May 7, 2000.

33. *UCANews*, March 13, 2000.

34. Author's interview.

35. *ZENIT*, March 14, 2000.

36. *UCANews*, September 20, 2000.

37. Xiaokang Su and Luxiang Wang, *Deathsong of the River: A Reader's Guide to the Chinese TV Series Heshang*, trans. and ed., Richard W. Bodman and Pin P. Wan (Ithaca, N.Y.: Cornell East Asia Series, 1991).

38. Madsen, *China's Catholics*, pp. 25–26.

39. Ibid., p. 32.

40. *UCANews*, October 3, 2000.

41. John Pomfret and Philip P. Pan, *Washington Post Foreign Service*, August 5, 2001: "Expanding its use of torture and high-pressure indoctrination, China's Communist Party has gained the upper hand in its protracted battle against the banned Falungong spiritual movement, according to government sources and Falungong practitioners. As a result, they say, large numbers of people are abandoning the group that presented the party with its most serious challenge since the 1989 student-led protests in Tiananmen Square."

42. *Vatican Information Service*, October 24, 2001.

43. *People's Daily Online*, October 31, 2001.

—————— 11 ——————

Politics of Partial Marketization
State and Class Relations in Post-Mao China

Kyung-Sup Chang

Introduction

A core aspect of the post-Mao reform in China is to induce or allow market-oriented economic behavior from various production units and individuals and institute market-based relations between them. In rural areas, economic institutional decollectivization has made peasants resume individual farming and other private production activities. The economic outcomes of such activities are now determined not just by parameters set by the state, such as state procurement prices for grain, but increasingly by market situations, that is, the demand and supply of grain, petty-manufactured goods, and personal services both at the local and the national level. In urban areas, strenuous efforts have been made to institute labor market principles into collective and state enterprises. Increasingly, workers are denied political entitlement to permanent employment and instead asked to accept pay cuts, temporary or permanent layoffs, and so forth. However, many adaptive people can now acquire new employment opportunities in various types of private and joint-venture enterprises or initiate their own private ventures.

These changes have added up to a situation where the constraints and directions imposed by the state on the economic activities of various social groups are gradually replaced by the risks and opportunities of the market economy. This also means a fundamental transformation of the core conditions and processes by which the inter-class relations among various rural, urban, and political classes are shaped. Under the pre-reform economic system of state commandism, the competing interests of these groups used to be coordinated and/or manipulated through the political and bureaucratic channels of the state. That is, inter-class relations in the pre-reform era were formed "through the state." In the post-Mao era, market-oriented reform has created new arenas and processes for inter-class relations beyond state control. However, the state has not entirely withdrawn its control of inter-class relations any more than the program of marketization has been fully implemented. Instead, marketization—or withdrawal of state intervention—has been unevenly pursued and fulfilled across different industries and regions.

This uneven marketization or destatization has in effect led to a sort of favoritism by which the state preferentially protects the vested interests of state-dependent groups such as workers in state enterprises, political and administrative cadres, and entrepreneurs with political connections while the interests of grassroots groups in marketized sections are subject to the uncertainty and instability of the market economy as well as discrimination in the allocation of public economic resources. For instance, worker-peasant disparities in the levels of income and living standard have rather increased in favor of workers, while the general performance of the urban economy has been much poorer than that of the rural economy. Also, a sort of privatization of the privatization process has occurred as many cadres and former cadres have consciously attempted to convert their political or administrative authority over the collective economy into their private wealth or entrepreneurial opportunities. In this context, it is well understood among Chinese people that attaining some access to (and sometimes control over) state power is a key to economic success. Of course, many persons have been able to achieve private economic success without any state support. But these successful persons (*xianfu jieceng*) account for a tiny minority of the population and inevitably need political protection to deal with local neighbors' feeling of relative deprivation.

Class differentiation and economic inequality in the market economy alone can be considered a serious retrogression from the socialist ideal of equal and communal prosperity.[1] When state engagement is observed to be responsible for even worse tendencies of class differentiation and economic inequality, there is a serious possibility that people's frustration and resistance is expressed not only against richer neighbors but also much more crucially against the state (and its local agents). In this context, state authority can easily be identified with economic injustice. Such grassroots sentiment has already been expressed in numerous peasant riots and worker protests across the country. Theoretically, political democratization now can be considered a precondition for economic justice although the party-state leadership in Beijing tends to show a different perspective that a strong authoritarian leadership is needed to curb politically induced economic injustice.

Class restructuring and its concomitant change in the state-society relationship in China's market socialist reform are social phenomena unprecedented in human as well as Chinese history and thus difficult to explain on the basis of existing theory. To overcome this intellectual lacuna, a state-centered explanation of class relations is hereby presented and applied to the social realities of reform-era China. This is an effort to explain the conflation of class problems and the state-society relationship by showing that class relations are formed and adjusted "through the state." The state-centered explanation of class relations refuses to regard class relations as the competition and conflict among social classes separated from state power. Instead, it emphasizes that class order is critically shaped by the "access to state power" of each social class. In China's market-oriented economic reform, state power has not been replaced by market principles but reinvigorated through strategic selection of the operational scope and direction of market principles. As a sort of "partial marketization" has occurred, class relations are centered on state-dependent adoption/exclusion of market principles.

Theoretical and Historical Backgrounds: Access to State Power and Class Relations

Inequality and class conflict in the supposedly classless society of post-revolutionary China were noted not only by critical scholars and intellectuals but also by the supreme leader, Mao Zedong himself. In fact, Mao argued that socialism in China had engendered contradictions of its own, which would require new stages of revolutionary political struggle. In an address delivered in 1957, Mao indicated two types of contradictions—namely, between enemies and us (people) and among people themselves.[2] The contradictions between enemies and people were supposedly revealed by the resistance of reactionary groups to the socialist transformation of post-revolutionary Chinese society as well as to the earlier socialist revolution. The contradictions among people themselves, on the other hand, were the disharmony and conflict that emerged among various social groups and elements even after the revolution and the basic socialist transformation had been completed. To Mao, these contradictions among people themselves necessitated additional political efforts beyond what Marx, Lenin, and Stalin had suggested—that is, "permanent" revolutionary struggle as materialized in such instances as the Great Leap Forward and the Cultural Revolution.

In detail, the contradictions among people themselves were found: among workers, among peasants, among intellectuals, between workers/peasants and intellectuals, between workers and national bourgeoisie, among national bourgeoisie, and between people and their government.[3] The contradictions between people and their government, in turn, were found: among the competing interests of the state, collectives, and individuals, between democracy and centralism, between leaders and the led, and between bureaucratic cadres and people. These contradictions among people themselves supposedly evinced that there existed, in socialist China, conflictual relations and inequalities among various groups and classes that hinged on various occupational, political, administrative, and regional statuses.

While Mao's analysis of the class conflict and inequality in post-revolutionary China is no less convincing than that of professional scholars, a further characterization of the class relations and group categories he used should be made. In China, the positions and inter-relations of party and state cadres, intellectuals, workers of urban state and collective enterprises, peasants of rural collective farms, and former class enemies and their offspring were not built as Max Weber conceptualized as market-based class properties (in capitalist society) but as state-set or state-dependent properties in a political and economic system comprehensively organized and tightly directed by the state. This proposition, however, should not be interpreted as a mere repetition of the totalitarianism argument. What matters decisively here is "access to state power." While state power in the context of supposedly proletarian dictatorship and the state-command economy was overwhelming, there was always fierce competition among different social and political groups to magnify their connection to and influence on it.[4]

Each social group's access to state power is either formally institutionalized through the political and administrative framework for governance and economic management or informally pursued through individual relationships or collective political pressure.[5] For instance, the privileges of urban residents over peasants, particularly in the pre-reform era, were institutionally ensured by the politico-economic system, which entitled most urban residents to employment in state enterprises (and thus to state-guaranteed high remuneration and welfare benefits) and coerced peasants to undertake stagnant collective farming at their own risk. Private entrepreneurs in the reform era, by contrast, have to cultivate various informal clientelistic relations with party and government cadres if they want to acquire a business permit in lucrative areas and secure production materials and bank loans at administratively determined favorable terms.

Access to state power may be compared with what Vivienne Shue calls the "reach of the state" into society or what Peter Evans calls the social "embeddedness of the state." Shue argues, "Chinese socialist state builders of the Mao era seem to have looked . . . for ways to domesticate localist loyalties, to incorporate them into state socialist structures, and turn them, where possible, into a positive force for socialist development."[6] To be an effective force in social transformation and economic development, even the Maoist state had to respect local social structures and relations but, whenever feasible, utilized them for a maximum mobilization of grassroots efforts. In state-led capitalist industrializing economies, according to Evans, the ability of the state to penetrate social organizations and relations and manipulate them for effective policy implementation has been a key to national economic success.[7] When these efforts are made by the state, the streams of influence and pressure form a two-way traffic in which social groups try to capitalize on the social penetration of the state to advance their own interests.

The social reach and embeddedness of the state will sound more convincing if the state, which has emerged out of, but become independent from, society repenetrates and sometimes accommodates social structure and redirects social change to achieve its autonomous goals; whereas access to state power will be more persuasive if social and political groups, which have been formed or allowed to form by the state, influence the state back to expedite their class interests. The social reach and embeddedness of the state are concepts that seem to have theoretically evolved out of the neo-Marxian debate on state autonomy and capacity. These concepts are offered to show that the state is not simply autonomous from class interests but persuades, reorganizes, and, where inevitable, compromises with them. Access to state power is a theoretical concern that extends from the Marxist critique of "degenerated party-state dictatorship" over producer classes in socialist societies.[8] Using this concept helps to understand that various social and political groups not only recognize the monolithic authority of the state but also attempt to influence or collude with it to promote their class interests.

Chinese people's concern about access to state power was not historically unprecedented. In traditional China, Wakeman observes, "first, that gentry status could be reduced to a common denominator—power-holding through office or access to power-holders—and, second, that people who spoke or thought in ways we now identify with the high culture of China were better able to protect their local interests than those who did not share this language and way of life with Chinese officialdom."[9] He also notes that "Corporate interest groups did, of course, exist, but they were usually outside the limits of acceptable political behavior." Seeking the support or influence of the state in managing social relations is nothing to blame politically or morally in China's corporatist historical tradition.[10]

In post-revolutionary China, competition and checks in gaining, maintaining, and aggrandizing access to state power came to constitute a lively corporatist political society (rather than a totalitarian machine society), of which rich historical documentation is available. Cadres at various divisions and levels of party-state office were busy not only in capitalizing on their official authority for their own benefits (or against the interests of peasants and workers under their supervision) but also in establishing connections to cadres in higher state offices.[11] Workers in urban enterprises were always considered politically more threatening by the party-state and thus endowed with larger influence on macroeconomic policies of the state than peasants in collective farms, making worker-peasant material disparities ever wider.[12] Managers and workers/peasants in urban enterprises and rural collective farms competed hard to win the support of unit party leadership, while party cadres themselves were always concerned about the competing goals of economic performance and political stability.[13] A total denial of access to state power was made toward former class enemies and their offspring, who could not expect to join cadredom at any level or receive any preferential treatment in allocation of jobs and benefits in their work units.[14]

Most of these tendencies and policies were rather reinforced during the Cultural Revolution, a political project intended to eradicate the contradictions of class conflict and inequality in socialist China. Ironically, the political upheaval was settled in a manner that made state power more personified in individual political leaders than ever. The political motif of transforming the bureaucratic socialist system into a democratic and organic one rather became responsible for the arbitrary use of state power by individual leaders whose primary concern was to bolster their political position in various state and party organizations. A concomitant trend was that social and political groups began to compete even harder to forge and strengthen particularistic ties with the state power elite.[15]

These observations lead to a conclusion that the particular historical constellations of class relations in post-revolutionary China can be understood only when access to state power as materialized in various distinct ways is fully taken into account. Class relations were forged and transformed "through the state." The legacy of this state-shaped class structure is still evident in post-Mao or reform-era China, despite the fact that now state power is often expressed in terms of market economic outcomes.

Reform as Partial Marketization and Class Relations

The characteristics and directions of post-Mao reform in China have been changing constantly despite the recent official declaration of building a "socialist market economy." Nevertheless, it will be safe to say that Chinese reform has been centered on step-by-step changes in economic institutions and policies, as opposed to the experience of the former Soviet Union and East European countries where abrupt political transitions triggered no less radical economic changes. Very broadly, there are two main dimensions of China's economic system transition, that is, privatization and/or rationalization of production organizations at the micro-level and institutionalization of market transactions of labor, consumer goods, capital goods, enterprise ownership rights, finance, as well as welfare services at the macro-level. While China's reform is hailed as the most successful case of post-socialist economic development, results have been highly mixed across different industries, regions, and policy domains.

Two points need to be made to caution against any hasty generalization on the nature or outcome of post-Mao economic reform. First, the contents and courses of actual reform have never been fully planned in advance by the state. Instead, reform has been a constant trial-error-revision sequence as shaped by the tense interplay between the pragmatist state leadership and various social and political groups concerning individual and collective economic interests. Second, institutionalization of the market, while it certainly signals reduction of the plan, is by no means linked to replacement of the state in the macrocoordination of economic activities. The authority and role of the state are now evinced not only through the bureaucratic control of economic activities and resources but also through the (mal)functioning of market dynamics. As a corollary, state-society interaction now takes place both through bureaucracy and market.

These two tendencies have been jointly responsible for the emergence of a "partially marketized economic system" in which the degrees and/or directions of marketization of commodities, services, and labor critically affect the competing class interests of various groups and individuals. In a certain aspect, this uneven marketization has a macroeconomic rationale as the party-state leadership intends to pursue reform without spurning the economic and political utility of pre-reform economic institutions all at once.[16] In reality, however, partial marketization has ramified into a sort of favoritism by which the party-state preferentially protects the vested interests of state-dependent groups such as workers in state enterprises, cadres in party and state organizations, and entrepreneurs with political connections, while the interests of grassroots groups in marketized sections are subject to the uncertainty and instability of market conditions as well as discrimination in the allocation of public economic resources. Of course, marketization sometimes works to promote new economic opportunities and windfall profits for certain groups while others under bureaucratic control have to carry on hopeless nonmarket economic activities.

Symptoms of partial marketization are abundant in post-Mao China. A very sketchy look at the current industrial and employment structure will enable the reader to realize that full-scale market forces operate only in some segments of the Chinese economy, for instance, in private and foreign enterprises and in family farms. Labor markets do exist but their effect is nullified in regards to legal urban residents with tenured jobs. In contrast, rural-to-urban migrants, called *mingongchao,* are subject to all the adverse impacts of marketization. Even marketization of social services accruing to the demise or decline of socialist work units, simultaneously as welfare units, has occurred unevenly. Consequently, all rural families and individuals have to suddenly rely on paid services and goods from markets while most urban families and individuals are still assured basic protection of their welfare needs. Ownership of industrial and commercial enterprises has also been subjected to partial marketization as shareholding arrangements and sales are allowed and sometimes encouraged only in those industries and enterprises without strategic economic or political importance. Also, there has been the *shuanggui* (dual track) price system for a significant number of consumer and producer goods, which consists of administered low prices and market-set high prices. Banks have two types of loans which are offered according to market and administrative criteria correspondingly. In fact, the list of related examples is almost inexhaustible.

Some of these symptoms may simply be transitory phenomena which will evaporate as time goes by or deregulation proceeds. But an overall impression is that partial marketization in reform-era China is not merely an outcome of "gradual" marketization. China's partially marketized economic system has an economic as well as political logic of its own and will last for a considerable period of time. An important part of such logic is derived from the fact that pre-reform corporatist political society still prevails with a critical influence on the contents and directions of reform policies. The competition among different social and political groups to magnify their connection to and influence on state power is as fierce as in the pre-reform era and has serious ramifications in the scope and manner of marketization. After reckoning what outcomes will arise when market principles enter their economic domains, these groups attempt to facilitate, obstruct, or deflect the marketization process by staging political pressure on or bribing party and state offices. In China's partially marketized economy, the contents and degrees of marketization affect competing class interests decisively. To the extent that the marketization process is a task of the state itself, class relations in reform-era China continue to be forged and transformed "through the state." The following section presents details on this feature of post-Mao Chinese society.

Class Structure and Relations in Partially Marketized China

Peasants, Workers, and Mingongchao: *Dual Dualism*

Reform has transformed China's eight hundred million peasant population from collective laborers in People's Communes into family-based private farmers. Although the prime means of production, that is, land, is still

ollectively owned and rent to them for a certain limited period for indi-
idual cultivation, their class status is not much different from their pre-
evolutionary ancestors. It is true that nonagricultural sectors both in rural
and urban areas have absorbed rural surplus labor at an amazing speed, but
amily farmers still constitute the dominant class category in contemporary
China. As they have changed from collective farm workers into autonomous
economic producers, Chinese peasants are now confronted with both new
opportunities for wealth creation and structural uncertainties emanating from
the market economy.[17]

The social and economic autonomy of Chinese peasants accruing to agricultural decollectivization has been expressed, most explosively, in their
vibrant desire for quitting agriculture and/or leaving villages.[18] Given the
extreme shortage of farmland supply, most of the rural families had difficulty
in securing mere subsistence safely. Ever since the communist party-state
suddenly withdrew its long-held suppression of nonagricultural economic
activities by peasants and gradually allowed them short-term migration and
commuting to nearby towns and small cities, nonagricultural employment
and rural exodus have increased at dramatic rates.[19] While a majority of peasant-
turned-workers are employed in rural collective industries (*xiangzhenqiye*),
an increasing number of unprepared masses—dubbed *mangliu* (blind flow)—
have entered big cities, causing various social and economic problems.[20] In a
situation where more and more regular urban residents (with the urban residence permit called *hukou*) have to accept layoffs, pay cuts, and job delays
amidst the desperate urban economic reform, these new, unallowed, and un-
welcome entrants are not easily absorbed into the urban economy. However,
the Chinese urban economy has already increased its reliance on village-provided abundant and cheap migrant labor, called *mingongchao,* to an irrevers-
ible extent. These migrant, and often circulating, workers, constitute neither a
peasant class nor an urban working class, but are influenced simultaneously
by the socioeconomic situation of both urban and rural areas.[21]

For most of the urban workers whose work units such as state and collective enterprises continue to exist, their class status of (socialist) wage laborer
can be considered to be maintained, at least, on surface. However, with the
managerial rationalization of state and collective enterprises being the most
crucial task of urban economic reform, various experiments with new forms
of management and ownership have inevitably affected the social and economic status of urban workers. In particular, the pressure on these socialist
enterprises for profitability and financial independence has led to a rapid
destabilization of workers' employment conditions, so that their difference
from the employment conditions of workers in capitalist economies is quickly
decreasing.[22] Furthermore, those enterprises which have decided to accept

foreign companies' investment are concomitantly exposed to capitalist labor relations as a condition for such investment, thereby causing local Chinese workers deep anxiety.[23] Nonetheless, the changes in the living conditions and employment status of urban workers, whose potential for political disruption is unparalleled, are given perhaps the most serious consideration by the communist party-state.

While all grassroots *renmin*, whether peasants or urban workers, have experienced fundamental and abrupt transformations in their social and economic status, urban workers are somehow provided by the state with various shock-absorbing mechanisms against such changes.[24] This is evinced most clearly by the fact that the income level and living standard of urban workers have widened the already substantial leads over those of peasants during a period when the rural economy has far excelled the urban economy in its performance.[25] This ironic phenomenon derives from the fact that the state has risked a serious financial burden to cover the huge and chronic deficits of urban state enterprises and thus protect the employment status and welfare benefits of workers therein. By contrast, the state has refused to approximate, that is, adjust upward, its procurement prices for farm products to the actual market prices since the mid-1980s, thereby aggravating the profitability crisis of agriculture.[26]

Furthermore, even marketization (commodification) of social services and security mechanisms, resulting from the demise or reform of socialist production units, has taken place unevenly.[27] Most regular urban residents still expect, not in vain, that their basic welfare needs should be met mainly through enterprise-level social security programs; whereas the deconstruction of the communal welfare mechanisms amid agricultural decollectivization has forced most peasants to use commodified services in the market at their own expense.[28] In addition, the state has been spending enormously every year to provide price subsidies exclusively for regular urban residents' foodstuffs and other basic consumer goods, so that their living standards may not deteriorate amidst the rampant and sustained inflation. In the mid-1980s, such subsidies alone amounted close to the total state spending on national defense.[29] These preferential measures of the state have enabled regular urban workers to expand their superior socioeconomic status over peasants even when their state enterprises are in chronic and hopeless deficit.

The state-imposed inequality between regular urban workers and peasants is systematically reproduced, within urban areas, as the inequality between regular urban workers and migrant workers from rural villages. Confronted with the continuous stagnation in agricultural productivity and household income, a rapidly increasing number of Chinese peasants have shown natural reactions of quitting agriculture and/or leaving villages.[30] In fact, the reformist state leadership has adopted social and economic policies hat allow and sometimes encourage such reactions of peasants. However, once peasants enter urban places, their migrant status (or illegal worker status) results in various kinds of social and economic discrimination by the state and urban enterprises that are determined to protect the exclusive employment and welfare benefits of regular urban residents.[31] While a labor market has been formally instituted as part of the economic reform, adverse impacts are effectively contained or diluted with regard to regular urban residents who have a practical entitlement to lifetime employment. The effort at marketization of labor relations within state and collective enterprises, that is, *laodonghetongzhi* (labor contract system), has been only partially successful in its actual implementation.[32] In the early period of the labor contract system (i.e., the mid-to-late 1980s), enterprise managers and local governments could not overcome the staunch resistance of workers to cancellation of their permanent job security (secularly called *tiefanwan*); more recently, workers have gradually accepted the status of contract laborer, however, with the actual content of their contracts ensuring their *tiefanwan* in a different (contractual) disguise.[33] As far as labor relations for regular urban residents are concerned, the Chinese economy remains only partially marketized. By contrast, migrant workers are required to endure all kinds of social and economic hardships germinated from the "segmented" market economy, even when such endurance is not likely to guarantee stable permanent employment. Furthermore, it is extremely difficult, if not impossible, for migrant workers to acquire adequate social services even at their own expenses, while such services are guaranteed to regular urban residents as a sort of (urban) citizenship right.[34]

If it is considered that migrant workers constitute the common communal entity with their family members remaining in villages, there seems to exist a dual inequality structure between urban and rural people created and buttressed by the state.[35] This "dual dualism" of the state manifests itself not only in the class relations between peasants (and their migrating relatives) and urban workers but also in the class relations peasants and urban workers form correspondingly with their employers. That is, while regular urban workers have been allowed to maintain their socialist employment relations and work conditions within state and collective enterprises, village-provided migrant workers are compelled to form strict market relations with various types of enterprises and entrepreneurs under the most adverse, discriminatory conditions.

Peasant-Workers in Xiangzhenqiye: *Local Entrepreneurial Collectivism*

There has been an explosive growth of the rural population employed in village and township-owned enterprises, called *xiangzhenqiye*, since the early

1980s.[36] Post-Mao reform gave birth to rural-based, labor-intensive industries on such a massive scale that more than one hundred twenty million
peasants came to find jobs at various ranks and functions therein. In its social
and political—not to mention economic—significance, this depeasantizatio
trend surpasses any other long-term social transformations accruing to eco
nomic reform whether in rural or urban areas. Even in the economic domair
as widely known, the growth of these rural industries is by far the most im
portant, and perhaps the only sustained, economic success of the Chines
reform. With all the economic difficulties generated from inefficient and defi
cit-making urban state enterprises and stagnant family farms, this rural in
dustrial sector alone has been almost exclusively responsible for China'
economic overheating since the mid-1980s.

On the surface, this rural industrial growth may be described as a familia
process of Lewisian industrialization based on abundant rural surplus la
bor.[37] But, the entrepreneurial initiative, regional distribution, organizationa
structure, and internal class relations of these rural industries are quite dis
tinct from those observed in other societies. In particular, if seen from the
Lewisian perspective, there is a crucial missing link in this industrializatior
process, that is, the initial absence of urban-originated capital and entrepreneurship (to be combined with rural surplus labor). Instead, the tripartite
interactions among peasants, local states, and the central party-state leadership came to fill such an economic vacuum and led to a rural-contained but
autonomous industrialization by peasant communities. This spawned a unique
process of market-oriented industrialization without typical capitalist social
transformation.

On the part of the peasants, who have acquired substantial social and economic autonomy and income growth amidst the agricultural decollectivization
and upward price adjustments of farm products during the early to mid-1980s,
they were equipped not only with abundant surplus labor to be utilized in
nonagricultural sectors but also with desire *and* purchasing capacity for new
consumer goods, cash surplus to be invested in nonagricultural ventures,
farm-produced raw materials to be processed, and sometimes self-initiated
individual or collective entrepreneurship.[38] Thus, peasants were linked to
the new industries not just as passive labor sellers but also as the main con-
sumers, investors, raw-material providers, and entrepreneurs/managers. As a
consequence, many of the rural industrial enterprises can be considered "la-
bor-managed firms," with which societies like the former Yugoslavia tried to
build a new line of socialist economy.[39]

These efforts and initiatives of peasants did not result in isolated and dispersed trials—as Karl Marx would have predicted of "a sack of isolated po-
tatoes"—but came to drive a rebirth of rural economic collectivism across

China. This was not so much because Chinese peasants were ideologically awakened as because local collective units (villagers' committees) and state organs (*xiang* governments) were actively engaged in organizing, managing, and financing the new industrial enterprises. On the part of local leaders and cadres, running rural industries is no new experience since they had been in charge of many rural industries set up under Mao Zedong's initiative during the Great Leap Forward and the Cultural Revolution.[40] This time, however, is different in that rural industries are the only identifiable collective economic basis on which their positional benefits as well as the communal financial resources can be secured and marketization of the rural as well as the national economy has opened up a wide array of economic opportunities in which their entrepreneurial leadership can be practiced. Compared to the pre-reform era, rural economic collectivism in the reform era is much more pragmatic, and, concomitantly, much less political. Rural cadres and leaders across China have tried to prepare a favorable political and administrative environment for new industrial ventures, renovate or build factories, set up corporate organizations, mobilize villagers' economic resources, secure financial and/or technical cooperation from urban or foreign enterprises, and staff or appoint the management of rural industrial enterprises.[41] As a result of their active and comprehensive efforts, most of the rural industries remain collective production units, which are not just nominally but practically village or township-run and in which class distinctions and antagonism between peasant-workers and managers are not salient. This entrepreneurial leadership or intervention of the local state, however, sometimes makes room for politically mustered economic exploitation, as many despotic local elites have not reserved their greed in abusing their authority over employees and assets in rural industries.

Both economically and politically, rapid rural industrialization as has proceeded in the post-Mao era gives a huge relief to the central state leadership. The most formidable economic (and inevitably political) task of the Dengist regime on the eve of reform was to feed and employ the massive rural surplus labor of at least two hundred million without aggravating the urban economic problems of widespread deficits and overemployment in state and collective enterprises.[42] Agricultural reforms such as institutional decollectivization and upward adjustment of farm producer prices had only a short-term effect in improving the material fate of the then eight hundred million peasant population. In this situation, a strategy of "third sector" development was pursued. Rural communities were allowed and even encouraged to develop various nonagricultural industries and ventures within their own localities, but without relying on other localities or the central state for financial and other resources. A sort of "contained industrialization" has been sought by the Beijing government, as underemployed and undernourished peasants were expected to be economically absorbed by nonagricultural enterprises within their own localities, or at least outside the already congested big cities.[43] It has been hoped that the massive rural labor surplus be released into nonagricultural sectors without forging a direct, hostile market relation with urban workers who are now confronted with their own troubles of layoffs, unemployment, and so on. So far, this hope has not been betrayed too badly. However, the central state leadership has at least indirectly pitted the interests of rural and urban industries—and inevitably those of rural and urban industrial workers—against each other. For it has frequently intervened in the competition of the two sectors for scarce capital, raw materials, energy, and skills, mostly to the advantage of the urban sector.

In sum, while agricultural decollectivization led to the demise of rural collective institutions, local economic collectivism is still thriving in rural enterprises owned and managed by villages, townships, and towns. These collectively owned but market-oriented rural industries are tightly controlled by local leaders and cadres, whereas labor power, investment funds, and commodity demand are secured mostly from grassroots peasants. The central state leadership in Beijing, which is keen to the need to develop alternative sources of economic growth and labor absorption other than stagnant agriculture and inefficient state industries, hopes that this self-generated, labor-intensive rural industrialization continues to reduce rural labor surplus and improve rural income without burdening the urban economy. Local state entrepreneurship combined with the peasants' economic autonomy and motivation has been responsible for the almost overnight creation of a huge rural industrial population, in which class relations are highly distinct.

Private Entrepreneurs: Political Managerialism

While private farmers and workers of state and collective enterprises still account for an overwhelming majority of the Chinese population, those who belong to various newly formed private economic units are rapidly increasing in their size and proportion. The new economic units include: *getihu* (individual or family-based economic operations, sometimes with a few hired hands, engaged mostly in petty service trade); *siyingqiye* (privately run small enterprises with a certain limit on the size of hired workers); foreign-invested enterprises; Chinese-foreign joint venture enterprises, among other entities. As these new economic units can start their operations without adopting the socialist principles of ownership and management, the class characteristics of their workers, managers, and investors are not fundamentally different from those of their counterparts in a capitalist system. Sometimes these new economic units enter into joint management and/or investment with state or collective enterprises. In such cases, workers, managers, and investors of the joint ventures take on extremely complicated class characteristics reflecting the systemic attributes of the combined enterprises. For these reasons, Chinese society in the reform era shows one of the most complex class structures in human history.

Among the new classes arising out of the economic system changes, it is perhaps private entrepreneurs who have the most crucial ramifications for the systemic nature of the new Chinese society. Their formation and growth could potentially imply the emergence of a new elite or ruling group in the Chinese class structure. As of the mid-1990s, however, almost all of these private entrepreneurs were either small enterprise owners who participated in everyday management in person or managers of medium- or large-size enterprises whose capital share was only nominal or absent.[44] Thus, these groups clearly fall short of any economic ruling class corresponding to the bourgeoisie in capitalist society.[45]

Just as the ownership and managerial characteristics of newly formed enterprises in the reform era are exceptionally complicated, those entrepreneurs who own and/or manage such enterprises have extremely complex class characteristics.[46] Nonetheless, no matter whether they belong to collective, private, or joint-ownership enterprises, most of the contemporary Chinese entrepreneurs may not be considered professional managers who are equipped with such economic rationality and managerial skills as are needed for improving corporate profitability in a pure market economy. On the contrary, Chinese entrepreneurs have to act as political/administrative troubleshooters if their enterprises are to survive in China's partially marketized economic system. They have to keenly analyze the areas and manners in which the state intervenes in or combines with the market economy and then persuade or even bribe policymakers and cadres to induce administrative decisions favorable to their own enterprises.[47] In addition, they have to handle the corporate sociopolitical climate—composed of workers, local residents, enterprise-level party cadres besides themselves—in such a direction as to minimize any political costs incurring complaints and resistance from these constituencies.[48] To undertake these functions efficiently, even private entrepreneurs have to attain the attribute of an able political/administrative coordinator who can skillfully secure access to state power and take advantage of it whenever necessary.[49] If a Chinese entrepreneur has been successful even without a rational economic attitude and professional managerial capacity, he/she may possess at least good skills for political/administrative maneuvers. In this context, any entrepreneur who has a past career as a party or state cadre will have a most useful leverage in corporate management because they can utilize their *guanxi* (connections) with currently incumbent cadres.

The current Chinese economy has: the *shuanggui* (dual track) system by which two prices, market-cleared (higher) and administratively set (lower) correspondingly, co-exist for many raw materials, producer goods, and consumer goods; the dual loaning system by which loans are provided at two different interest rates, market-cleared (higher) and administratively set (lower), depending on the sources of funds; and the preferential taxation system by which various corporate taxes are reduced or exempt by the criteria set by the central and local governments. Those private entrepreneurs who, thanks to their precious access to state power, can acquire materials, machinery, and funds at the administratively set, much cheaper costs and avoid taxes lawfully may not be classified as the same social class as those who cannot—at least, not by the political criteria.[50] In addition, if privatization or marketization of a certain economic sector is expected to produce a windfall of monopoly profits, a capable Chinese entrepreneur should be able to secure an exclusive right to market entrance by mobilizing political support from patron cadres and state offices. This type of strategic market entrance has been most distinctly performed by the so-called *taizidang* (party of princes) entrepreneurs who have abused their politically powerful parents' authority in various monopolistic private ventures. The phenomenal economic outcomes of these rent-seeking behaviors, fostered by state power, are well illustrated by the phenomenon of numerous private enterprises growing hundreds times larger over several years. The rent-seeking alliance between the state and private entrepreneurs, while it is different from the classic role of the capitalist state to support the capitalist class in its class conflict with labor, still tends to sacrifice the interests of grassroots people because it often caters to the unjustified private interests of private entrepreneurs by further distorting the partially marketized, distorted economic system.

Even when private entrepreneurs do not pursue rent-seeking activities through their collusion with cadres, they still have to maintain tender relations with them in order to minimize various "nonbusiness transaction costs" incurring everyday political and administrative interferences.[51] In addition, when private entrepreneurs deal with the complaints and resistance of workers, local residents, and cadres, they should be able to secure political support from higher-level party and government authorities to minimize further political damages to business. It is true that many entrepreneurs have been impressively successful in their private business even without the direct support from or collusion with party and state offices. However, such cases of clean success constitute an extremely rare minority, and even their success is not readily justified in the eyes of poor neighbors, not to mention in the eyes of suspicious cadres. Thus, political protection, if not outright political collusion, is a minimum condition for private business.[52] Successful private entrepreneurs in reform-era China, most of whom have shown distinct talent in strategic dependence on or skillful co-opting with state power, constitute as much a political as an economic class.

Party-State Cadres: Class Against Itself

China's market-oriented reform has been accompanied by a strenuous effort to minimize the political and administrative intervention of the state in economic sectors and production units under the doctrine of managing the economy "according to economic principles." Consequently, party and state cadres who were accustomed to political supervision and control of the economy are now asked to be reborn suddenly as purely economic functionaries (i.e., professional managers) or to strengthen specialized functions as pure administrators or party politicians.[53] Such adaptations, of course, are far from easy, so that many unprepared cadres, especially old ones, have been weeded out politically.[54] However, there is no empirical ground for believing that reform has structurally weakened the ruling class status of party and state cadres. To the contrary, reform has led to a situation in which state power is exercised in a more expansive and complex manner, in particular, through its allocation of various private economic opportunities.[55] That is, many state and party cadres have tried to convert their political power into economic wealth by usurping the limited opportunities for wealth accumulation themselves or assigning such opportunities to their relatives, close friends, or political clients in secrecy.[56]

China's reform, as compared to those politically driven reforms in Russia and the East European countries, is often referred to as one centered on or confined to the economy. But, although it is seldom proclaimed too loudly, there have been a series of political and administrative actions taken to induce a rational apportionment of state power and to create an adequate institutional environment for private economic activities. That is, even if the communist party has not given up its monopoly over political power, many measures have been taken to supervise and control the exercise of power by organizations and cadres at various levels of the party-state hierarchy.[57] More specifically, the kernel of Deng Xiaoping's striving for political and administrative reform consisted of, on the one hand, separation of the functions and authorities of the state and the communist party and, on the other hand, substitution of cadres who are young and professionally qualified for those who are not. The principal program in this regard is a new system of state civil service, that is, *guojiagongwuyuan*.[58] The formation of a modern administrative class by training and empowering professional civil servants with rational attitudes is considered an indispensable condition for the firm rooting and sustained development of the market economic system. These professional administrators are then expected to pursue their individual advancement by performing a good leadership function for economic development and social stability.

However, if cadres behave such that their formal status as state managers and their private status as exclusive interest seekers diverge rampantly, the institution of the state may degenerate from a civil mechanism for providing public goods into a private tool for suppressing and exploiting grassroots people. This possibility, while it is rather commonplace in human history, has become a serious reality in reform-era China. Numerous former and current cadres at various levels of the party-state hierarchy have not hesitated to abuse their political influence and administrative authority over the rapidly restructuring (privatizing) national and local economies in order to receive illegal fees and kickbacks from private entrepreneurs, initiate their own business in secrecy, and preferentially support their clique's business. These acts constitute what may be called the "privatization of the privatization process."[59] Although the privatization of many nationally owned production organizations and resources may be considered an indispensable task for the market-oriented economic transition, the particular privatization process should be undertaken in such a rational and impartial manner as to facilitate national economic development and collective welfare improvement most effectively. Only when this is possible can the communist political regime reinforce its power basis through a sort of "instrumental legitimacy" for economic development and can individual cadres maintain their class status as political and administrative leaders. However, concrete realities in reform-era China show that too many cadres have tried to realize their class interests not by fulfilling their political and administrative leadership roles effectively, but by abusing the state power entrusted to them to gain personal wealth.[60]

The basic conditions for a stable and lasting political survival of the communist regime have been dismantled much more seriously by its agents at various ranks than by dissident social groups like students and intellectuals. The party-state is taken hostage to the self-defeating class interests of its local agents, that is, privately minded, myopic cadres engaged in corruption, so that their legitimacy for political leadership is seriously atrophying. From a long-term perspective, since the politically buttressed class status of party and state cadres presupposes the political survival of the communist regime itself, China's political ruling class is (ab)using state power against itself. This means that the political legacy of Stalinist state socialism—the nomenclature class, which through its domination of the bureaucratic command economy, practically privatized the collectively owned means of production and exploited grassroots workers and peasants economically, approximating the bourgeois class in capitalist society—is reproduced in a more complicated manner in China's partially marketized economic system.

Democratization: Class Politics against Market or State?

The market economy has been associated with alienation, inequality, and poverty in most societies. China's "socialist market" economy does not appear to be an exception. However, Chinese grassroots people, let alone intellectuals, tend to conceive the increasing inequality and alienation as fundamentally rooted in the undemocratic attitude and behavior of the party-state elite. Perhaps the Western historical experience of democratization is a scholarly and intellectual issue with a limited political significance for the Chinese people, but the grassroots disagreement with the communist leadership presents a formidable obstacle to the sustainability of market socialist dictatorship. It has already become part of many grassroots people's casual street chatter to blame and curse the communist party—of course, not in the presence of cadres or security officers—for everyday economic hardships and wrongs.

From the previous analysis of state-interwoven class relations, it is rather obvious why disadvantaged underclasses regard the undemocratic state (or its local agents) as the main cause of inequality, alienation, and even poverty in an era of market economy. The impoverishing, disequalizing, and alienating effects of the market economy are too often intertwined with the decisions of state organs and the acts of party-state cadres. In fact, in the mind of grassroots people, the sectoral bias, self-interest, and outright corruption of policy makers and local cadres appear much more horrifying than any inherent tendencies of the market economy to cause inequality and alienation. In market socialist China, democratization is a goal of grassroots class politics that is pursued much more seriously against state power than against the market economy.

Against this background, most of the grassroots grievances, resistances, and even riots have broken out against local cadres or the communist party-state itself, rather than against any purely market-based *nouveau riche.* Peasants in many inland provinces rioted against corrupt and extorting local cadres.[61] In many big cities, unemployed and impoverished groups of people have staged rallies against their local and/or central government for their economic mishaps.[62] During the Tiananmen uprising in 1989, many disenchanted workers, peddlers, and even small entrepreneurs sympathized with (and sometimes joined) students in the demand for political democratization.[63] Of course, incidents of struggle against ungenerous rich neighbors and harsh employers are not infrequent. Even in such cases, there often lies grievances against local cadres, who have either implicitly or explicitly sided with the hated rich neighbors and merciless employers in everyday social and economic affairs.

Even if people at the grassroots may not have such a refined consciousness about their democratic political rights as students and intellectuals, they nonetheless feel that the democratization of state power will enhance economic justice in an era of a state-embedded market economy. At the least, close supervision and strict punishment of corrupt, biased, and despotic cadres in their localities and work units are eagerly asked for. Such grassroots political sentiment may not be articulated in a coherent class ideology or organization, but the sheer number of similarly critical people alone—a factor, according to Xueguang Zhou, that leads to collective action through the "large numbers" effect—poses a formidable political threat to the Chinese communist regime.[64] This is why the current leader, Jiang Zemin, has launched anti-corruption campaigns again and again. Even if he may not be successful in actually controlling corruption, it can be the most appealing act of the supreme leader in the eyes of most grassroots persons. The anti-corruption campaigns are thus a form of class politics catering to the desire of grassroots peasants, workers, and peasant-workers.[65]

Notes

1. Deng Xiaoping clarified his position on such problems as early as 1978, by proposing his *xianfu* (getting rich early) argument. He remarked, "it should be accepted that certain areas, enterprises, workers, and peasants attain high income and affluent life through industrious attitude and efficient management" (Deng Xiaoping, *Deng Xiaoping wenxuan, 1975–1982* (Selected Writings of Deng Xiaoping, 1975–1982) (Beijing: Renmin Chubanshe, 1983), p. 142. In the subsequent reform process, however, Deng's bold position was overshadowed by political concerns linked to various types of inequalities. After the Tiananmen incident in June 1989, Deng had to reiterate his emphasis to pacify worries about a setback in reform by saying in his famous *nanxun jianghua* (southern round lecture) "areas which develop first (thanks to favorable conditions) will lead undeveloped areas and ultimately prosper together" (Deng Xiaoping, *Deng Xiaoping wenxuan III* (Selected Writings of Deng Xiaoping III) (Beijing: Renmin Chubanshe, 1993), p. 374. Deng's remarks, however, could not prevent his conservative political rivals and various social groups from voicing critical views on reform-generated inequalities.

2. See Mao Zedong (Mao Tse-tung), *Selected Readings from the Works of Mao Tsetung* (Beijing: Foreign Languages Press, 1971), pp. 432–479.

3. The contradictions between the people and their government were part of the contradictions among the people themselves because the government belonged to the people.

4. This line of theoretical interest is most closely related to Mancur Olson's thesis. In Olson's *The Logic of Collective Action* (New York: Schocken, 1971), he argues that the competition among various social groups in a democratic society to induce favorable government policies concerning the use of public resources is usually won

y the group of big business runners because their smaller number allows them to
coordinate their interests tightly and carry out a most effective lobbying to government offices and parliamentary committees. However, the access to state power in
post-Mao China appears to be affected more sensitively by the political group dynamics and ideology inherited from the Maoist era than by such immediate social ecologi-
al conditions for political actions as emphasized by Olson (i.e., group size, etc.).

5. Xueguang Zhou, in his "Unorganized Interests and Collective Action in Communist China" (*American Sociological Review* 58, no.1 [1993]: 54–73), argues that a
ight institutional structure has governed the state-society relationship in China such
that any collective action (against state power) based on "organized interests" is extremely difficult. However, his argument does not preclude the possibility that this
institutional structure can serve as a mechanism through which various social groups
seek state support in advancing their "undefiant" group interests.

6. Vivienne Shue, *The Reach of the State: Sketches of the Chinese Body Politic*
Stanford, Calif.: Stanford University Press, 1988), p. 71.

7. Peter Evans, *Embedded Autonomy: States, Firms and Industrial Transformation* (Princeton: Princeton University Press, 1995).

8. See Leon Trotsky, *The Revolution Betrayed* (New York: Pathfinder, 1972),
Milovan Djilas, *The New Class: An Analysis of the Communist System* (New York:
Praeger, 1957), and Michael Voslensky, *Nomenklatura: The Soviet Ruling Class* (Gar-
den City, N.Y.: Doubleday, 1984).

9. Frederic Wakeman, Jr., "Mr. Wang vs. Mr. Chen: A High Ch'ing Parable," in
Robert F. Dernberger et al., eds., *The Chinese: Adapting the Past, Facing the Future*
(Ann Arbor: Center for Chinese Studies, University of Michigan, 1991), p. 255.

10. Ibid.

11. Richard Kraus, *Class Conflict in Chinese Socialism* (New York: Columbia
University Press, 1981).

12. Peter Nolan and Gordon White, "Urban Bias, Rural Bias, or State Bias? Urban-
Rural Relationship in Post-Revolutionary China," *Journal of Development Studies*
20, no. 1 (1984): 52–81.

13. See Andrew Walder, *Communist Neo-Traditionalism: Work and Authority in
Chinese Industry* (Berkeley: University of California Press, 1986), and Jean Oi, *State
and Peasant in Contemporary China: The Political Economy of Village Government*
(Berkeley: University of California Press, 1989).

14. Hong Yung Lee, *The Politics of the Chinese Cultural Revolution* (Berkeley:
University of California Press, 1978).

15. See Walder, *Communist Neo-Traditionalism*, and Oi, *State and Peasant*.

16. In an informal discussion, Justin Yifu Lin and I came to agree on this aspect of
Chinese reform.

17. Kyung-Sup Chang, "China's Rural Reform: The State and Peasantry in Constructing a Macro-Rationality," *Economy and Society* 21, no. 4 (1992): 430–452.

18. Kyung-Sup Chang, "The Peasant Family in the Transition from Maoist to
Lewisian Rural Industrialisation," *Journal of Development Studies* 29, no. 2 (1993):
220–244.

19. See Shengzu Gu, *Feinonghua yu chengzhenhua yanjiu* (Study of Deagricul-
turalization and Urbanization) (Hangzhou: Zhejiang Renmin Chubanshe, 1991), and
Kyung-Sup Chang, "China's Urbanization and Development Before and After Economic Reform: A Comparative Reappraisal," *World Development* 22, no. 4 (1994):
601–613.

20. Sen-dou Chang, "The Floating Population: An Informal Process of Urbanisation in China," *International Journal of Population Geography* 2, no. 3 (1996): 197–214.

21. Jiusheng Kang, "The Part-Work and Part-Farm Population and the Shift of the Agricultural Labor Force," *Chinese Sociology and Anthropology* 21, no. 2 (1989) 58–68.

22. Minghua Zhao and Theo Nichols, "Management Control of Labour in State-Owned Enterprises: Cases from the Textile Industry," *China Journal,* no. 36 (1996) 1–21.

23. Kyung-Sup Chang, "The Remaking of the Chinese Working Class: Shandong Workers in *Reverse Proletarianization.*" Unpublished research report.

24. Michael Korzec, *Labor and the Failure of Reform in China* (New York: St. Martin's, 1992).

25. Kyung-Sup Chang, "Economic Privatism and New Patterns of Inequality in Post-Mao China," *Development and Society* 29, no. 2 (2000): 23–54.

26. Louis Putterman, "Dualism and Reform in China," *Economic Development and Cultural Change* 40, no. 3 (1992): 467–494.

27. In pre-reform China, where nationally effective programs for social security were absent, socialist production units such as state enterprises and collective farms had also functioned as welfare provision units for their workers and peasants. Consequently, the recasting or demise of these production units in the reform era unavoidably threatens the welfare status of their workers.

28. Deborah Davis, "Chinese Social Welfare: Policies and Outcomes," *China Quarterly,* no. 119 (1989): 577–597.

29. The Chinese government would not hide such spending even in its formal budget tabulation as published in the *Zhongguo tongji nianjian* (Statistical Yearbook of China) series.

30. Chang, "The Floating Population."

31. Chang, "The Remaking of the Chinese Working Class."

32. Sukhan Jackson, "Labor Issues in China," in Sukhan Jackson, ed., *Contemporary Developments in Asian Industrial Relations* (Sydney: Industrial Relations Research Center, University of New South Wales, 1994), pp. 55–76.

33. Chang, "The Remaking of the Chinese Working Class."

34. In some areas, migrants have responded to this adverse situation by setting up their own communal networks and institutions for emergency relief, education, and other services. See Chang, "The Floating Population."

35. The bondage between migrant workers and their family members in villages is not only a moral and cultural phenomenon but also a crucial economic phenomenon in labor-intensive industrialization. On the one hand, the immediate motivation for migration is to relieve the economic burden of their family under land shortage and/or earn additional family income. On the other hand, when migrant workers have difficulty in attaining an adequately paying permanent job, village-remaining family members often support them with living and training expenses, foodstuffs, and other essentials. See C. Meillassoux, *Maidens, Meal and Money: Capitalism and the Domestic Community* (New York: Cambridge University Press, 1981). About the Chinese context, see Chang, "The Peasant Family in the Transition."

36. See Ding Guoguang, *Xiangzhen qiye lun* (Study of Township and Village Enterprises) (Beijing: Zhongguo Caizheng Jingji Chubanshe, 1993), and Christopher Findlay, Andrew Watson, and Harry Wu, eds., *Rural Enterprises in China* (New York: St. Martin's, 1994).

37. See Chang, "The Peasant Family in the Transition" for the Lewisian and the uniquely Chinese nature of post-Mao rural industrialization.

38. Ibid.

39. Pat Howard, *Breaking the Iron Rice Bowl: Prospects for Socialism in China's Countryside* (Armonk, N.Y.: M.E. Sharpe, 1988).

40. Carl Riskin, *China's Political Economy: The Quest for Development Since 1949* (New York: Oxford University Press, 1987).

41. Findlay, Watson, and Wu, eds., *Rural Enterprises in China.*

42. Kyung-Sup Chang, "China's Urbanization and Development Before and After Economic Reform: A Comparative Reappraisal," *World Development* 22, no. 4 (1994): 601–613.

43. Alice Goldstein, Sidney Goldstein, and Shengzu Gu, "Rural Industrialization and Migration in the People's Republic of China," *Social Science History* 15, no.3 (1991): 289–314.

44. Kristen Parris, "Private Entrepreneurs as Citizens: From Leninism to Corporatism," *China Information* 10, no. 3/4 (1995): 1–28.

45. In a similar vein, Gil Eyal, Ivan Szelenyi, and Eleanor Townsley, in their "The Theory of Post-Communist Managerialism" (*New Left Review*, no. 222 [1997]: 91), observe that "Former socialist managers are tempted to acquire business ownership . . . the dominant trend in managerial buy-outs is still petty bourgeoisification, as former socialist managers become small-business operators, but in a small fraction of cases, managers acquire enough ownership in large firms to control them as owners, especially if they can coordinate their action with other members of management who hold significant ownership stakes."

46. David L. Wank, "Private Business, Bureaucracy, and Political Alliance in a Chinese City," *Australian Journal of Chinese Affairs,* no. 33 (1995): 55–71.

47. Yasheng Huang, "Web of Interests and Patterns of Behaviour of Chinese Local Economic Bureaucracies and Enterprises during Reforms," *China Quarterly*, no. 123 (1990): 431–458.

48. Andrew Walder, "Factory and Manager in an Era of Reform," *China Quarterly*, no. 118 (1989): 242–264.

49. Dorothy Solinger, *China's Transition from Socialism: Statist Legacies and Market Reforms, 1980–1990* (Armonk, N.Y.: M.E. Sharpe, 1993).

50. Wank, "Private Business, Bureaucracy, and Political Alliance."

51. Ibid.

52. Parris, "Private Entrepreneurs as Citizens."

53. Hong Yung Lee, *From Revolutionary Cadres to Party Technocrats in Socialist China* (Berkeley: University of California Press, 1991).

54. Richard Latham, "The Implications of Rural Reforms for Grass-Roots Cadres," in Elizabeth Perry and Christine Wong, eds., *The Political Economy of Reform in Post-Mao China* (Cambridge, Mass.: Harvard University Press, 1985), pp. 157–173.

55. Oi, *State and Peasant*; Richard Levy, "Corruption, Economic Crime and Social Transformation since the Reforms: The Debates in China," *Australian Journal of Chinese Affairs,* no. 33 (1995): 1–25.

56. Even in abrupt market transitions in East Central Europe, according to Eyal, Szelenyi, and Townsley ("The Theory of Post-Communist Managerialism," p. 84), there is "reproduction of the managerial elite," a phenomenon which "runs directly counter to theoretical expectations that cadres would lose economic power in a transition to market economies." They interpret this continuity on the basis of the "cultural

capital" or "technical know-how" supposedly possessed by former cadres, professionals, as well as dissident intellectuals. In China, where the communist party-state has maintained its monopoly power, political office is still the most important basis for the superior economic status of current and former cadres, although their human capital does help them in their social transformation into private entrepreneurs or professional managers.

57. Lee, *From Revolutionary Cadres to Party Technocrats.*

58. Hong Yung Lee, "The Civil Service System and Political Reforms in China," *Asia Journal* 3, no. 2 (1996): 1–22.

59. In Russia, such distortion of the privatization process is often called "nomenklatura privatization" in that it has been led by former nomenklatura members.

60. Levy, "Corruption, Economic Crime and Social Transformation since the Reforms."

61. In particular, peasants in Sichuan Province staged numerous revolts against local cadres in the 1990s.

62. For instance, I noticed during my visit that residents of Shenyang, a rapidly decaying heavy industrial metropolis, launched a monthly downtown demonstration to complain about their economic mishaps.

63. Levy, "Corruption, Economic Crime and Social Transformation since the Reform."

64. Zhou, "Unorganized Interests and Collective Action in Communist China."

65. Another aspect of the anti-corruption campaigns, often pointed out in the foreign news media, is that Jiang's political rivals and their followers have been pursued and punished in these campaigns. This high-level political infighting, however, is not incompatible with the class politics for grassroots persons.

The Editor and Contributors

Alvin Y. So is a professor in the Division of Social Science at the Hong Kong University of Science and Technology. He recently published *Hong Kong's Embattled Democracy* (1999); *Asia's Environmental Movements* (co-editor, M.E. Sharpe, 1999); *The Chinese Triangle of Mainland China, Taiwan, and Hong Kong* (co-editor, 2001); *Survey Research in Chinese Societies* (co-editor, Oxford, 2001); and *Crisis and Transformation in China's Hong Kong* (co-editor, M.E. Sharpe, 2002).

Kam Wing Chan is a professor of geography at the University of Washington. He received a Ph.D. degree from the University of Toronto. He is the author of *Cities with Invisible Walls* (1994) and has written extensively on China's urbanization, migration, the household registration system, labor market, and economic development. He has also served as a consultant for the Asian Development Bank, International Labour Office, World Bank, United Nations, and the PRC Government.

Kyung-Sup Chang is a professor of sociology at Seoul National University. He has served as the editor of *Development and Society* since 1999. His work on Chinese development and social change has appeared in *World Development, Journal of Development Studies, Economy and Society, Rationality and Society*, and others. He is currently preparing a monograph entitled *Ruralism: Reinterpretation of China's Post-Collective Development.*

Carsten A. Holz is a professor in the Division of Social Science of the Hong Kong University of Science and Technology. His research interests are financial and macroeconomic aspects of China's economic reforms.

Hsin-Huang Michael Hsiao is a research fellow at the Institute of Sociology and director of the Asia-Pacific Research Program (APRP), Academia Sinica, and a professor of sociology at National Taiwan University. He has written widely on the transformation of Taiwan's social structure, social movements, and civil society. His recent publications include *East Asian Middle Classes in Comparative Perspective* (editor, 1999); *Taiwan's Social Welfare Movements Since the 1980s* (editor, 2000); *Changes in Southeast Asia* (editor, 2000); *Chinese Business in Southeast Asia* (co-editor, 2001); and *Exploration of the Middle Classes in Southeast Asia* (editor, 2002).

Ping-Chun Hsiung, is an associate professor, Division of Social Sciences, University of Toronto, Scarborough College. His research interests include feminist theories, research methodology, and epistemology; social changes in Chinese societies; and NGOs and civil society in Taiwan and China. Hsiung's publications include *Living Rooms as Factories: Class, Gender, and the Satellite Factory System in Taiwan*; and *Chinese Women Organizing: Cadres, Feminists, Muslims, Queers* (co-edited M. Jaschok and C. Milwertz, 2001).

James Kai-sing Kung teaches the economics of rural China and property rights economics in the Division of Social Science at the Hong Kong University of Science and Technology. His research interests include the economic history of both early twentieth century and communist China, and the relationship between property rights, economic development, and its distributive consequences in contemporary rural China. He has published in a number of professional journals, including *Economic Development and Cultural Change*, *Journal of Comparative Economics*, *Journal of Development Studies*, and *The China Journal*, as well as having written a number of book chapters in edited volumes on China's economic reforms.

George C.S. Lin, associate professor, Department of Geography, University of Hong Kong, is the author of *Red Capitalism in South China: Growth and Development of the Pearl River Delta* (1997) and many articles. His current research interests include urban and regional development in South China, and system and land use transformation in rural China, and transnationalism and the geography of the Chinese diaspora.

Yi-min Lin is associate professor of social science at the Hong Kong University of Science and Technology. He does research on the contemporary Chinese political economy. He is the author of *Between Politics and Markets: Firms, Competition, and Institutional Change in Post-Mao China* (2001).

Richard Madsen is professor of sociology at the University of California, San Diego. His most recent books include *Meaning and Modernity* (co-edited with William Sullivan, Ann Swidler, and Steven Tipton); *Unofficial China* co-edited with Perry Link and Paul Pickowicz); *China's Catholics*; and *China and the American Dream.*

Suzanne Ogden is a professor in the Department of Political Science at Northeastern University in Boston, Massachusetts, and a research associate at the Fairbank Center for East Asian Research, Harvard University. She works primarily on issues of democratization, with a focus on the interrelationship between culture, development, and political development. Her *Inklings of Democracy in China* was published in 2002. Professor Ogden is also the author of *China's Unresolved Issues: Politics, Development and Culture* (1989, 1992, 1995), as well as *Global Studies: China* (2001), now in its ninth edition.

Tian Zhu is an assistant professor in the Division of Social Science at the Hong Kong University of Science and Technology. He received a Bachelor of Science degree from Tsinghua University, an M.A. degree from Beijing University, and a Ph.D. in economics from Northwestern University. His research focuses primarily on Chinese economic reforms and the economics of organization. He has written a number of articles on the ownership restructuring of state-owned enterprises in China.

Index

Accommodation approach, 42
Activism
  grassroots politics
    Anhui Province, 8, 34–35
    developmental state, 8, 9–10, 22
    institutional transformation, 31, 33–34,
      36–37, 38–39, 43
    partial marketization politics, 283–84
    See also Gender politics
Age, labor migration, 117, 128
Agency problem, 211, 223n.69
Agricultural Bank of China (ABC)
  financial crisis, 185, 186–87*t*, 217n.14
  loan reform, 189, 193, 218n.21, 219n.23
    decision-making, 193–94, 219n.26
    profitability reform, 194–98
Agricultural production
  competition, 21
  developmental state, 8–10, 11
  Dongguan (Guangdong Province), 89,
    94–95, 97, 98
  Fujian Province investment, 136
  labor migration, 128–30
  See also Property rights
Agricultural reform
  developmental state, 8–9
  institutional transformation
    cumulative pressure thesis, 32, 34–36
    local initiative thesis, 30–31
    pace-setting mechanisms, 36–37, 39,
      54n.68
    See also Family production policy; Property
      rights
All-China Federation of Industry and
  Commerce, 149–50
Anhui Province
  institutional transformation, 8, 34–35,
    54n.69
  labor migration, 119, 120, 127–28
Apparel industry, 93, 141
Asian financial crisis, 20–21
  See also Economic reform assessment
Asset management companies (AMCs)
  government financial reform, 210, 223n.65
  state bank reform, 185, 193, 198, 219n.23
Associations. *See* Autonomous social
  organizations; Business associations

Authoritarianism
  developmental state characteristics, 18
  Fujian Province social transformation, 144
  gender politics, 163
  nationalism, 226
Automobile industry, 142
Autonomous social organizations, 143–45,
  148
Autonomy
  developmental state characteristics, 18
  Fujian Province civil society
    intellectuals, 145
    local government, 154–55
    private business, 145, 146, 148, 150
    social structure transformation, 145, 146,
      148, 150, 154–55
    Taiwan investment, 150, 153
  Fujian Province social transformation,
    143–44
Aviation Bureau (Fujian Province), 140

Banking industry. *See* Economic reform
  assessment; *specific banks*; State bank
Bank of China (BoC)
  financial crisis, 185, 186–87*t*, 217n.14,
    218n.15
  loan reform, 189, 193, 218n.21, 219n.23
    decision-making, 193–94, 219n.26
    profitability reform, 194–98
Bank of Communications, 199
Baogan daohu, 66, 76n.21
Belgium, labor migration, 116
Big bang approach, 43–44
Bonds, 193, 210–11
Bottom-up strategy, 11, 19, 33–34, 102
Boxer Rebellion, 246, 260
Brigade enterprises, 9
Business associations, 147, 148–50, 155–56
Business networks, 140, 142, 164, 167

Canada, labor migration, 116
Cannonization. *See* Religious evolution
Capital investment, 83, 128–29
  See also Foreign investment
Capitalism
  developmental state strategies, 11–12
  gender politics, 168–69

Foreign trade
  exports *(continued)*
    export-oriented industrialization, 3, 7, 8
    Fujian Province investment, 137, 141
    Pearl River Delta, 85
  imports
    developmental state, 3, 7, 11, 12
    import processing (Guangdong
      Province), 90–91, 94
    import-substitution, 3, 7
  institutional transformation
    cumulative pressure thesis, 35
    liberalization, 39, 44
    pace-setting mechanisms, 37
    sustaining mechanisms, 46–48
  trade surplus, 4–5
  See also Dongguan (Guangdong Province)
Forestry industry, 136
Formosa Plastics, 142
Fourth World Conference on Women (1995),
  163, 164
France, nationalism, 238
Free riders, 63, 66
Fujian Province
  developmental state strategies, 12
  overview, 12, 16–17
  regional integration, 81–82
  Special Economic Zone (SEZ), 81–82
Fujian Province civil society
  autonomy
    intellectuals, 145
    local government, 154–55
    private business, 145, 146, 148, 150
    social structure transformation, 145, 146,
      148, 150, 154–55
  conclusions, 157–59
  corporatism
    developmental state sustainability, 16–17
    private business, 148–50
    state relations, 148–50
  Fuzhou, 153
  global capitalism, 145
  intellectuals
    autonomy, 145
    class conflict, 151–52
    democratization, 151–52
    liberalism, 151–52
    managerial class, 150–52
    middle class, 150–53
    population percentage, 152
    private business contrast, 150–52
    professional class, 150–52
    state relations, 145, 150–53
  local government
    autonomy, 154–55
    decentralization policy, 154
    private business alliance, 155–56
    semi-austerity policy, 154
    state conflict, 154
    state relations, 153–56

Fujian Province civil society
  local government *(continued)*
    suburban development areas, 153, 154
    tax revenue, 154
  private business
    autonomy, 145, 146, 148, 150
    business associations, 147, 148–50,
      155–56
    business owner class, 146–50
    class conflict, 151–52
    conservative strategy, 147–48, 150,
      152–53
    corporatism, 148–50
    democracy movement (1989), 147–48
    getihu enterprises, 146
    industrialization, 146
    intellectual contrast, 150–52
    joint ventures, 146
    local government alliance, 155–56
    middle class, 146
    political corruption measures, 147–48
    political nepotism measures, 147–48
    siying qiye enterprises, 146, 147–48
    social structure transformation, 145–47
    state alliance, 146–48
    state relations, 145–50
    state suppression, 149
    working class, 146
  Quanzhou, 154
  Shanghan, 156
  social inequality
    agricultural industry, 156–57
    income distribution, 156–57
    rural/urban divide, 156–57
    social welfare, 157
  social structure transformation
    autonomous social organizations,
      144–45, 148
    autonomy, 145, 146, 148, 150, 154–55
    business owner class, 146–50
    class conflict, 151–52
    intermediary structures, 152
    middle class, 146, 150–53
    private business, 145–47
    social inequality, 157
    working class, 146
  state relations
    business associations, 147, 148–50,
      155–56
    business conservatism, 147–48, 150,
      152–53
    corporatism, 148–50
    decentralization policy, 154
    democracy movement (1989), 147–48
    intellectuals, 145, 150–53
    local government, 153–56
    marketization, 144–45, 146
    open door policy, 144–45, 146
    private business, 145–50
    semi-austerity policy, 154